Lecture Notes in Computer Science 13504

More information about this series at https://link.springer.com/bookseries/558

Chen-Mou Cheng · Mitsuaki Akiyama (Eds.)

Advances in Information and Computer Security

17th International Workshop on Security, IWSEC 2022
Tokyo, Japan, August 31 – September 2, 2022
Proceedings

 Springer

Editors
Chen-Mou Cheng
BTQ AG
Vaduz, Liechtenstein

Mitsuaki Akiyama 🆔
NTT
Tokyo, Japan

ISSN 0302-9743   ISSN 1611-3349 (electronic)
Lecture Notes in Computer Science
ISBN 978-3-031-15254-2   ISBN 978-3-031-15255-9 (eBook)
https://doi.org/10.1007/978-3-031-15255-9

This Springer imprint is published by the registered company Springer Nature Switzerland AG
The registered company address is: Gewerbestrasse 11, 6330 Cham, Switzerland

Preface

The Seventeenth International Workshop on Security (IWSEC 2022) was held as a hybrid event, both online and onsite, in Tokyo, Japan, between August 31 and September 2, 2022. It was co-organized by the Technical Committee on Information Security in Engineering Sciences Society (ISEC) of the Institute of Electronics, Information and Communication Engineers (IEICE) and the Special Interest Group on Computer Security (CSEC) of the Information Processing Society of Japan (IPSJ).

Following IWSEC's tradition, this year we also had two tracks, Track A: Cryptography and Track B: Cybersecurity and Privacy with two separate Program Committees. In total we received 34 submissions, 23 to Track A and 11 to Track B, each of which was then reviewed in a double-blind fashion by three to four experts in the pertinent fields. After comprehensive review and shepherding, we accepted 12 papers, nine in Track A and three in Track B, and included their revised and refined versions in this publication. Among them the Best Paper Award went to "Efficient Multiplication of Somewhat Small Integers Using Number-Theoretic Transforms" by Hanno Becker, Vincent Hwang, Matthias J. Kannwischer, Lorenz Panny, and Bo-Yin Yang; and the Best Student Paper Award went to "On Extension of Evaluation Algorithms in Keyed-Homomorphic Encryption" by Hirotomo Shinoki and Koji Nuida.

We are grateful to all those who contributed to the success of IWSEC 2022 during this difficult time of the COVID-19 pandemic. In particular, we would like to thank all authors for submitting their works to the workshop, and we express our deepest appreciation to the members of the Program Committees and the external reviewers for their thorough reviews and in-depth discussions leading to the workshop's excellent program. Last but not least, we would like to thank the general co-chairs, Noboru Kunihiro and Yuji Suga, for their supreme leadership, as well as all members of the Organizing Committee for the great work resulting in the successful event.

September 2022

Chen-Mou Cheng
Mitsuaki Akiyama

Organization

General Co-chairs

Noboru Kunihiro   University of Tsukuba, Japan
Yuji Suga   Internet Initiative Japan Inc., Japan

Program Committee Co-chairs

Chen-Mou Cheng   BTQ AG, Liechtenstein
Mitsuaki Akiyama   NTT, Japan

Poster Chair

Hiroki Kuzuno   Kobe University, Japan

Publication Chair

Junji Shikata   Yokohama National University, Japan

Local Organizing Committee

Hiroshi Tsunoda   Tohoku Institute of Technology, Japan
Hyungrok Jo   Yokohama National University, Japan
Kaisei Kajita   Japan Broadcasting Corporation, Japan
Kazumasa Shinagawa   Ibaraki University, Japan
Masaya Yasuda   Rikkyo University, Japan
Minako Ogawa   Fujitsu Ltd., Japan
Toshiya Shimizu   Fujitsu Laboratories Ltd., Japan
Takeshi Nakai   Toyohashi University of Technology, Japan
Xuping Huang   Advanced Institute of Industrial Technology, Japan
Yasuhiko Ikematsu   Kyushu University, Japan
Yasuhiro Murasaki   Japan Broadcasting Corporation, Japan
Yohei Watanabe   University of Electro-Communications, Japan
Yuntao Wang   Osaka University, Japan

Program Committee

Track A: Cryptography

Shi Bai	Florida Atlantic University, USA
Chi Cheng	China University of Geosciences, China
Sherman S. M. Chow	Chinese University of Hong Kong, Hong Kong
Keita Emura	NICT, Japan
Chun-I Fan	National Sun Yat-sen University, Taiwan
Hector Hougaard	Osaka University, Japan
Takanori Isobe	University of Hyogo, Japan
Yuichi Komano	Toshiba Corporation, Japan
Po-Chun Kuo	BTQ AG, Lichtenstein
Yining Liu	Guilin University of Electronic Technology, China
Florian Mendel	TU Graz, Austria
Kirill Morozov	University of North Texas, USA
Koji Nuida	Kyushu University, Japan
Dipanwita Roy Chowdhury	IIT Kharagpur, India
Bagus Santoso	University of Electro-Communications, Japan
Peter Schwabe	Ruhr-University Bochum, Germany
Daniel Slamanig	Austrian Institute of Technology, Austria
Willy Susilo	University of Wollongong, Australia
Yangguang Tian	University of Surrey, UK
Yuntao Wang	Osaka University, Japan
Bo-Yin Yang	Academia Sinica, Taiwan
Kazuki Yoneyama	Ibaraki University, Japan
Rui Zhang	Chinese Academy of Sciences, China
Thomas Espitau	NTT, Japan

Track B: Cybersecurity and Privacy

Gregory Blanc	Telecom SudParis, France
Herve Debar	Telecom SudParis, France
Josep Domingo-Ferrer	Universitat Rovira i Virgili, Spain
Koki Hamada	NTT, Japan
Hiroki Kuzuno	Kobe University, Japan
Frederic Majorczyk	DGA MI and CentraleSupelec, France
Toshiki Shibahara	NTT, Japan
Yuji Suga	Internet Initiative Japan Inc., Japan
Giorgos Vasiliadis	Hellenic Mediterranean University, Greece
Takumi Yamamoto	Mitsubishi Electric Corporation, Japan
Josep Balasch	KU Leuven, Belgium

Additional Reviewers

Ravi Anand
Carles Anglés-Tafalla
Zhenzhen Bao
Cristòfol Daudén-Esmel
Christian Doczkal
Shiuan Fu
Lorenzo Grassi
Akira Ito
Ziming Jiang
Kaisei Kajita
Fukang Liu
Jack P. K. Ma
Alireza Mehrdad

Qian Mei
Yusuke Naito
Takeshi Nakai
Partha Sarathi Roy
Simona Samardjiska
Kazumasa Shinagawa
Erkan Tairi
Yang Tao
Han Wang
Harry W. H. Wong
Rui Xu
Shota Yamada
Yongjun Zhao

Contents

Advanced Cryptography

Mathematical Cryptography

Efficient Multiplication of Somewhat Small Integers Using Number-Theoretic Transforms

Hanno Becker[1](✉), Vincent Hwang[2,3](✉), Matthias J. Kannwischer[3](✉), Lorenz Panny[3](✉), and Bo-Yin Yang[3](✉)

[1] Arm Research, Cambridge, UK
hanno.becker@arm.com
[2] National Taiwan University, Taipei, Taiwan
vincentvbh7@gmail.com
[3] Academia Sinica, Taipei, Taiwan
matthias@kannwischer.eu, lorenz@yx7.cc, by@crypto.tw

Abstract. Conventional wisdom purports that FFT-based integer multiplication methods (such as the Schönhage–Strassen algorithm) begin to compete with Karatsuba and Toom–Cook only for integers of several tens of thousands of bits. In this work, we challenge this belief, leveraging recent advances in the implementation of number-theoretic transforms (NTT) stimulated by their use in post-quantum cryptography. We report on implementations of NTT-based integer arithmetic on two Arm Cortex-M CPUs on opposite ends of the performance spectrum: Cortex-M3 and Cortex-M55. Our results indicate that NTT-based multiplication is capable of outperforming the big-number arithmetic implementations of popular embedded cryptography libraries for integers as small as 2048 bits. To provide a realistic case study, we benchmark implementations of the RSA encryption and decryption operations. Our cycle counts on Cortex-M55 are about 10× lower than on Cortex-M3.

Keywords: FFT-based multiplication · NTT · Arm processors · RSA

1 Introduction

The development of fast algorithms for arithmetic on big numbers is a well-established field of research. As with any computational problem, its study can be dissected into two parts: First, the analysis of the *asymptotic* complexity. Second, the analysis of *concrete* complexity for a chosen size of input. The results are often different: An algorithm may have inferior asymptotic performance but superior practical performance for a certain input size. The analysis of the "crossover point", that is, the input size at which an asymptotically faster algorithm also becomes practically faster, is an important question when moving from theory to practice. The present paper is about the evaluation of such a crossover point in the case of big number arithmetic on microcontrollers.

© The Author(s), under exclusive license to Springer Nature Switzerland AG 2022
C.-M. Cheng and M. Akiyama (Eds.): IWSEC 2022, LNCS 13504, pp. 3–23, 2022.
https://doi.org/10.1007/978-3-031-15255-9_1

The multiplication of big numbers can be performed in a variety of ways of decreasing asymptotic complexity and (unsurprisingly) increasing sophistication. At the base, so-called "schoolbook multiplication" approaches calculate the product of two n-limb numbers $(a_0, \ldots, a_{n-1})$ and $(b_0, \ldots, b_{n-1})$ by computing and accumulating all n^2 subproducts $a_i b_j$. While from a practical perspective, a lot of research has been conducted on the optimal *concrete* strategy, they all lead to an asymptotic complexity of $\mathcal{O}(n^2)$. Next, the Karatsuba method [KO63] and its generalization by Toom–Cook [Too63] lower the asymptotic complexity to $\mathcal{O}(n^{1+s})$ for varying $0 < s < 1$; for example, Karatsuba's method of computing

$$(a_0 + ta_1)(b_0 + tb_1) = a_0 b_0 + t^2 a_1 b_1 + t((a_0 + a_1)(b_0 + b_1) - a_0 a_0 - a_1 b_1)$$

leads to an asymptotic complexity of $\mathcal{O}(n^{\log_2 3}) \subseteq \mathcal{O}(n^{1.585})$. Moving further, starting with the famous Schönhage–Strassen algorithms [SS71], FFT-based integer multiplications achieve asymptotic complexity $\mathcal{O}(n \log n \log \log n)$ and better, and the long conjectured (and presumably final) complexity of $\mathcal{O}(n \log n)$ was only recently achieved in [HH21].

Despite its far superior asymptotic complexity, however, NTT-based integer multiplication is not used for number ranges found in contemporary public-key cryptography: In fact, quadratic multiplication strategies appear to be the most prominent choice in those contexts. At the same time, the past years have seen significant research and progress regarding fast implementation of the NTT, stimulated by their prominence in post-quantum cryptography. The primary objective of this paper is to evaluate how those optimizations affect the practical performance and viability of NTT-based big number arithmetic.

1.1   Results

We find that the crossover point for viability of NTT-based modular arithmetic is at around 2048 bits. More precisely, we compare to modular arithmetic implementations found in the popular TLS libraries BearSSL and Mbed TLS, and find that our NTT-based implementation outperforms both by 1.3×–2.2× on Cortex-M3 and by 1.8×–6.4× on Cortex-M55. We also notice that there is considerable optimization potential for the schoolbook multiplications in BearSSL and Mbed TLS—when this is implemented, 2048-bit NTT-based modular multiplication is only slightly better (1.1×) than schoolbook multiplication on Cortex-M3, and essentially equal on Cortex-M55. When moving to 4096-bit multiplication, however, our NTT-based implementation outperforms even those highly optimized schoolbook multiplications. We thus think that NTT-based modular arithmetic should be considered from 2048-bit onwards.

Software: Our Cortex-M3 code is available at https://github.com/ntt-int-mul/ntt-int-mul-m3. Our Cortex-M55 code will be made available soon at https://gitlab.com/arm-research/security/pqmx.

Related Work. Present-day general-purpose computer algebra systems switch to FFT-based multiplication only for very large numbers. For example,

GMP [GMP] uses Schönhage–Strassen when multiplying numbers with more than 3000–10000 limbs (i.e., at least 96 000 bits) depending on the platform.[1] However, when tailoring an implementation to a specific integer size and platform, the crossover point appears to be lower. Previous work on implementing RSA using Schönhage–Strassen [GKZ07] in hardware concluded that it can only outperform Karatsuba and Toom–Cook for key sizes larger than 48 000 bits. [Gar07] reports similar findings: It estimates Schönhage–Strassen to be competitive only for RSA key sizes above $2^{17} \approx 131\,000$ bits, several orders of magnitude beyond typical RSA parameter choices. To the best of our knowledge, there is no competitive implementation of real-world RSA using FFT-based integer multiplication.

Other Work. In addition to improvements to the efficiency of number-theoretic transforms, post-quantum cryptography has stimulated research into efficient schoolbook multiplication strategies for integers of a few hundred bits, as found in elliptic-curve or isogeny cryptography. It would be interesting to study and compare the performance of RSA based on the combination of Karatsuba and those new quadratic multiplication algorithms. Another avenue for further research is the evaluation of NTT-based arithmetic on high-end processors.

2   Preliminaries

2.1   RSA

The RSA (Rivest–Shamir–Adleman) cryptosystem [RSA78] was the most common public-key cryptosystem for decades and remains in widespread use, primarily with keys of 2048, 3072, or 4096 bits. We briefly recap how it works.

During key generation, a semiprime $N = pq$ with p and q of roughly equal size is generated. The public key is N and a small e to which power it is easy to raise, commonly $e = 2^{16} + 1$. We have $x^{k\phi(N)+1} \equiv x \pmod{N}$ for all x, k, where $\phi(N) = (p-1)(q-1)$ is the totient function. With $d \equiv e^{-1} \pmod{\phi(N)}$, the public map $x \mapsto x^e \bmod N$ is then inverted by the secret map $y \mapsto y^d \bmod N$, the secret key being d. Both encryption and signing primitives can be constructed based on this pair of public/private maps.

The private map can be evaluated using the Chinese Remainder Theorem (CRT) method, computing $x = y^d \bmod N$ by interpolating $x \equiv y^{d \bmod (p-1)} \pmod{p}$ and $x \equiv y^{d \bmod (q-1)} \pmod{q}$. Modular multiplications are commonly implemented using Montgomery multiplication, and modular exponentiation uses windowing methods (see Sect. 3).

2.2   FFT-Based Integer Multiplication

Numerous versions of FFT-based integer multiplications are known, but their blueprint is typically the following: First, find an FFT-based quasi-linear time

---

[1] https://gmplib.org/manual/FFT-Multiplication.

multiplication algorithm in a suitable polynomial ring. Second, find a means to reduce integer multiplication to the chosen kind of polynomial multiplications.

Starting with Schönhage–Strassen and Pollard [SS71, Pol71], numerous instantiations of this idea have been developed, using polynomials over $\mathbb{C}$, finite fields $\mathbb{F}_q$, integers modulo Fermat numbers $\mathbb{Z}/(2^{2^n}+1)\mathbb{Z}$, and also multivariate polynomial rings [HH21]. Here, we focus on NTT-based integer multiplication using polynomials in $\mathbb{Z}_q[X]/(X^n-1)$ with q a prime or bi-prime, which is close to [Pol71]. While variable-size integer multiplication requires recursive application of the above principle, it is not necessary for the integer sizes considered here.

Section 2.3 discusses how the NTT yields a quasi-linear multiplication in $\mathbb{Z}_q[X]/(X^n-1)$. We now explain the reduction from integer multiplication.

To turn a multiplication of $a, b \in \mathbb{Z}$ into a multiplication in $\mathbb{Z}_q[X]/(X^n-1)$, one first lifts a, b to integer *polynomials* $A, B \in \mathbb{Z}[X]$ along $f : \mathbb{Z}[X] \to \mathbb{Z}, X \mapsto 2^\ell$, the canonical choice being the radix-2^ℓ presentations of a, b. Since $f(AB) = ab$, it suffices to compute $AB \in \mathbb{Z}[X]$. To do so, one chooses q and n such that $AB \in \mathbb{Z}[X]$ is a canonical representative for the finite quotient $\mathbb{Z}_q[X]/(X^n-1)$, that is, it is of degree $< n$ with coefficients in $\{0, \ldots, q-1\}$. Under these circumstances, one can then uniquely recover AB from its image $g(AB) = g(A)g(B)$ under $g : \mathbb{Z}[X] \to \mathbb{Z}_q[X]/(X^n-1)$. We have thus reduced the computation of ab in $\mathbb{Z}$ to that of $g(A)g(B)$ in $\mathbb{Z}_q[X]/(X^n-1)$.

2.3   Number-Theoretic Transforms

The *number-theoretic transform* (NTT) is a generalization of the discrete Fourier transform, replacing the base ring $\mathbb{C}$ of the complex numbers by other commutative rings, commonly finite fields $\mathbb{F}_q$. In the present context, its value lies in the fact that it transforms convolutions into pointwise products in quasi-linear time, reducing the complexity of convolutions from quadratic to quasi-linear.

Definition. We're working over $\mathbb{Z}_q := \mathbb{Z}/q\mathbb{Z}$ for odd q and fix $\omega \in \mathbb{Z}_q$ an nth root of unity. We write $[n] := \{0, 1, \ldots, n-1\}$. The NTT [Für09, HH21] is the canonical projection $\mathbb{Z}_q[x]/\langle x^n-1\rangle \to \prod_i \mathbb{Z}_q[x]/\langle x-\omega^i\rangle$, which under the isomorphism $\mathbb{Z}_q[x]/\langle x-\omega^i\rangle \cong \mathbb{Z}_q, a(x) \mapsto a(\omega^i)$ can also be described as

$$\mathrm{NTT} : \mathbb{Z}_q[x]/\langle x^n-1\rangle \to \mathbb{Z}_q^n, \quad \mathrm{NTT}(a) := \big(a(1), a(\omega), \ldots, a(\omega^{n-1})\big).$$

If ω is a principal nth root of unity and n is invertible in $\mathbb{Z}_q$, this constitutes a ring isomorphism $\mathrm{NTT} : \mathbb{Z}_q[x]/\langle x^n-1\rangle \cong \mathbb{Z}_q^n$; in particular, we have $ab = \mathrm{NTT}^{-1}\big(\mathrm{NTT}(a) \cdot_\Pi \mathrm{NTT}(b)\big)$, where $\cdot_\Pi$ is the pointwise multiplication in $\mathbb{Z}_q^n$.

Fourier Inversion. Domain and codomain of the NTT can be identified via the isomorphism of $\mathbb{Z}_q$-modules (not rings) $\varphi : \mathbb{Z}_q[x]/\langle x^n-1\rangle \cong \mathbb{Z}_q^n, x^i \mapsto e_i$ (where e_i is the ith unit vector). This renders the resulting $\mathrm{NTT} : \mathbb{Z}_q^n \to \mathbb{Z}_q^n$ close to an involution: $\mathrm{NTT}^2 = \mathrm{mul}_n \circ \mathbf{neg}$, where $\mathrm{mul}_n : \mathbb{Z}_q^n \to \mathbb{Z}_q^n$ is pointwise multiplication with n and $\mathbf{neg} : \mathbb{Z}_q^n \to \mathbb{Z}_q^n$ sends e_i to $e_{\mathbf{neg}(i)}$ with $\mathbf{neg}(0) = 0$ and $\mathbf{neg}(i) = n - i$ for $i > 0$ (we don't distinguish between a permutation on

$[n]$ and the induced isomorphism on $\mathbb{Z}_q^n$). Another way of saying this is that $\mathrm{NTT}' : \mathbb{Z}_q[x]/\langle x^n - 1\rangle \cong \mathbb{Z}_q^n$ defined by $\mathrm{NTT}'(a) := \big(\boldsymbol{a}(1), \boldsymbol{a}(\omega^{-1}), \ldots, \boldsymbol{a}(\omega^{-(n-1)})\big)$ is, up to multiplication by n and application of φ, the inverse of $\mathrm{NTT} : \mathbb{Z}_q[x]/\langle x^n - 1\rangle \cong \mathbb{Z}_q^n$. This is the *Fourier Inversion Formula*, and the curious reader will find that it boils down to the orthogonality relations $\sum_j \omega^{ij} = n \cdot \delta_{i,0}$.

Fast Fourier Transform. The NTT can be calculated using the Cooley–Tukey (CT) FFT algorithm: For $n = 2m$, CT splits $\mathbb{Z}_q[x]/\langle x^{2m} - \zeta^2\rangle$ into $\mathbb{Z}_q[x]/\langle x^m - \zeta\rangle \times \mathbb{Z}_q[x]/\langle x^m + \zeta\rangle$ via $\mathrm{CT}(a + x^m b, \zeta) = (a + \zeta b, a - \zeta b)$ for a, b of degree $< m$—this is called a *CT butterfly*. The idea can be applied recursively, and for $n = 2^k$ we in particular obtain a map $\mathrm{NTT}_{\mathrm{CT}} : \mathbb{Z}_q[x]/\langle x^n - 1\rangle \cong \mathbb{Z}_q^n$ which is equal to $\mathtt{bitrev} \circ \mathrm{NTT}$, where $\mathtt{bitrev} : [2^k] \to [2^k]$ is the bitreversal permutation.

The CT strategy can also be applied for radices $r \neq 2$, performing one splitting $\mathbb{Z}_q[x]/\langle x^{rm} - \zeta^r\rangle \cong \prod_i \mathbb{Z}_q[x]/\langle x^m - \omega_r^i \zeta\rangle$ at a time. When applied recursively to a factorization $n = r_1 \cdots r_s$, the resulting map $\mathrm{NTT}_{\mathrm{CT}} : \mathbb{Z}_q[x]/\langle x^n - 1\rangle \cong \mathbb{Z}_q^n$ agrees with $\sigma(r_1, \ldots, r_s) \circ \mathrm{NTT}$, where $\sigma(r_1, \ldots, r_s)$ is given by

$$[n] \quad \cong \quad [r_1] \times \ldots \times [r_s] \xrightarrow{\text{reverse}} [r_s] \times \ldots \times [r_1] \quad \cong \quad [n]$$

where the first and last map are lexicographic orderings. Note that $\sigma(2, \ldots, 2) = \mathtt{bitrev}$, and $\sigma(r_1, \ldots, r_s)$ is an involution only if $(r_1, \ldots, r_s)$ is a palindrome.

Inverse NTT. For the computation of $\mathrm{NTT}_{\mathrm{CT}}^{-1}$, there are two approaches: First, one can invert CT butterflies via *Gentleman–Sande butterflies* $\mathrm{GS}(a, b, \zeta) = (a + b, (a - b)\zeta)$. Alternatively, one can leverage $\mathrm{NTT}_{\mathrm{CT}} = \sigma \circ \mathrm{NTT}$ and $\mathrm{NTT}^{-1} = \mathrm{mul}_{1/n} \circ \mathrm{NTT}'$ to compute $\mathrm{NTT}_{\mathrm{CT}}^{-1} = \mathrm{mul}_{1/n} \circ \mathrm{NTT}' \circ \sigma^{-1} = \mathrm{mul}_{1/n} \circ \sigma^{-1} \circ \mathrm{NTT}_{\mathrm{CT}}' \circ \sigma^{-1}$. If σ is an involution (e.g., if $n = 2^k$), this is $\mathrm{mul}_{1/n} \circ \sigma \circ \mathrm{NTT}_{\mathrm{CT}}' \circ \sigma^{-1}$ and can thus be implemented like $\mathrm{NTT}_{\mathrm{CT}}$ while implicitly applying the permutation σ; this leads to the implementation of $\mathrm{NTT}_{\mathrm{CT}}^{-1}$ as presented in [Abd+22, Figure 1], which does not require explicit permutations. For a general mixed-radix NTT, however, σ is not an involution, and an explicit permutation by σ^{-2} is needed; we avoid this via Good's trick, as explained in the next section.

GS butterflies lead to exponential growth for an exponentially shrinking number of coefficients, while CT butterflies yield linear growth for *all* coefficients. This impacts the amount and placement of reductions during $\mathrm{NTT}^{\pm 1}$.

Good's Trick. For $n = rs$ with coprime r, s, another strategy to computing NTT_n is computing the bottom edge in the commutative diagram

This has two benefits: First, if r, s are prime powers then $\mathrm{NTT}_{r/s}^{\pm 1}$ can be computed via CT as described above, avoiding non-involutive permutations. Second, fewer twiddle factors are needed for the computation of $\mathrm{NTT}_s \otimes \mathrm{NTT}_r$.

Incomplete NTTs. Denoting $R := \mathbb{Z}_q[x]/\langle x^n - 1 \rangle$ and $R_i := \mathbb{Z}_q[x]/\langle x - \omega^i \rangle$, the NTT splitting $\mathrm{NTT} : R \xrightarrow{\cong} \prod_i R_i$ transfers to any R-algebra: If S is an R-algebra, we have $S \cong S \otimes_R R \cong S \otimes_R \prod_i R_i \cong \prod_i S \otimes_R R_i$. The most common example are *incomplete NTTs*: The ring $S := \mathbb{Z}_q[y]/\langle y^{nh} - 1 \rangle$ is an algebra over its subring $R := \mathbb{Z}_q[y^h]/\langle y^{nh} - 1 \rangle \cong \mathbb{Z}_q[x]/\langle x^n - 1 \rangle$ to which the NTT applies, and so $S \cong \prod_i S \otimes_R \mathbb{Z}_q[y^h]/\langle y^h - \omega^i \rangle = \prod_i \mathbb{Z}_q[y]/\langle y^h - \omega^i \rangle$.

The benefits of using incomplete NTTs are: First, we only need an nth principal root of unity to partially split $\mathbb{Z}_q[y]/\langle y^{nh} - 1 \rangle$. Second, polynomial multiplication using incomplete NTTs and "base multiplication" in $\mathbb{Z}_q[y]/\langle y^h - \omega^i \rangle$ may be faster than for full NTTs and base multiplication in $\mathbb{Z}_q$.

We use incomplete NTTs for all parameter sets—see below.

Fermat Number Transforms. The Fermat number transform (FNT) is a special case of NTT where the modulus is a Fermat number $F_t := 2^{2^t} + 1$ [AB74]. For the coefficient ring $\mathbb{Z}_{F_t}$, we can compute a size-n NTT if n divides 2^{t+2}. If we choose 2 to be the principal 2^{t+1}th root of unity, then the twiddle factors for a size-$(t+1)$ Cooley–Tukey FFT are all powers of 2.

Since there are square roots for ± 2, we can choose a principal 2^{t+2}th root of unity ω with $\omega = \sqrt{2}$ and compute a size-2^{t+2} NTT [AB74]. Furthermore, if F_t is a prime, then we can compute a size-2^{2^t} NTT. Note that the only known prime Fermat numbers are $F_0, \ldots, F_4$.

2.4   Modular Reductions and Multiplications

(Refined) Barrett Reduction. Signed Barrett reduction approximates

$$a \bmod^{\pm} q = a - q \lfloor a/q \rfloor = a - q \left\lfloor a \tfrac{\mathrm{R}}{q}/\mathrm{R} \right\rceil \approx a - \lfloor a \cdot [\![\mathrm{R}/q]\!]/\mathrm{R} \rceil =: \mathbf{bar}_{q,\mathrm{R}}^{[\![\,]\!]}(a),$$

where $\mathrm{R} = 2^w$ is a power of 2 and $[\![\mathrm{R}/q]\!]$ is a precomputed integer approximation to $\tfrac{\mathrm{R}}{q}$. The quality of the resulting approximation $\mathbf{bar}_{q,\mathrm{R}}^{[\![\,]\!]}(a) \approx a \bmod^{\pm} q$—and in particular, the question of when it may in fact be an *equality*—depends on the value of w, and two choices for w are common, as we now recall.

First, $w = M$ where $M \in \{16, 32\}$ is the word or half-word size bitlength, allowing $\lfloor \tfrac{-}{\mathrm{R}} \rceil$ to be conveniently implemented using rounding high multiply instructions. We call this the "standard" Barrett reduction.

Second, $w = (M - 1) + \lfloor \log_2 q \rfloor$, which is maximal under the constraint that $[\![\mathrm{R}/q]\!]$ is a signed M-bit integer: This choice leads to higher accuracy of the approximation, but typically requires an additional instruction. We will henceforth call it the "refined" Barrett reduction. For standard Barrett reduction, both $[\![a]\!] := 2 \lfloor \tfrac{a}{2} \rfloor$ and $[\![a]\!] := \lfloor a \rceil$ can be useful, while for refined Barrett reduction, we always choose $[\![a]\!] = \lfloor a \rceil$ because of its tighter bound $|\lfloor a \rfloor - a| \leq \tfrac{1}{2}$.

Note that both "standard" and "refined" Barrett reductions are already known in the literature as Barrett reduction. We make this distinction for introducing an extension of the signed Barrett multiplication introduced by [Bec+22a].

(Refined) Barrett Multiplication. For two integers a, b and a modulus q, signed Barrett multiplication [Bec+22a] approximates

$$ab \bmod^{\pm} q = ab - q \left\lfloor \tfrac{ab}{q} \right\rceil = ab - q \left\lfloor a \tfrac{b\mathtt{R}}{q} / \mathtt{R} \right\rceil \approx ab - \left\lfloor a \cdot \left\lfloor \tfrac{b\mathtt{R}}{q} \right\rceil / \mathtt{R} \right\rceil q =: \mathbf{bar}_{q,\mathtt{R}}^{[\![\ ]\!]}(a, b),$$

where again $\mathtt{R} = 2^w$ is a power of 2 and $[\![b\mathtt{R}/q]\!]$ is a precomputed integer approximation to $\tfrac{b\mathtt{R}}{q}$. Previously, only the choice $w = M \in \{16, 32\}$ was considered. In analogy with refined Barrett reduction, we suggest to also consider $w = (M - 1) + \lfloor \log_2 q \rfloor - \lceil \log_2 |b| \rceil$, which again is maximal under the constraint that $[\![b\mathtt{R}/q]\!]$ is a signed M-bit integer. We call the resulting approximation to $ab \bmod^{\pm} q$ the "refined" Barrett multiplication.

We summarize the quality and size of Barrett reduction and multiplication:

Fact 1. Let $q \in \mathbb{N}$ be odd and $a, b \in \mathbb{Z}$ with $|a|, |b| < 2^{M-1}$ for $M \in \{16, 32\}$. Moreover, let $[\![-]\!] : \mathbb{Q} \to \mathbb{Z}$ be any integer approximation, i.e. $|x - [\![x]\!]| \leq 1$ for all $x \in \mathbb{Q}$, and put $t \bmod^{[\![\ ]\!]} q := t - q [\![t/q]\!]$.
   Then for $\mathtt{R} := 2^M$ we have $|\mathbf{bar}_{q,\mathtt{R}}^{[\![\ ]\!]}(a, b)| \leq \frac{a(b\mathtt{R} \bmod^{[\![\ ]\!]} q)}{\mathtt{R}} + \frac{\mathtt{R}}{2}$.

Proof. [Bec+22a, Corollary 2]   □

Fact 2. Let $q \in \mathbb{N}$ be odd and $a, b \in \mathbb{Z}$ with $|a|, |b| < 2^{M-1}$ for $M \in \{16, 32\}$. Moreover, pick $k \geq 1$ maximal s.t. $\varepsilon := |\lfloor b\mathtt{R}/q \rceil - b\mathtt{R}/q| \leq 2^{-k}$. Finally, set $\mathtt{R} := 2^w$ for $w := (M - 1) + \lfloor \log_2 q \rfloor - \lceil \log_2 |b| \rceil$. Then:
   If $\log_2 |a| < (M - 1) - (\lceil \log_2 |b| \rceil - (k - 1))$, then $\mathbf{bar}_{q,\mathtt{R}}^{[\![\ ]\!]}(a, b) = ab \bmod^{\pm} q$.

Restating Fact 2 in simple terms: Refined Barrett *reduction* (the special case $b = 1$) yields canonical representatives for *all* inputs a with $|a| < 2^{M-1}$. For a refined Barrett multiplication, the range of inputs for which $\mathbf{bar}_{q,\mathtt{R}}^{[\![\ ]\!]}(a, b)$ is guaranteed to be canonical is narrowed by the bitwidth of b; *however*, this can be compensated for by an exceptionally close approximation $b\mathtt{R}/q \approx \lfloor b\mathtt{R}/q \rceil$.

Proof of Fact 2. Setting $\delta := a \lfloor b\mathtt{R}/q \rceil / \mathtt{R} - ab/q$, it follows from the definition of ε and k that $|\delta| \leq |a|/2^{k+w}$. Since $\lfloor - \rceil$ changes its value only when crossing values of the form $\{\tfrac{2n+1}{2}\}$ for $n \in \mathbb{Z}$, for $\lfloor \tfrac{ab}{q} \rceil$ and $\left\lfloor \tfrac{a \lfloor \tfrac{b\mathtt{R}}{q} \rceil}{\mathtt{R}} \right\rceil = \lfloor \tfrac{ab}{q} + \delta \rceil$ to agree it is sufficient to show that $|\delta| < \min \left\{ \left| \tfrac{2n+1}{2} - \tfrac{c}{q} \right| \mid c, n \in \mathbb{Z} \right\} = \tfrac{1}{2q}$—the last equality holds since q is odd. Refined Barrett multiplication is thus guaranteed to yield the canonical representative of ab if $\tfrac{|a|}{2^{k+w}} < \tfrac{1}{2q}$, i.e. $|a| < \tfrac{2^{k+w-1}}{q}$. Plugging in $w = M - 1 + \lfloor \log_2 q \rfloor - \lceil \log_2 |b| \rceil$ and estimating $q < 2^{\lfloor \log_2 |q| \rfloor + 1}$, this follows provided $\log_2 |a| < (M - 1) - (\lceil \log_2 |b| \rceil - (k - 1))$, as claimed.   □

Example 1. Let $M = 32$, $q = 114826273$, and $b = 774$. Then $\lfloor \log_2 q \rfloor = 26$ and $\lceil \log_2 b \rceil = 10$, so $w = 47$. Moreover, $\varepsilon := |\lfloor b\text{R}/q \rceil - b\text{R}/q|$ satisfies $\varepsilon < 2^{-11}$. Thus, according to Fact 2, the refined Barrett multiplication $\mathbf{bar}^{\pm}_{q,\text{R}}(-, b)$ for $\text{R} := 2^{47}$ does therefore yield canonical representatives for all inputs a with $|a| < 2^{31}$: The exceptionally good approximation $\lfloor b\text{R}/q \rceil \approx b\text{R}/q$ makes up for the size of b.

Montgomery Multiplication. The Montgomery multiplication [Mon85] of a, b with respect to a modulus q and a 2-power $\text{R} > q$ is defined as $\mathbf{mont}^{+}_{q}(ab) = \text{hi}\,(a \cdot b + q \cdot \text{lo}\,(q' \cdot \text{lo}\,(a \cdot b)))$, providing a representative of $ab\text{R}^{-1}$ modulo q. Here, $q' = -q^{-1} \bmod \text{R}$, and lo and hi are extractions of the lower and upper $\log_2 \text{R}$ bits, respectively. Montgomery multiplication is defined and relevant for both small-width modular arithmetic such as modular arithmetic modulo a 16-bit or 32-bit prime, as well as large integer arithmetic as used, e.g., in RSA.

Multi-precision Montgomery Multiplication. Montgomery multiplication for big integers is implemented iteratively: For $a, b = \sum_i b_i \text{B}^i$, one computes a representative of $ab\text{B}^{-n}$ by writing $ab\text{B}^{-n} = \ldots (ab_2 + (ab_1 + (ab_0)\text{B}^{-1})\text{B}^{-1})\text{B}^{-1} \ldots$ and computing each $x \mapsto (x + ab_i)\text{B}^{-1}$ using a Montgomery multiplication w.r.t. B. Each such step involves the computation and accumulation of $P = x + ab_i$ and of $Q = ((x+ab_i)_0 q' \bmod \text{B})p$. If the products are computed separately, this is called *Coarsely Integrated Operand Scanning* (CIOS) [KAK96]. If $(x + ab_i)_0 q' \bmod \text{B}$ is computed first and then $P + Q$ is computed in one loop, it is called *Finely Integrated Operand Scanning* (FIOS).

Divided-Difference for Chinese Remainder Theorem (CRT). We compute polynomial products modulo $q_1 q_2$ by interpolating products modulo q_1 and q_2 using the divided-difference algorithm for CRT [Chu+21]: Let q_0, q_1 be two coprime integers and $m_1 := q_0^{-1} \bmod {}^{\pm}q_1$. For a system $u \equiv u_0 \pmod{q_0}, u \equiv u_1 \pmod{q_1}$ with $|u_0| < \frac{q_0}{2}, |u_1| < \frac{q_1}{2}$, we solve for u with $|u| < \frac{q_0 q_1}{2}$ by computing:

$$u = u_0 + ((u_1 - u_0)m_1 \bmod {}^{\pm}q_1)\, q_0. \tag{1}$$

2.5   Implementation Targets

We briefly explain our choice of implementation targets.

Cortex-M3. The Arm® Cortex®-M3 CPU is a low-cost processor found in a wide range of applications such as microcontrollers, automotive body systems, or wireless networking. It implements the Armv7-M architecture and features a 3-stage pipeline, an optional memory protection unit (MPU) and a single-cycle $32 \times 32 \to 32$-bit multiplier with optional 1-cycle accumulation or subtraction.

   We select the Cortex-M3 primarily for two reasons: First, it is a popular choice of MCU for automotive hardware security modules (e.g. Infineon AURIX TC27X). Second, its $32 \times 32 \to 64$ long multiplication instructions smull, smlal, umull, umlal have data-dependent timing and lead to timing side channels when used to process sensitive data. To avoid those, implementations need to use single-width multiplication instructions mul, mla, and mls instead. We expect this reduction of basic multiplication width to have a more significant impact on the runtime of classical multiplication than on (quasi-linear) NTT-based multiplication. A goal of the paper is to evaluate this intuitive assessment.

Cortex-M55. The Cortex-M55 processor is the first implementation of the Armv8.1-M architecture, with optional support for the M-Profile Vector Extension (MVE), or Arm® Helium™ Technology. It features a 5-stage pipeline when Helium is enabled, and except for some pairs of Thumb instructions, it is single issue. In addition to the Helium vector extension, it supports the Low Overhead Branch Extension, as well as tightly coupled memory (TCM) for both code and data, with a total Data-TCM bandwidth of 128-bit/cycle, 64-bit/cycle for CPU processing and 64-bit/cycle for concurrent DMA transfers. For a more extensive introductions to both the Armv8.1-M architecture and the Cortex-M55 CPU, we refer to [Bec+22b, Section 3] and the references therein.

We select the Cortex-M55 for the following reasons: First, due to its support for SIMD vector processing, it is an exciting and powerful new implementation target—the cryptographic capabilities of which are still to be explored. Second, the authors are not aware of means to vectorize classical umaal-based multiplication strategies using MVE, while in contrast it has been demonstrated in [Bec+22b] that the NTT is amenable for significant speedup using MVE. We are thus curious to understand how a vectorized NTT-based integer multiplication fares compared to classical umaal-based integer multiplication.

3 Implementations

3.1 High-Level Strategy

We implement Montgomery multiplication on top of NTT-based large integer multiplication, the latter as described in Sect. 2.2. This is in contrast to CIOS/FIOS approaches for iterative Montgomery multiplication, which never need to compute the double-width product of two large integers.

We pick $\mathtt{R} = 2^{\ell \cdot n/2}$, which in contrast to $\mathtt{R} = 2^N$ aligns taking the low and high half w.r.t. $\mathtt{R}$ with taking the low resp. high halves of polynomials.

NTT-based large integer multiplication involves a considerable amount of precomputation, such as chunking and NTT. Since each Montgomery multiplication involves three integer multiplications—$a \cdot b$, $t := q' \cdot (a \cdot b)_{\text{low}}$, and $p \cdot t$—two of which involve static factors p and p', we buffer their precomputations. We also make use of asymmetric multiplication [Bec+22a] and refer to the resulting NTT and base multiplication as $\mathtt{NTT}_{\text{heavy}}$ and $\mathtt{basemul}_{\text{light}}$.

Algorithm 1, Algorithm 2 and Appendix E describe our modular multiplication strategy in more detail. Appendix B explains how to perform the non-trivial precomputation of $p^{-1} \bmod \mathtt{R}$ for our large choice of $\mathtt{R}$.

Algorithm 1:	**Algorithm 2:**
Montgomery squaring using NTTs	Montgomery multiplication using NTTs

Input: p, $aR \bmod p$,
$\quad\quad \hat{p}^{-1} = \mathtt{NTT}(\mathtt{chk}(p^{-1} \bmod 2^k))$,
$\quad\quad \hat{p} = \mathtt{NTT}(\mathtt{chk}(p))$
Output: $c = a^2 R \bmod p$

1: $\hat{a} = \mathtt{NTT}(\mathtt{chk}(a))$
2: $t = \mathtt{dechk}(\mathtt{NTT}^{-1}(\hat{a} \circ \hat{a}))$
3: $\hat{t} = \mathtt{NTT}(\mathtt{chk}(t \bmod 2^k))$
4: $l = \mathtt{dechk}(\mathtt{NTT}^{-1}(\hat{t} \circ \hat{p}^{-1}))$
5: $\hat{l} = \mathtt{NTT}(\mathtt{chk}(l \bmod 2^k))$
6: $r = \mathtt{dechk}(\mathtt{NTT}^{-1}(\hat{l} \circ \hat{p}))$
7: $c = \frac{t}{2^k} - \frac{r}{2^k}$
8: **if** $c < 0$ **then** $c = c + p$
9: **return** c

Input: $aR \bmod p$, $bR \bmod p$
$\quad\quad \hat{p}^{-1} = \mathtt{NTT}(\mathtt{chk}(p^{-1} \bmod 2^k))$,
$\quad\quad \hat{p} = \mathtt{NTT}(\mathtt{chk}(p))$
Output: $c = a \cdot b \cdot 2^{-k} \bmod p$

1: $\hat{a} = \mathtt{NTT}(\mathtt{chk}(a))$
2: $\hat{b} = \mathtt{NTT}(\mathtt{chk}(b))$
3: $t = \mathtt{dechk}(\mathtt{NTT}^{-1}(\hat{a} \circ \hat{b}))$
4: $\hat{t} = \mathtt{NTT}(\mathtt{chk}(t \bmod 2^k))$
5: $l = \mathtt{dechk}(\mathtt{NTT}^{-1}(\hat{t} \circ \hat{p}^{-1}))$
6: $\hat{l} = \mathtt{NTT}(\mathtt{chk}(l \bmod 2^k))$
7: $r = \mathtt{dechk}(\mathtt{NTT}^{-1}(\hat{l} \circ \hat{p}))$
8: $c = \frac{t}{2^k} - \frac{r}{2^k}$
9: **if** $c < 0$ **then** $c = c + p$
10: **return** c

3.2 Parameter Choices

Recall from Sect. 2.2 that the Schönhage–Strassen algorithm involves lifting N-bit numbers to $\mathbb{Z}[X]$ along $X \mapsto 2^\ell$ and computing their product in $\mathbb{Z}_q[X]/(X^n - 1)$ using the NTT. We now describe our choices of N, ℓ, n, q; they were found by manually tailoring the algorithm to the given target architectures.

First, if we divide our inputs into ℓ-bit chunks, we need $n \geq 2 \lceil \frac{N}{\ell} \rceil$; otherwise, we cannot lift from $\mathbb{Z}_q[X]/(X^n - 1)$ back to $\mathbb{Z}_q[X]$. For performance, we also want n so that NTT-based polynomial multiplication is fast, e.g., a 2-power. Hence, we may deliberately choose $n > 2 \lceil \frac{N}{\ell} \rceil$ and pad with zeros when needed.

Secondly, the coefficients of the product of two dimension-$(n/2)$ polynomials with ℓ-bit coefficients are bounded by $\frac{n}{2} \cdot 2^{2\ell}$, so we need $q \geq \frac{n}{2} \cdot 2^{2\ell}$ to be able to lift from $\mathbb{Z}_q[X]$ back to $\mathbb{Z}[X]$. However, we also need to pick q so that $\mathbb{Z}_q$ has a principal nth root of unity, as otherwise the NTT is not defined. We pick $q = q_1 q_2$ a bi-prime and compute modulo q_1 and q_2 separately via CRT; using two half-size moduli maps to the available hardware multipliers better than a single larger q. Table 1 presents our choices, and we explain them in detail now.

On the Cortex-M3, we use chunks of $\ell = 11$ bits, so $\lceil \frac{N}{\ell} \rceil = 187$ for $N = 2048$ and $\lceil \frac{N}{\ell} \rceil = 373$ for $N = 4096$, but pick slightly larger $n = 384 > 2 \lceil \frac{N}{\ell} \rceil$ for $N = 2048$ and $n = 768 > 2 \lceil \frac{N}{\ell} \rceil$ for $N = 4096$ since both are dimensions for which a fast NTT can be implemented. Next, we need $q_1 q_2 \geq 192 \cdot 2^{22}$ for $N = 2048$ and $q_1 \cdot q_2 \geq 384 \cdot 2^{22}$ for $N = 4096$; we pick $(q_1, q_2) = (12289, 65537)$ for $N = 2048$, and $(q_1, q_2) = (25601, 65537)$ for $N = 4096$. The Fermat prime $q_2 = 65537$ allows particularly fast NTT computation using the FNT, while the other prime is chosen to be the smallest admissible prime for which a 128th (resp. 256th) primitive root of unity exists.

Table 1. Parameters

Cortex-M3				
bits (N)	chunking (ℓ)	poly length (n)	NTT	modulus $q = q_1 \cdot q_2$
2048	11 bits	384	$128 = 2^7$	$12289 \cdot 65537$
4096	11 bits	768	$256 = 2^8$	$25601 \cdot 65537$
Cortex-M55				
bits (N)	chunking (ℓ)	poly length (n)	NTT	modulus $q = q_1 \cdot q_2$
2048	22 bits	192	$64 \cdot 3 = 2^6 \cdot 3$	$114\,826\,273 \cdot 128\,919\,937$
4096	22 bits	384	$128 \cdot 3 = 2^7 \cdot 3$	$114\,826\,273 \cdot 128\,919\,937$

On the Cortex-M55, we use chunks of $\ell = 22$ bits, so $\lceil \frac{N}{\ell} \rceil = 94$ for $N = 2048$ and $\lceil \frac{N}{\ell} \rceil = 187$ for $N = 4096$, but again pick slightly larger $n = 192 > 2 \lceil \frac{N}{\ell} \rceil$ for $N = 2048$ and $n = 384 > 2 \lceil \frac{N}{\ell} \rceil$ for $N = 4096$ since those are NTT-friendly dimensions. For $q = q_1 q_2$, we pick $114\,826\,273 \cdot 128\,919\,937$ for both $N = 2048$ and $N = 4096$. Those choices are motivated as follows: First, we have $q \approx 2^{53.7} > 2^{51.58} \approx \frac{384}{2} \cdot 2^{44}$. In fact, since we even have $q > 4 \cdot (\frac{384}{2} \cdot 2^{44})$, we can recover the coefficients in the *sum* of two polynomial products as the *signed* canonical representatives of their image in $\mathbb{Z}_q$. The former allows saving one CRT during the Montgomery multiplication, while the latter means that we don't need a signed-to-unsigned conversion after the signed CRT. Second, q_1, q_2 are carefully chosen so that $(q_2 \bmod q_1)^{-1}$ in $\mathbb{Z}_{q_2}$ is amenable to refined Barrett multiplication—in fact, since $(q_2 \bmod q_1)^{-1} = 774$, this is what we observed in Example 1. Thirdly, both $q_1 - 1$ and $q_2 - 1$ are multiples of 96 and thus support incomplete dimension-96 NTTs. Finally, $q_1, q_2 < 2^{27}$ are small enough that during the dimension-96 NTTs, no explicit modular reduction is necessary.

3.3 Chunking and Dechunking

We need to convert between multi-precision integers and polynomials, which we refer to as "chunking" chk() and "dechunking" dechk(). chk() takes an N-bit multi-precision integer and splits it into n chunks of ℓ bits each, viewed as the coefficients of a polynomial. In other words, we lift along $\mathbb{Z}[X] \to \mathbb{Z}, X \mapsto 2^\ell$. dechk() converts a polynomial to a multi-precision integer by evaluating the polynomial at $X = 2^\ell$. As the coefficients of polynomials may grow beyond 2^ℓ during computation, this requires carrying through the entire polynomial and packing into a multi-precision integer.

3.4 Modular Exponentiation and Table Lookup

For the private-key operations, we use square-and-multiply with Algorithms 1 and 2 to implement constant-time exponentiation with a fixed window size of

w bits. This requires constant-time table lookups, and choosing the optimal w depends on the relative costs of a modular multiplication compared to such lookups: The cost of a lookup scales linearly in the table size 2^w, whereas the number of required multiplications only scales proportionally to $1/w$. We have determined that $w = 6$ is the fastest choice for both Cortex-M3 and Cortex-M55 and both 2048 and 4096 bits. We note that memory consumption will be an increasing concern as w grows, since the lookup table contains 2^w entries—exponentially large in w. In turn, reducing w will incur only a mild performance penalty while allowing for a significant reduction in the table size.

It may seem at first that storing the table entries in NTT domain should be preferable. However, the much larger size of elements in NTT domain results in drastically slower table lookups, which in our implementation clearly outweighs the cost of transforming to NTT domain on the fly after each load. Thus, our implementation stores the table entries as integer values.

For the public-key operation, we use a straightforward square-and-multiply for the fixed public exponent $2^{16}+1$ which is overwhelmingly common in practice.

3.5 Implementation Details for Cortex-M3

Our Cortex-M3 NTT implementation relies on a code generator written in Python, featuring a bounds checker which determines when it should insert reductions, and which aborts if it cannot guarantee the correctness of the computation. The result is a set of fully unrolled assembly implementations of NTT, inverse NTT, base multiplication and squaring, for configurable moduli.

The code generator uses the same high-level structure for FNTs and "generic" NTTs, the main difference being in the reductions. The generator also recognizes multiplications by power-of-two constants and converts them to shifts when appropriate; this is one of the main optimizations employed by FNTs.

Number-Theoretic Transforms. We use incomplete NTTs of lengths $384 = 2^7 \cdot 3$ and $768 = 2^8 \cdot 3$. Both NTTs are implemented for the prime moduli $q_1 = 12289$ ($q_1 = 25601$) and $q_2 = 65537$, which by CRT correspond to a single NTT of the same length modulo $q_1 \cdot q_2$. We use CT butterflies for the forward NTT and GS butterflies for the inverse. Layers are merged as appropriate[2] to eliminate unnecessary store-load pairs. The base multiplication is a straightforward polynomial multiplication in a ring of the form $\mathbb{Z}_q[X]/(X^3 - \zeta)$. The CRT computation after the inverse NTTs is applied to each coefficient separately and follows Eq. 1.

"General" Number-Theoretic Transform. For most moduli including $q_1 = 12289$ and $q_1 = 25601$, we use a combination of (signed) Montgomery multiplication (Appendix A, Algorithm 4) and (signed) Barrett reductions (Appendix A, Algorithm 3). The Barrett reduction comes in two variants, the difference consisting

---

[2] The layers are merged as $4 + 3$ resp. $4 + 2 + 2$ in the forward NTTs, exploiting that the upper half of the input coefficients are zero, and $3 + 2 + 2$ resp. $3 + 3 + 2$ in the inverse NTTs. Register pressure prohibits more aggressive merging.

in the optional addition of R/2 before the right shift. Skipping the addition is faster, but results in worse reduction quality.

Fermat Number Transform. For the Fermat prime $q_2 = 2^{16} + 1 = 65537$, we use variants of the "FNT reduction" shown in Appendix A, Algorithm 5. Depending on the desired reduction quality, the algorithm is either applied (1) as written, or (2) with its input offset by 2^{15} and the output correspondingly offset by -2^{15}, or (3) followed by a conditional subtraction of $2^{16} + 1$ if the output is $> 2^{15}$. Method (2) produces a representative in $\{-2^{16} + 1, 2^{16} - 1\}$, while the output of method (3) is a canonical symmetric representative, i.e., lies in $\{-2^{15}, ..., 2^{15}\}$. Methods (2) and (3) are equally fast if the constant 2^{15} can be kept in a low register throughout. If register pressure renders this undesirable, method (2) provides a convenient "intermediate" solution between the very fast FNT reduction and the canonical symmetric reduction.

Constant-Time Lookup. We use predicated moves to extract the desired table entry in a "striding" fashion: For each slice of four 32-bit words, the respective part of each table entry is loaded and conditionally moved into a set of target registers using a `itttt eq; moveq; moveq; moveq; moveq` instruction sequence. The target registers are stored after processing all entries. Compared to the alternative of traversing the table entry by entry, this finalizes each output word immediately, and no partial outputs have to be stored and reloaded.

3.6   Implementation Details for Cortex-M55

Pipeline Efficiency. As explained in [Bec+22b], Cortex-M55 is a *dual-beat* implementation of MVE; that is, most MVE instructions execute over two cycles. To still achieve a Instructions per Cycle (IPC) rate of more than 0.5 without costly dual-issuing logic, Cortex-M55 supports *instruction overlapping* for neighboring vector instructions, provided they use different execution resources. The balance and ordering of instructions is therefore crucial for performance. We find that all our core subroutines have a good balance between load/store, addition and multiplication instructions and can be carefully arranged to maximize instruction overlapping, achieving an IPC > 0.9. Table 5 provides details.

Number-Theoretic Transform. We implement incomplete NTTs of degree $96 = 3 \cdot 32$ and $192 = 3 \cdot 64$ via Good's trick, using CT butterflies and Barrett multiplication throughout. Algorithm 6 is a translation of Barrett multiplication into MVE. No explicit modular reductions are necessary during NTT or NTT^{-1}, as we confirm using a script tracking the bounds of modular representative throughout the NTT, applying Fact 1 repeatedly.

Base Multiplication. The incomplete NTTs leave us with base multiplications in rings of the form $\mathbb{Z}_q[X]/(X^4 - \zeta)$ with a < 32-bit prime q, which we implement essentially using the method of [Bec+22b]: A polynomial $\boldsymbol{a} = a_0 + a_1 X + a_2 X^2 +$

$a_3 X^3$ is first expanded into a sequence $\tilde{a} = (a_0, \ldots, a_3, \zeta a_0, \ldots, \zeta a_3)$, and 64-bit representatives of the coefficients of $\boldsymbol{a} \cdot \boldsymbol{b}$ are computed as dot products of (b_3, b_2, b_1, b_0) with length-4 subsequences of $\tilde{a}$, using vmalaldav. Here, we instead compute $\tilde{a} = \frac{1}{n}(a_0, \ldots, a_3, \zeta a_0, \ldots, \zeta a_3)$, where n is the incomplete NTT degree, taking care of the scaling by $\frac{1}{n}$ as part of the base multiplication.

CRT. We vectorize the divided-difference interpolation (1), producing chunked outputs. We allow non-reduced inputs and compute canonical reductions u_0' of u_0 and of $(u_1 - u_0')m_1$ as part of the CRT rather than at the end of NTT^{-1}. For the computation of $(u_1 - u_0')m_1$, we use refined Barrett multiplication, leveraging our choice of primes. The long multiplication $((u_1 - u_0')m_1 \bmod {}^{\pm}q_1) q_0$ is computed via vmul[h], aligned to the 2^ℓ-boundary via $(a, b) \mapsto (a \bmod 2^\ell, b \cdot 2^{32-\ell} + \lfloor a/2^\ell \rfloor)$ (note $|b_i| < 2^{\lceil 52.7 \rceil - 32} = 2^{21}$, so $|2^{10} b_i| < 2^{31}$), and the low part added to u_0'. This results in a non-canonical chunked presentation of the CRT interpolation with 32-bit values, which are finally reduced to $< 2^\ell + 2^{32-\ell} = 2^{22} + 2^{10}$ via $a_i \mapsto (a_i \bmod 2^\ell) + \lfloor a_{i-1}/2^\ell \rfloor$. We found that the slight non-canonicity of the coefficients does not impact functional correctness, while enabling vectorization of the above routine—a perfect reduction, in turn, is inherently sequential.

Constant Time Lookup. In contrast to Cortex-M3 we do not use predicated move operations: A block of loads followed by a block of predicated moves allows for only very little instruction overlapping. Instead, we use load-multiply-accumulate sequences with secret constant 0/1 for the conditional moves, achieving very good instruction overlapping. Overall, we obtain a constant-time lookup of 5184 cycles for a table of 8192-bytes—26% over the theoretical minimum of 8192/2 cycles necessary to load each table entry once with a 64-bit data path. See Sect. C.

As our data resides in uncached Data-TCM, it is tempting to consider a plain load for a constant time lookup. We strongly advise against this: While access to D-TCM is *typically* single-cycle, it's not in general: On Cortex-M55 a D-TCM load with secret address could happen concurrently with a DMA transfer and trigger a memory bank conflict depending on the addresses being loaded. While this particularly issue could be circumvented in our present context, it might be problematic on future microarchitectures, and it appears prudent to simply stick to the principle that memory access patterns should not rely on secret data.

4   Results

4.1   Benchmark Environment

Cortex-M3. We use the STM32 Nucleo-F207ZG with the STM32F207ZG Cortex-M3 core with 128 kB RAM and 1 MB flash. We clock the Cortex-M3 at 30 MHz (rather than the maximum frequency of 120 MHz) to void having any flash wait states when fetching code or constants from flash. We place the stack in SRAM1 (112 kB) only since it results in slightly better performance. We use libopencm3[3] and some hardware abstraction code is taken from pqm3[4].

---

[3] https://github.com/libopencm3/libopencm3.
[4] https://github.com/mupq/pqm3.

Table 2. Performance of our NTTs and FNTs in cycles

Cortex-M3							
(N, n)	q	NTT	$\text{NTT}_{\text{heavy}}$	basemul	basesqr	$\text{basemul}_{\text{light}}$	NTT^{-1}
(2048, 384)	12289	12409	14692	7053	6101	5949	15130
	65537	7635	9631	7181	6488	5563	11090
(4096, 768)	25601	31491	35805	13808	11386	11729	36227
	65537	19892	23697	14062	12160	10957	25015

Cortex-M55							
(N, n)	q	NTT	$\text{NTT}_{\text{heavy}}$	basemul	basesqr	$\text{basemul}_{\text{light}}$	NTT^{-1}
(2048, 192)	114 826 273	814	1441	1500	–	880	900
	128 919 937						
(4096, 384)	114 826 273	2027	3230	2894	–	1696	2195
	128 919 937						

We use the SysTick counter for benchmarking. We use `arm-none-eabi-gcc` version 11.2.0 with `-O3`.

Cortex-M55. We make use of the Arm MPS3 FPGA prototyping board with an FPGA model of the Cortex-M55r1 (AN552). Both the prototyping board and the FPGA model are publicly available[5]. Qemu supports a previous revision of the image (AN547) and can be used for running our code as well. However, for meaningful benchmarks, the FPGA board is required. We make use of the tightly coupled memory for code (ITCM) and data (DTCM). The core is clocked at the default frequency of 32 MHz. We use the PMU cycle counter for benchmarking. We use `arm-none-eabi-gcc` version 11.2.0 with `-O3`.

4.2 NTT and FNT Performance

Table 2 contains the cycle counts for our core transformations. For the Cortex-M3, we implement four different transforms using specialized code for each combination of size and modulus. This allows us to minimize the number of explicit modular reductions taking into account the size of the modulus and its twiddles, and also to have a much faster FNT (modulo 65537) than the NTTs modulo 12289 and 25601. For the Cortex-M55 and a given size, the same code is used for both moduli with different precomputed constants; since no explicit modular reductions are required, we do not see prime-specific optimization potential. Base squaring and multiplication are the same, as we do not see optimization potential for squaring.

---

[5] https://developer.arm.com/tools-and-software/development-boards/fpga-prototyping-boards/download-fpga-images.

Table 3. Performance of modular multiplication, squaring, exponentiation in cycles. expmod$_{\text{public}}$ is a modular exponentiation with the exponent 65537. expmod$_{\text{private}}$ is a modular exponentiation with a private n-bit exponent.

	n	mulmod	sqrmod	expmod$_{\text{public}}$	expmod$_{\text{private}}$
Cortex-M3					
This work		220 047	196 830	4 227 473	494 923 435
This work (FIOS)	2048	234 041	–	4 912 705	543 648 872
BearSSL [Bear]		283 038	–	18 350 210	718 347 177
This work		510 708	454 128	9 752 690	2 250 748 647
This work (FIOS)	4096	926 523	–	19 458 326	4 228 661 467
BearSSL [Bear]		1 102 151	–	70 443 207	5 505 856 187

	n	mulmod	sqrmod	expmod$_{\text{public}}$	expmod$_{\text{private}}$
Cortex-M55					
This work		21 330	19 701	389 482	50 085 366
This work (FIOS)	2048	20 260	–	426 707	50 683 718
MbedTLS [Mbed]		41 443	–	884 416	108 441 240
BearSSL [Bear]		83 517	–	5 400 650	217 123 645
This work		47 660	43 620	861 450	218 110 707
This work (FIOS)	4096	73 316	–	1 540 685	358 080 308
MbedTLS [Mbed]		152 371	–	3 223 797	755 391 521
BearSSL [Bear]		328 801	–	21 254 533	1 646 834 048

4.3 Modular Arithmetic: Multiplication, Squaring, Exponentiation

Table 3 presents timings for our modular arithmetic routines.

For Cortex-M3, we compare with BearSSL [Bear] (v0.6, i15 implementation) which to our knowledge is the only library claiming to be constant-time on the Cortex-M3. We also consider a handwritten FIOS implementation (Sect. 2.4).

On Cortex-M55, we compare to BearSSL v0.6 (i31 implementation), to Mbed TLS [Mbed] v3.1.0, and to our own handwritten FIOS implementation. The BearSSL implementation compiles down to umlal, while the Mbed TLS implementation uses CIOS (Sect. 2.4) with umaal-based inline assembly.

We find that our implementations outperform Mbed TLS and BearSSL significantly for both 2048-bit and 4096-bit parameters. Moreover, for Cortex-M3, our NTT-based implementation is also slightly faster than the handwritten FIOS implementation for 2048-bit, and considerably faster for 4096-bit.

Somewhat surprisingly, the umaal-based handwritten FIOS is much faster than the umaal-based CIOS in Mbed TLS, and on par with our NTT-based implementation for 2048-bit. For 4096-bit, however, the NTT-based implementation prevails.

The optimization potential between `umaal`-based FIOS and CIOS lies within memory accesses: Mbed TLS' CIOS assembly does not leverage the 64-bit data path of Cortex-M55, and merging of loops in FIOS also saves accesses. We reported this optimization potential to the Mbed TLS team.[6]

Figure 1 shows the distribution of cycles spent in one modular multiplication.

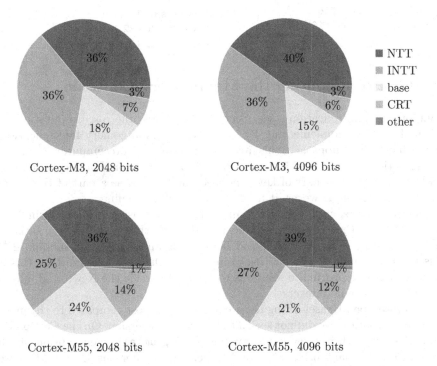

Fig. 1. Clock cycles spent on the subroutines of a single modular multiplication.

A   Reduction Algorithms for Cortex-M3 and Cortex-M55

Algorithm 3: $(\log_2 \mathtt{R})$-bit Barrett reduction on Cortex-M3.	**Algorithm 4:** 16-bit Montgomery multiplication on Cortex-M3.
Input: a $= a$	**Input:** $(\mathtt{a}, \mathtt{b}) = (a, b 2^{16} \bmod^{\pm} q)$
Output: a $= a \bmod^{\pm} q$	**Output:** a $= ab \bmod^{\pm} q$
1: `mul t, a, `$\lceil \mathtt{R}/q \rfloor$	1: `mul a, a, b`
2: *(optional)* `add t, t, #(R/2)`	2: `mul t, a, `$-q^{-1} \bmod^{\pm} 2^{16}$
3: `asr t, t, #`$\log_2 \mathtt{R}$	3: `sxth t, t`
4: `mls a, t, `q`, a`	4: `mla a, t, `q`, a`
	5: `asr a, a, #16`

---

[6] See https://github.com/ARMmbed/mbedtls/issues/5666
   and https://github.com/ARMmbed/mbedtls/issues/5360.

Algorithm 5: FNT reduction on Cortex-M3.
Input: a = a
Output: a = a mod$^\pm$ 65537 $\in$ $[-32767, 98303]$
1: ubfx t, a, #0, #16
2: sub a, t, a, asr#16

Algorithm 6: Barrett multiplication on Cortex-M55.
Input: $(\mathtt{a}, \mathtt{b}, \mathtt{b'}) = \left(a, b, \frac{\lfloor b2^{32}/q \rfloor_2}{2} \right)$
Output: a = ab mod$^\pm$ q
1: vmul.s32 l, a, b
2: vqrdmulh.s32 h, a, b'
3: vmla.s32 l, h, q

B   On Precomputing the Montgomery Constant

Montgomery multiplication (see Sect. 2.4) requires the precomputation of q^{-1} mod R. When implementing RSA via "large" Montgomery multiplication, rather than a FIOS approach, this means that we need to precompute n^{-1} mod R for encryption and p^{-1} mod R and q^{-1} mod R for decryption. For decryption this can be computed as a part of key generation and stored as a part of the secret key. For encryption, however, it needs to be computed online.

Modular inversion x^{-1} mod 2^r can be performed using "Hensel lifting": If $xy - 1 = 2^k a$, so that y is an inverse to x modulo 2^k, then $y' = 2y - x^2 y$ satisfies $xy' - 1 = -(xy-1)^2 = 2^{2k} a^2$, and hence y' is an inverse of x modulo 2^{2k}. This yields x^{-1} mod 2^k after $\mathcal{O}(\log k)$ iterations. One may observe that this is the sequence of approximate solutions to $xy = 1$ for x via the Newton–Raphson method in the 2-adic integers.

We prototyped Hensel-lifting to assess its relative cost compared to the modular exponentiation; we did not seek a fully optimized version. On the Cortex-M3 we implement both a variable-time variants using umlal for encryption and a constant-time variant using mla for key generation. For the Cortex-M55, we achieve the best performance using umaal. We list the performance in Table 4. We see that already a basic implementation has only a small performance overhead compared to an exponentiation (e.g., < 5% for RSA-4096).

Table 4. Performance of Hensel lifting; numbers for RSA-4096 in bold.

k	Cortex-M3		Cortex-M55
	mla (constant-time)	umlal (variable-time)	umaal (constant-time)
2112	**85 337**	45 326	**12 430**
4224	313 695	**163 107**	**38 575**

C   Table Lookup

Algorithm 7:
Conditional move on Cortex-M3

```
1: ldr.w a, [tbl, #4]
2: ldr.w b, [tbl, #8]
3: ldr.w c, [tbl, #12]
4: ldr.w d, [tbl], #16
5: cmp.n idx, #dst
6: itttt.n EQ
7: moveq.w a, A
8: moveq.w b, B
9: moveq.w c, C
10: moveq.w d, D
```

Algorithm 8:
Overlapping-friendly conditional
accumulation on Cortex-M55

```
1: cmp idx, #dst
2: cset mask, EQ // idx == dst
3: vldrw.u32 t, [tbl], #16
4: vmla.s32 A, t, mask
5: vldrw.u32 t, [tbl], #16
6: vmla.s32 B, t, mask
7: vldrw.u32 t, [tbl], #16
8: vmla.s32 C, t, mask
9: vldrw.u32 t, [tbl], #16
10: vmla.s32 D, t, mask
```

D   Pipeline Efficiency of Cortex-M55 Implementation

Table 5 shows Performance Monitoring Unit (PMU) statistics for the subroutines of our Cortex-M55 modular exponentiation ($N = 4096$). We use ARM_PMU_CYCCNT, ARM_PMU_INST_RETIRED, ARM_PMU_MVE_INST_RETIRED, and ARM_PMU_MVE_STALL for counting cycles, retired instructions, retired MVE instructions, and MVE instructions causing a stall, respectively. We derive the rate of Instructions per Cycle (IPC), as well as ARM_PMU_MVE_INST_RETIRED/ARM_PMU_MVE_STALL as a measure of the MVE overlapping efficiency. Despite most MVE instructions running for 2 cycles, instruction overlapping allows achieving an IPC > 0.9.

Table 5. Performance Monitoring Unit statistics for Cortex-M55 implementation.

Primitive	Cycles	Instructions	Instructions per Cycle (IPC)	MVE instructions	MVE stalls	MVE efficiency
NTT	2027	1936	0.95	1876	27	98.6%
NTT$_{heavy}$	3231	3017	0.93	2742	130	96.0%
NTT^{-1}	2195	2128	0.96	2072	9	99.6%
basemul	2894	2737	0.94	2500	109	95.6%
basemul$_{light}$	1695	1659	0.97	1634	6	99.6%
CRT	4287	4216	0.98	3563	13	99.6%
Table lookup	5184	4816	0.92	4132	12	99.7%

E   High-level Multiplication Structure

See Fig. 2.

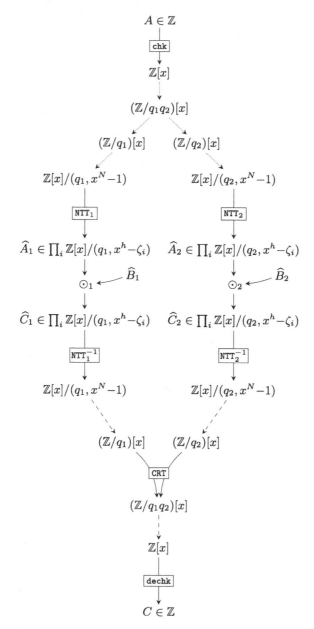

Fig. 2. High-level structure of our integer multiplication algorithm. Finely dotted arrows denote a conceptual reinterpretation with no change in representation. Dashed arrows denote a canonical choice of lift, e.g., a representative of minimal degree for polynomials or a smallest non-negative representative for integers.

References

[AB74]   Agarwal, R.C., Burrus, C.S.: Fast convolution using Fermat number transforms with applications to digital filtering. IEEE Trans. Signal Process. **22**(2), 87–97 (1974)

[Abd+22] Abdulrahman, A., et al.: Multi-moduli NTTs for Saber on Cortex-M3 and cortex-M4. IACR Trans. Cryptogr. Hardw. Embed. Syst. **2022**(1), 127–151 (2022)

[Bear]   Pornin, T.: BearSSL: a smaller TLS/SSL library

[Bec+22a] Becker, H., et al.: Neon NTT: faster Dilithium, Kyber, and Saber on Cortex-A72 and Apple M1. IACR Trans. Cryptogr. Hardw. Embed. Syst. **2022**(1), 221–244 (2022)

[Bec+22b] Becker, H., et al.: Polynomial multiplication on embedded vector architectures. IACR Trans. Cryptogr. Hardw. Embed. Syst. **2022**(1), 482–505 (2022)

[Chu+21] Chung, C.-M.M., et al.: NTT multiplication for NTT-unfriendly rings: new speed records for Saber and NTRU on Cortex-M4 and AVX2. IACR Trans. Cryptogr. Hardw. Embed. Syst. **2021**(2), 159–188 (2021)

[Für09]   Fürer, M.: Faster integer multiplication. SIAM J. Comput. **39**(3), 979–1005 (2009)

[Gar07]   García, L.C.C.: Can Schönhage multiplication speed up the RSA decryption or encryption? In: MoraviaCrypt 2007 (2007)

[GKZ07]   Gaudry, P., Kruppa, A., Zimmermann, P.: A GMP-based implementation of Schönhage-Strassen's large integer multiplication algorithm. In: ISSAC 2007, pp. 167–174. ACM (2007)

[GMP]   Free Software Foundation. The GNU Multiple Precision Arithmetic Library

[HH21]   Harvey, D., van der Hoeven, J.: Integer multiplication in time $O(n \log n)$. Ann. Math. **193**(2), 563–617 (2021)

[KAK96]   Koc, C.K., Acar, T., Kaliski, B.S.: Analyzing and comparing Montgomery multiplication algorithms. IEEE Micro **16**(3), 26–33 (1996)

[KO63]   Karatsuba, A., Ofman, Y.: Multiplication of multidigit numbers on automata. Soviet Phys. Doklady **7**, 595–596 (1963). Translated from Doklady Akademii Nauk SSSR, vol. 145, no. 2, pp. 293–294, July 1962

[Mbed]   Arm Ltd., Mbed TLS

[Mon85]   Montgomery, P.L.: Modular multiplication without trial division. Math. Comput. **44**(170), 519–521 (1985)

[Pol71]   Pollard, J.M.: The fast Fourier transform in a finite field. Math. Comput. **25**, 365–374 (1971)

[RSA78]   Rivest, R., Shamir, A., Adleman, L.: A method for obtaining digital signatures and public-key cryptosystems. Commun. ACM **21**(2), 120–126 (1978)

[SS71]   Schönhage, A., Strassen, V.: Schnelle Multiplikation großer Zahlen. Computing **7**(3–4), 281–292 (1971)

[Too63]   Toom, A.L.: The complexity of a scheme of functional elements realizing the multiplication of integers. Soviet Math. Doklady **3**, 714–716 (1963)

On Linear Complexity of Finite Sequences: Coding Theory and Applications to Cryptography

Edoardo Persichetti$^{(\boxtimes)}$ⓘ and Tovohery H. Randrianarisoaⓘ

Florida Atlantic University, Boca Raton, FL 33434, USA
{epersichetti,trandrianarisoa}@fau.edu

Abstract. We define two metrics on vector spaces over a finite field using the linear complexity of finite sequences. We then develop coding theory notions for these metrics and study their properties. We give a Singleton-like bound as well as constructions of subspaces achieving this bound. We also provide an asymptotic Gilbert-Varshamov-like bound for random subspaces. We show how to reduce the problem of finding codewords with given Hamming weight into a problem of finding a vector of a given linear complexity. This implies that our new metric can be used for cryptography in a similar way to what is currently done in the code-based setting.

Keywords: Linear code · Linear complexity · Periodic linear complexity · Gilbert-Varshamov · Signature scheme

1 Introduction

Code-based Cryptography was informally born in 1978, when Robert J. McEliece proposed a new cryptosystem based on the hardness of decoding linear codes (binary Goppa codes) in the Hamming metric [20]. The advantage of this approach is that cryptosystems of this kind are considered safe against adversaries with access to quantum computers. More precisely, there is no known quantum algorithm that can decode a random linear code in polynomial time. After 40 years of cryptanalysis, the cryptosystem is still considered to be secure, as a general framework. However, the protocol requires the use of relatively large public keys, which may be undesirable in certain applications.

To address the key size issue, it was initially suggested to use different families of linear codes, as well as "structured" linear codes (e.g. [10,19,24]). After several years and various unsuccessful attempts, the field has stabilized, and one can say that code-based encryption/key-establishment protocols are going to be crystallized (also thanks to NIST's Standardization effort [23]) into one of two main categories: the original McEliece framework (with only minor improvements that do not affect security, e.g. [22]) or protocols based on structured parity-check codes such as QC-MDPC [21]. The former, although with its well-known limitations, provides a safe choice relying on 40 years of security history [1]. The latter,

C.-M. Cheng and M. Akiyama (Eds.): IWSEC 2022, LNCS 13504, pp. 24–44, 2022.
https://doi.org/10.1007/978-3-031-15255-9_2

instead, represents the opposite trend, namely a choice aimed at a performance advantage, which however fails to fully explore some security aspects [3].

The situation is different for code-based signature schemes, for which a satisfactory solution has yet to be found; it is worth noting that the few code-based signature schemes submitted to NIST's process were all either broken, or withdrawn. This has prompted a large body of work in recent years, trying to circumvent the traditional issues by either relying on a different coding problem [7,11] or leveraging innovative frameworks [14–16] in the Hamming metric. As we will show, the notion of weight for vectors is closely related to the notion of linear complexity for sequences. This motivates us to study the linear complexity of sequences as a new metric for coding theory, with an eye towards cryptographic applications.

1.1 Overview

Let $\mathbb{F}_q$ be the finite field of size q. We recall some notions from coding theory in the Hamming metric. Let $\mathbf{x} = (x_1, \cdots, x_n) \in \mathbb{F}_q^n$. The *Hamming weight* $w_H(\mathbf{x})$ of $\mathbf{x}$ is the number of non-zero entries of $\mathbf{x}$. If $\mathbf{x}$ and $\mathbf{y}$ are two elements of $\mathbb{F}_q^n$, we define the *Hamming distance* between $\mathbf{x}$ and $\mathbf{y}$ as $d_H(\mathbf{x}, \mathbf{y}) = w_H(\mathbf{x} - \mathbf{y})$. A *linear code* $\mathcal{C}$ of length n over $\mathbb{F}_q$ is a subspace of $\mathbb{F}_q^n$ paired with the distance d_H. The *minimum distance* of a linear code $\mathcal{C}$ is the smallest value of $d_H(\mathbf{x}, \mathbf{y})$ for any two distinct codewords $\mathbf{x}, \mathbf{y} \in \mathcal{C}$.

The most important parameters for a linear code $\mathcal{C}$ are the size q of the base field, the length n, the dimension k and minimum distance d of the code. We denote such code by $[n, k, d]$ and the field is assumed to be understood. One has to optimize the choice of these parameters for applications. For example, one typically wants to construct codes that have simultaneously large dimension and large minimum distance, while the base field should preferably be as small as possible (binary field for example). A trade-off between the minimum distance and the dimension should be considered, as captured by the Singleton bound.

Theorem 1 (Singleton bound). *Let $\mathcal{C}$ be an $[n, k, d]$ linear code over $\mathbb{F}_q$. Suppose that d is the minimum distance of $\mathcal{C}$. Then,*

$$d \leq n - k + 1.$$

Due to this, we want to have codes which maximize both the dimension and the minimum distance of the codes. Thus we want to have codes for which the inequality in the above definition is an equality. Such codes are defined as follows.

Definition 1. *An $[n, k, d]$ linear code $\mathcal{C}$ which attains the Singleton bound i.e. $d = n - k + 1$, is called a* Maximum Distance Separable (MDS) *code.*

There exist explicit instances of maximum distance separable codes. One easy construction is given by the following. Let $n = q - 1$ and let $\alpha = (\alpha_1, \cdots, \alpha_n)$

be a vector having as entries all the distinct non-zero elements of $\mathbb{F}_q$. We define the evaluation map as

$$ev_\alpha : \mathbb{F}_q[x] \to \mathbb{F}_q^n$$
$$f(x) \mapsto (f(\alpha_1), \cdots, f(\alpha_n))$$

Let $\mathbb{F}_q[x]_{<k}$ be the vector space of all polynomials of degree at most $k - 1$. Then the image $\mathcal{C} = ev_\alpha(\mathbb{F}_q[x]_{<k})$ is an MDS code. This comes from the fact that a polynomial of degree at most $k - 1$ can have at most $k - 1$ roots. The code we just described is called *Reed-Solomon* code.

It is this relation between the property of the roots of polynomials and the weights of vectors which is interesting for us. The following theorem is a consequence of the König-Rados Theorem [18, Chap. 6].

Theorem 2. *Let* $\mathbb{F}_q^* = \{\alpha_1, \ldots, \alpha_{q-1}\}$ *and let* $f(x) = a_0 + a_1 x + \cdots + a_{q-2} x^{q-2}$ *be a polynomial over* $\mathbb{F}_q$. *If* $f(x)$ *has* $q - 1 - r$ *roots, then* $(f(\alpha_1), \cdots, f(\alpha_{q-1}))$ *has (Hamming) weight* r *and the periodic sequence* $\overline{(a_0, \cdots, a_{q-2})}$ *has linear complexity* r *i.e. there exist* $c_0, \ldots, c_{r-1} \in \mathbb{F}_q$ *such that*

$$a_{i+r \bmod (q-1)} = \sum_{j=0}^{r-1} c_j a_{i+j \bmod (q-1)}, \quad \forall i \in \mathbb{N}$$

and r *is the smallest for such integer.*

Through Theorem 2, we can relate the linear complexity of a periodic sequence with the Hamming weight of a vector. However, we have only periodic sequences with period $q - 1$. This raises the following question: what happens if we consider sequences $(a_0, \ldots, a_n)$ of any length not necessarily equal to $q - 1$? Even more generally, what is the situation with any type of sequences which are not necessarily assumed to be periodic? We will answer these questions in the next sections. Our goal is to provide a theory of the linear complexity of subspaces of sequences. Such a theory can in fact be used as a basis to consider new code-based cryptosystems based on the linear complexity of sequences.

1.2   Our Contribution

Using rank metric in lieu of the Hamming metric is a popular trend in code-based cryptography, occasionally leading to interesting results [2,4]. While this approach is not always completely satisfactory and its security is still not fully explored [5,6,25], it does hint at the possibility of using other metrics for building protocols, which provides additional motivation for our work. In this paper, we strive to show that the metric connected to the linear complexity of finite sequences is viable to build cryptographic schemes. To do that, we first carefully develop the necessary coding theory notions, beginning in Sect. 2 by describing linear-feedback shift registers and some of their properties. We then present the definition of linear complexity for both arbitrary finite sequences and sequences with a fixed period. Accordingly, in Sect. 3, we define two new metrics on $\mathbb{F}_q^n$ by considering the linear complexity of finite sequences and periodic sequences with a fixed period. We give a Singleton-like bound with respect to the new metrics and we construct optimal subspaces i.e. subspaces that achieve the bound. In the interest of space, these subspaces and their applications are described in Appendix B. We then move on to studying hard problems in this metric, which is a fundamental step to apply the metric to cryptography. Thus, in Sect. 4, we show that, given a subspace of $\mathbb{F}_q^n$, the problem of finding codewords with a given linear complexity is NP-complete. We do this for both finite and periodic sequences. The result is achieved by reducing the problem of finding a codeword with given Hamming weight to a problem of finding vectors with given linear complexity. In Sect. 5, we describe further properties of the linear complexity of sequences. We give an asymptotic Gilbert-Varshamov-like bound, which shows that most subspaces have large minimum distance with respect to the linear complexity. Furthermore, we describe techniques for solving the hard problems introduced earlier, which effectively constitute attack techniques for the schemes, and analyze their complexity. Finally, in Sect. 6 we describe a sample application to the cryptographic setting, by adapting a construction of Feneuil et al. [15] and explaining why its formulation in terms of linear complexity provides a computational advantage.

2   Linear-Feedback Shift Registers

We fix a finite field $\mathbb{F}_q$ where q is a power of a prime.

Definition 2. *A* Linear-Feedback Shift Register (LFSR) *of order l over $\mathbb{F}_q$ is an infinite sequence (a_i) over $\mathbb{F}_q$ such that there are fixed $c_j \in \mathbb{F}_q$, $j = 0, \ldots, l-1$ with,*

$$a_{i+l} = \sum_{j=0}^{l-1} c_j a_{i+j}, \quad \forall i \in \mathbb{N}.$$

The feedback polynomial *associated to (a_i) is $f(z) = z^l - \sum_{j=0}^{l-1} c_j z^j$.*

Definition 3. *Let (a_i) be an LFSR over $\mathbb{F}_q$. The* generating function *$A(z)$ associated to (a_i) is the formal power series*

$$A(z) = \sum_{i=0}^{\infty} a_i z^i.$$

Given an LFSR over $\mathbb{F}_q$ with feedback polynomial $f(z)$ and generating function $A(z)$, one can show [18, Chap. 8] that for some polynomial $g(z)$ of degree $l - 1$ at most, we have

$$A(z) = \frac{g(z)}{f^*(z)},$$

where f^* is the reciprocal polynomial given by $f^*(z) = z^l f\left(\frac{1}{z}\right)$.

Definition 4 (Linear Complexity). *Given a non-zero finite sequence* $(a_i) = (a_0, \cdots, a_{n-1}) \in \mathbb{F}_q^n$, *the* linear complexity $\mathfrak{L}(a_i)$ *of the sequence is the smallest* l *such that*

$$a_{i+l} = \sum_{j=0}^{l-1} c_j a_{i+j}, \quad \forall i, \ 0 \leq i \leq n-l-1,$$

for some fixed $c_j \in \mathbb{F}_q$. *We set* $\mathfrak{L}(\mathbf{0}) = 0$, *where* $\mathbf{0} = (0, \ldots, 0)$.

Another family of sequences are periodic sequences.

Definition 5 (n-periodic Linear Complexity). *Let* n *be a positive integer. An infinite sequence* (a_i) *is called* n-periodic *if for all* $i \geq 0$, $a_{i+n} = a_i$. *Such sequences are written as* $\overline{(a_0, \ldots, a_{n-1})}$. *The linear complexity of the sequence is defined as*

$$\mathfrak{L}_p \overline{(a_0, \ldots, a_{n-1})} = \mathfrak{L}(a_0, \ldots, a_{n-1}, a_0, \ldots, a_{n-1}).$$

Remark 1. It is possible that an n-periodic sequence is l-periodic for some $l < n$. The context tells us what period we consider for our sequences.

Given a finite sequence, it is possible to compute the shortest LFSR that produces it. This can be done using the Berlekamp-Massey algorithm in $\mathcal{O}(n^2)$ field operations in $\mathbb{F}_q$ [18, Chap. 8]. Furthermore, if the linear complexity of the sequence is $n/2$, then n successive terms of the sequence are enough to uniquely find the shortest shift register.

We have the following property for the linear complexity of finite sequences.

Proposition 1. *Let* $(a_i) = (a_0, \cdots, a_{n-1})$ *be a finite sequence over* $\mathbb{F}_q$. *Then* $\mathfrak{L}(a_i) \leq n$. *Furthermore the only sequences attaining the bound* n *are of the form* $(0, \cdots, 0, a)$, *with* $a \in \mathbb{F}_q^*$.

Proof. We can just use an LFSR with (a_i) as initial state so that the maximum linear complexity is at most n. It is obvious that $(0, \cdots, 0, a)$ has linear complexity n. Finally, if $(a_i) = (a_0, \cdots, a_{n-1})$ is such that $a_j \neq 0$ for some j with $0 \leq j \leq n-2$, then by taking $c_i = 0$ except when $i = j$, where $c_j = a_{n-1}/a_j$, we prove that $a_{n-1} = \sum_{j=0}^{n-2} c_j a_j$ so that the linear complexity is at most $n-1$. $\square$

The corresponding property for periodic sequences is given in the following proposition.

Proposition 2. *Let* $\overline{(a_i)} := \overline{(a_0, \cdots, a_{n-1})}$ *be an* n-periodic sequence over $\mathbb{F}_q$. *Then* $\mathfrak{L}_p \overline{(a_i)} \leq n$.

Proof. It is enough to show that the LFSR defined by the coefficients in $\mathbb{F}_q$, $(c_0, \ldots, c_{n-1}) = (1, 0, \ldots, 0)$ generates the periodic sequence with initial input $(a_0, \ldots, a_{n-1})$. Thus the linear complexity is smaller or equal to n. $\square$

Remark 2. Unlike the case of finite sequences, there can be periodic sequences other than $\overline{(0, \cdots, 0, a)}$, with $a \in \mathbb{F}_q^*$ that attain the bound in the proposition.

As an example, we can use Theorem 2. Start with a codeword in $\mathbb{F}_q^n$ with Hamming weight $n = q - 1$: then, the corresponding polynomial will have coefficients which form an n-periodic sequence of linear complexity n.

The key property of the linear complexity of sequences which will be used later is the following.

Theorem 3. *Let (a_i) and (b_i) be two finite sequences of the same length. If $(c_i) = (a_i) + (b_i)$, then*

$$\mathfrak{L}(c_i) \leq \mathfrak{L}(a_i) + \mathfrak{L}(b_i).$$

Proof. With a slight abuse of notation, we denote by (a_i) (resp. (b_i)) the LFSR generating the finite sequence (a_i) (resp. (b_i)). Suppose that these LFSR have generating functions

$$\frac{g_a(z)}{f_a^*(z)} \text{ and } \frac{g_b(z)}{f_b^*(z)},$$

respectively. Then the generating function of the LFSR generating (c_i) is

$$\frac{g_a(z)f_b^*(z) + g_b(z)f_a^*(z)}{f_a^*(z)f_b^*(z)}.$$

Thus, (c_i) can be generated by an LFSR with the feedback polynomial $f_a(z)f_b(z)$. It follows that the linear complexity of the sequence is at most $\mathfrak{L}(a_i) + \mathfrak{L}(b_i)$. $\qquad\square$

Corollary 1. *Let $\overline{(a_i)}$ and $\overline{(b_i)}$ be two finite periodic sequences of the same period. If $\overline{(c_i)} = \overline{(a_i)} + \overline{(b_i)}$, then*

$$\mathfrak{L}_p\overline{(c_i)} \leq \mathfrak{L}_p\overline{(a_i)} + \mathfrak{L}_p\overline{(b_i)}.$$

3   Coding Theory Using Linear Complexity

Let $\mathbb{F}_q$ be a finite field and let n be a positive integer. We will consider vectors in $\mathbb{F}_q^n$ and embed them with two different metrics using the linear complexity of finite (resp. periodic) sequences.

Definition 6. *Let $\mathbf{a} = (a_0, \cdots, a_{n-1}) \in \mathbb{F}_q^n$ and $\mathbf{b} = (b_0, \cdots, b_{n-1}) \in \mathbb{F}_q^n$ be two finite sequences of n elements of $\mathbb{F}_q$ each. Then we define two distances on $\mathbb{F}_q^n$ as*

$$d_1(\mathbf{a}, \mathbf{b}) = \mathfrak{L}((a_i) - (b_i)) \text{ and } d_2(\mathbf{a}, \mathbf{b}) = \mathfrak{L}_p(\overline{(a_i)} - \overline{(b_i)}).$$

It is easy to see that both maps define a distance. We only show it for d_1, but the proof for d_2 is similar.

(i)   By definition $d_1(\mathbf{a}, \mathbf{b}) = 0 \Leftrightarrow \mathbf{a} = \mathbf{b}$.
(ii) By definition of $\mathfrak{L}$, $\mathfrak{L}(a_i) \geq 0$.
(iii) The symmetry is obvious, i.e. $d_1(\mathbf{a}, \mathbf{b}) = d_1(\mathbf{b}, \mathbf{a})$.

(iv) For the triangular inequality,

$$
\begin{aligned}
d_1(\mathbf{a}, \mathbf{b}) &= \mathfrak{L}((a_i) - (b_i)) \\
&= \mathfrak{L}((a_i) - (c_i) + (c_i) - (b_i)) \\
&\leq \mathfrak{L}((a_i) - (c_i)) + \mathfrak{L}((c_i) - (b_i)), \text{ by Theorem 3} \\
&= d_1(\mathbf{a}, \mathbf{c}) + d_1(\mathbf{c}, \mathbf{b}).
\end{aligned}
$$

Thus, d_1 indeed defines a distance of $\mathbb{F}_q^n$. In a similar fashion, d_2 also defines a distance.

As in traditional coding theory, we can define a subset of $\mathbb{F}_q^n$ and fix a metric d_j, $j = 1, 2$ on this set. We will derive basic coding results for this context.

Definition 7. *Let S be a subset of $\mathbb{F}_q^n$ together with a distance $d \in \{d_1, d_2\}$. The minimum distance d of S is the minimum of $d(\mathbf{a}, \mathbf{b})$ for distinct $\mathbf{a}, \mathbf{b} \in S$. We describe the parameters of S as $[n, |S|, d]$. In case S is a k-dimensional subspace of $\mathbb{F}_q^n$, then d is the minimum linear complexity of the non-zero sequences in S and we say S is an $[n, k, d]$ code with this metric.*

Next, we inspect the bounds on a $[n, |S|, d]$-subset of $\mathbb{F}_q^n$.

Theorem 4 (Singleton Bound). *Let $\mathbb{F}_q$ be a finite field of size q. Let $S \subset \mathbb{F}_q^n$ be a set of elements of $\mathbb{F}_q^n$ together with a distance $d \in \{d_1, d_2\}$, with minimum distance d with respect to the metric. Then $|S| \leq q^{n-d+1}$.*

Proof. It is clear that for any finite sequence (a_i), $\mathfrak{L}(a_i) \leq \mathfrak{L}_p\overline{(a_i)}$ and therefore, for any $\mathbf{a}$ and $\mathbf{b}$ in $\mathbb{F}_q^n$, $d_1(\mathbf{a}, \mathbf{b}) \leq d_2(\mathbf{a}, \mathbf{b})$. Thus it is enough to show the thesis for the distance d_2. We define the linear map ϕ as

$$
\phi : \mathbb{F}_q^n \rightarrow \mathbb{F}_q^{n-d+1}
$$

$$
(a_0, \cdots, a_{n-1}) \rightarrow \begin{pmatrix} 1 \dots 1 \end{pmatrix} \begin{pmatrix} a_0 & \cdots & a_{n-d} & a_{n-d+1} & \cdots & a_{n-1} \\ \vdots & \ddots & \vdots & \vdots & \ddots & \vdots \\ a_{d-1} & \cdots & a_{n-1} & a_0 & \cdots & a_{d-2} \end{pmatrix}
$$

This map is constrained to be injective on S, otherwise (if two sequences $\mathbf{a}$ and $\mathbf{b}$ were mapped to the same image) then $\mathbf{a} - \mathbf{b}$ would be mapped to zero. In this case, if we write $\mathbf{a} - \mathbf{b} = (c_0, \dots, c_{n-1})$, then

$$
\begin{pmatrix} 1 \cdots 1 \end{pmatrix} \begin{pmatrix} c_0 & \cdots & c_{n-d} & c_{n-d+1} & \cdots & c_{n-1} \\ \vdots & \ddots & \vdots & \vdots & \ddots & \vdots \\ c_{d-1} & \cdots & c_{n-1} & c_0 & \cdots & c_{d-2} \end{pmatrix} = \begin{pmatrix} 0 \cdots 0 \end{pmatrix}.
$$

Thus the last row is a linear combination of the previous rows. But this would imply that $\mathfrak{L}_p\left(\overline{(a_i) - (b_i)}\right) \leq d - 1$ i.e. $d_2(\mathbf{a}, \mathbf{b}) \leq d - 1$. This contradicts the minimum distance of S. By injectivity, we must have that $|S| \leq |(\mathbb{F}_q^{n-d+1})|$. $\square$

Note that in this proof, instead of using $(1 \cdots 1)$, we can use any vector with 1 as last entry. These operations are equivalent to the puncturing operation on codes. Namely, using $(0 \cdots 0\ 1)$ is analogue to puncturing at the first $d - 1$ positions.

Remark 3. In case $\mathcal{S}$ is linear of dimension k over $\mathbb{F}_q$, then the Singleton bound is $k \leq n - d + 1$.

To conclude this section, we mention the existence of structures that achieve the Singleton bound. We call these *Optimal Sets of Sequences*, and describe them briefly in Appendix B.

4   Linear Complexity Coset Weight Problems

Given that our initial motivation was the possibility of an application to cryptography, in this section we show that the problem of decoding random linear codes with respect to the linear complexity metrics d_1 and d_2 is a difficult problem. Namely, we show that some problems related to the linear complexity are NP-complete. Recall that a decisional problem $\mathcal{P}$ is said to be in NP if, for any instance of $\mathcal{P}$ with a positive answer, there is an algorithm which can verify the solution in polynomial time. A problem $\mathcal{P}$ is called NP-hard if any problem in NP can be reduced to $\mathcal{P}$ in polynomial time. If a problem is both NP and NP-hard, then it is called NP-complete. NP-complete problems are considered to be intractable. One example of an NP-complete problem, which is relevant for us, is the following (where we indicate (I) for Input and (Q) for Question).

Coset Weight Problem (CWP):

(I) A matrix $\mathbf{H} \in \mathbb{F}_q^{r \times n}$, a vector $\mathbf{b} \in \mathbb{F}_q^r$ and a non negative integer ω.
(Q) Is there a vector $\mathbf{a} \in \mathbb{F}_q^n$ such that $w_H(\mathbf{a}) \leq \omega$ and $\mathbf{a}\mathbf{H}^\top = \mathbf{b}$?

CWP was proven to be NP-complete in [13]. However, the statement in [13] is proved only for the binary field. A more general statement with arbitrary field size is proved in [8]. For our theory, we want to show that the following problems related to the linear complexity are NP-complete.

Linear Complexity Coset Weight Problem (LCCWP):

(I) A matrix $\mathbf{H} \in \mathbb{F}_q^{r \times n}$, a vector $\mathbf{b} \in \mathbb{F}_q^r$ and a non-negative integer ω.
(Q) Is there a vector $\mathbf{a} \in \mathbb{F}_q^n$ such that $\mathfrak{L}(\mathbf{a}) \leq \omega$ and $\mathbf{a}\mathbf{H}^\top = \mathbf{b}$?

Periodic Linear Complexity Coset Weight Problem (PLCCWP):

(I) A matrix $\mathbf{H} \in \mathbb{F}_q^{r \times n}$, a vector $\mathbf{b} \in \mathbb{F}_q^r$ and a non-negative integer ω.
(Q) Is there a vector $\mathbf{a} \in \mathbb{F}_q^n$ such that $\mathfrak{L}_p(\mathbf{a}) \leq \omega$ and $\mathbf{a}\mathbf{H}^\top = \mathbf{b}$?

To show that these decision problems are NP-complete, we first show that CWP can be reduced to PLCCWP. Then we show that PLCCWP can be reduced to LCCWP. To begin, we show a reduction from CWP to a more specialized problem, which we state below. Its difference with CWP is that the size of the field $\mathbb{F}_q$ is not arbitrary but it is fixed to be $q = n + 1$.

Fixed-Field Coset Weight Problem (FFCWP):

(I) A matrix $\mathbf{H} \in \mathbb{F}_q^{r \times (q-1)}$, a vector $\mathbf{b} \in \mathbb{F}_q^r$ and a non negative integer ω.

(Q) Is there a vector $\mathbf{a} \in \mathbb{F}_q^{q-1}$ such that $w_H(\mathbf{a}) \leq \omega$ and $\mathbf{a}\mathbf{H}^\top = \mathbf{b}$?

The result is proven in the following theorem.

Theorem 5. *FFCWP is NP-complete.*

Proof. The fact that FFCWP is NP is easy to see. Next, we transform an instance of CWP to an instance of FFCWP. Let $\mathbf{H} \in \mathbb{F}_q^{r \times n}$, $\mathbf{b} \in \mathbb{F}_q^r$ and ω a non-negative integer from an instance of CWP. Let $Q = q^{\lceil \log_q(n+1) \rceil}$. It is clear that $Q \geq n+1$. If $Q > n+1$, then construct the matrix $\mathbf{H}_1 \in \mathbb{F}_Q^{r \times (Q-1)}$ by appending columns of zeros to the matrix $\mathbf{H}$. Finding $\mathbf{a} \in \mathbb{F}_q^n$ such that $w_H(\mathbf{a}) \leq \omega$ and $\mathbf{a}\mathbf{H}^\top = \mathbf{b}$ is reduced to finding $(\mathbf{a}|\mathbf{0}) \in \mathbb{F}_q^{Q-1}$ such that $w_H(\mathbf{a}) \leq \omega$ and $(\mathbf{a}|\mathbf{0})\mathbf{H}_1^\top = \mathbf{b}$. Now, if there was a polynomial-time algorithm which solves FFCWP, we could use it to find $\mathbf{a}_1$ such that $\mathbf{a}_1\mathbf{H}_1^\top = \mathbf{b}$. Note that $\mathbf{a}_1$ can still be a vector over $\mathbb{F}_Q$. However, we show that we can use this to get a solution over $\mathbb{F}_q$. Due to the form of $\mathbf{H}_1$, we may assume that $\mathbf{a}_1 = (a_1, \ldots, a_n, 0, \ldots, 0)$. Now, let $Tr_{Q/q}$ be the trace function corresponding to the finite extension $\mathbb{F}_Q/\mathbb{F}_q$. We also denote by $Tr_{Q/q}(\mathbf{x})$, for any vector $\mathbf{x}$ over $\mathbb{F}_Q$, where the trace map is applied individually on the entries of $\mathbf{x}$. Then, since the matrix $\mathbf{H}_1$ and the vector $\mathbf{b}$ have entries in $\mathbb{F}_q$, we have that

$$(Tr_{Q/q}(a_1), \ldots, Tr_{Q/q}(a_n), 0, \ldots, 0)\mathbf{H}_1^\top = Tr_{Q/q}\left((\mathbf{a}|\mathbf{0})\mathbf{H}_1^\top\right) = Tr_{Q/q}(\mathbf{b}) = \mathbf{b}.$$

This gives us $(Tr_{Q/q}(a_1), \ldots, Tr_{Q/q}(a_n))\mathbf{H}^\top = \mathbf{b}$ where the vector given by $(Tr_{Q/q}(a_1), \ldots, Tr_{Q/q}(a_n))$ has entries over $\mathbb{F}_q$. Notice that the trace over $\mathbb{F}_q/\mathbb{F}_q$ can be computed in polynomial time. Therefore a polynomial-time algorithm solving FFCWP also solves CWP in polynomial time. Since CWP is NP-complete, it is NP-hard, from which it follows that FFCWP must also be NP-hard, and hence NP-complete. $\qquad\square$

Remark 4. Switching from the field $\mathbb{F}_q$ of size q to the field $\mathbb{F}_Q$ with $Q = q^{\lceil \log_q(n) \rceil}$ does not increase the difficulty of the problem exponentially. Indeed, instead of working over the field $\mathbb{F}_q$, we just work on a field of size $Q \sim n$.

We now use the result in Theorem 5 to show that PLCCWP is also NP-complete. First of all, note that it is easy to see that PLCCWP is in NP. Next, we will need to translate the notion of Hamming distance into the notion of linear complexity. For that we recall the results from Sect. 1.

Let q be a power of a prime. Theorem 2 says that if $f(x) = f_0 + f_1 x + \cdots + f_{q-2} x^{q-2}$ is a polynomial over a finite field $\mathbb{F}_q$ of size q, then the number of roots of $f(x)$ in $\mathbb{F}_q^*$ is given by $q - 1 - \omega$, where $\mathfrak{L}_p\overline{(f_0, f_1, \ldots, f_{q-2})} = \omega \leq q - 1$.

Another tool that we need is how to convert a vector into a polynomial. That is done via the interpolation using a Vandermonde matrix. Suppose that we have a finite field with q elements $\mathbb{F}_q = \{0, b_1, \ldots, b_{q-1}\}$. Then the following Vandermonde matrix is invertible.

$$
V = \begin{pmatrix}
1 & 1 & \ldots & 1 \\
b_1 & b_2 & \ldots & b_{q-1} \\
b_1^2 & b_2^2 & \ldots & b_{q-1}^2 \\
\vdots & \vdots & \ddots & \vdots \\
b_1^{q-2} & b_2^{q-2} & \ldots & b_{q-1}^{q-2}
\end{pmatrix}.
\tag{1}
$$

Thus for any $(c_1, \ldots, c_{q-1}) \in \mathbb{F}_q^{q-1}$, there is a unique polynomial $f_0 + f_1 x + \cdots + f_{q-2} x^{q-2}$ such that $f(b_i) = c_i$. This can be computed via $(f_0, \ldots, f_{q-2}) = (c_1, \ldots, q_{q-1}) V^{-1}$. We denote the map by

$$
\phi : \qquad \mathbb{F}_q^{q-1} \to \mathbb{F}_q^{q-1}
\tag{2}
$$
$$
(c_1, \ldots, c_{q-1}) \mapsto (f_0, \ldots, f_{q-2})
$$

Now, let us see how we can convert a linear code into a subspace of periodic sequences. Suppose that we have a finite field $\mathbb{F}_q$ with q elements. Assume that $\mathcal{C} \subset \mathbb{F}_q^{q-1}$. Let $\mathbf{c} = (c_1, \cdots, c_{q-1}) \in \mathbb{F}_q^{q-1}$. If we assume that $\{a_1, \cdots, a_{q-1}\} = \mathbb{F}_q^*$, then, via the map in Eq. (2), any $\mathbf{c}$ can be written as

$$
\mathbf{c} = (f(a_1), \cdots, f(a_{q-1})),
$$

for some polynomial $f(x)$ of degree $q-2$ over $\mathbb{F}_q$. Using Theorem 2 and the above discussion, we see that the Hamming weight of $\mathbf{c}$ is the same as the periodic linear complexity $\mathfrak{L}_p(f_0, f_1, \ldots, f_{q-2})$. Therefore, we have the following correspondence.

$$
\left\{ \begin{array}{c} \text{Codewords } \mathbf{c} \text{ in } \mathbb{F}_q^{q-1} \\ \text{using the Hamming weight} \end{array} \right\} \Leftrightarrow \left\{ \begin{array}{c} \text{Finite sequences } \mathbf{c}V^{-1} \text{ in } \mathbb{F}_q^{q-1} \\ \text{using the linear complexity} \end{array} \right\}
\tag{3}
$$

Now, with FFCWP, we have a parity-check matrix $\mathbf{H} \in \mathbb{F}_q^{r \times (q-1)}$ and a vector $\mathbf{b} \in \mathbb{F}_q^r$. We want to find $\mathbf{c} \in \mathbb{F}_q^{q-1}$ such that $\mathbf{c}\mathbf{H}^\top = \mathbf{b}$ and $w_H(\mathbf{c}) \leq \omega$. Using the Vandermonde matrix in Eq. (1) and the correspondence (3), we can write $\mathbf{c} = \mathbf{a}V$. Thus $\mathbf{a}V\mathbf{H}^\top = \mathbf{b}$. So if we set $\mathbf{H}_1 = V\mathbf{H}^\top$, then the problem is equivalent to finding $\mathbf{a} \in \mathbb{F}_q^{q-1}$ such that $\mathbf{a}\mathbf{H}_1^\top = \mathbf{b}$ and $\mathfrak{L}_p(\mathbf{c}) \leq \omega$. In other words, solving FFCWP over $\mathbb{F}_q^{q-1}$, can be reduced to solving PLCCWP over $\mathbb{F}_q$.

Theorem 6. *Solving PLCCWP is at least as hard as solving FFCWP.*

Since by Theorem 5, solving a general instance of FFCWP is NP-complete, we can also conclude that solving PLCCWP is NP-hard. Thus, we have the following theorem.

Theorem 7. *PLCCWP is NP-complete.*

Now, because we know that $\mathfrak{L}_p(a_1,\ldots,a_n) = \mathfrak{L}(a_1,\ldots,a_n,a_1,\ldots,a_n)$, we can reduce an instance of PLCCWP to an instance of LCCWP in the following manner. Suppose we are looking for $\mathbf{a}$ such that $\mathfrak{L}_p(\mathbf{a}) = \omega \le n$ and $\mathbf{a}\mathbf{H}^\top = \mathbf{b}$. This can be interpreted as looking for $(\mathbf{a}|\mathbf{a})$ such that $\mathfrak{L}(\mathbf{a}|\mathbf{a}) = \omega \le n$ and $(\mathbf{a}|\mathbf{a})\mathbf{H}_1^\top = (\mathbf{b}|\mathbf{0})$, where

$$\mathbf{H}_1 = \left[\begin{array}{c|c} \mathbf{H} & \mathbf{0} \\ \hline \mathbf{I}_n & -\mathbf{I}_n \end{array}\right]$$

If there were an algorithm solving LCCWP, then we could use it with the parity-check matrix $\mathbf{H}_1$ and syndrome $(\mathbf{b}|\mathbf{0})$ to find a solution $(\mathbf{a}_1|\mathbf{a}_2)$. The identity matrix $\mathbf{I}_n$ in $\mathbf{H}_1$ ensures that $\mathbf{a}_1 = \mathbf{a}_2$, so we find a solution of the form $(\mathbf{a}|\mathbf{a})$ and therefore we get a solution to PLCCWP. Thus, we have the following theorem.

Theorem 8. *LCCWP is NP-complete.*

From Theorem 2, we have seen that there is a correspondence between linear complexity and Hamming weight. As we have seen in this section, the problem of decoding in the Hamming metric can be translated into a problem of decoding with linear complexity, where the period of the sequences is fixed. It is therefore natural to ask if we can do the converse. It is not straightforward to use the previous results. Namely, when we start with a finite field $\mathbb{F}_q$ with the Hamming metric, we end up with the field $\mathbb{F}_Q$ with the linear complexity, for $Q = q^l$, and the period of the finite sequence is fixed to be $n = Q^l - 1$. Thus, for the converse, if we start with periodic sequences with period n such that $n+1$ is not a power of a prime, we cannot use the above correspondence. However, we are going to show that, with a more general version of Theorem 2, we are still able to switch from periodic linear complexity to Hamming metric. We begin with the following.

Proposition 3 ([12]). *Let $\mathbb{F}_q$ be a finite field and let w be a primitive n-th root of unity lying in $\mathbb{F}_{q^m}$ for some m. The linear complexity of $\mathfrak{L}_p\overline{(a_0,\ldots,a_{n-1})}$ with $a_i \in \mathbb{F}_q$ is equal to the Hamming weight of $(c_0,\ldots,c_{n-1})$, where $c_i = \sum_{j=0}^{n-1} w^{-ij}a_j$.*

By the previous proposition, if one starts with a subspace of $\mathbb{F}_q^n$ embedded with the n-periodic linear complexity, then one can transform the problem to a Hamming-metric version over the field $\mathbb{F}_{q^m}$ in a straightforward way. In this case, the problem can be easily translated to a problem with Hamming metric, the theoretic results from Hamming metric can be translated into results in the periodic linear complexity metric. Hence, from here on, we focus on finite sequences that are not restricted to a fixed period and are measured with the distance d_1.

5   Properties of Linear Complexity

As we have seen, one can compute the linear complexity of a sequence using the Berlekamp-Massey algorithm. Thus, if a sequence has small linear complexity, one can easily find an LFSR generating this sequence. Due to this fact, we usually want to have sequences with large linear complexity. Therefore, one important question is to know how many finite sequences have large linear complexity. Another motivation for this section is that knowing the number of sequences with a given linear complexity is important for the security aspect of a code-based cryptosystem using linear complexity as metric. In the vast majority of the traditional code-based cryptosystems, in fact, one has to randomly generate error vectors with a fixed Hamming weight. We may think of the same by replacing the Hamming weight by linear complexity. In order to parametrize the security of such scheme, one again needs to know the number of sequences with a given linear complexity. When we consider finite sequences, there is already an answer to this question [17]. As mentioned in the last paragraph of the previous section, we are only interested in finite sequences without fixed periods. Thus, we will only use the linear complexity $\mathcal{L}$ and the distance $d = d_1$.

Theorem 9 ([17]). *Let* $\omega \leq n$ *be positive integers. Then, the number of sequences* $(a_i) = (a_1, \ldots, a_n)$ *having length* n *and linear complexity* $\mathcal{L}(a_i) = \omega$ *over a finite field* $\mathbb{F}_q$ *of size* q *is given by*

$$\begin{cases} 1 & \text{if } \omega = 0, \\ q^{2\omega-1}(q-1) & \text{if } \omega \leq \lfloor \frac{n}{2} \rfloor, \\ q^{2(n-\omega)}(q-1) & \text{if } \omega > \lfloor \frac{n}{2} \rfloor. \end{cases}$$

Theorem 10. *Given two integers* $\omega \leq n$*, the number* $b(n, \omega)$ *of finite sequences* $(a_i) = (a_1, \ldots, a_n)$ *having length* n *and linear complexity* $\mathcal{L}(a_i)$ *at most* ω *over a finite field* $\mathbb{F}_q$ *of size* q *is*

$$\begin{cases} 1 & \text{if } \omega = 0, \\ \dfrac{q^{2\omega+1}+1}{q+1} & \text{if } \omega+1 \leq n-\omega, \\ \dfrac{1-q^{2(n-\omega)}}{1+q} + q^n & \text{if } n-\omega \leq \omega. \end{cases}$$

Proof. Direct computation from Theorem 9. □

Since we also know the size of balls with respect to the linear complexity from Theorem 10, we can give a formula for the sphere packing bound.

Theorem 11 (Sphere Packing Bound). *Let* S *be a set of sequences of length* n *and with minimum distance* d*. Then*

$$|S| \leq \begin{cases} \dfrac{q^n(q+1)}{q^{2\lfloor \frac{d-1}{2} \rfloor}+1} & \text{if } 2\lfloor \frac{d-1}{2} \rfloor \leq n-1, \\ \dfrac{q^n(q+1)}{1-q^{2(n-\lfloor \frac{d-1}{2} \rfloor)}+(1+q)q^n} & \text{if } 2\lfloor \frac{d-1}{2} \rfloor > n-1. \end{cases}$$

Proof. This is a direct consequence of Theorem 10 and uses the fact that the union of the spheres of radius $\lfloor \frac{d-1}{2} \rfloor$ centered at the sequences in S is a disjoint union. □

Our next theorem is the analogue to the Gilbert-Varshamov bound.

Theorem 12 (Gilbert-Varshamov Bound for Linear Complexity). *Let $d \leq n$ be positive integers. Let $A_q(n, d)$ be the size of the largest possible subset $\mathcal{S}$ of $\mathbb{F}_q^n$ with minimum distance d with respect to the metric d_1. Then*

$$\begin{cases} A_q(n, d) = q^n & \text{if } d = 1, \\ A_q(n, d) \geq \dfrac{q^n(q+1)}{q^{2d-1}+1} & \text{if } d \leq n - d + 1, \\ A_q(n, d) \geq \dfrac{q^n(q+1)}{1 + q^n(q+1) - q^{2(n-d-1)}} & \text{if } d \geq n - d + 2. \end{cases}$$

Proof. We follow the proof in the classical Hamming metric. When $d = 1$, the result is trivial. Suppose that $|\mathcal{C}| = A_q(n, d)$. Because of the maximality of $\mathcal{S}$, any elements of $\mathbb{F}_q^n$ should be contained in a ball $B(\mathbf{x}, d - 1)$, with center $\mathbf{x}$ and radius $d - 1$, for some $\mathbf{x} \in \mathcal{S}$. Thus $\mathbb{F}_q^n = \cup_{\mathbf{x} \in \mathcal{S}} B(\mathbf{x}, d - 1)$. Thus, we have $|\mathbb{F}_q^n| \leq |\mathcal{S}| b(n, d - 1)$. The results follow from Theorem 10. $\qquad\square$

The following is a version of the Gilbert-Varshamov bound for linear spaces of sequences.

Theorem 13 (Gilbert-Varshamov Bound for Linear Spaces). *Let $d \leq n$ be positive integers. Let $\mathcal{D}_q(n, d)$ be the dimension of the largest possible subspace $\mathcal{S}$ of $\mathbb{F}_q^n$ with minimum distance d with respect to the metric d_1. Then*

$$\begin{cases} \mathcal{D}_q(n, d) = n & \text{if } d = 1, \\ \mathcal{D}_q(n, d) \geq \log_q\left(\dfrac{q^n(q+1)}{q^{2d-1}+1}\right) & \text{if } d \leq n - d + 1, \\ \mathcal{D}_q(n, d) \geq \log_q\left(\dfrac{q^n(q+1)}{1 + q^n(q+1) - q^{2(n-d-1)}}\right) & \text{if } d \geq n - d + 2. \end{cases}$$

Proof. Again, the case $d = 1$ is trivial. For a non-zero vector $\mathbf{x} \in \mathbb{F}_q^n$, we denote by $\langle \mathbf{x} \rangle$, the one-dimensional $\mathbb{F}_q$-space generated by $\mathbf{x}$. Now, if $\mathcal{S}$ has maximal dimension, say k, then for any element $\mathbf{x} \in \mathbb{F}_q^n \backslash \mathcal{S}$, the space $\mathcal{S} +_{\mathbb{F}_q} \langle \mathbf{x} \rangle$ should contain an elements of linear complexity smaller than d. Thus, there is $\mathbf{a} \in \mathcal{S}$ and $b \in \mathbb{F}_q^*$ such that $\mathbf{a} + b\mathbf{x}$ has linear complexity at most $d - 1$. Thus $\mathbf{x} \in B(\mathbf{a}, d - 1)$. On the other hand, if $\mathbf{x} \in \mathcal{S}$ then $\mathbf{x} \in B(\mathbf{x}, d - 1)$. Thus we get to the same proof of the previous theorem: $\mathbb{F}_q^n = \cup_{\mathbf{x} \in \mathcal{S}} B(\mathbf{x}, d - 1)$. The results follow. $\qquad\square$

The bounds in Theorems 11, 12 and 13 were given for the reader to compare to the case of linear codes equipped with the Hamming metric. However, we have already seen a bound on the maximum size of set of sequences with a given minimum distance (see Theorem 4) and we have shown that the bound is attained for any parameters and without restriction on the base field. Now, we want to give a criteria for the optimal subspaces of sequences. To do this, for any integer $t < n$ and a vector $\mathbf{b} = (b_1, \ldots, b_t)$, we define the matrix $\mathbf{M_b} \in \mathbb{F}_q^{n \times (n-t)}$ by

$$\mathbf{M_b} = \begin{pmatrix} b_1 & 0 & \cdots & 0 \\ \vdots & b_1 & \cdots & 0 \\ b_t & \vdots & \ddots & \vdots \\ -1 & b_t & \ddots & b_1 \\ 0 & -1 & \ddots & \vdots \\ \vdots & \ddots & \ddots & b_t \\ 0 & \cdots & 0 & -1 \end{pmatrix}$$

Theorem 14. *Let $\mathcal{S}$ be an $[n,k]$ subspace of sequences over $\mathbb{F}_q$ and let $k \leq n - d + 1$. Let $\mathbf{G}$ be a generator matrix of $\mathcal{S}$. Then the following statements are equivalent:*

(i) The minimum distance of $\mathcal{S}$ is d.
(ii) There exists a vector $\mathbf{c} = (c_1, \ldots, c_d) \in \mathbb{F}_q^d$ such that $\mathbf{GM_c}$ has rank strictly smaller than k. Furthermore, $\mathbf{GM_b}$ has full rank k for any vector $\mathbf{b} = (b_1, \ldots, b_{d-1}) \in \mathbb{F}_q^d$.

Proof. Suppose that the minimum distance is d. Because no element of $\mathcal{S}$ has linear complexity smaller than d, then if $\mathbf{a} = (a_1, \ldots, a_n) \in \mathcal{S}$ no coefficients $\mathbf{b} = (b_1, \ldots, b_{d-1})$ can generate $\mathbf{a}$ with initial state $a_1, \ldots, a_{d-1}$. Thus we have that $(m_1, \ldots, m_k)\mathbf{GM_b} \neq \mathbf{0}$ for any $(m_1, \ldots, m_k) \in \mathbb{F}_q^k$. Therefore $\mathbf{GM_b} \in \mathbb{F}_q^{k \times (n-d)}$ has no left kernel i.e. it has full rank k. In a similar fashion, if there is a codeword of linear complexity d, then we can find $\mathbf{c} = (c_1, \ldots, c_d)$ such that $\mathbf{GM_c} \in \mathbb{F}_q^{k \times (n-d)}$ has non-empty left kernel and thus its rank is smaller than k. The converse can be proved using the same idea in reverse fashion. □

Corollary 2. *Let $\mathcal{S}$ be an $[n, k, d]$ subspace of sequences over $\mathbb{F}_q$. Then $\mathcal{S}$ is optimal, i.e. $d = n - k + 1$, if and only if $\mathbf{GM_b} \in \mathbb{F}_q^{k \times k}$ is invertible for any $\mathbf{b} = (b_1, \ldots, b_{n-k}) \in \mathbb{F}_q^{n-k}$. In particular $\mathcal{S}$ has a generator matrix of the form $\mathbf{G} = [\mathbf{X}|\mathbf{I}_k]$.*

Proof. A direct consequence of Theorem 14. □

The previous corollary gives a characterization of optimal subspaces of sequences. Our next step is to give a bound on the minimum distance of random subspaces. This follows a method analogous to the asymptotic Gilbert-Varshamov bound in the Hamming metric case (See [9] for example).

Fix a positive integer $1 \leq d \leq n$. Let $\mathbf{G}$ be a matrix in $\mathbb{F}_q^{k \times n}$ chosen uniformly at random. Suppose that $\mathcal{S}_\mathbf{G}$ is the row space of $\mathbf{G}$. Let P be the probability that the minimum distance $d(\mathcal{S}_\mathbf{G})$ of $\mathcal{S}_\mathbf{G}$ is strictly smaller than d i.e.

$$P = Prob\,(d(\mathcal{S}_\mathbf{G}) < d) = Prob\,(\exists \mathbf{x} \in \mathbb{F}_q^k \backslash \{\mathbf{0}\} \colon \mathcal{L}(\mathbf{xG}) < d)$$

It is clear that

$$P \le \sum_{\mathbf{x} \in \mathbb{F}_q^k \setminus \{\mathbf{0}\}} Prob\left(\mathfrak{L}(\mathbf{xG}) < d\right).$$

Now, because $\mathbf{G}$ is a uniformly random variable, so is $\mathbf{xG}$. Thus

$$Prob\left(\mathfrak{L}(\mathbf{xG}) < d\right) = \frac{b(n, d-1)}{q^n}.$$

Thus

$$P \le (q^k - 1)\frac{b(n, d-1)}{q^n}.$$

Thus we have the following theorem.

Theorem 15. *Let $\mathbf{G}$ be a random $(k \times n)$ matrix over $\mathbb{F}_q$ and let $\mathcal{S}_{\mathbf{G}}$ be the row space of $\mathbf{G}$ over $\mathbb{F}_q$. Let $d < n/2$ be the minimum distance of $\mathcal{S}$ and let $\epsilon > 0$, where $k = n - 2d - \epsilon$. Then $Prob\left(d(\mathcal{S}_{\mathbf{G}}) < d\right) \le \frac{2}{q^2 q^{\epsilon n}}$.*

Proof. Let $P = Prob\left(d(\mathcal{S}_{\mathbf{G}}) < d\right)$. From the previous paragraph, we have

$$P \le (q^k - 1)\frac{b(n, d-1)}{q^n}.$$

Because $d/n < 1/2$, then by Theorem 10,

$$P \le (q^k - 1)\frac{q^{2d-1} + 1}{(q+1)q^n} \le \frac{2q^k q^{2d-1}}{q^{n+1}}$$

Thus

$$P \le \frac{2}{q^2 q^{n-k-2d}},$$

and the result follows.   □

Now, in Theorem 15, $q^{-\epsilon n}$ decreases exponentially with respect to n. Thus, we can conclude the following.

Corollary 3. *With high probability, a random $k \times n$ matrix over $\mathbb{F}_q^n$ generates a space of sequences with minimum distance at least $\frac{n-k}{2}$.*

6   Cryptographic Applications

In this section, we illustrate one possible application of our theory to cryptography. Namely, we show how a recent signature scheme by Feneuil et al. [15], which uses the popular "MPC-in-the-head" paradigm, can be formulated in terms of linear complexity, and how this leads to an improvement. Due to space constraints, we are not able to describe the signature scheme in full; instead, we summarize the relevant part of the scheme, and present our proposed modification.

Let $\mathbf{H}$ be a parity-check matrix of a random $[n,k]$ code and let $\mathbf{y} \in \mathbb{F}_q^{n-k}$. For the purpose of verification, a prover wants to prove that he knows $\mathbf{x} \in \mathbb{F}_q^n$ such that $\mathbf{x}\mathbf{H}^T = \mathbf{y}$ and $w_H(\mathbf{x}) \leq w$. The prover does not want to reveal information about $\mathbf{x}$. Note that, by taking $\mathbf{H} = [\mathbf{H}'|\mathbf{I}_{n-k}]$, we can write $(\mathbf{x}_A|\mathbf{x}_B)\mathbf{H}^T = \mathbf{y}$ for $\mathbf{x} = (\mathbf{x}_A|\mathbf{x}_B)$. In this case, $\mathbf{x}_A$ uniquely determines $\mathbf{x}$ from $\mathbf{y}$ and $\mathbf{H}$.

Following the notation of [15], let $\mathbb{F}_{\text{poly}}$ be a finite extension of $\mathbb{F}_q$ such that $n \leq |\mathbb{F}_{\text{poly}}|$ and let $\{\gamma_1, \ldots, \gamma_n\}$ be distinct elements of $\mathbb{F}_{\text{poly}}$. Let $S(X) \in \mathbb{F}_{\text{poly}}[X]$ be the polynomial interpolation of the points (γ_i, x_i). It is easily seen that the condition $w_H(\mathbf{x}) \leq r$ is equivalent to $S(x)$ having at least $n - w$ roots in $\{\gamma_1, \cdots, \gamma_n\}$. In [15], it is shown that this is equivalent to the existence of two polynomials $P, Q \in \mathbb{F}_{\text{poly}}[X]$ such that $Q \cdot S - P \cdot F = 0$, where $\deg P \leq w - 1$, $\deg Q = w$ and $F = \prod_{i=1}^n (X - \gamma_i)$. In order to prove his knowledge, the prover does the following.

(1) Write $\mathbf{x}_A = \sum_{j=1}^N \mathbf{x}_A^{(j)}$. These define $\mathbf{x} = \sum_{j=1}^N \mathbf{x}^{(j)}$ and ensures that the syndrome relation $\mathbf{x}\mathbf{H}^T = \mathbf{y}$ is satisfied. The elements of these sums are what we call the shares in the MPC protocol.

(2) Find the interpolation polynomial $S^{(j)}(X)$ using the points $(\gamma_i, x_i^{(j)})$, where $i = 1, \ldots, n$ and $\mathbf{x}^{(j)} = (x_1^{(j)}, \ldots, x_n^{(j)})$. By the linearity of the Lagrange interpolation, $S(X) = \sum_{j=1}^N S^{(j)}(X)$.

(3) Write $Q(X) = \sum_{j=1}^N Q^{(j)}(X)$.

(4) Write $(P \cdot F)(X) = \sum_{j=1}^N (P \cdot F)^{(j)}(X)$.

(5) To verify that $Q(X)S(X) = (P \cdot F)(X)$. One can verify that $Q(r_l)S(r_l) = (P \cdot F)(r_l)$ for $1 \leq l \leq r$ and r_j elements of an extension $\mathbb{F}_{\text{points}}$ of $\mathbb{F}_{\text{poly}}$.

(6) To make this verification without revealing $Q(r_l)$ and $S(r_l)$, one needs to use the decompositions $Q(r_l) = \sum_{j=1}^N Q^{(j)}(r_l)$, $S(r_l) = \sum_{j=1}^N S^{(j)}(r_l)$ and $(P \cdot F)(r_l) = \sum_{j=1}^N (P \cdot F)^{(j)}(r_l)$ in an MPC protocol.

For full details about the usage of these steps in a zero-knowledge protocol for syndrome decoding, we refer the reader to [15].

In Step (2), the prover is required to make several of interpolations to find the polynomials $S^{(j)}(X)$. These computations negatively affect the performance of the scheme. In the following, we explain how to use a system with periodic linear complexity as metric, and completely avoid the interpolation steps, thereby considerably speeding up the scheme of [15]. In the remaining part of this section, we set $n = q - 1$ and therefore we can also choose $\mathbb{F}_{\text{poly}} = \mathbb{F}_q$.

Let $\mathbf{H}$ be a parity check matrix of a random $[n,k]$ code and let $\mathbf{y} \in \mathbb{F}_q^{n-k}$. Now, a prover wants to show that he knows $\mathbf{a} \in \mathbb{F}_q^n$ such that $\mathbf{a}\mathbf{H}^T = \mathbf{y}$ and $\mathcal{L}_p(\mathbf{a}) \leq w$, without revealing information about $\mathbf{a}$. Again, we take $\mathbf{H} = [\mathbf{H}'|\mathbf{I}_{n-k}]$ and we can write $(\mathbf{a}_A|\mathbf{a}_B)\mathbf{H}^T = \mathbf{y}$ for $\mathbf{a} = (\mathbf{a}_A|\mathbf{a}_B)$.

By Theorem 2 and Eq. (3), if $\mathbf{a} = (a_0, \ldots, a_{n-1})$ and $S(X) = \sum_{i=0}^{q-2} a_i X^i$, then $w_H(S(\gamma_0), \ldots, S(\gamma_{q-2})) = \mathfrak{L}_p(\mathbf{a})$, where $\mathbb{F}_q^* = \{\gamma_0, \ldots, \gamma_{n-1}\}$. Using the same method as before, showing that $\mathfrak{L}_p(\mathbf{a}) \le w$ is therefore the same as showing the existence of two polynomials $P, Q \in \mathbb{F}_{\text{poly}}[X]$ such that $Q \cdot S - P \cdot F = 0$, where $\deg P \le w - 1$, $\deg Q = w$ and $F = \prod_{i=1}^{n}(X - \gamma_i)$. The difference with the scheme in the Hamming metric is that the polynomial $S(X)$ is already defined by $\mathbf{a}$. Thus, no interpolation is needed, as claimed. In general, these are the steps the prover needs to follow.

(1') Write $\mathbf{a}_A = \sum_{j=1}^{N} \mathbf{a}_A^{(j)}$. This defines $\mathbf{a} = \sum_{j=1}^{N} \mathbf{a}^{(j)}$ and ensures that the syndrome relation $\mathbf{a}\mathbf{H}^T = \mathbf{y}$ is satisfied. The elements of these sums are the shares in the MPC protocol.

(2') The coefficients of $\mathbf{a}^{(j)}$ define a polynomial $S^{(j)}(X)$. By linearity, we have $S(X) = \sum_{j=1}^{N} S^{(j)}(X)$.

(3') Write $Q(X) = \sum_{j=1}^{N} Q^{(j)}(X)$.

(4') Write $(P \cdot F)(X) = \sum_{j=1}^{N}(P \cdot F)^{(j)}(X)$.

(5') To verify that $Q(X)S(X) = (P \cdot F)(X)$, one can verify that $Q(r_l)S(r_l) = (P \cdot F)(r_l)$ for $1 \le l \le r$ and r_j elements of an extension $\mathbb{F}_{\text{points}}$ of $\mathbb{F}_{\text{poly}}$.

(6') To perform this verification without revealing $Q(r_l)$ and $S(r_l)$, one needs to use the decompositions $Q(r_l) = \sum_{j=1}^{N} Q^{(j)}(r_l)$, $S(r_l) = \sum_{j=1}^{N} S^{(j)}(r_l)$ and $(P \cdot F)(r_l) = \sum_{j=1}^{N}(P \cdot F)^{(j)}(r_l)$ in an MPC protocol.

As mentioned above, since in this setting we have $n = q - 1$ and $\mathbb{F}_{\text{poly}} = \mathbb{F}_q$, Eq. (3) shows that syndrome decoding of the form $\mathbf{x}\mathbf{H}^T = \mathbf{y}$ and $w_H(\mathbf{x}) \le w$ is equivalent to syndrome decoding of the form $\mathbf{a}\mathbf{H}_1^T = \mathbf{y}$. In this regard, the parameter sets for the Hamming metric are exactly the same parameter sets for the periodic linear complexity metric. In order to find the best parameters for a security of the scheme with the linear complexity, we can therefore use parameters from the Hamming metric. We can for example use a similar set of parameters as in the Variant 3 described in [15], working on a field $\mathbb{F}_q = \mathbb{F}_{\text{poly}} = \mathbb{F}_{256}$, and using a code of length $n = q - 1 = 255$ and dimension $k = 128$. The weight of the secret key $\mathbf{a}$ in this case is $w = 80$. An implementation of the scheme of [15] in this new metric is planned as future work, as well as a translation to the (non-periodic) linear complexity setting.

Acknowledgements. Part of this work was supported by SNF grant no. 169510 when T. Randrianarisoa was at the University of Zurich. The work is also partially funded by the National Science Foundation (NSF) grant CNS-1906360.

A   The Berlekamp-Massey Algorithm

Algorithm 1. Berlekamp-Massey

1: **procedure** BM($s_0, \cdots, s_{n-1}$)
2:     $f(z) \leftarrow 1$, $A(z) \leftarrow 1$,
3:     $L \leftarrow 0$, $m = -1$, $e \leftarrow 1$
4:     **for** i from 0 to $n - 1$ **do**
5:         $d \leftarrow s_i + \sum_{j=1}^{L} f_j s_{i-j}$
6:         **if** $d \neq 0$ **then**
7:             $B(z) \leftarrow f(z)$
8:             $f(z) \leftarrow f(z) - (d/e)A(z)z^{i-m}$
9:             **if** $2L \leq i$ **then**
10:                 $L \leftarrow i + 1 - L$
11:                 $m \leftarrow i$
12:                 $A(z) \leftarrow B(z)$
13:                 $e \leftarrow d$
14:             **end if**
15:         **end if**
16:     **end for**
17:     **return** L and $f(z)$
18: **end procedure**

B   Optimal Sets of Sequences

Definition 8 (Optimal Sets of Sequences). *We call a set $S \subset \mathbb{F}_q^n$ an Optimal Set of Sequences (OSS) (resp. Optimal Set of Periodic Sequences (OSPS)) if the minimum distance with respect to the metric d_1 (resp. d_2) of S reaches the bound of the previous theorem i.e. if S has elements of length n and minimum distance d and $\sharp S = q^{n-d+1}$.*

Example 1. Let S be the set of sequences of length n over a finite field $\mathbb{F}_q$ defined by

$$S = \{(0, \cdots, 0, a_1, \cdots, a_k) : a_i \in \mathbb{F}_q\}.$$

Then, S is both an OSS an OSPS of dimension k. That is because the sequences cannot be generated by an LFSR of length smaller than $n - k + 1$ except when it is the zero sequence.

The nice property of using the set of sequences with the linear complexity as a metric is that, in opposite to maximum distance separable codes in the Hamming metric, we can have an optimal set of sequences for any parameters. The construction works even for the binary field. Furthermore, the decoding of OSS given in Examples 1 is straightforward. They are similar and we will only describe it for the OSS in Example 1. First let us look at the unique decoding property.

Proposition 4. *Suppose that S is an $[n, M, d]$ set of sequences. Suppose that $\mathbf{y} \in \mathbb{F}_q$ is equal to $\mathbf{x} + \mathbf{e}$, where $\mathbf{x} \in S$ and $\mathfrak{L}(\mathbf{e}) < \frac{d}{2}$. Then, the decomposition $\mathbf{x} + \mathbf{e}$ is unique.*

Proof. If $\mathbf{y} = \mathbf{x}_1 + \mathbf{e}_1 = \mathbf{y}_2 + \mathbf{e}_2$, then $\mathbf{x}_1 - \mathbf{x}_2 = \mathbf{e}_2 - \mathbf{e}_1$. Therefore $d(x_1, x_2) = \mathfrak{L}(\mathbf{e}_2 - \mathbf{e}_1)$. By Theorem 3, $d(x_1, x_2) \leq \mathfrak{L}(\mathbf{e}_2) + \mathfrak{L}(\mathbf{e}_1) < d$. This is in contradiction with the minimum distance of S.

Let S, of dimension k, be the OSS in Example 1. Suppose that we know $\mathbf{y} = \mathbf{x} + \mathbf{e}$ with $\mathbf{x} \in S$ and $\mathfrak{L}(\mathbf{e}) < \frac{n-k+1}{2}$. By Proposition 4, we know that $\mathbf{e}$ is unique. Since the $n - k$ first entries of $\mathbf{x}$ are equal to zero. Then we know the first $n - k$ entries of $\mathbf{e}$. Now, since $\mathfrak{L}(\mathbf{e}) < \frac{n-k+1}{2}$, we can uniquely recover the LFSR generating $\mathbf{e}$ by using Berlekamp-Massey. on the first $n - k$ entries of e. We are therefore able to produce the whole $\mathbf{e}$ and then we compute $\mathbf{x} = \mathbf{y} - \mathbf{e}$. By Proposition 4, the resulting $\mathbf{x}$ is the only correct original codeword.

C   Application for Decoding Reed-Solomon Codes

We can use linear complexity to get a decoding algorithm for Reed-Solomon coded (see Sect. 1). Let $\mathbb{F}_q^* = \{\alpha_1, \ldots, \alpha_n\}$, where $n = q - 1$. The Reed Solomon code $\mathcal{C}$ is defined as

$$\mathcal{C} = \{(f(\alpha_1), \ldots, f(\alpha_n)) \colon f(x) \in \mathbb{F}_q[x], \deg f(x) \leq k - 1\}.$$

Assume that the received codeword is $\mathbf{c} + \mathbf{e}$ and $w_H(\mathbf{e}) \leq \frac{n-k+1}{2}$. By Theorem 2, $\mathbf{c}$ corresponds to a polynomial $f_{\mathbf{c}}$ of degree at most $k - 1$, and $\mathbf{e}$ corresponds to a polynomial $f_{\mathbf{e}}$ of degree at most $q - 2$. The first step of decoding is to interpolate $\mathbf{c} + \mathbf{e}$ to get $f_{\mathbf{c}} + f_{\mathbf{e}}$. Now, since $f_{\mathbf{c}}$ has degree at most $k - 1$, the last $n - k + 1$ coefficients of $f_{\mathbf{e}}$ are the same as the last $n - k + 1$ coefficients of $f_{\mathbf{c}} + f_{\mathbf{e}}$. Since $\mathbf{e}$ has Hamming weight smaller or equal to $\frac{n-k+1}{2}$, the coefficients of $f_{\mathbf{e}}$ has linear complexity $t \leq \frac{n-k+1}{2}$. In particular the last $n - k + 1$ coefficients of $f_{\mathbf{e}}$ is generated by an LFSR of length t at most. Now, given that $t \leq \frac{n-k+1}{2}$ and since we know $n - k + 1$ coefficients, the Berlekamp-Massey algorithm gives the shortest LFSR generating these coefficients. The same LFSR also generates the whole array of coefficients of $f_{\mathbf{e}}$ periodically, and so we can recover the whole of $f_{\mathbf{e}}$ using simple linear algebra. Finally, evaluating f_e at $(\alpha_1, \ldots, \alpha_n)$ gives us $\mathbf{e}$.

References

1. Albrecht, M.R., et al: Classic McEliece: conservative code-based cryptography. https://classic.mceliece.org/
2. Aguilar Melchor, C., et al.: RQC - Rank Quasi-Cyclic. http://pqc-rqc.org/
3. Aragon, N., et al.: BIKE: Bit Flipping Key Encapsulation. https://bikesuite.org/
4. Aragon, N., Blazy, O., Gaborit, P., Hauteville, A., Zémor, G.: Durandal: a rank metric based signature scheme. In: Ishai, Y., Rijmen, V. (eds.) EUROCRYPT 2019. LNCS, vol. 11478, pp. 728–758. Springer, Cham (2019). https://doi.org/10.1007/978-3-030-17659-4_25

5. Bardet, M., et al.: An algebraic attack on rank metric code-based cryptosystems. In: Canteaut, A., Ishai, Y. (eds.) EUROCRYPT 2020. LNCS, vol. 12107, pp. 64–93. Springer, Cham (2020). https://doi.org/10.1007/978-3-030-45727-3_3

6. Bardet, M., et al.: Improvements of algebraic attacks for solving the rank decoding and MinRank problems. In: Moriai, S., Wang, H. (eds.) ASIACRYPT 2020. LNCS, vol. 12491, pp. 507–536. Springer, Cham (2020). https://doi.org/10.1007/978-3-030-64837-4_17

7. Barenghi, A., Biasse, J.-F., Persichetti, E., Santini, P.: LESS-FM: fine-tuning signatures from the code equivalence problem. In: Cheon, J.H., Tillich, J.-P. (eds.) PQCrypto 2021 2021. LNCS, vol. 12841, pp. 23–43. Springer, Cham (2021). https://doi.org/10.1007/978-3-030-81293-5_2

8. Barg, S.: Some new NP-complete coding problems. Problemy Peredachi Informatsii 30(3), 23–28 (1994). ISSN 0555-2923

9. Barg, A.: Complexity issues in coding theory. In: Pless, V., Brualdi, R., Huffman, W. (eds.) Handbook of Coding Theory, chap. 7, pp. 649–754. Elsevier, New York (1998). ISBN 978-0-444-50088-5

10. Berger, T.P., Cayrel, P.-L., Gaborit, P., Otmani, A.: Reducing key length of the McEliece cryptosystem. In: Preneel, B. (ed.) AFRICACRYPT 2009. LNCS, vol. 5580, pp. 77–97. Springer, Heidelberg (2009). https://doi.org/10.1007/978-3-642-02384-2_6

11. Biasse, J.-F., Micheli, G., Persichetti, E., Santini, P.: LESS is more: code-based signatures without syndromes. In: Nitaj, A., Youssef, A. (eds.) AFRICACRYPT 2020. LNCS, vol. 12174, pp. 45–65. Springer, Cham (2020). https://doi.org/10.1007/978-3-030-51938-4_3

12. Blahut, R.E.: Transform techniques for error control codes. IBM J. Res. Dev. 23(3), 299–315 (1979). ISSN 0018-8646

13. Berlekamp, E., McEliece, R., van Tilborg, H.: On the inherent intractability of certain coding problems (corresp.). IEEE Trans. Inf. Theory 24(3), 384–386 (1978). ISSN 0018-9448

14. Feneuil, T., Joux, A., Rivain, M.: Shared Permutation for Syndrome Decoding: New Zero-Knowledge Protocol and Code-Based Signature. Cryptology ePrint Archive, Report 2022/188 (2022). https://ia.cr/2021/1576

15. Feneuil, T., Joux, A., Rivain, M.: Syndrome decoding in the head: shorter signatures from zero-knowledge proofs. Cryptology ePrint Archive, Report 2022/188 (2022). https://ia.cr/2022/188

16. Gueron, S., Persichetti, E., Santini, P.: Designing a practical code-based signature scheme from zero-knowledge proofs with trusted setup. Cryptography 6(1), 5 (2022)

17. Gustavson, F.G.: Analysis of the berlekamp-massey linear feedback shift-register synthesis algorithm. IBM J. Res. Dev. 20(3), 204–212 (1976). https://doi.org/10.1147/rd.203.0204. ISSN 0018-8646

18. Lidl, R., Niederreiter, H.: Finite Fields, 2nd edn. Cambridge University Press, Cambridge (1996). ISBN 0-521-39231-4/hbk

19. Misoczki, R., Barreto, P.S.L.M.: Compact McEliece keys from Goppa codes. In: Jacobson, M.J., Rijmen, V., Safavi-Naini, R. (eds.) SAC 2009. LNCS, vol. 5867, pp. 376–392. Springer, Heidelberg (2009). https://doi.org/10.1007/978-3-642-05445-7_24

20. McEliece, R.: A public-key cryptosystem based on algebraic coding theory. Deep Space Network Progress Report 44:114116 (1978)

21. Misoczki, R., Tillich, J., Sendrier, N., Barreto, P.: MDPC-McEliece: new McEliece variants from moderate density parity-check codes. In: 2013 IEEE International Symposium on Information Theory, pp. 2069–2073, July 2013. ISSN 2157-8095

22. Niederreiter, H.: Knapsack type cryptosystems and algebraic coding theory. Prob. Control Inf. Theory. Problemy Upravlenija i Teorii Informacii **15**, 19–34 (1986)

23. NIST. https://csrc.nist.gov/projects/post-quantum-cryptography. Accessed 9 June 2022

24. Persichetti, E.: Compact McEliece keys based on quasi-dyadic Srivastava codes. J. Math. Cryptol. **6**(2), 149–169 (2012)

25. Samardjiska, S., Santini, P., Persichetti, E., Banegas, G.: A reaction attack against cryptosystems based on LRPC codes. In: Schwabe, P., Thériault, N. (eds.) LATINCRYPT 2019. LNCS, vol. 11774, pp. 197–216. Springer, Cham (2019). https://doi.org/10.1007/978-3-030-30530-7_10

System Security and Threat Intelligence

Methods of Extracting Parameters of the Processor Caches

Sihao Shen[1,2], Zhenzhen Li[1,2], and Wei Song[1,2(✉)] (iD)

[1] State Key Laboratory of Information Security, Institute of Information
Engineering, CAS, Beijing, China
`songwei@iie.ac.cn`
[2] School of Cyber Security, University of Chinese Academy of Sciences,
Beijing, China

Abstract. As attack scenarios and targets are constantly expanding,
cache side-channel attacks have gradually penetrated into various daily
applications and brought great security risks. The success of a cache
side-channel attack relies heavily on the pre-knowledge of some important parameters of the target cache system. Existing methods for reading
cache parameters have their limits. In this paper, a series of tests are proposed to extract cache parameters at runtime, which provides a method
for launching existing cache side-channel attacks in some restricted cases
and reduces the cost of attacks. They have been used to extract cache
parameters on four processors using three different architectures, as well
as in a restricted virtual machine environment. The extracted parameters
match with the publicly available information, including some parameters unavailable from the CPUID instruction.

Keywords: hardware security · cache side-channel · micro-architecture

1 Introduction

Cache side-channel attacks have become an important way of leaking critical
information in modern computer systems, especially after their employment in
the Meltdown [1] and Spectre attacks [2]. The attack scenario has been broadened
from a single core to multicore processors, virtual machines (VMs) [3] and trusted
execution domains [4–6]. The targets of attacks also grow from just the secrets
of crypto-algorithms to users' private data [7,8], the mapping of virtual and
physical address spaces [9] and manipulating data bits in memory [10].

The success of a cache side-channel attack relies heavily on the pre-knowledge
of some important parameters of the target cache system. The *access latency* of
the target cache is used as the time reference for inferring cache states [11]. The
size of a cache and the *number of cache sets* affect the probability in finding
an address conflicting with the target address [12]. Attacking using the minimal
eviction set is crucial for a clean and stealth attack [13], while the size of this
eviction set is decided by the *number of ways* in each cache set in set-associative
caches [12,13]. The *replacement policy* asserts significant impact on the way of

© The Author(s), under exclusive license to Springer Nature Switzerland AG 2022
C.-M. Cheng and M. Akiyama (Eds.): IWSEC 2022, LNCS 13504, pp. 47–65, 2022.
https://doi.org/10.1007/978-3-031-15255-9_3

using eviction sets. For permutation-based policies [14], such as the widely used pseudo LRU (Least Recently Used) [15], sequentially accessing an eviction set is sufficient to dislodge the target. However, repeated and complicated accessing methods are required when scan-resistant policies, such as RRIP (Re-Reference Interval Prediction) [16], are adopted by modern processors [17]. In addition, it is found that the replacement policy also decides the optimal method for searching eviction sets [18].

Before launching the actual attack, attackers need to collect the aforementioned parameters with some investigation. Some parameters, such as the size of cache, might be publicly available if the processor information can be precisely identified through the CPUID instruction of x86-64 or the lscpu command on Linux. Other parameters, usually the access latency of individual cache levels, could be calculated by running tests on the target system [11,13,19]. However, the existing methods have some limitations. Not all architectures provide the CPUID instruction. Even when it is available to user land, it might be virtualized to mask the cache related information or even provide wrong information [20]. System commands, such as lscpu, might not be available as attackers have no method to open a shell. Testing the access latency at runtime might be problematic if all high-resolution timers, like the RDTSC of x86-64, are disabled [21]. Finally, attacks might be launched in a restricted environment [7] where attackers have almost no direct access to machine level instructions or resources.

To address these issues, this paper proposes a series of tests to extract the required cache parameters at runtime. These tests do not rely on accessing any of the files, commands and instructions leaking the cache information or the processor model. Instead of utilizing existing timing sources on the target system, a high-resolution timer is created and utilized to measure the access latency of all cache levels. *Consequently, these tests have the potential to be ported across different computer architectures and running in restricted environments, which provides a method for launching existing cache side-channel attacks in some restricted cases and reduces the cost of attacks.* In fact, we have already run the same tests on four processors over three different instruction sets (ISAs) including x86-64, AArch64 and RISC-V, as well as in a virtual machine environment. The tests have successfully extracted almost all the aforementioned cache parameters, including some parameters unavailable from the CPUID instruction.

2 Background

2.1 Cache Architecture

In modern processors, caches adopt a multi-level hierarchical structure. Taking the recent Intel processors as an example, level-one (L1) and level-two (L2) caches are privates caches accessible only by the local core, while level-three cache (L3 $) acting as the LLC (last-level cache), is shared by all cores. Normally, caches located near the processor core pipeline (inner caches), such as L1 $, operate at a higher speed and smaller size than those far away from the core (outer caches), such as the LLC. A memory access always starts from the inner caches and inquires the outer caches only when data misses in the inner ones.

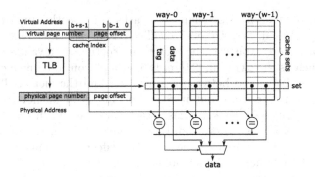

Fig. 1. A virtually indexed and physically tagged cache

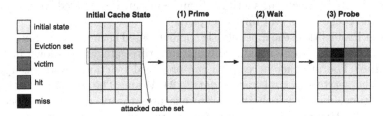

Fig. 2. Process of Prime+Probe attack

Almost all caches use a set-associative internal structure. The cache space is divided into cache sets and each set contains multiple ways of fixed sized cache blocks. Figure 1 depicts a virtually indexed and physically tagged cache normally used as the L1 \$. The 2^s cache sets are indexed by a segment of the virtual address (VA[b+s-1:b]) while the lower b bits (VA[b-1:0]) are used as the cache block offset and the higher bits (VA[63:12] assuming the 4 KB page size) are used by the translate lookaside buffer (TLB) for generating the physical page number also used as the tag for the cache way matching. Each cache set contains w cache blocks, i.e., w ways. When accessing a data, a cache set is selected by the VA and all cache blocks inside this set are simultaneously checked with the tag provided by the TLB. If the data is cached, one of the cache blocks would match with the tag; otherwise, the data is uncached (a miss) and will be fetched from the outer cache. Consequently, this missing block is stored in the cache set at either an unoccupied way or a cache block, chosen by a replacement policy, is evicted to the outer cache to make a room.

2.2 Cache Side-Channel Attacks

Cache side-channel attacks are based on the difference in time, where the latency is small when an attacker accesses a cached address but large when this address is evicted from the cache [22, 23]. Attackers can obtain a lot of sensitive information from this time difference, which leads to information leakage.

Commonly used cache side-channel attacks are mostly divided into two categories: flush-based attacks and conflict-based attacks. The flush-based attacks [24–26] require explicit cache control instructions to invalidate the target cache block, such as the `clflush` [24] on x86, in addition to requiring the target cache block must be shared between the attacker and the victim. This type of attack is simple and accurate but it relies too much on memory sharing and cache control instructions, making this attack unsuccessful in many restricted situations. If either of the above conditions is not satisfied, the attacker could launch conflict-based attacks to achieve similar effect [12]. This type of attack exploits the fact that each cache set holds only a fixed number of cache blocks, and blocks mapped to the same set conflict with each other [27–30]. The attacker can thus control the state of a cache set by occupying it completely. After the victim program is executed, victim information can be inferred by rechecking whether the cache set is still fully occupied.

Prime+Probe [31] is the most classic conflict-based cache side-channel attack. The attack process can be roughly divided into three stages, as shown in Fig. 2: **(1) Prime**: The attacker accesses a pre-prepared eviction set to occupy the target cache set to evict all victim data. **(2) Wait**: The attacker waits for a period of time, during which the victim executes the program and reoccupies the cache. **(3) Probe**: The attacker accesses the eviction set again and records the access latency. If the victim accesses the target cache set while waiting, some of the attacker's cache blocks are evicted from the target cache set. They must be reloaded from memory during probe resulting prolonged access latency.

In a conflict-based cache side-channel attack, an important step is to construct the eviction set, which consists of a collection of (virtual) addresses that are all congruent to each other with the target address [12,13], i.e., all mapping to the same cache set.

Definition 1. If and only if two virtual addresses x and y map to the same cache set, $Set(x) = Set(y)$ [13], but are not on the same cache block, $Cb(x) \neq Cb(y)$, then the addresses x and y are said to congruent to each other:

$$Congruent(x, y) \Longleftrightarrow Set(x) = Set(y) \land Cb(x) \neq Cb(y) \tag{1}$$

Definition 2. $[x]$ denotes the collection of all congruent addresses with address x. Suppose the number of ways for the cache set is w. For a target address x, a collection of virtual addresses S is an eviction set for x if $x \notin S$, and at least w addresses in S are congruent with x [13]:

$$x \notin S \land |[x] \cap S| \geq w \tag{2}$$

3   Threat Model

We assume unprivileged attackers with the ability to launch a multi-thread program on the target system and allocate consecutive memory in the virtual memory space. All files, commands and instructions that might leak the cache

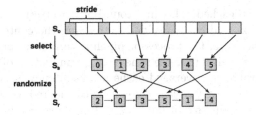

Fig. 3. Construct the randomized sequence of addresses

Algorithm 1: Latency measurement

---

1 **function** *latency(S_r)*
2   *start = timer()*
3   **foreach** *p* **in** S_r **do** *p = *p*
4   **return** *(timer() − start)/len(S_r)*
5 **end**

---

information or the processor model has been disabled on the target system, attackers cannot get these information directly by reading files or executing commands such as lscpu. Attackers cannot directly launch a flush-based attack. The parameters of the target platform are not known to attackers in advance and need to be obtained through actual measurements. Attackers may be in a virtual environment. Meanwhile, sources of high-resolution timers, such as the RDTSC of x86-64, might be removed or made unusable.

4 Measuring Cache Access Latency

The access latency of a cache is the foremost crucial parameter required for time side-channels while also the easiest one to obtain. It is therefore chosen as the first cache parameter to be extracted.

4.1 Random Cache Scan

The main idea of estimating the access latency of a cache is by measuring the overall latency of accessing a pre-constructed sequence of addresses. In order to accurately measure the access latency while effectively circumventing the various optimization implemented in modern processors, the access latency is averaged from the overall time of traversing a long and randomized sequence of addresses S_r constructed according to Fig. 3 [17]. A consecutive memory space S_o is initially allocated from the virtual address space. According to a predefined stride, a consecutive address sequence S_s is constructed from S_o and then randomized to form the final S_r. A final step is to link S_r into a linked-list by storing the next address in the memory pointed by the current address, which is the key in disabling instruction level parallelism as described by Algorithm 1.

Before actually extracting the cache access latency using Algorithm 1, S_r is accessed for multiple times to ensure the maximum number of addresses of

S_r have already been cached. The final round of traverse is a timed run. Inside the traverse, the next address is decided by reading the content of the current address (line 3); therefore, the processor pipeline cannot accurately predict the next address and the overall traverse time is an accumulation of individual memory accesses. Naturally, the averaged cache access latency is averaged from the overall time. Conceptually, this latency can be considered as the optimal cache performance for a certain size of data (S_o) after the cache system is properly warmed. The detailed method to extract the cache access latency of individual cache levels will be revealed in Sect. 5.

4.2   A Portable Timer

The latency of cache accesses ranges from a couple to several hundreds of nanoseconds [11]. To accurately measure this latency, especially for the L1 caches, we need high-resolution timers. On x86-64 processors, such a timer can be conveniently built from the RDTSC instruction. Other processor architectures are nevertheless lack of such high-resolution source of time in user land. We summarize the applicable architectures of commonly used timer resources and their approximate accuracy in Table 2 in Sect. 6.

In order to achieve the portability across architectures, we choose to construct a virtual time stamp (VTS) as firstly introduced in [32] for all processors. The detailed method is illustrated in Algorithm 2. Assuming the processor under test is a multicore processor, a separated child timer thread is attached to a unique core, which does nothing else but constantly increases a global counter cnt. In the main thread, the latency measurement process then utilizes cnt as a wall clock for timing. Since self-increasing is usually faster than memory accesses, this wall clock should be quick enough as long as it is not disturbed by context switching.[1] Additionally, each time the global variable cnt is incremented, it requires accessing memory twice. Actually, it is possible to reduce the number of memory accesses by executing the self-increment operation directly through assembly instructions [28]. This means that the global variable cnt can be incremented faster in the same time, thus improving the resolution. The actual resolution of this virtual time stamp is evaluated in Sect. 6.

Furthermore, we did not attach threads to a certain core (without using CPU affinity) in the actual experiments. According to our observations, the probability of threads being migrated to other cores is very low and is a small probability event. If the counting thread has core migration, we believe that there will be an impact on the clock accuracy within a short period of time when the migration occurs, but these effects will be averaged over multiple samples in the experiment and have little effect on the final result. Of course, using CPU affinity to attach the counting thread on one core will improve the accuracy of the algorithm, but it will also inevitably reduce the cross-platform capability of the algorithm.

---

[1] Such context switching can be detected by software as it usually leads to outstanding measurement errors.

Algorithm 2: Virtual time stamp

---
1 global variable $cnt \leftarrow 0$
2 //child timer thread
3 **while**($true$) **do** $cnt + +$
4
5 //main thread
6 **function** $latency'(S_r)$
7       $start = cnt$
8   **foreach** p **in** S_r **do** $p = *p$
9   **return** $(cnt - start)/len(S_r)$
10 **end**

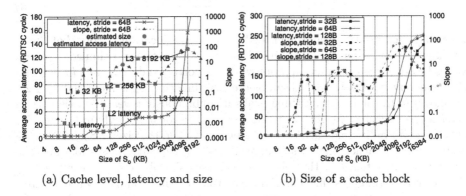

(a) Cache level, latency and size   (b) Size of a cache block

Fig. 4. Extracting basic parameters using random cache scan

5   Methodology of Extraction

This section describes the series of tests used to extract individual cache parameters. To better illustrate the details of each test, we provide actual test results collected from an Intel i7-3770 using RDTSC as the timing source. In addition, the virtual time stamp are used as the timer to detect replacement policies in Figs. 6 and 7 since ARM and RISC-V architecture processors are involved. The experimental results of using the virtual time stamp and running on other more recent processor architectures are revealed in Sect. 6.

5.1   Cache Size and Latency of All Levels

The parameter extraction starts with a series of cache scans using a relatively small stride (such as 64 B) but with different sizes of S_o. An exemplary test on an Intel i7-3770 is depicted in Fig. 4a. The number of cache levels, the access latency and the size are the first batch of parameters to be extracted.

When S_o is smaller than the size of L1 \$, the access latency l denotes the L1 access latency as all accesses hit in L1 \$. When S_o grows well beyond the size of L1 \$, nearly all access miss in L1 because the long scan pattern leaves no locality for the L1 \$ to explore. Consequently, all accesses are served by the L2 \$ and l equates to the access latency of the L2 \$. Similarly, we can extract the

L3 access latency using an even larger S_o. However, we need to first figure out the sizes of individual cache levels.

According to Fig. 4a, the latency l increases with S_o at a varying speed. When S_o grows just surpassing the size of a cache, l jumps from the access latency of the current level to the next. The number of cache levels can be extracted by counting the number of these latency jumps. It is found that such jumps can be clearly detected by analyzing the slope curve, which measures the first order of derivative of l calculated as:

$$f(i) = \frac{l_{i+1} - l_i}{2} + \frac{l_i - l_{i-1}}{2} \tag{3}$$

where $f(i)$ denotes the increasing speed of l at x-axis location i. Note that the x-axis and the y-axis for the slope curve in Fig. 4a are both logarithmized. We use x-axis location i as the function input while the corresponding S_o and l are l_i and $S_{o,i}$ respectively. A value of l is sampled every time that S_o is increased by $\sqrt{2}$.[2] As shown in the slope curve, three peaks unambiguously reveal the existence of three levels of caches. More interestingly, the peaks locate exactly in the vicinity of the sizes of individual caches. This is because when the size of S_o exceeds the cache size, the cache generates a large number of capacity misses [33] and the average access latency of the sequence increases sharply. Using the related S_o of a peak as a rough estimation and correcting it using common sense, such as the number of sets should be 2'power, we can infer the sizes of individual cache levels. Moreover, the latency of a cache level can be estimated using the latency l_i at location of the lowest $f(i)$ related to the cache level.

5.2   Size of a Cache Block

A cache block is the smallest portion of data being communicated between caches. Although almost all modern processors adopt a uniformed block size of 64 bytes to ease the implementation of cache coherence, some processors use non-64 uniformed block size or even different block sizes across cache levels. We cannot simply assume that the block size is 64 bytes universally.

The way to extract the block size at a certain cache level is to pinpoint a match between the block size and a stride. If the chosen stride is smaller than the block size, each cache block has multiple addresses contained in S_r while only one address is contained if the stride is equal to or larger than the block size. When S_o grows just beyond the cache size, part of cache accesses begin to miss and the average latency starts to rise. In this situation, the average access latency using a smaller stride is lower than using a larger stride. Since multiple addresses of the same cache block is contained in S_r using a small stride and a whole cache block is refilled when missed, each cache refill is effectively a prefetch

---

[2] Introducing extra samples in between each pair of basis points ($\times 2$) sharpens the peaks in the slope curve, which makes the peaks easy to detect but leads to long running time. As a trade-off, only one extra sample is added at the middle ($\sqrt{2}$) of the basis points on the logarithmized x-axis.

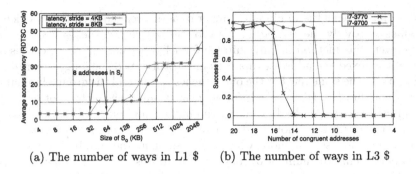

(a) The number of ways in L1 $ (b) The number of ways in L3 $

Fig. 5. Extracting the number of ways

for the remaining addresses not yet accessed to the same block, which then leads to the reduced latency. If we sweep stride from a small value to a value larger than the block size, a gradual rise of the latency curve should be observable until the stride is equal to the block size. Any further increase on stride results in a similar latency curve. Consequently, the first stride fails to raise the latency curve is equal to the block size.

In our test, the stride is gradually doubled from 8 to 256 bytes. The latency curves for strides from 32 to 128 bytes are depicted in Fig. 4b. The Intel i7-3770 adopts a uniformed block size of 64 bytes. The latency using a stride of 32 bytes is indeed lower than the latency of stride 64 and 128 bytes while the latency curve of the latter mostly identical. However, it is difficult to check whether two curves are identical by a program. Instead, we check whether the peaks of two slope curves are co-located with a small error. Also shown in Fig. 4b, the peaks of the slope curves of stride 64 and 128 bytes perfectly co-located for all cache levels, which reveals that all cache levels use the same block size of 64 bytes. The extra benefit of using the slope curve is the enlarged distance between peaks. For the peaks using stride less than 64 bytes, the height of the peak is noticeably lower and the location is pushed rightwards, thanks to the much milder latency jumps produced by them.

5.3   Number of Cache Ways and Sets

The random cache scan can be used to extract the number of ways in a L1 cache set provided the L1 $ is set-associative. As shown in Fig. 5a, the latency curve moves rightwards when the stride grows beyond 4 KB. This is because all the addresses in the 32 KB S_r (stride $= 4$ KB) are congruent [13] and mapped to the same cache set due to the hardwired cache set index VA[b+s-1:b] as illustrated in Fig. 1, and they are just enough to fill the whole set. When the stride increased to 8 KB, the number of addresses is halved. To fill the whole set then requires a S_r covering 64 KB. Note that the size S_r divided by the stride is both 8 for the two cases, revealing the number of ways in the L1 $ is 8. We can explain it from another angle. Since the L1 $ is virtually indexed, by choosing addresses with the same stride, we effectively create an eviction set for a set. Detecting the shift of curve thus reveals the minimum number of addresses required for an eviction set, which is exactly the number of ways for set-associative caches [13,34]. However, this method is only suitable for L1 $ because all outer caches are physically indexed and addresses apart from the same stride on longer guaranteed of mapping to the same set. For the outer caches, we extend the group elimination search algorithm [13,34] to search for congruent addresses instead of using the random cache scan. At the beginning, the number of congruent addresses a is large enough to fill the whole set to create an eviction set. However, it cannot create an eviction set anymore when a is less than the number of ways. By gradually reducing the number of congruent addresses in an eviction set, we can derive the minimum number of addresses, which is also the number of ways. Figure 5b shows the results of extracting the number of ways of the L3 $ on both i7-3770 and a latest i7-9700. When the number of addresses is set to less than the minimum number (the number of ways), the success rate of finding an eviction set immediately drops to zero. The result clearly reveals that the numbers of ways are 16 and 12 for the L3 $ on Intel i7-3770 and i7-9700 respectively.

The detailed steps is illustrated in Algorithm 3. The input candidate set C is divided into $a + 1$ groups (a is the number of congruent addresses). Since the eviction set contains a congruent addresses, there must be a certain group among the $a + 1$ groups that does not contain the addresses in the eviction set. For each group G, if the target address x can still be evicted after removing it from the candidate set C, it means that the addresses in the group G are irrelevant to the eviction set, then remove the group G. Conversely, keep the group G and continue to detect whether the next group G can be removed. Until a group G that can be removed from the candidate set C is found, then the current round of detection is ended. The remaining candidate set C continues to be divided into $a + 1$ groups to start the next round of detection until the number of congruent addresses in C is exactly equal to a, thus the eviction set S is successfully obtained.

Finally, since cache size equates the production of number of sets, number of ways and block size, it is straightforward to calculate the number of sets once the other three parameters are extracted, i.e. $cache\ size = set * way * block\ size$.

5.4   Replacement Policy

In a cache side-channel attack, dislodging the target address by traversing an eviction set is literally a thrashing access pattern [16] whose effectiveness is closely related to the replacement policy adopted by the target cache. A couple of traverses are usually enough for *permutation-based* policies, such as LRU [35]. Increasing the number of traverses is sufficient to defeat *random* replacement policies. Complicated traverse algorithms [12] would be required for *scan-resistant* policies, such as RRIP [16,36]. Instead of detecting the exact types of policies [19], this paper tries to classify replacement policies into three categories: permutation-based, random and scan-resistant policies.

It is relatively easy to differentiate permutation and non-permutation policies. Figure 6 depicts the jump of access latency when S_r grows beyond the size of the L1 $ on Intel i7-3770 and the HiFive unleashed board (RISC-V processor). The virtual time stamp is used to measure the access latency. As indicated

---

Algorithm 3: Group elimination search

Input: C, candidate set; x, target address; a, number of congruent addresses.
Output: S, eviction set for x.

```
 1 function group_ reduction(s, x, a)
 2 |   while |C| > a do
 3 |   |   G_1, ..., G_{a+1} ← split(C, a + 1)
 4 |   |   i ← 1
 5 |   |   while ¬ TEST (C\G_i, x) do
 6 |   |   |   i ← i + 1
 7 |   |   end
 8 |   |   C ← C\G_i
 9 |   end
10 |   S ← C
11 |   return S
12 end
```

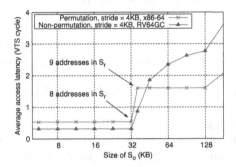

Fig. 6. Differentiating permutation and non-permutation policies

by the result, the two L1 \$ certainly adopts different replacement policies. Intel i7-3770 likely uses a permutation-based policy because the access latency suddenly increases when S_r just grows beyond the cache size (32 KB), indicating the cache scan with 9 addresses can easily dislodge all the 8 cache blocks. As for the RISC-V processor, much more congruent addresses are required for evicting the whole cache set, denoting the use of a non-permutation policy.

To further differentiate scan-resistant and random policies, we have done a modified cache scan as described by Fig. 6 in [17] on the RISC-V processor whose caches adopting non-permutation policies. The sequence S_r is divided into a short and a long sequence. The short sequence should fit in the target cache and are initially traversed multiple times to mimicking a access pattern with temporal locality. The whole sequence is then used in a normal cache scan but only the access latency of the short sequence is measured. If a scan-resistant policy is adopted, addresses belonging to the long sequence are replaced before the short ones, and the latency curve is pushed rightwards, as described in [17].

In summary, permutation and non-permutation policies are detected using a normal cache scan. A permutation policy is used if the latency curve shows a narrow and sharp jump at the size of the cache; otherwise, a non-permutation policy is used. A modified cache scan is then applied. If the latency curve of the short sequence is noticeably pushed rightwards from the size of the cache, a scan-resistant policy should be used; otherwise, it is likely to be a random one.

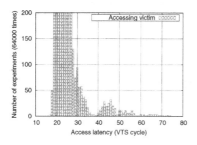 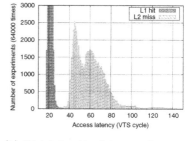

(a) Detecting if victim is evicted from L2 \$

(b) Obtaining the latency of accessing memory

Fig. 7. Detecting the random replacement policy by latency distributions

Furthermore, there is a way to verify the use of a random policy by calculating whether the substitution rate is completely random through a large number of repeated experiments. Take the L2 \$ on the Jetson Nano (ARM architecture) as an example, the number of its ways is 16. If the L2 \$ adopts uses a random policy, then the probability of successfully evicting the target address to memory should be only 1/16 when using a congruent address to evict the target address. By repeating the experiment we can obtain this probability and thus infer whether the cache adopts a random policy. We first need to find two addresses called attacker and victim that map to the same cache set on both L1 and L2 \$. Then the eviction set of attacker and victim is constructed. Each address in the eviction set must be in the same set as these two addresses in L1 \$ but in a different set in L2 \$, in order to ensure that no additional noise is introduced when evicting the target address to the L2 \$.

First, access the eviction set to evict the victim to the L2 \$, and then re-access the eviction set to evict the attacker to the L2 \$ as well. Since attacker and victim are congruent with each other, victim may be evicted from the L2 \$ to memory during this process. Finally, the state of the victim in the cache is inferred according to its access latency. The above experiments were performed 64,000 times and the access latency of the victim was counted. This experiment uses the virtual time stamp as the timer and the results are shown in Fig. 7a. According to the analysis, the probability that the attacker successfully evicts the victim to memory is 1/16 (the reciprocal of the numbers of ways for the L2 \$) if the L2 \$ adopts a random policy. In this case, the access latency of victim is the time it takes to fetch data from memory.

To obtain the access latency of memory, we need to count the cache access latency in different states. A certain target address is accessed multiple times to make it cached, and then it is evicted from the cache through the cache flush instruction. These two different states of access latency are recorded and the results are shown in Fig. 7b. We can intuitively obtain the access latency of memory (L2 miss) is about 30 or more.[3]

We then calculated the frequency of access latency greater than 30 in Fig. 7a, which is about 1/18 of the total number of experiments (the practically possible number of ways closest to this value is 16). Only the random policy has a replacement rate of 1/16, so we can infer that the L2 $ does adopt a random policy based on this result. This experiment exploits the law of large numbers, i.e., repeating the experiment many times under the same conditions, the frequency of a random event will approximate its probability. That is why we need a sufficient number of experiments to ensure accuracy, and this also brings a long time-consuming problem. How to detect the random policy more quickly and accurately is also one of our subsequent research goals.

6   Experiment Results

We have chosen four representative processors using three different architectures to conduct the experiments. The processor information is illustrated in Table 1. Besides the relatively old i7-3770, a latest i7-9700 processor is also tested. We have also managed to run the tests on two non-x86 processors which we have access to. One is a Jetson Nano board mounted with an Arm Cortex-A57 processor and the other one is a HiFive Unleashed board mounted with a SiFive u540 processor. All processors run a Linux operating system while tests are compiled with the default GNU GCC compiler. In order to further verify the usability of this method in some restricted environments, such as cloud computing, browser sandboxes, etc., we installed a virtual machine on the i7-9700 processor and performed the same cache parameter extraction experiments in the virtual machine environment.

The methods of measuring time varies across architectures and the commonly used time resources are shown in Table 2. The resolution may vary within the same architecture due to extra factors such as dynamic frequency scaling. Among them, the RDTSC register has the highest precision, which can reach 0.3 ns on the i7-9700 processor, but it is only applicable to the x86 architecture. The ARM architecture can use the cntvct_el0 register for timing, which has an accuracy of about 52 ns on the Jetson Nano processor. Both the time and cycle registers can be used for timing on the RISC-V architecture, and their accuracy is 1 µs and 1 ns respectively on HiFive Unleashed processor. While the virtual time stamp we used is applicable to all three architectures above.

We verify the resolution of the virtual time stamp by calculating the increase of the global variable *cnt* during a certain runtime period, the details are as follows: In the main thread, we accurately control the running time through a sleep function and record the increment of the global variable *cnt* in the child timer thread during this period. Dividing the running time by the increment produces the resolution of the virtual time stamp, which indicates how long

---

[3] This latency is not consistent with Table 3 as extra delay is caused by the operations to clean states at the beginning of each test.

Table 1. Processor information and timer resolution

	Intel	Intel	Intel (VM)	Jetson Nano	Unleashed
Processor	i7-3770	i7-9700	i7-9700	Cortex-A57	SiFive u540
Arch.	x86-64	x86-64	x86-64	ARMv8.0-A	RV64GC
OS	Ubuntu 16.04	Ubuntu 18.04	Ubuntu 16.04	Ubuntu 18.04	OpenEmbeded
GCC ver.	5.4	5.4	5.4	7.5	10.2
Resolution	1.9ns	1.2ns	1.2ns	5.0ns	11.0ns

Table 2. Comparison of time resources under different architectures

	RDTSC	cntvct_e10	time	cycle	virtual time stamp (VTS)
Arch.	x86	ARM	RISC-V	RISC-V	x86/ARM/RISC-V
Resolution	0.3ns	52.0ns	1.0us	1.0ns	1.2-11.0ns

it takes for the global variable *cnt* to increase by one unit. In addition, the child timer thread will increase the single-core CPU overhead to over 90%, thus this timer runs at the highest frequency. The resolution achieved by the virtual time stamp method is revealed on the final row of Table 1. It is shown that the virtual time stamp achieves nanosecond resolution on all processors. All of the experiment results provided in this section are collected from tests using this virtual time stamp.

Taking the virtual time stamp as the precise timer, we extract the access latency at all cache levels by scanning the random address sequence on the four processors. The specific latency as well as its slope variation is shown in Fig. 8 and Table 3 along with the extracted cache parameters. Although the L1 access latency on all processors is less than the resolution of the virtual time stamp, the latency of the L2 $ is always longer than 1. Note that the we only need to differentiate a L1 hit from miss, as long as the measured difference between the L1 and L2 latency is longer than 1, the resolution of the virtual time stamp is high enough.

Intel processors normally adopt a three-level cache hierarchy but only two levels are found on the two non-x86 processors. The proposed tests successfully produce an estimation on all cache parameters except for the numbers of sets and ways for the L2 $ on Intel processors. These L2 $ caches are found to be physically indexed caches. As described in Sect. 5.3, the test extracts the number of ways by trying to figure out the minimum number of congruent addresses needed by an eviction set. However, the group elimination algorithm [12] suffers from significant error rate and fails to produce any eviction sets. With some investigation, we suspect the L2 $ on these Intel processors might be non-inclusive with regarding to the L1 $.

The non-inclusive structure means that when the data in the upper-level cache is evicted, this evicted data will be written back to the next-level. It ensures that the current cache only holds data that is not in the upper-level cache. The design and implementation of non-inclusive cache are more complex but improve security by making the eviction set construction much more difficult [37]. The current trend in cache design is a shift from inclusive to non-inclusive, such

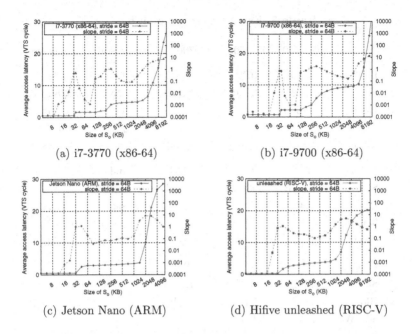

(a) i7-3770 (x86-64)

(b) i7-9700 (x86-64)

(c) Jetson Nano (ARM)

(d) Hifive unleashed (RISC-V)

Fig. 8. Extracting cache latency through virtual time stamp (VTS)

as Intel's Skylake architecture, which has designed the L3 $ as a non-inclusive structure. Although it is reported possible to construct eviction sets for L3 $ using directory-based coherence policy [37], it is unlikely for a non-inclusive and private L2 $ to use directory. Finding eviction sets on it thus remains an open question requiring further research.

In the virtual machine environment, we extracted the same cache parameters as the i7-9700 processor in the normal environment except for the number of ways for the L3 $. This is because the two-layer address translation mechanism in the virtual machine (VM VA to host VA, and then from host VA to host PA) leads to an increase in TLB pressure and a significant increase in miss rate. Previous studies have shown that this noise can significantly affect the success rate of the eviction set search algorithm [38]. It was found that the existing opensourced algorithms, such as the group elimination algorithm [13] and the random algorithm [12], cannot work directly in the virtual environment for the time being. How to address such problems in a restricted environment is also one of our future work.

We have compared the extracted parameters against the information available from CPUID and lscpu. All the parameters match with the publicly available information while the correctness on the extracted types of replacement policies remains unclear. It is partially verified by a separate research [19] that the Intel processors do adopt scan-resistant policies on the L3 $ and even the L2 $ for recent processors. Whether the L2 $ of i7-3770 indeed adopting a scan-resistant policy would need further investigation. Some counter-intuitive results

Table 3. Extracted cache parameters

		i7-3770	i7-9700	i7-9700 (VM)	Jetson	Unleashed
	Latency	0.59	0.72	0.73	0.52	0.31
	Size	32KB	32KB	32KB	32KB	32KB
L1	Block	64B	64B	64B	64B	64B
	Set/Way	64/8	64/8	64/8	256/2	64/8
	Replace	permu.	permu.	permu.	permu.	random
	Latency	1.76	2.18	2.21	3.34	3.63
	Size	256KB	256KB	256KB	2MB	2MB
L2	Block	64B	64B	64B	64B	64B
	Set/Way	?	?	?	2048/16	1024/32
	Replace	scan-res.	scan-res.	scan-res.	random	permu.
	Latency	5.58	8.83	8.94		
	Size	8MB	12MB	12MB		
L3	Block	64B	64B	64B		
	Set/Way	8192/16	16384/12	?		
	Replace	scan-res.	scan-res.	scan-res.		

are found on the RISC-V processors as it uses a random replacement policy on the L1 $. Since the L1 $ has high performance requirements, permutation-based replacement policies (such as LRU, etc.) are usually adopted. We have double-checked our experiment result. The opensourced implementation of the SiFive u540 (Rocket-Chip) does show the possibility to set the policy to random for L1 $ but it is still an odd choice for performance concerns.

7   Conclusion

A series of tests have been proposed in this paper to extract the cache parameters crucial for cache side-channel attacks. With the help of a virtual time stamp timer, the proposed tests have the potential to be ported across different computer architectures and running in restricted environments, which provide a method for launching existing cache side-channel attacks in some restricted cases and reduces the cost of attacks. We have conducted experiments on four representative processors using three different architectures, as well as in a virtual machine environment. Nearly all cache parameters have been extracted except for the number of ways of the L2 $ on Intel processors because these caches are suspected non-inclusive, which makes the construction of the eviction set extremely difficult. All the extracted parameters match with the publicly available information using CPUID and lscpu. How to effectively construct an eviction set in a non-inclusive cache or virtual machine environment is currently a challenge in the field of cache side-channel attacks, which is also one of our next research goals.

Acknowledgements. The HiFive Unleashed board was kindly borrowed from Xiongfei Guo. This work was partially supported by the National Natural Science Foundation of China under grant No. 62172406 and No. 61802402, the CAS Pioneer Hundred Talents Program, and internal grants from the Institute of Information Engineering, CAS. Any opinions, findings, conclusions, and recommendations expressed in this paper are those of the authors and do not necessarily reflect the views of the funding parties.

References

1. Lipp, M., et al.: Meltdown: reading kernel memory from user space. In: Proceedings of the USENIX Security Symposium, August 2018, pp. 973–990 (2018)
2. Kocher, P., et al.: Spectre attacks: exploiting speculative execution. In: Proceedings of the IEEE Symposium on Security and Privacy, May 2019, pp. 19–37 (2019)
3. Ristenpart, T., Tromer, E., Shacham, H., Savage, S.: Hey, you, get off of my cloud: exploring information leakage in third-party compute clouds. In: Proceedings of the ACM Conference on Computer and Communications Security, November 2009, pp. 199–212 (2009)
4. Brasser, F., Müller, U., Dmitrienko, A., Kostiainen, K., Capkun, S., Sadeghi, A.-R.: Software grand exposure: SGX cache attacks are practical. In: Proceedings of the USENIX Workshop on Offensive Technologies, August 2017
5. Hähnel, M., Cui, W., Peinado, M.: High-resolution side channels for untrusted operating systems. In: Proceedings of the USENIX Annual Technical Conference, July 2017, pp. 299–312 (2017)
6. Schwarz, M., Maurice, C., Gruss, D., Mangard, S.: Fantastic timers and where to find them: high-resolution microarchitectural attacks in JavaScript. In: Proceedings of the International Conference on Financial Cryptography and Data Security, January 2017, pp. 247–267 (2017)
7. Oren, Y., Kemerlis, V.P., Sethumadhavan, S., Keromytis, A.D.: The spy in the sandbox: practical cache attacks in JavaScript and their implications. In: Proceedings of the ACM SIGSAC Conference on Computer and Communications Security, October 2015, pp. 1406–1418 (2015)
8. Page, D.: Theoretical use of cache memory as a cryptanalytic side-channel. Cryptology ePrint Archive (2002)
9. Gras, B., Razavi, K., Bosman, E., Bos, H., Giuffrida, C.: ASLR on the line: Practical cache attacks on the MMU. In: Proceedings of the Network and Distributed System Security Symposium, February 2017
10. Kim, Y., et al.: Flipping bits in memory without accessing them: an experimental study of DRAM disturbance errors. In: Proceedings of the International Symposium on Computer Architecture, June 2014, pp. 361–372 (2014)
11. Hund, R., Willems, C., Holz, T.: Practical timing side channel attacks against kernel space ASLR. In: Proceedings of the IEEE Symposium on Security and Privacy, May 2013, pp. 191–205 (2013)
12. Song, W., Liu, P.: Dynamically finding minimal eviction sets can be quicker than you think for side-channel attacks against the LLC. In: Proceedings of the International Symposium on Recent Advances in Intrusion Detection, September 2019, pp. 427–442 (2019)

13. Vila, P., Köpf, B., Morales, J.: Theory and practice of finding eviction sets. In: Proceedings of the IEEE Symposium on Security and Privacy, May 2019 (2019)
14. Jain, A., Lin, C.: Cache Replacement Policies. Morgan & Claypool Publishers, San Rafael (2019)
15. Berg, C.: PLRU cache domino effects. In: Proceedings of the International Workshop on Worst-Case Execution Time Analysis, June 2006
16. Jaleel, A, Theobald, K.B., Steely, S.C.Jr., Emer, J.S.: High performance cache replacement using re-reference interval prediction (RRIP). In: Proceedings of the International Symposium on Computer Architecture, June 2010, pp. 60–71 (2010)
17. Wong, H.: Intel Ivy Bridge cache replacement policy, January 2013. http://blog.stuffedcow.net/2013/01/ivb-cache-replacement/
18. Qureshi, M.K.: New attacks and defense for encrypted-address cache. In: Proceedings of the International Symposium on Computer Architecture, June 2019, pp. 360–371 (2019)
19. Vila, P., Ganty, P., Guarnieri, M., Köpf, B.: CacheQuery: learning replacement policies from hardware caches. In: Proceedings of the ACM SIGPLAN Conference on Programming Language Design and Implementation, June 2020, pp. 519–532 (2020)
20. Nakajima, J., Mallick, A.K.: Hybrid-virtualization – enhanced virtualization for Linux. In: Linux Symposium, vol. 2, June 2007, pp. 87–96 (2007)
21. Martin, R., Demme, J., Sethumadhavan, S.: TimeWarp: rethinking timekeeping and performance monitoring mechanisms to mitigate side-channel attacks. In: Proceedings of the International Symposium on Computer Architecture, June 2012, pp. 118–129 (2012)
22. Deng, S., Xiong, W., Szefer, J.: A benchmark suite for evaluating caches' vulnerability to timing attacks. In: Proceedings of the International Conference on Architectural Support for Programming Languages and Operating Systems, 2020, pp. 683–697 (2020)
23. Ge, Q., Yarom, Y., Cock, D., Heiser, G.: A survey of microarchitectural timing attacks and countermeasures on contemporary hardware. J. Cryptogr. Eng. **8**(1), 1–27 (2016). https://doi.org/10.1007/s13389-016-0141-6
24. Yarom, Y., Falkner, K.: FLUSH+RELOAD: a high resolution, low noise, L3 cache side-channel attack. In: Proceedings of the USENIX Security Symposium, 2014, pp. 719–732 (2014)
25. Zhang, X., Xiao, Y., Zhang, Y.: Return-oriented flush-reload side channels on arm and their implications for android devices. In: Proceedings of the ACM SIGSAC Conference on Computer and Communications Security, 2016, pp. 858–870 (2016)
26. Zhang, Y., Juels, A., Reiter, M.K., Ristenpart, T.: Cross-tenant side-channel attacks in PaaS clouds. In: Proceedings of the ACM SIGSAC Conference on Computer and Communications Security, 2014, pp. 990–1003 (2014)
27. Osvik, D.A., Shamir, A., Tromer, E.: Cache attacks and countermeasures: the case of AES. In: Pointcheval, D. (ed.) CT-RSA 2006. LNCS, vol. 3860, pp. 1–20. Springer, Heidelberg (2006). https://doi.org/10.1007/11605805_1
28. Lipp, M., Gruss, D., Spreitzer, R., Maurice, C., Mangard, S.: ARMageddon: cache attacks on mobile devices. In: Proceedings of the USENIX Security Symposium, 2016, pp. 549–564 (2016)
29. Yan, M., Gopireddy, B., Shull, T., Torrellas, J.: Secure hierarchy-aware cache replacement policy (SHARP): defending against cache-based side channel attacks. In: Proceedings of the ACM/IEEE Annual International Symposium on Computer Architecture, pp. 347–360. IEEE (2017)

30. Irazoqui, G., Eisenbarth, T., Sunar, B.: S$A: a shared cache attack that works across cores and defies VM sandboxing - and its application to AES. In: Proceedings of the IEEE Symposium on Security and Privacy, pp. 591–604. IEEE (2015)

31. Liu, F., Yarom, Y., Ge, Q., Heiser, G., Lee, R.B.: Last-level cache side-channel attacks are practical. In: Proceedings of the IEEE Symposium on Security and Privacy, May 2015, pp. 605–622. IEEE (2015)

32. Percival, C.: Cache missing for fun and profit. In: BSD Conference Ottawa (2005)

33. Smith, A.J.: Cache memories. ACM Comput. Surv. **14**(3), 473–530 (1982)

34. Song, W., Li, B., Xue, Z., Li, Z., Wang, W., Liu, P.: Randomized last-level caches are still vulnerable to cache side-channel attacks! But we can fix it. In: Proceedings of the IEEE Symposium on Security and Privacy, May 2021

35. Abel, A., Reineke, J.: Reverse engineering of cache replacement policies in intel microprocessors and their evaluation. In: Proceedings of the IEEE International Symposium on Performance Analysis of Systems and Software, pp. 141–142. IEEE (2014)

36. Qureshi, M.K., Jaleel, A., Patt, Y.N., Steely, S.C., Emer, J.: Adaptive insertion policies for high performance caching. ACM SIGARCH Comput. Arch. News **35**(2), 381–391 (2007)

37. Yan, M., Sprabery, R., Gopireddy, B., Fletcher, C.W., Campbell, R.H., Torrellas, J.: Attack directories, not caches: side-channel attacks in a non-inclusive world. In: Proceedings of the IEEE Symposium on Security and Privacy, May 2019, pp. 888–904 (2019)

38. Genkin, D., Pachmanov, L., Tromer, E., Yarom, Y.: Drive-by key-extraction cache attacks from portable code. In: Preneel, B., Vercauteren, F. (eds.) ACNS 2018. LNCS, vol. 10892, pp. 83–102. Springer, Cham (2018). https://doi.org/10.1007/978-3-319-93387-0_5

KDPM: Kernel Data Protection Mechanism Using a Memory Protection Key

Hiroki Kuzuno[1]([✉])[iD] and Toshihiro Yamauchi[2][iD]

[1] Graduate School of Engineering, Kobe University, Kobe, Japan
kuzuno@port.kobe-u.ac.jp
[2] Faculty of Natural Science and Technology, Okayama University, Okayama, Japan
yamauchi@okayama-u.ac.jp

Abstract. The kernel data of an operating system kernel can be modified through memory corruption by exploiting kernel vulnerabilities. Memory corruption allows privilege escalation and defeats security mechanisms. The kernel control flow integrity verifies and guarantees the order of invoking kernel codes. The kernel address space layout randomization randomizes the virtual address layout of the kernel code and data. The additional kernel observer focuses on the unintended privilege modifications to restore the original privileges. However, these existing security mechanisms do not prevent writing to the kernel data. Therefore, kernel data can be overwritten by exploiting kernel vulnerabilities. Additionally, privilege escalation and the defeat of security mechanisms are possible.

We propose a kernel data protection mechanism (KDPM), which is a novel security design that restricts the writing of specific kernel data. This mechanism protects privileged information and the security mechanism to overcome the limitations of existing approaches. The KDPM adopts a memory protection key (MPK) to control the write restriction of kernel data. The KDPM with the MPK ensures that the writing of privileged information for user processes is dynamically restricted during the invocation of specific system calls. To prevent the security mechanisms from being defeated, the KDPM dynamically restricts the writing of kernel data related to the mandatory access control during the execution of specific kernel codes. Further, the KDPM is implemented on the latest Linux with an MPK emulator. We also evaluated the possibility of preventing the writing of privileged information. The KDPM showed an acceptable performance cost, measured by the overhead, which was from 2.96% to 9.01% of system call invocations, whereas the performance load on the MPK operations was 22.1 ns to 1347.9 ns.

1 Introduction

The operating system (OS) kernel encounters threats, in which privileges may be escalated and security mechanisms may be defeated. The user process of the adversary exploits the kernel code containing vulnerabilities (i.e., vulnerable

C.-M. Cheng and M. Akiyama (Eds.): IWSEC 2022, LNCS 13504, pp. 66–84, 2022.
https://doi.org/10.1007/978-3-031-15255-9_4

kernel code), thereby corrupting the memory. Thus, privileged information can be modified and kernel data of the security mechanism can be altered to gain full administrator privileges. By modifying the kernel data related to mandatory access control (MAC), the user acquires administrator privileges and circumvents the MAC restrictions [1,2].

The following are the countermeasures that can prevent kernel attacks via vulnerable kernel code. Kernel control flow integrity (KCoFI) inspects the order of code execution [3] to restrict the kernel code from being illegally invoked [4]. Kernel address space layout randomization (KASLR) randomizes the virtual addresses of the kernel code and kernel data in the kernel memory space to foil attacks [5], whereas the additional kernel observer (AKO) detects unintentional rewriting in response to the changes in the privileged information of user processes against a privilege escalation attack [6].

These mitigate the kernel data from being illegally modified via kernel vulnerabilities. However, if the kernel memory is successfully corrupted, kernel data can be overwritten. We consider that a running kernel does not restrict the writing of kernel data in the kernel mode. Existing approaches do not control the write restrictions of kernel data related to privileged information and security mechanisms. Therefore, an adversary can gain full administrator privileges.

In this study, we propose a kernel data protection mechanism (KDPM), which is a novel security capability that dynamically controls the write restrictions of specific kernel data as protected kernel data. Figure 1 provides an overview of the KDPM, which determines whether system calls and kernel codes have write permission of the kernel data in the kernel layer. To ensure kernel data protection and managing write restrictions, the KDPM adopts the Intel memory protection key (MPK), which is a protection keys for supervisor (PKS). A PKS provides a protection key that handles write restrictions for each page of kernel data.

The KDPM assumes that the user process of an adversary invokes a vulnerable kernel code which attempts to modify the kernel data related to privileged information or security mechanism. The KDPM focuses the mitigation of the illegal overwritten of these kernel data. The privileged information is changed by specific system calls and the policy of MAC is modified by specific kernel codes. Moreover, the function pointers of the MAC are never modified at the running kernel. The KDPM provides a straightforward application of the PKS to maintain simple design of the kernel data protection. Additionally, the KDPM combines the characteristics of system calls, kernel code behavior, and hardware features. The limitation of the KDPM is a little difficult to support frequently modified kernel data.

The KDPM has two implementations that focus on the different types of kernel attacks. Implementation 1 is a general purpose for the protection of privileged information to prevent privilege escalation. This allows user processes to write to protected kernel data only when write-permitted system calls are invoked. Implementation 2 protects the kernel data of the security mechanism (e.g., MAC) to prevent security mechanism from being defeated. This reduces overheads to limit the write restriction timing of protected kernel data.

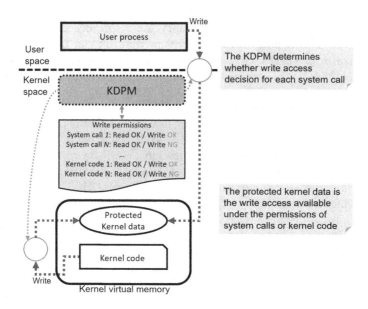

Fig. 1. Overview of the kernel data protection mechanism

Further, Implementation 2 allows the protected kernel data to be written only when executing a write-permitted kernel code.

- **Implementation 1**: To prevent a privilege escalation attack, Implementation 1 controls the write restriction of privileged information in each write-permitted system call to protect the privileged information of user processes.
- **Implementation 2**: Implementation 2 controls the write restriction of the kernel data related to the security mechanism in each write-permitted kernel code to prevent the defeating security mechanism attack.

Intel CPUs containing a PKS are not available as of March 2022 and will be implemented on the next generation CPUs; however, a PKS is available in the QEMU environment [7]. This study is an early application of the forthcoming PKS to protect kernel data. The following are the contributions of this study:

1. We designed the KDPM that protects the kernel data in the running kernel to prevent privilege escalation and defeat of security mechanism attacks through vulnerable kernel code. The implementations of the latest Linux kernel use a PKS to handle the write restriction of the kernel code during a specific system call or specific kernel code execution.
2. To evaluate the KDPM, we confirmed that the kernel with Implementation 1 can prevent the modification of privileged information by the adversary's user process. Additionally, we confirmed that the kernel with Implementation 2 can prevent the defeat of security mechanisms. The overhead of Implementation 1 requires latency of system call ranging from 2.96% to 9.01%, and the

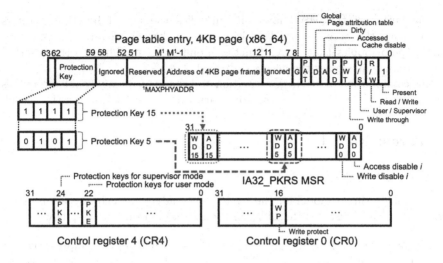

Fig. 2. Intel memory protection key [8]

processing time for the kernel with Implementation 2 for writing the PKS is 22.1 ns. Furthermore, reading the register operation requires 30.5 ns, and writing the register operation requires 1347.9 ns.

2   Background

2.1   Memory Protection Key

Intel CPU provides an MPK, which is a security feature provided to control read and write restrictions on a page basis, that is, page table entry (PTE) [8]. The MPK includes protection keys for userspace (PKU) and the protection key right for user mode register for the user mode. In addition, the MPK includes PKS and IA32_PKRS_MSR register (hereinafter, PKRS) for the kernel mode.

As shown in Fig. 2, the PTE has 16 4-bit protection keys (Pkeys), and the 32-bit flag (two bits per Pkey: write disable (WD) and access disable (AD)) controls the read and write restriction for each Pkey

The read and write restriction for Pkey i ($0 \leq i \leq 15$) is performed via the register. If the value of bit AD $i \times 2$ is 0, read is allowed. In contrast, if the value of bit AD $i \times 2$ is 1, read is not allowed. Additionally, if the value of bit WD $i \times 2{+}1$ is 0, write is allowed; and if the value of bit WD $i \times 2{+}1$ is 1, write is not allowed.

2.2   Kernel Vulnerability

Kernel vulnerabilities are improper implementations that lead to kernel attacks [9]. Privilege escalation forcibly invokes kernel codes that modify privileged information [10–12]. Specifically, the variable cred of the kernel data that stores privileged information is overridden from the normal user to the administrator [13].

The defeat of the MAC forcefully modifies the list of function pointers that manage the access control decisions in the kernel. Meanwhile, the variable `selinux_hooks` that stores function pointers, is modified to the inserted kernel codes that bypass the access control [1,2].

The combination of privilege escalation and the MAC being disabled provides full administrator capability to the adversary with no restrictions on the kernel.

3 Threat Model

3.1 Environment

We assumed a threat model for the KDPM. The adversary acquires administrator privileges and disables the MAC in the target environment as follows:

- Adversary: An adversary gains normal user privileges, attempts privilege escalation, and defeats the MAC via the PoC code that exploits kernel vulnerabilities.
- Kernel: A kernel contains kernel vulnerabilities that can be exploited for privilege escalation and defeating the MAC. Existing security mechanisms (e.g., KCoFI, KASLR, and AKO) are not applied.
- Kernel vulnerability: A kernel vulnerability is the presence of a vulnerable kernel code that exploits kernel memory corruption.
- Attack targets: Attack targets are kernel data related to privileged information of user process (e.g., user id) and kernel data of the MAC (e.g., function pointers and access policies).

3.2 Scenario

The adversary induces the attack that executes the PoC code as the user process exploits the vulnerable kernel code. The following are the details of an attack:

1. Privilege escalation attack
   The user process of the adversary forcefully rewrites user privileges to gain administrator privileges for attaining full control of the computer.
2. Defeating security mechanisms
   The user process of the adversary forcefully disables the MAC by replacing the function pointer of the kernel code with one that does not make access decisions.

4 Design

4.1 Concept

To manage write restrictions on specified kernel data, we designed the KDPM to satisfy the following requirement:

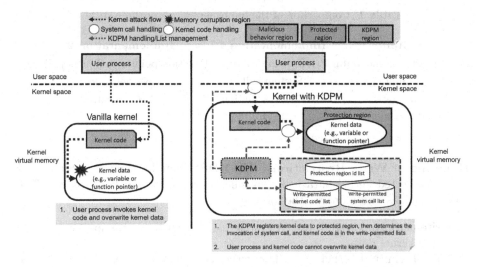

Fig. 3. Design overview of the KDPM

– Requirement: Prevent privilege escalation and defeat of security mechanisms
  by illegally modifying kernel data via kernel vulnerabilities. The kernel must
  control the write restrictions of kernel data for specific system calls and kernel
  codes on the running kernel. The kernel data can be written only when system
  calls are invoked and the authorized kernel codes are executed.

4.2 Approach

The KDPM supports the kernel data as protected kernel data (e.g., variable or
function pointer) and the identifier to satisfy the aforementioned requirement.
Figure 3 shows an overview of the KDPM that supports the linking of the identifier to the write-permitted system calls and write-permitted kernel code.

Protected Kernel Data: The following are the definitions of protected kernel
data and identifiers:

– Protected kernel data: The kernel data of the user process (e.g., privileged
  information) and security mechanisms (e.g., the function pointer and access
  policy).
– Identifier: The identifier is used to set the write restrictions of the protected
  kernel data. For controlling the write restriction, the identifier is associated with the protected kernel data, write-permitted system call, and write-
  permitted kernel code.

The kernel with the KDPM provides a list of protected kernel data and
corresponding identifiers in advance at the time of booting. Additionally, the
kernel data for each user process generation is assumed to be protected.

Table 1. Comparison of the implementations of the KDPM

Item	Implementation 1	Implementation 2
Protected kernel data	Privilege information	Function pointer & Access policy
Handling	System call	Kernel code
Mitigation	Privilege escalation	MAC defeating
Performance	High	Low

Handling of Write Restrictions: The KDPM handles the write restrictions of the protected kernel data using specific system calls and kernel codes. The KDPM defines and manages the following:

– Write-permitted system call: A system call has write permission for the protected kernel data.
– Write-permitted kernel code: The kernel code is authorized to write to the protected kernel data.

The KDPM disables write restrictions during a write-permitted system call is issued or write-permitted kernel code is executed. At the end of the write-permitted system call or write-permitted kernel code execution, the KDPM enables the write restriction to the protected kernel data.

5 Implementation

In this study, the KDPM is implemented on Linux with the x86_64 CPU architecture. Table 1 presents the protected kernel data and write control timing according to the implementations. The following are the implementation details:

– Implementation 1: This manages the protected kernel data containing privileged information and write-permitted system calls that change the privileges of the user process. Even if a user process attempts a privilege escalation, the privilege information cannot be written during the execution of another system call.
– Implementation 2: This manages protected kernel data related to the MAC (e.g., the Linux Security Module (LSM)) and write-permitted kernel code that changes the security policy or access control decision. Even if the user process attempts to defeat the MAC, the function pointer of the kernel code related to the LSM and security policy in the kernel data cannot be written during another kernel code execution. It is internal to the kernel and has little impact on the performance of user processes.

5.1 Protected Kernel Data Management

Implementations 1 and 2 equally manage the protected kernel data and the processes that handle page faults.

Table 2. Protected kernel data and write-permitted system call of Implementation 1

Item	Description
Protected kernel data	User ID (e.g., uideuidfsuidsuid)
	Group ID (e.g., gidegidfsidsgid)
Write-permitted system call	execve, setuid, setgid, setreuid, setregid
	setresuid, setresgid, setfsuid, setfsgid

Protected Kernel Data: A Linux kernel with implementations that support an identifier is set to the protected kernel data, which is arranged on one page (4 KB), and the PKS handles the write restriction.

- Identifier: Implementations control the write restriction of the protected kernel data and identification number i. The identification number i is the same as the value of the Pkey i (4 bit) of PTE.
- Write restriction control: Implementations use the identification number i of the protected kernel data to control Pkey i of the PKRS. If the value of WDi in the PKRS is set to 1, write access is restricted; however, if WDi is set to 0, write access is permitted.

The handling of write restrictions by the implementations with the PKRS is a different process (for details, see Sects. 5.2 and 5.3).

Page Fault Handling: The kernel with implementations supports the page fault handler functions `do_page_fault` and `do_double_fault` to identify illegal page references of protected kernel data by the PKS. In the Linux kernel, a page fault (i.e., error number 35) is a violation of the write protection on a page of Pkey. The implementations do not allow writing to the protected kernel data, and these send a `SIGKILL` to the target user process using the function `force_sig_info`.

5.2   Implementation 1

Figure 4 presents an overview of Implementation 1. Implementation 1 protects the privilege information for each user process. It manages the list of protected kernel data and that of write-permitted system calls.

Protected Kernel Data: Implementation 1 generates a dedicated page (4 KB) as protected kernel data when a user process is created. The dedicated page stores the privileged information of the user process provided in Table 2. The list of write-permitted system calls is also protected and write restriction control is performed by the PKS at the kernel startup.

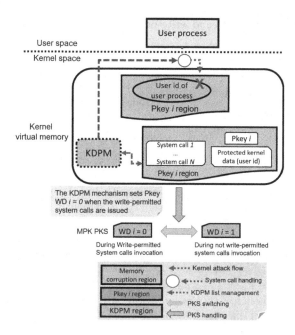

Fig. 4. Implementation 1 of the KDPM

Handling of Write Restrictions: Implementation 1 admits the system calls that change the privileged information (Fig. 2). The process of controlling the write restrictions of the protected kernel data using Pkey is as follows:

1. The kernel identifies a system call invoked by a user process.
2. The kernel determines if the system call number is included in the list of write-permitted system calls.
   (a) For write-permitted system calls: the kernel sets the protected kernel data with the write-enable permission by the PKRS.
3. The execution of the system call is continued.
4. After the system call: the kernel restores the protected kernel data and is set to the write-disable permission by the PKRS.

5.3   Implementation 2

Figure 5 presents an overview of Implementation 2. Implementation 2 adopts the write-permitted kernel code of the LSM and supports the list of kernel data related to the LSM and that of the write-permitted kernel codes. Implementation 2 handles the write restrictions for the protected kernel data when executing write-permitted kernel codes that change the access control policy and access control decision.

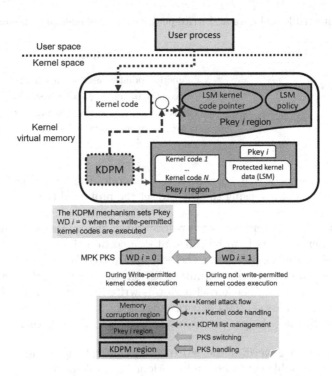

Fig. 5. Implementation 2 of the KDPM

Protected Kernel Data: Table 3 presents the kernel data to be protected in Implementation 2. Additionally, `selinux_hooks` is a variable that stores function pointers that are part of the kernel data related to the LSM, and `selinux_state` is a variable that stores the access control policy. Furthermore, the list of write-permitted kernel codes is protected by write restriction control using the PKS.

Handling of Write Restrictions: Implementation 2 stores the function pointer of the kernel data related to the LSM, and the list of write-permitted kernel codes is set during the booting of the kernel. Table 3 also presents the kernel codes to be included in the list of write-permitted kernel codes.

The following procedure is used to control the restrictions on the write-permitted kernel code using the PKS:

1. The kernel invokes the kernel code of Implementation 2 during the execution of the write-permitted kernel code.
2. The kernel code of Implementation 2 determines whether the caller belongs to a write-permitted kernel code.

Table 3. Protected kernel data and write-permitted kernel code of Implementation 2

Item	Description
Protected kernel data	Function pointer (e.g., selinux_hooks)
	Security policy (e.g., selinux_state)
Write-permitted kernel code	Kernel functions in the selinux_hooks
	avc_init, avc_insert, avc_node_delete, avc_node_replace

(a) In the case of a write-permitted kernel code, the kernel performs write restriction control using the PKS to set the protected kernel data as write enabled.

(b) The kernel registers the write restriction of the protected kernel data in the timer and sets it to be called after a certain time.

3. The kernel continues processing the write-permitted kernel code.
4. Before the end of the write-permitted kernel code, the kernel code of Implementation 2 is called. The kernel performs write restriction using the PKS to set the protected kernel data as write disabled.
5. The kernel finishes the processing of the write-permitted kernel code.

Implementation 2 verifies the write restriction setting using the timer to prevent write as enable continued unintentionally. Implementation 2 also checks the number of kernel code invocations to determine whether the write restriction enabled and disabled are the same. Further, Implementation 2 verifies whether the duration of write enable exceeds the specified time. The timer is a complementary feature to prevent missing of the configuration of the PKS protection setting. This timer usually requires sufficient time to miss it between starting and finishing the execution of the write-permitted kernel code.

6   Evaluation

6.1   Security Capability

The security capability evaluation validates whether the kernel with the KDPM adequately protects privileged information.

1. Prevention of privilege escalation attack
   A kernel vulnerability that can be exploited for a privilege escalation attack is introduced into the Linux kernel. We evaluate the kernel with Implementation 1, which enables the write restriction of the privileged information of user processes. This prevents an adversary from performing a privilege escalation attack.
2. Preventing the defeat of security mechanism
   We evaluate the kernel with Implementation 2, which enables the write restriction of kernel data of the LSM to prevent MAC defeat.

6.2 Performance Evaluation

In performance evaluation, we investigate whether the kernel and user processes are affected by Implementation 1 and the effect of the PKS operations used in Implementation 2.

1. Measurement of the kernel performance overhead
   To measure the performance of the Linux kernel with Implementation 1, the benchmark software calculates the overhead of the system call invocation latency.
2. Measurement of PKS performance overhead
   To measure the performance of the PKS in the KDPM, we measure the processing time of the PKS operations in the Linux kernel with Implementation 2.

6.3 Evaluation Environment

Equipment: We evaluated the PoC code and kernel using a physical machine equipped with an Intel (R) Core (TM) i7-7700HQ (2.80 GHz, x86_64) processor with 16 GB memory.

The security capability evaluation was implemented on a virtual machine because QEMU 6.0.91 supports the PKS. However, the PKS is not available as of January 2022 on the Intel CPU. The guest OS on QEMU was Debian 10.2, and Implementations required 15 source files and 431 lines for Linux kernel 5.3.18. The PKS performance for Implementation 2 was evaluated using a measurement program that required 165 lines for Linux kernel 5.3.18.

Implementation: To evaluate the security capability, a kernel vulnerability was introduced into the Linux kernel using a PoC code [14] that leads to privilege escalation via memory corruption through the system call number 350. Additionally, the Linux kernel module (LKM) attempted to overwrite the LSM function pointer to defeat the MAC on the running kernel:

- **Privilege escalation:** Vulnerable kernel code 1 refers to CVE-2017-6074 [14], which was implemented as a system call `sys_kvuln01`. The PoC code exploits the vulnerable kernel code to overwrite the privileged information of a user process for privilege escalation.
- **Defeating security mechanism:** A customized LKM attempts to overwrite the function pointer of the kernel code that manages the LSM file access permission to circumvent the MAC decision.

6.4 Security Capability Evaluation Result

Prevention of Privilege Escalation Attack: The security evaluation result for the adversary's user process is shown in Fig. 6. In line 3, the kernel captures the original system call (i.e., system call number 350) with process ID 1661. The kernel indicates 0×8, which indicates that the write disable (WD) of Pkey 1 is

1. [*] start vulnerable system call (sysnum: 350) invocation
2. [364.203190] vulnerable system call invocation
3. [364.203227] sysnum: 0x15e (350)
4. [364.203275] PID: user process 1661
5. [364.203309] PKS PRIV: enable pks currently
6. [364.203405] read_pkrs for CPU 0: 0x8
7. [364.203496] sys_kvuln01 current privileges 1: uid=33 euid=33 gid=33

8. [*] process uid, euid, gid, and egid are changed to 0
9. [*] kernel catches the page fault regarding protection key
10. [364.204186] PKS: protection keys hw error code 35, pkey 1
11. HW error code 35 (0b100011)
12. Page fault error code bits: from Linux v5.3.18 : arch/x86/include/asm/trap_pf.h
    1. bit 0 == 1: protection fault, X86_PF_PROT
    2. bit 1 == 1: write access, X86_PF_WRITE
    3. bit 5 == 1: protection keys block access, X86_PF_PK
13. [364.204232] read_pkrs for CPU 0: 0x8
14. [364.212966] killing target PID: 1661

Fig. 6. Prevention of a privilege escalation attack

1. [*] LKM attempts to find the function pointer of the LSM
2. [286.118427] selinux_hooks[56].hook.file_permission Address ffffffff81e77c18
3. [286.213409] PKS PRIV: enable pks currently
4. [286.214513] read_pkrs for CPU 0: 0x8
5. [*] LKM tries to overwrite the function pointer of the LSM
6. [*] kernel catches the page fault regarding protection key
7. [286.216821] PKS: protection keys hw error code 35, pkey 1
8. HW error code 35 (0b100011)
9. Page fault error code bits: from Linux v5.3.18 : arch/x86/include/asm/trap_pf.h
    1. bit 0 == 1: protection fault, X86_PF_PROT
    2. bit 1 == 1: write access, X86_PF_WRITE
    3. bit 5 == 1: protection keys block access, X86_PF_PK
10. [286.221232] read_pkrs for CPU 0: 0x8

Fig. 7. Prevention of a MAC defeat

enabled. In line 10, the kernel catches a page fault (i.e., error number 35) when writing to the page that stores the privileged information with Pkey 1. The page fault indicates a write protection violation of a page protected by the Pkey. In line 14, the kernel sends SIGKILL to the user process of the adversary.

Preventing the Defeat of Security Mechanism: The security evaluation result of the LKM is shown in Fig. 7. In line 2, the LKM attempts to find one of the function pointers of selinux_hooks. In line 5, LKM attempts to overwrite the function pointer of selinux_hooks. In line 7, the kernel catches a page fault (i.e., error number 35) when writing to the page storing the function pointer with Pkey 1. The page fault indicates a write protection violation of a page protected by Pkey.

From the security evaluation results, we confirmed that the Linux kernel with the KDPM prevents privilege escalation attacks and avoids the defeat of security mechanism. The KDPM correctly manages the Pkey and detect memory corruption of the vulnerable kernel code.

6.5 Performance Evaluation Result

Measurement of the Kernel Processing Overhead: The system call overhead was measured using LMbench benchmark software. A vanilla kernel was

Table 4. System call invocation overhead of Implementation 1 (μs)

System call	Vanilla kernel	Implementation 1	Overhead
fork+/bin/sh	227111.28	236738.69	9627.41 (4.24%)
fork+execve	12780.0566	13931.6703	1151.6136 (9.01%)
fork+exit	10837.0729	11285.5603	448.4874 (4.14%)
open/close	1302.5639	1334.5312	41.9672 (2.95%)
read	168.8898	180.4594	11.5696 (6.85%)
write	164.2567	176.4273	12.1705 (7.41%)
fstat	195.0063	203.7508	8.7445 (4.48%)
stat	613.7426	631.9393	18.1966 (2.96%)

Table 5. Overhead of PKS operations (ns)

Instruction	Implementation 2
Pkey write	30.5
PKRS read	22.1
PKRS write	1347.9

compared with the kernel with Implementation 1. LMbench was executed 10 times to calculate the average system call latency.

LMbench performs 54 invocations of the system call for fork+/bin/sh, 4 invocations for fork+execve, 2 invocations for fork+exit and open/close, and the other is 1 invocation. Table 4 shows the overhead of the system call. The highest and lowest overheads are fork+execve with 9.01% and stat with 2.96%, respectively.

Measurement of PKS Operations: The Linux kernel with Implementation 2 invokes the Pkey write of the PTE and read and write of the PKRS. The measurement program was repeated 10,000 times, and the average value was calculated. Table 5 shows the cost of the PKS operations. The write of Pkey required 30.5 ns; PKRS read required 22.1 ns, and PKRS write required 1347.9 ns.

7 Discussion

7.1 Security Capability Consideration

We demonstrated that the kernel with the KDPM can detect and prevent PoC codes through a kernel vulnerability with a privilege escalation attack and an LKM with a defeat of security mechanisms. In addition, we confirmed that the kernel and user process operations were not affected by the operation that restricts the writing of kernel data. The evaluation result confirms that the

KDPM can dynamically control read restrictions by appropriately setting the PKS. The KDPM only allows system calls for permissions to change privileges and kernel codes for modifying access control information. Therefore, the KDPM prevents the illegal modification of privileged information and kernel code related to access control.

Additionally, the KDPM mitigates the threat from the latest kernel vulnerabilities (e.g., zero-day attack) before the kernel patch is released. Because the KDPM manages a small number of write-permitted system calls and kernel codes. It ensures that the system call or kernel code of a zero-day attack can be manually removed from the write-permitted lists for the protected kernel data to reduce the potential of a kernel attack.

Moreover, analyzing the security capability of the implementations requires the inspection of memory access sequences from the attack of the actual memory corruption kernel vulnerability that performs the illegal modification of kernel data for additional evaluation.

7.2   Performance Consideration

The performance evaluations reveal that the kernel with the implementations requires overhead in kernel processing and read control by the PKS. The duration required for the PKS operations of Implementations 1 and 2 are the same.

The difference of performance costs for each implementation, Implementation 1 determines whether a system call number is allowed to be written. The user process affects the execution time of the system call and generates privileged information of the user process. Meanwhile, Implementation 2 determines the write-permitted kernel code for processing each access control mechanism. We consider that Implementation 2 has an impact on kernel processing when access control decisions are necessary.

To inspect the performance costs of the implementations, we consider the measurements of overheads for practical applications or an evaluation of other benchmark software, such as UnixBench and SPEC.

7.3   Limitation

Design Limitation: We consider that the PKS is lightweight for protecting kernel data. However, if multiple kernel data share a Pkey, the effects of the write available timing during asynchronous processing should be determined due to interrupts and exceptions in the kernel.

If a kernel vulnerability is discovered and an attack is successful, the vulnerable kernel code may have contained a write-permitted system call or write-permitted kernel code. This is a case of circumventing of the KDPM, which allows the modification of protected kernel data.

The design of the KDPM retains the static information in the list of write-permitted system calls and that of write-permitted kernel codes for the kernel. Customizing both lists is difficult and requires additional permissions for the running kernel or kernel modules. We consider the modification of both lists through a kernel component (e.g., kernel module or extended Berkley Packet Filter).

Implementation Limitation: The limitation of the PKS is that the number of Pkeys is 16. The 0th Pkey is used as the initial value of the PTE. The kernel data to be protected must be managed using 15 Pkeys. As the number of types of kernel data to be protected is limited, an appropriate classification of kernel data should be considered when applying the KDPM.

Additionally, Implementation 2 requires an additional kernel process for the restriction of kernel data, which adds to the performance load and requires kernel modifications. Additionally, the timer of Implementation 2 may induce the kernel instability owing to the write permission being forcefully disabled before the write-permitted kernel code is terminated. We require the consideration that the investigation for the time of kernel code execution to adjust the actual value of the timer setting.

7.4 Portability

The portability of the KDPM to other OSs must be considered. The KDPM relies on the PKS, which requires the implementation of virtual memory space with a PTE in the OS that supports an Intel CPU.

8 Related Work

User Process Data Protection Using the MPK: For data protection using the MPK in applications, libmpk provides a flexible library that supports user processes. This can manipulate the protected data using the PSU [15]. ERIM is proposed as a separation method for the protected user process data into different user processes using PSUs [16].

Kernel Data Protection Using the MPK: To protect the kernel code and kernel data using the MPK in the kernel, xMP proposes a security mechanism that provides multiple domains. These contain pages of kernel memory space that are allocated using the PKU. The virtual machine monitor (VMM) manages domains via Pkeys [17]. Additionally, libhermitMPK proposes a security mechanism to protect against unauthorized reading and writing by dividing and managing the kernel code and data into multiple Pkeys [18].

Prevention of Malicious Code Execution: To prevent illegal kernel code execution in the kernel, the control flow integrity (CFI) [3], which verifies the order of program function calls, is applied [19]. To apply the CFI to the kernel, KCoFI is proposed as a security mechanism for preserving the integrity of the order of invoking kernel codes as the original architecture [4].

Table 6. Comparison of kernel protection approaches and types of target vulnerability (C.: code execution, M.: memory corruption) [20]

Feature	libhermitMPK [18]	xMP [17]	KCoFI [4]	KDPM
Protection	Entire kernel	Entire kernel	Kernel behavior	Kernel data
Granularity	Kernel code	VM	Kernel code	System call & Kernel code
Implementation	In-kernel	VMM monitoring	In-kernel	In-kernel
Limitation	Kernel code security	VMM overhead	Original Architecture	Pkey number
Target Vulnerability	M.	M.	C.	M.

8.1 Comparison

Table 6 presents a comparison of the KDPM with existing security mechanisms [4,17,18].

Furthermore, libhermitMPK separates the kernel into two regions (i.e., Safe/Unsafe) using Pkeys [18]. The running kernel code can only read and write to kernel data belonging to the same region. In addition, xMP manages the kernel memory space of the guest OS kernel into multiple domains using Pkeys. The kernel codes and kernel data are assigned forcefully for each domain through the VMM [17]. Although libhermitMPK and xMP show that kernel data can be overridden if the same Pkey is assigned to a vulnerable kernel code and overhead using the VMM, the KDPM assigns Pkeys only to the protected kernel data to separately control system calls and kernel codes from the write restrictions of the kernel data.

KCoFI adopts the CFI for kernel processing that corresponds with the asynchronous behavior to handle the interruption and context switch of tasks [4]. Although KCoFI prevents the invocation of illegal kernel code, kernel memory corruption is not covered. If an attacker executes an arbitrary code in the kernel mode, the KDPM protection may be defeated. We recommend applying the CFI to the kernel with the KDPM to prevent hardware security defeat. Therefore, the CFI verifies the order of invocation of kernel codes to prevent the illegal execution of the kernel code, which attempts to controls hardware registers. The kernel with the KDPM preserves the kernel data protection.

9 Conclusion

An adversary can achieve privilege escalation and the defeat of security mechanisms by corrupting the kernel memory. KCoFI, KASLR, and AKO are kernel attack countermeasures that mitigate and prevent the threat of kernel attacks. However, vulnerable kernel codes can still modify the kernel data at the kernel layer.

In this paper, we proposed a novel security design of a KDPM that manages write restrictions on specific kernel data. The KDPM enables the kernel to control write privileges on PTEs using the MPK PKS in the running kernel by the CPU. We compared the KDPM with existing approaches. From the two implementations of the KDPM, Implementation 1 protects the privileged information of the user process to prevent privilege escalation, whereas Implementation 2 protects the kernel data of the MAC to prevent the defeat of security mechanisms.

In the evaluation, we introduced a kernel vulnerability that can be exploited for privilege escalation attacks and demonstrated the restriction capability for the writing of privileged information of the user processes. The performance evaluation showed that the overhead for invoking system call on Linux with Implementation 1 ranged from 2.96% to 9.01%, and the PKS operations overhead on Linux with Implementation 2 ranged from 22.1 ns to 1347.9 ns.

In future studies, to prevent vulnerable kernel code execution and illegal modification of kernel data due to the principle of security risk and performance overhead, researchers can provide the design of lightweight security mechanism that combines the verification of kernel code execution sequence and the write protection of kernel data at the adequate timing to mitigate kernel attacks.

Acknowledgment. This work was partially supported by the Japan Society for the Promotion of Science (JSPS) KAKENHI Grant Number JP19H04109 and JP22H03592.

References

1. Exploit Database: Nexus 5 Android 5.0 - Privilege Escalation. https://www.exploit-db.com/exploits/35711/. Accessed 21 May 2019
2. grsecurity: super fun 2.6.30+/RHEL5 2.6.18 local kernel exploit. https://grsecurity.net/~spender/exploits/exploit2.txt. Accessed 21 May 2019
3. Abadi, M., Budiu, M., Erlingsson, U., Ligatti, J.: Control-flow integrity principles, implementations, and applications. In: Proceedings of the 12th ACM Conference on Computer and Communications Security, pp. 340–353. ACM (2005). https://doi.org/10.1145/1609956.1609960
4. Criswell, J., Dautenhahn, N., Adve, V.: KCoFI: complete control-flow integrity for commodity operating system kernels. In: Proceedings of the IEEE Security and Privacy, pp. 292–307. IEEE (2014). https://doi.org/10.1109/SP.2014.26
5. Shacham, H., Page, M., Pfaff, B., Goh, E., Modadugu, N., Boneh, D.: On the effectiveness of address-space randomization. In: Proceedings of the 11th ACM Conference on Computer and Communications Security, pp. 298–307. ACM (2004). https://doi.org/10.1145/1030083.1030124
6. Yamauchi, T., Akao, Y., Yoshitani, R., Nakamura, Y., Hashimoto, M.: Additional kernel observer: privilege escalation attack prevention mechanism focusing on system call privilege changes. Int. J. Inf. Secur. **20**(4), 461–473 (2020). https://doi.org/10.1007/s10207-020-00514-7
7. Bonzini, P.: [PATCH] target/i86: implement PKS. https://lore.kernel.org/qemu-devel/20210127093540.472624-1-pbonzini@redhat.com/. Accessed 18 Aug 2021
8. Intel Corporation: Intel(R) 64 and IA-32 Architectures Software Developer's Manual. https://www.intel.com/content/www/us/en/developer/articles/technical/intel-sdm.html. Accessed 18 Aug 2021
9. Chen, H., Mao, Y., Wang, X., Zhow, D., Zeldovich, N., Kaashoek, F.M.: Linux kernel vulnerabilities-state-of-the-art defenses and open problems. In: Proceedings of the Second Asia-Pacific Workshop on Systems, pp. 1–5. ACM (2011). https://doi.org/10.1145/2103799.2103805

10. CVE-2016-4997. https://cve.mitre.org/cgi-bin/cvename.cgi?name=CVE-2016-49 97. Accessed 10 May 2019
11. CVE-2016-9793. https://cve.mitre.org/cgi-bin/cvename.cgi?name=CVE-2016-97 93. Accessed 10 June 2019
12. CVE-2017-1000112. https://cve.mitre.org/cgi-bin/cvename.cgi?name=CVE-201 7-1000112. Accessed 10 June 2019
13. CVE-2017-16995. https://cve.mitre.org/cgi-bin/cvename.cgi?name=CVE-2017-16 995. Accessed 10 June 2019
14. CVE-2017-6074 (2017). https://cve.mitre.org/cgi-bin/cvename.cgi?name=CVE-2017-6074. Accessed 16 Sep 2021
15. Park, S., Lee, S., Xu, W., Moon, H., Kim, T.: libmpk: software abstraction for intel memory protection keys (Intel MPK). In: Proceedings of the 2019 USENIX Annual Technical Conference, pp. 241–254. USENIX (2019). https://dl.acm.org/doi/10.5555/3358807.3358829
16. Vahldiek-Oberwagner, A., Elnikety, E., Duarte, O.N., Sammier, M., Druschel, P., Garg, D.: ERIM: secure, efficient in-process isolation with protection keys (MPK). In: Proceedings of the 28th USENIX Conference on Security Symposium, pp. 1221–1238. USENIX (2019). https://dl.acm.org/doi/10.5555/3361338.3361423
17. Proskurin, S., Momeu, M., Ghavamnia, S., Kemerlis, P.V., Polychronakis, M.: xMP: selective memory protection for kernel and user space. In: Proceedings of the 2020 IEEE Symposium on Security and Privacy, pp. 563–577. IEEE (2020). https://doi.org/10.1109/SP40000.2020.00041
18. Sung, M., Olivier, P., Lankes, S., Ravindran, B.: Intra-unikernel isolation with intel memory protection keys. In: Proceedings of the 16th ACM SIGPLAN/SIGOPS International Conference on Virtual Execution Environments, pp. 143–156. ACM (2020). https://doi.org/10.1145/3381052.3381326
19. Edge, J.: Control-flow integrity for the kernel. https://lwn.net/Articles/810077/. Accessed 8 Jan 2022
20. Linux Vulnerability Statistics. https://www.cvedetails.com/vendor/33/Linux.html. Accessed 5 July 2019

CyNER: Information Extraction from Unstructured Text of CTI Sources with Noncontextual IOCs

Shota Fujii[1,2]([✉]) [iD], Nobutaka Kawaguchi[1], Tomohiro Shigemoto[1], and Toshihiro Yamauchi[3] [iD]

[1] Research & Development Group, Hitachi, Ltd., Kanagawa, Japan
shota.fujii.xh@hitachi.com
[2] Graduate School of Natural Science and Technology, Okayama University, Okayama, Japan
[3] Faculty of Natural Science and Technology, Okayama University, Okayama, Japan

Abstract. Cybersecurity threats have been increasing and growing more sophisticated year by year. In such circumstances, gathering Cyber Threat Intelligence (CTI) and following up with up-to-date threat information is crucial. Structured CTI such as Structured Threat Information eXpression (STIX) is particularly useful because it can automate security operations such as updating FW/IDS rules and analyzing attack trends. However, as most CTIs are written in natural language, manual analysis with domain knowledge is required, which becomes quite time-consuming.

In this work, we propose CyNER, a method for automatically structuring CTIs and converting them into STIX format. CyNER extracts named entities in the context of CTI and then extracts the relations between named entities and IOCs in order to convert them into STIX. In addition, by using key phrase extraction, CyNER can extract relations between IOCs that lack contextual information, such as those listed at the bottom of a CTI, and named entities. We describe our design and implementation of CyNER and demonstrate that it can extract named entities with the F-measure of 0.80 and extract relations between named entities and IOCs with the maximum accuracy of 81.6%. Our analysis of structured CTI showed that CyNER can extract IOCs that are not included in existing reputation sites, and that it can automatically extract IOCs that have been exploited for a long time and across multiple attack groups. CyNER is thus expected to contribute to the efficiency of CTI analysis.

Keywords: Cyber Threat Intelligence · Information Extraction · Named Entity Recognition · Relation Extraction · STIX

1 Introduction

Cybersecurity threats have been increasing and growing more sophisticated year by year. In such circumstances, gathering Cyber Threat Intelligence (CTI) and following up with up-to-date threat information is crucial. For example, CTI

C.-M. Cheng and M. Akiyama (Eds.): IWSEC 2022, LNCS 13504, pp. 85–104, 2022.
https://doi.org/10.1007/978-3-031-15255-9_5

contains information on new vulnerabilities, malware, attackers' methods, and countermeasures against them. Indicator Of Compromise (IOC) is often included as an indicator for detecting attacks, and consists of, for example, IP addresses, URLs of suspicious sites, and hash values of malware. By utilizing this information for the detection rules of firewalls and intrusion detection systems, attacks can be detected in advance. Thus, by appropriately extracting and utilizing the information of the malware, vulnerability, and IOCs contained in CTI, it is possible to construct detection rules and analyze attack trends.

CTI is often first distributed as unstructured data in media such as blogs, news sites, and social networking sites. There is a time lag between the release of such information and its structuring—sometimes up to a month or more [22]. Therefore, in order to keep up with the latest threat information, it is necessary to analyze and utilize unstructured data. However, more than 60,000 CTIs are published every month [13], and it is not realistic to analyze all of them manually. In addition, since many CTIs are written in natural language, it is difficult to simply implement machine processing on them. In such circumstances, it is important to structure a CTI written in natural language into a form that can be processed by machines, and to support efficient analysis.

To resolve these challenges, some studies [21,32] have tried to analyze unstructured CTIs by constructing dictionaries or ontologies. However, in the security field, new words tend to be generated because of new malware or vulnerabilities, so their continuous maintenance is not easy. In addition, since IOCs such as URLs and IP addresses have a fixed format, they can be extracted by using regular expressions, but they often lack contextual information such as what kind of malware or attacker they are being used by. It is difficult to use such noncontextual information for analysis and to judge whether it is applicable as a detection rule or not. Therefore, it is important to add contextual information such as malware name and attacker name to the IOC.

Other research has examined machine learning, probabilistic method, and graph mining to perform robust information extraction for unknown words and to provide meaning to IOCs. For example, [42] matches Common Vulnerabilities and Exposures (CVE) summaries with Common Platform Enumeration (CPE) through machine learning-based Named Entity Recognition (NER) with high accuracy. In addition, iACE [18] attempts to extract contextual information about IOCs using graph mining. These studies mitigate the aforementioned difficulties with maintaining dictionaries and ontologies and the lack of contextual information. On the other hand, these methods, including the above-mentioned research, assumed that words related to IOCs appear in the neighborhood of IOCs. As for the semantics of IOCs, there are many cases in which IOCs are listed at the bottom of a CTI after the main topic is described. In such cases, the context of the IOCs is missing, and the existing methods, which assume that IOCs and their related words appear in the same neighborhood, cannot give proper context to the IOCs.

To solve these problems, we propose CyNER, a method for structuring CTIs using Natural Language Processing (NLP) techniques such as NER and Relation Extraction (RE). The proposed method aims to improve the efficiency of analysis by extracting named entities that should be focused on in the context of cybersecurity, such as malware names, vulnerability names, and IOCs. CyNER also aims to structure CTIs in a way that maintains contextual information by extracting relations between named entities. In addition, by estimating the topics mentioned in a CTI through key phrase extraction and associating them with IOCs, we can give contextual information such as relevant malware names and vulnerability names to IOCs lacking context, which is not possible with the existing methods. This makes it possible to link noncontextual IOCs to relevant malware or vulnerability names, which is difficult to extract with existing methods [18,45] that assume that technical terms associated with IOCs will appear in the same sentence. Moreover, we aim to improve the usability of the data by structuring them in a general-purpose format of Structured Threat Information eXpression (STIX) [30]. This makes it possible, for example, to conduct crossover analysis for threat information that is dispersed across different information sources. Although there are studies that cross-analyze already structured information such as blocklists and threat feeds [17,23], it is difficult for existing studies to cross-analyze unstructured threat information due to the existence of IOCs separated from the main texts as mentioned above. The contributions of this paper are as follows.

- By extracting named entities and relations between named entities from unstructured CTIs, CyNER automatically structures them in the STIX 2.1 format. In addition, by extracting key phrases from CTI and associating them with noncontextual IOCs, we can extract relations that have no relation in the neighborhood, which is not done in existing RE methods.
- The evaluation with our dataset showed that both the named entities and noncontextual IOCs could be extracted. We found that the F-measure for NER can be improved by up to 2.4 points by using a language model trained on a domain corpus for structuring CTI, compared to using a general-purpose language model. In addition, we were able to link entities to noncontextual IOCs with an accuracy of up to 81.65%.
- Using CyNER, we structured 52,292 CTIs from 34 sources, extracted 270,047 IOCs, and conducted a crossover analysis. In this analysis, the following facts were revealed and the possibility of using CyNER was demonstrated.
  - We compared the coverage of the IOCs extracted by CyNER with that of existing reputation services, and showed that CyNER can extract IOCs that are not included in the existing services.
  - We found that 19,010 IOCs were reported continuously, and some were exploited by multiple attack groups for more than a year.

2 Background and Challenges

2.1 Cyber Threat Intelligence

As mentioned earlier, threat information, called CTI, and especially structured CTI, has an important role to play in conducting security operations. In this context, various structured formats for cyber security have been developed for the purpose of machine-readable security information and information sharing in a common format. There is OpenIOC [20], which specializes in IOCs, and STIX [30] and MISP [27], which cover a wider range of information. For example, STIX consists of two parts: SDO (STIX Domain Object), which is an object of domain terms in the context of cyber security, and SRO (STIX Relationship Object), which is a relationship between SDOs.

The infrastructure for sharing such information is also being developed. Facebook ThreatExchange [8], the Defense Industrial Base Cybersecurity Information Sharing Program [7], and Automated Indicator Sharing [5] are frameworks for sharing reliable information among member organizations. There are also public frameworks for sharing IOCs, such as AlienVault OTX [1], OpenCTI [33], and MISP. However, a structured CTI for sharing in these frameworks needs to be created separately.

2.2 NLP

Information extraction is an NLP task in which structured data are extracted from unstructured documents. This task consists of various technologies such as NER, which extracts named entities from sentences, and RE, which extracts relations between named entities.

In recent years, high accuracy in information extraction has been achieved by using language models such as Word2Vec [24] to convert words or sentences into numerical expressions called distributed representations, which are then used as input for various tasks. In particular, Bidirectional Encoder Representations from Transformers (BERT) [6] and applied language models based on BERT have achieved high performance in a variety of tasks. There are also a number of later improved models, such as RoBERTa [19] for higher accuracy and ALBERT [16] for lighter weight.

2.3 Challenges

As mentioned above, structured CTI is useful and the infrastructure for sharing it is being developed. On the other hand, since most CTI is written in natural language, unstructured CTI needs to be structured. In this case, it is desirable to structure the CTI in a common format (as discussed in Sect. 2.1) so that we can utilize the various functions that have been developed, such as visualization and linkage with security appliances. Therefore, the goal of this research is to automatically convert CTI into a common format. In order to achieve this, the following issues need to be addressed.

Challenge 1: The complexity of terms. As mentioned above, new terms are developed every day, so extracting terms using a dictionary is not easy because it requires continuous maintenance of the dictionary. In addition, there are multiple terms that have the same meaning (e.g., "C&C" and "C2", "APT10" and "menuPass". In addition, some unique expressions overlap with common words (e.g., meltdown).

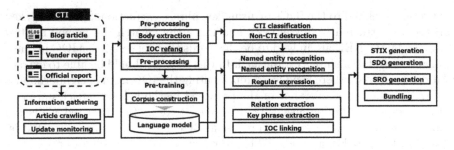

Fig. 1. Overview of CyNER.

Challenge 2: Extraction of distant relationships. In natural language of the general domain, named entities with relations often co-occur in the same or neighboring sentences, and existing RE methods often use the same sentence or a few neighboring sentences as the search range of relations [11,26,34,40]. This is not true, however, for CTI. For example, a specific malware threat is described in detail in the text, and the IOCs related to the malware are listed at the bottom of the CTI. In this case, the IOCs at the bottom of the CTI should be associated with name of the malware as a named entity, but since the IOCs are located far from the name of the malware, it is difficult to extract this relation using existing RE methods. In fact, when we examined the 270,047 IOCs we collected, more than half of them (144,430) were separated from the main texts (e.g., bullet points). Thus, it is necessary to implement a method for extracting such distant relations and restore the context of "noncontextual" IOCs.

3   Design and Implementation

3.1   Basic Idea and Overview

As discussed, while CTI structured according to a common format has various advantages, the construction cost is high and it is not practical to manually structure all unstructured CTIs. Therefore, our proposed method aims to automatically structure CTIs in a common format to support efficient analysis. To accomplish this, we need to solve the two challenges mentioned in Sect. 2.3.

First, to solve *Challenge 1*, we use BERT and related methods for NER. BERT is a machine learning-based method that can extract a greater number of new words compared to dictionary-based methods. In addition, unlike previous word representation methods such as Word2Vec, BERT can construct word representations that take into account the context. This increases the likelihood of recognizing words with equivalent meaning even if they are different. In addition, BERT learns embedded representations on a sub-word basis, not on a word basis. This is expected to increase the likelihood of recognizing unique expressions by subword, even if the word is new.

In order to solve *Challenge 2*, we assume that the noncontextual IOCs are related to the words that represent the CTI in question, and extract the distant relationships related to the IOCs by using key phrase extraction. Specifically, key phrases are extracted from the CTI, and those that match the named entities extracted by the NER are judged to be the words that represent the IOC in question, and the relationship is established. In this way, we should be able to extract relations even when there is no word representing the IOC in the neighborhood.

Figure 1 shows the overview of the proposed method. First, articles are collected from sites that publish CTI, and then text in the collected CTIs are preprocessed for the later stage of processing. Then, only CTIs are extracted by classifying the articles, and non CTIs are rejected. After that, information that should be described as STIX is extracted by NER and RE. Finally, the extracted information is formatted as STIX.

In the following sections, we describe the details of the processing for each step.

3.2 Information Gathering

First, CyNER gathers candidates of CTI from various websites such as blogs and official reports. CyNER initially crawls all CTI-related webpages and gathers all articles. In this paper, we chose several major websites and implemented a crawler and parser tailored for each. In addition, to prevent duplication of articles and overload of target websites, CyNER gathers only updated articles. To do so, updated articles are gathered by using RSS feeds in cases where target websites provide RSS. Otherwise, CyNER parses CTI-providing pages and verifies whether the articles are new or not. After that, CyNER gathers only new articles.

3.3 Preprocessing

In this step, CyNER carries out preprocessing for text in the gathered CTIs. Web articles often include non-CTI information such as html tags, advertisements, and navigation bars, so CyNER extracts body texts for deleting any unnecessary information.

Next, CyNER performs refang on the IOCs. *Refang* means to returning defanged IOCs to their original form, e.g., converting "example[.]com" into "example.com". In doing so, IOCs can be extracted by regular expression. The refang mechanism is implemented by defining refanging rules (such as replacing "[.]" with "."") in advance and then using rule-based search and replace. One of the refang rules is removing brackets. All refang rules are shown in the Appendix B.

After this preprocessing, the collected information is processed to make it suitable for the later stage of NLP. Specifically, the extracted text is divided into sentences so that it can be processed by the language model.

3.4 Pretraining

As mentioned above, BERT and other pre-trained language models are widely available and can be used for NER. On the other hand, it is known that pre-training

Table 1. Named entity list.

STIX object	Extracted items	Description	Examples	Extraction method
Attack pattern	name	Attack pattern name	Spear Phishing	NER
Campaign	name	Campaign name	Operation Aurora	NER
Threat actor	name	Threat actor name	APT10	NER
Identity	name	Name	Hitachi, Ltd.	NER
Indicator	pattern	IOC	URL, hash, etc.	Regular expression
Malware	labels	Malware type	Ransomware	NER
	name	Malware name	WannaCry	NER
Tool	name	Tool name	Metasploit	NER
Vulnerability	name	Vulnerability name	CVE-2014-0160	Regular expression
			HeartBleed	NER

on a domain-specific corpus in a specialized field improves the accuracy of various tasks based on the model in question [4]. Therefore, we aim to improve the accuracy of NER by constructing our own pre-training model using the domain corpus of the cyber security field.

In order to build a pre-training model for the cyber security domain, we first crawl web pages that publish CTI and collect them as candidates for the domain corpus to be used as training data for building the language model. Next, we remove unnecessary information from the collected CTI to extract sentences for training. Specifically, in order to extract the main text, we remove unnecessary information such as HTML tags and JavaScript. In addition, even in the body part, there are still some sentences such as headings and bullets that are not necessary for learning. Therefore, referring to the literature [35], we remove the unnecessary information by the following process to make a domain corpus.

- Pages with less than 5 sentences
- Lines with less than 3 words
- Lines that may be signatures such as *snort* (lines starting with "{" or "$")

Finally, the domain corpus constructed so far is used for pre-training to build the language model. By using the above method, we aim to improve the accuracy of NER for structuring CTI.

3.5 CTI Classification

Some of the blogs and official pages that provide CTIs include articles introducing products and seminars. Since these are not CTIs, we reject them by constructing a binary classifier to determine whether they are CTIs or not. Our binary classifier consists of the aforementioned pre-trained BERT and a fully-connected layer that outputs whether the input document is a CTI or not.

3.6 Named Entity Recognition

To modify the corpus that has been processed up to this point into a form suitable for NLP, NER is performed. We first define the items to be extracted as extended

Table 2. Relation rule list.

Subject	Object	Relation
Indicator_pattern	Attack_pattern_name	
- Hash value	Campaign_name	indicates
- File name	Malware_name	
	Threat_actor_name	
Malware_name	Indicator - URL - IP address	communicates-with

named entities (Table 1). As mentioned earlier, CyNER carries out structuring according to the STIX 2.1 format. Therefore, we define the named entities in a form corresponding to the objects (SDOs) in STIX. As already described, formatted named entities (e.g., IP addresses, URLs, and CVE numbers) are extracted by regular expressions. In addition, other named entities are extracted by the NER model, which is implemented by fine-tuning *huggingface* [41] pre-trained models (BERT, RoBERTa, and ALBERT) for NER, the same as CTI classification.

3.7   Relation Extraction

By extracting the relationships between the named entities extracted in the previous step, CyNER acquires the contextual information. The definition of the relationship between IOCs and named entities is provided in Table 2. This definition is aligned with the SRO of STIX 2.1. CyNER firstly extracts relationships by existing method such as [18] for named entities located at same sentence. Here, on the basis of the policy described in Sect. 3.1, CyNER also attempts to extract the relationships between named entities and independent IOCs (Fig. 2). The specific process flow is as follows.

1. Among the IOCs extracted with regular expressions in the NER step, extract those independently listed, e.g., located alone at the bottom of a CTI, as candidates for RE.
2. Extract the top 10 key phrases that represent the CTI by using a key phrase extraction technique.
3. Among the extracted named entities, compare the named entities that can have a relationship with the IOCs with the key phrases, and associate the one that matches the top key phrase with the IOC as having the predefined relationship. The properties of the named entities that can have a relationship with the IOCs are attack_pattern, campaign_name, malware_name, and threat_actor_name. In other words, each IOC is assigned a relationship with up to four named entities.

With the above process, we can extract relationships between named entities and "noncontextual" IOCs, which are difficult to extract with existing methods.

As a key phrase extraction method, we used MultipartiteRank [2], which had the highest accuracy for our test data among the several methods we implemented and compared. The details are described in Sect. 4.

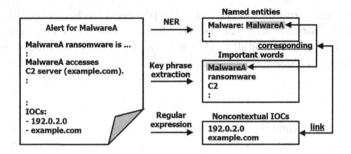

Fig. 2. Extraction method for noncontextual IOCs of CTI.

3.8 STIX Generation

STIX is generated using the named entities and their relationships extracted in the previous process. Specifically, first, the named entities extracted in the NER step are converted into the corresponding SDOs. Next, the relations extracted in the RE step are converted into SROs that define the relations among STIX objects. Finally, a STIX object is created for each CTI using a bundle object that groups STIX objects.

4 Evaluation

4.1 Experimental Setup

We implemented a prototype of CyNER according to the design described above and conducted the following two evaluations.

1. **Named Entity Recognition Accuracy.** CyNER attempts to extract the named entities (shown in Table 1) using a fine-tuned language model for SDO extraction; therefore, the accuracy of the NER is evaluated in terms of the precision, recall, and F-measure. In doing so, we will also test whether the accuracy is improved by pre-training language models using domain corpora.
2. **Relation Extraction Accuracy.** CyNER extracts relations between named entities and noncontextual IOCs of CTIs by comparing the results of NER with those of key phrase extraction. We evaluate the correctness of this RE. We then implement several key phrase extraction methods and evaluate which one is most suitable for this task.

In addition, we use CyNER to structure and analyze CTI. In this way, we verify the possibility of using CyNER for CTI-based security operations. Specifically, we also conducted the following evaluations.

3. **IOC coverage.** CyNER extracts named entities from unstructured CTI and associates them with IOCs. We compare and evaluate whether the coverage of IOCs and information associated with IOCs extracted by CyNER is as good as that of the de facto service. Specifically, we compare VirusTotal, a service for evaluating IOCs, and AlienVault OTX, a platform for sharing structured CTIs.

4. Time-series information. By using the proposed method, we can handle the time-series information of CTI and IOCs from the past to the present in a unified manner. Therefore, we analyze CTI and IOC from the viewpoint of time series and examine the possibility of using them.

4.2   Dataset

To conduct each of the evaluations described in the previous section, we selected 34 sites that distribute CTIs on the basis of existing studies and interviews with practitioners (detailed in the Appendix A). We implemented a crawler for each site and collected 75,652 CTI candidates published between June 2001 and December 2020, and then constructed the following datasets for evaluation. In all evaluations, data before 2019 were used for training and data after 2019 were used for testing. The labeling of the data was done independently by the author, who are experts in the field of cyber security. In addition, CTIs for labeling were randomly selected as described below, but those that contain few named entities were excluded.

– *Dataset for training language models.* The collected CTIs were subjected to the preprocessing described in Sect. 3.3 and then made into a domain corpus for language model training. The dataset consists of about 3,000,000 lines totaling about 320 MB.
– *Dataset for NER.* We randomly picked up the collected CTIs and prepared 100 CTIs annotated with named entities. This dataset consists of 13,479 sentences, 193,027 words, and 4,562 named entities in total.
– *Dataset for extracting IOC relations.* We randomly picked up the collected CTIs and prepared 100 CTIs that include at least one IOC. This dataset contains 2,371 IOCs.
– *Dataset of structured CTI.* Among the 75,652 CTIs mentioned above, 52,292 CTIs are evaluated by the CTI classifier in this section. The number of unique IOCs associated with named entities by CyNER is 270,047, and it consists 50,323 hashs, 184,349 URLs, and 35,375 IP addresses. Note that URLs in the Alexa Top 10,000 and private IP addresses defined in RFCs are excluded because they are highly likely to be false positives.

4.3   Result

Evaluation 1: Named Entity Recognition Accuracy. In this evaluation, 70 articles (70%) were used for training and 30 for verification. The training data were further divided into a 70% training set and a 30% validation set for training. For the models, we used BERT and its later variants, RoBERT and ALBERT, which are representative of the pre-training models available in huggingface. For each model, we used large, which has more parameters and higher accuracy, and base, which is lighter. In addition, in order to compare machine learning-based models with dictionary-based methods, dictionary-based NER was used as a baseline. Specifically, we registered named entities in the training data into a dictionary and

Table 3. NER accuracy of each model.

Method	Model	Precision	Recall	F-measure
Dictionary [12,18,21,32,45]	-	0.74	0.56	0.65
CRF [29,42]	-	0.68	0.68	0.68
BERT [37]	bert-base-uncased	0.81	0.70	0.75
	bert-large-uncased	0.78	0.73	0.75
	roberta-base	0.78	0.73	0.76
	roberta-large	0.85	0.74	0.78
	albert-base	0.84	0.73	0.77
	albert-large	0.84	0.70	0.77
CyNER	bert-base-uncased	0.81	0.76	0.78
(BERT fine-tuned by domain corpus)	bert-large-uncased	0.78	0.76	0.77
	roberta-base	0.81	0.79	0.80
	roberta-large	**0.80**	**0.80**	**0.80**
	albert-base	0.81	0.74	0.78
	albert-large	0.80	0.74	0.78

Table 4. Accuracy of relation extraction.

Method	Accuracy (%)
PositionRank	77.22
TopicRank	69.59
MultipartiteRank	81.65

Table 5. IOC coverage of each platform.

IOC type	Method	Total	Existed	(rate)	Did not exist	(rate)
SHA256	CyNER	1,000	1,000	(100%)	0	(0.0%)
	VT	1,000	906	(90.6%)	94	(9.4%)
	OTX	1,000	25	(2.5%)	975	(97.5%)
IPv4	CyNER	1,000	1,000	(100%)	0	(0.0%)
	VT	1,000	998	(99.8%)	2	(0.2%)
	OTX	1,000	195	(19.5%)	805	(80.5%)

extracted named entities from the validation data using the dictionary. As another baseline, we used the NER model with CRF, which is a well-known conventional method. We trained each model for 200 epochs. The final accuracy of both models is shown in Table 3, which includes the values of the data for validation.

First, we can see that the accuracy of all machine learning-based models was higher than that of the baseline dictionary. In order to determine the effect of pre-training with the domain corpus, we evaluated the accuracy with and without the domain corpus for each model except the baseline. The results without the domain corpus are listed in the *BERT* row, and the results with the domain corpus are listed in the *CyNER* row. From the experimental results, we can see that the F-measure improved in all the models, with a maximum improvement of about 2.4 points in *bert-base-uncase* (from 0.7523 to 0.7760). In addition, roberta-large had the highest accuracy among all models with an F-measure of 0.8012. This result confirms that pre-training with domain corpora can improve the accuracy of NER in the field of cyber security. Note that the following evaluations and analyses are conducted using CyNER with roberta-large.

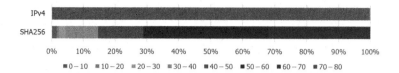

Fig. 3. Number of AV detections for IOCs included in VirusTotal.

Evaluation 2: Relation Extraction Accuracy. In this evaluation, we selected PositionRank [10], TopicRank [3], and MultipartiteRank [2] as the key phrase extraction methods and measured the percentage of correct answers when performing the relation extraction described in Sect. 3.7 using each method. In this case, only nouns, proper nouns, and adjectives were used as candidates for key phrases. We then compared the list of extracted key phrases with the list of unique expressions, and extracted those that matched as related words. The percentage of correct answers in this evaluation is shown in Table 4. MultipartiteRank had the highest percentage of correct answers, at 81.65%. The accuracy of PositionRank was almost the same, at 77.22%. Both methods favored words close to the beginning of the sentence, which suggests that key phrases related to IOCs in CTI have a high co-occurrence with words close to the beginning of the sentence. These results demonstrate that BERT is suitable for CTI classification, RoBERTa for NER, and MultipartiteRank for relation extraction.

4.4 IOC Coverage

In this evaluation, we checked whether or not the IOCs extracted by CyNER were included in VirusTotal and OTX, and compared their coverage. We randomly selected IOCs that were associated with one or more malware. The properties of the IOCs are the hash value of the malware (SHA256) and the communication destination (IPv4 address). In addition, we selected 1,000 hash values and 1,000 communication destinations, and used them for comparison.

First, Table 5 shows the results of the coverage evaluation. In this evaluation, we compared the coverage of VirusTotal and OTX based on 1,000 SHA256 and 1,000 IPv4 addresses each which are associated with the malware families extracted by CyNER. The coverage of OTX was 2.5% for SHA256 and 19.5% for IPv4, which is relatively low, probably due to the fact that OTX relies heavily on manual and expert registration. In contrast, the coverage of VirusTotal was 90.6% for SHA256 and 99.8% for IPv4, which included most of the IOCs extracted by CyNER. Since the number of contributors to VirusTotal is larger than that of OTX, it is assumed that most of the IOCs listed in the public CTI, which is the source of information for CyNER, have already been submitted. However, among the IOCs extracted by CyNER, there were some that were not included in either service, so it is useful to be able to structure such IOCs automatically and with contextual information by linking them to malware families.

Next, we compared the results in terms of the amount of information. First, although OTX lacks some coverage (as described above), it can be tagged

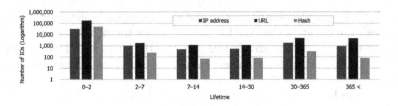

Fig. 4. Lifetime for each type of IOC.

manually and often contains the same amount of information or more than CyNER. In addition, VirusTotal can scan the target with dozens of AV products and URL scanners. The results of these scans are shown in Fig. 3.

Most of the files (SHA256) were detected by more than 30 AV products, which means that the results can be used to estimate with high accuracy whether the target is malware or not. In contrast, for the communication destination (IPv4), almost all of them were detected by fewer than ten engines, and it is not easy to estimate whether the target is malicious or not using only these results. This may be indirectly due to the fact that it is not easy to determine whether the target is malicious or not by simple scanning due to cloaking and the use of non-well-known ports. We also verified whether malware families can be estimated based on the scan results of VirusTotal using AVCLASS [38]. Of the 906 samples included in VirusTotal, we were able to estimate the malware family for about 40% as well as CyNER, but not for the remaining 60%. This can be attributed to the lack of information associated with the malware family, since some specimens and AV engines were detected with generic names such as *Generic.Trojan*. In addition, although samples that download malware in the latter stage were related to a specific malware family in a series of attacks, they were detected only as "Downloader" in isolation, and thus, similarly, no information related to the malware family could be obtained. On the other hand, CyNER can link IOCs to malware families in CTI, so it is highly possible to determine whether a malware is malicious or not regardless of whether it is SHA256 or IPv4. In addition, since CyNER links IOCs to attacks mentioned in CTI without depending on the nature of the sample, it is possible to link even Downloader to malware families that were dropped in the later stages.

4.5 Time-Series

In this section, we analyze IOC from the view point of time-series. For each IOC, the date when it was first reported by CTI and the date when it was last reported were recorded, and the difference in the number of days between them was defined as the observation period. The observation period was defined as the difference in the number of days between the two dates. Figure 4 shows the results of the survey divided by the type of IOC (IP address, URL, and hash), and the observation period plotted by its length. As we can see, most of the observation periods are within the range of 0 to 2 days for all the IOC types. In particular, 49,527 hash values, or more than 98% of all IOCs, fall within this range. This is probably due to the fact that it is relatively easy to detect malware based on hash values. Moreover, because hash values can be changed by variants, malware with the same hash tends not to be used for a long time. In addition, many of the URLs and IP addresses have a short observation period, suggesting that they are used and discarded after each attack.

On the other hand, although not the majority, 19,010 cases had an observation period of more than three days, and some of them were reported for a long period of time, especially for URLs and IP addresses. For example, 59[.]188[.]0[.]197 was an IP address that had been observed for a relatively long period of time (792 days). This IP address was reported as the C2 server in the spear phishing attack of the *Temper Panda* group in 2014. The IP address was later reported to have been used in an attack by the same group in 2015, suggesting that it is one of the attack infrastructures that the group has been continuously exploiting. The same IP address was also reported to have been used in an attack by the *APT16* group in 2015, suggesting that the attack infrastructure may be shared by multiple attack groups. Thus, it is possible that we can automatically extract more dangerous IOCs by extracting IOCs that have been observed for a long time.

5   Discussion

5.1   Practicality

Due to resource constraints, there is a real need to add only those threats that are of a higher level to the block list. For such a requirement, CyNER can be used to select those that are associated with a specific threat, or those that have been reported over a long period of time or across multiple sources. In addition, CyNER can be used to present long-term IOCs in chronological order, or to present IOCs that have been reported across multiple sources, which is expected to improve the efficiency of operations for the aforementioned requirements. In addition, since the IOCs are structured as STIX, which is a common format, it is expected that the utilization by existing libraries (e.g., visualization by STIX Visualizer [31]) and the automatic linkage with the security appliance can be utilized.

On the other hand, there are some points that need to be considered in practical use. Although we used the F-measure uniformly in this accuracy evaluation, the accuracy that we consider important differs depending on the task. For example, for manual incident response, coverage is important even if false positives are tolerated. In contrast, when creating a block list, true positives are important because it is undesirable to over-detect normal communication. It is therefore necessary to choose which indicators are important depending on the task. In addition, it has been suggested that CTI potentially contains false positives [17] so it may be desirable to introduce a separate filter for sensitive applications against false positives.

5.2   Limitation

False Positives and False Negatives. If the URL or IP address is defanged using an unknown method, there is a possibility that it cannot be refanged and cannot be extracted using regular expressions. However, in most cases, the defanging method is standardized for each CTI site, so we assume it is possible to deal with the problem by establishing a refang rule for each site.

In CyNER, all IOCs included in a CTI are handled flatly, and all IOCs are linked to a word that represents the CTI. In other words, the proposed method is likely to be incompatible with CTIs containing multiple topics in a single CTI, such as weekly reports.

Information Sources. In this paper, we focused on blogs and official announcements as CTI sources, but CTIs are published in other forms as well. One major CTI source is SNS, e.g., Twitter. Therefore, a lot of research has focused on collecting CTI from SNS: [39] gathers the vendor's patch release information from SNS, and [28] gathers threats or vulnerability information from SNS. In SNS analysis research, there are a number of unique challenges, e.g., texts are shorter than common articles, so extracting information is difficult [28,39], or fake information is potentially included, and verification is necessary [43]. Of course, intelligence in SNS has its advantages, primarily in that it is more prompt than in blogs; thus, in the future, we plan to extend CyNER for the importation of other sources for intelligence promptness and coverage. In addition, although 34 sources were used in this study, the information obtained in this experiment is not necessarily coverage, since other sources may exist.

5.3 Research Ethics

When collecting CTIs for evaluation in this paper, a certain interval was set for each access when information was obtained from the same site. In addition, as described in the design section, we checked for updates to the articles, and if there were none, we did not attempt further access. These measures reduce the unnecessary load on the CTI distribution site.

6 Related Work

Structuring CTI. Prior research has attempted to structure unstructured data by creating dictionaries and ontologies [21,32]. In [32], cyber ontologies and their extensions for malware were discussed. In addition, [21] argued the importance of developing a multi-layered cyber threat intelligence ontology. However, in the security field, continuous maintenance of dictionaries and ontologies is not easy because new words are often created due to the emergence of new malware, the discovery of vulnerabilities, and the assignment of code names. CyNER mitigates this challenge by using machine learning-based information extraction. Also, in [21], it was pointed out that existing ontologies lack expressiveness and coverage due to a lack of development.

To mitigate these issues, some studies have attempted to structure unstructured data by machine learning-based or probabilistic method-based natural language processing, similar to the proposed method [14,15,18,29,36]. In particular, iACE [18] attempted to extract not only named entities but also contextual information related to IOCs by using graph mining. However, the relationships with distant IOCs were not extracted, in contrast to our own work.

NLP in Cybersecurity. In addition to the aforementioned structuring, a number of studies have focused on the use of CTI. FeatureSmith [44] generates features by text mining CTI and automatically builds a model to detect Android malware. [9] is another method for automatically constructing threat detection rules from CTI. TTPDrill [12] conducts text mining for CTI and assigns the descriptions to TTPs and Cyber Kill Chains, and ChainSmith [45] estimates the roles of IOCs extracted from CTI. POIROT [25] performs Threat Hunting by graphing and comparing audit logs and CTI, respectively; Extractor [37] automates the graphing of CTI. However, the objectives of these studies did not involve structuring CTI, and none of them carried out crossover analyses of CTI. Although they have different goals, all these methods use natural language processing techniques to analyze and utilize CTI in the same way as CyNER.

Crossover Analysis for CTI. There are also several studies that attempt to perform crossover analysis of CTIs. [23] investigated IP addresses and domains in multiple blocklists and found that many IOCs are unique to a single list. [17] similarly investigated multiple blocklists. We focus on CTI in its unstructured state rather than blocklists, and conduct crossover analysis after structuring it.

7   Conclusion

In this paper, we proposed CyNER, a method to automatically convert CTIs written in natural language into STIX, with the aim of improving the efficiency of analysis. CyNER extracts named entities and relations between named entities from CTI and then automatically structures them into STIX 2.1 format. Key phrases are extracted in units of CTI and then associated with noncontextual IOCs. This enables the extraction of relations that have no relation in the neighborhood, which is not possible in previous RE methods.

We extracted 270,047 IOCs from 52,292 CTIs of 34 information sources using CyNER, and conducted a crossover analysis. The results showed that CyNER can extract IOCs that are not included in the existing reputation services. We also found that 19,010 IOCs are continuously reported and that some IOCs are exploited across multiple attack groups for more than a year. From the above results, it is expected that CyNER will contribute to the efficiency of CTI analysis. Future work will include improving the accuracy of each task and evaluating CyNER on larger datasets.

A   Source of CTI

Table 6 shows 34 sources of CTIs used by CyNER. We're very grateful to all of the CTI publishers.

Table 6. Source websites of CTIs.

#	Publisher	URL
1	Avast Blog	https://blog.avast.com/
2	Certego	http://www.certego.net/en/news/
3	Checkpoint	https://blog.checkpoint.com/
4	Cisco Talos	https://blog.talosintelligence.com/
5	Cofense	https://cofense.com/blog/
6	Crowdstrike	https://www.crowdstrike.com/blog/category/threat-intel-research/
7	Cylance	https://threatvector.cylance.com
8	Dancho Danchev's Blog	https://ddanchev.blogspot.com/
9	Dynamo	https://blog.dynamoo.com/
10	FireEye Blogs, Threat Research	https://www.fireeye.com/blog/threat-research.html
11	Fox-it	https://blog.fox-it.com/
12	Hexacorn	http://www.hexacorn.com/blog/
13	ICS-CERT, advisories	https://ics-cert.us-cert.gov/advisories
14	ICS-CERT, alerts	https://ics-cert.us-cert.gov/alerts
15	InQuest Blog	http://blog.inquest.net/blog/
16	Kaspersky lab, securelist	https://securelist.com/
17	krebs on security	https://krebsonsecurity.com/
18	malware-trafic-analysis	https://www.malware-traffic-analysis.net/
19	Malwarebytes Labs, Threat Analysis	https://blog.malwarebytes.com/category/threat-analysis/
20	MalwareMustDie	http://blog.malwaremustdie.org/
21	McAfee Threat Center	http://www.mcafee.com/us/threat_center/
22	Naked Security	https://nakedsecurity.sophos.com/
23	360 Netlab Blog	http://blog.netlab.360.com/
24	paloalto cybersecurity	https://researchcenter.paloaltonetworks.com/cybersecurity-2/
25	Sucuri	https://blog.sucuri.net/
26	Symantec	https://symantec.com/blogs/threat-intelligence
27	TaoSecurity	https://taosecurity.blogspot.com/
28	The Hacker News	https://thehackernews.com/
29	Threatpost	https://threatpost.com/blog/
30	TrendLabs Security Intelligence Blog	https://blog.trendmicro.com/trendlabs-security-intelligence/
31	US-CERT, alerts	https://www.us-cert.gov/ncas/alerts
32	Webroot	https://www.webroot.com/blog/
33	WeLiveSecurity	https://www.welivesecurity.com/
34	Zscaler blogs	https://www.zscaler.com/blogs/research

B   Refang Rules

Table 7 shows all the refang rules implemented in CyNER.

Table 7. Refang and defang rules.

Category	Before refanging	After refanging
URL	"hccp", "hxxp", "hXXp", "xxxx", "[http]"	"http"
URL	"hxxps", "xxxxx", "[https]"	"https"
URL	"http ://", "http//", "http:///"	"http://"
URL	"https ://", "https//", "https:///"	"https://"
URL	":// "	"://"
URL	"\/"	"//"
URL	"[www]", "(www)"	"www"
IPv4/URL	"(.)", "[.[", "].]", "[dot]", "(dot)", "[punkt]", "(punkt)", "DOT", "DOT"	"."
IPv4/URL	" .com"	".com"
IPv6/URL	"[:]"	":"

References

1. AlienVault: Open Threat Intelligence (2021). https://otx.alienvault.com/
2. Boudin, F.: Unsupervised keyphrase extraction with multipartite graphs. In: Proceedings of the 2018 Conference of the North American Chapter of the Association for Computational Linguistics: Human Language Technologies, vol. 2 (Short Papers). pp. 667–672 (2018)
3. Bougouin, A., et al.: TopicRank: graph-based topic ranking for keyphrase extraction. In: Proceedings of the Sixth International Joint Conference on Natural Language Processing, pp. 543–551 (2013)
4. Chalkidis, I., et al.: LEGAL-BERT: the muppets straight out of law school. In: Findings of the Association for Computational Linguistics: EMNLP 2020, pp. 2898–2904 (2020)
5. CISA: Automated Indicator Sharing (AIS) (2021). https://www.us-cert.gov/ais
6. Devlin, J., et al.: BERT: pre-training of deep bidirectional transformers for language understanding. In: Proceedings of the 2019 Conference of the North American Chapter of the Association for Computational Linguistics: Human Language Technologies, vol. 1 (Long and Short Papers), pp. 4171–4186 (2019)
7. DoD: Defense Industrial Base Cybersecurity Information Sharing Program (2021). https://dibnet.dod.mil/portal/intranet/
8. Facebook: Facebook ThreatExchange Overview (2021). https://developers.facebook.com/programs/threatexchange/
9. Feng, X., et al.: Understanding and securing device vulnerabilities through automated bug report analysis. In: Proceedings of the 28th USENIX Conference on Security Symposium. pp. 887–903. SEC 2019 (2019)
10. Florescu, C., et al.: PositionRank: an unsupervised approach to keyphrase extraction from scholarly documents. In: Proceedings of the 55th Annual Meeting of the Association for Computational Linguistics (vol. 1: Long Papers), pp. 1105–1115 (2017)
11. Gupta, P., et al.: Neural relation extraction within and across sentence boundaries. Proc. AAAI Conf. Artif. Intell. **33**(01), 6513–6520 (2019)
12. Husari, G., et al.: Ttpdrill: automatic and accurate extraction of threat actions from unstructured text of CTI sources. In: Proceedings of the 33rd Annual Computer Security Applications Conference, pp. 103–115. ACSAC 2017 (2017)
13. IBM: IBM Watson to Tackle Cybercrime (2016). https://newsroom.ibm.com/2016-05-10-IBM-Watson-to-Tackle-Cybercrime?lnk=hmhm
14. Jones, C.L., Bridges, R.A., Huffer, K.M.T., Goodall, J.R.: Towards a relation extraction framework for cyber-security concepts. In: Proceedings of the 10th Annual Cyber and Information Security Research Conference. CISR 2015 (2015)
15. Joshi, A., et al.: Extracting cybersecurity related linked data from text. In: 2013 IEEE Seventh International Conference on Semantic Computing, pp. 252–259 (2013)
16. Lan, Z., et al.: ALBERT: a lite BERT for Self-supervised Learning of Language Representations. In: International Conference of Learning Representations. CISR 2020 (2020)
17. Li, V.G., et al.: Reading the tea leaves: a comparative analysis of threat intelligence. In: 28th USENIX Security Symposium (USENIX Security 2019), pp. 851–867 (2019)
18. Liao, X., et al.: Acing the IOC game: toward automatic discovery and analysis of open-source cyber threat intelligence. In: Proceedings of the 2016 ACM SIGSAC Conference on Computer and Communications Security, pp. 755–766. CCS 2016 (2016)

19. Liu, Y., et al.: Roberta: a robustly optimized BERT pretraining approach. CoRR abs/1907.11692 (2019)
20. Mandiant: OpenIOC (2013). https://github.com/mandiant/OpenIOC_1.1
21. Mavroeidis, V., et al.: Cyber threat intelligence model: an evaluation of taxonomies, sharing standards, and ontologies within cyber threat intelligence. In: 2017 European Intelligence and Security Informatics Conference (EISIC), pp. 91–98 (2017)
22. McNeil, N., et al.: Pace: pattern accurate computationally efficient bootstrapping for timely discovery of cyber-security concepts. In: 2013 12th International Conference on Machine Learning and Applications, vol. 2, pp. 60–65 (2013)
23. Metcalf, L., et al.: Blacklist ecosystem analysis: Spanning Jan 2012 to June 2014. In: Proceedings of the 2nd ACM Workshop on Information Sharing and Collaborative Security, pp. 13–22. WISCS 2015 (2015)
24. Mikolov, T., et al.: Efficient estimation of word representations in vector space. In: 1st International Conference on Learning Representations, ICLR 2013, Workshop Track Proceedings (2013)
25. Milajerdi, S.M., et al.: Poirot: aligning attack behavior with kernel audit records for cyber threat hunting. In: Proceedings of the 2019 ACM SIGSAC Conference on Computer and Communications Security, pp. 1795–1812. CCS 2019 (2019)
26. Min, B., et al.: Ensemble semantics for large-scale unsupervised relation extraction. In: Proceedings of the 2012 Joint Conference on Empirical Methods in Natural Language Processing and Computational Natural Language Learning, pp. 1027–1037 (2012)
27. MISP project: MISP - Open Source Threat Intelligence Platform & Open Standards For Threat Information Sharing (2021). https://www.misp-project.org/
28. Mittal, S., et al.: Cybertwitter: using twitter to generate alerts for cybersecurity threats and vulnerabilities. In: 2016 IEEE/ACM International Conference on Advances in Social Networks Analysis and Mining (ASONAM), pp. 860–867 (2016)
29. Mulwad, V., et al.: Extracting information about security vulnerabilities from web text. In: 2011 IEEE/WIC/ACM International Conferences on Web Intelligence and Intelligent Agent Technology, vol. 3, pp. 257–260 (2011)
30. OASIS: Introduction to STIX (2021). https://oasis-open.github.io/cti-documentation/stix/intro.html
31. OASIS: STIX Visualizer (2021). https://oasis-open.github.io/cti-stix-visualization/
32. Obrst, L., et al.: Developing an ontology of the cyber security domain. In: STIDS, pp. 49–56 (2012)
33. OpenCTI-Platform: OpenCTI (2021). https://github.com/OpenCTI-Platform/opencti
34. Peng, N., et al.: Cross-sentence n-ARY relation extraction with graph LSTMS. Trans. Assoc. Comput. Linguist. 5, 101–115 (2017)
35. Raffel, C., et al.: Exploring the limits of transfer learning with a unified text-to-text transformer. J. Mach. Learn. Res. 21(140), 1–67 (2020)
36. Ramnani, R.R., et al.: Semi-automated information extraction from unstructured threat advisories. In: Proceedings of the 10th Innovations in Software Engineering Conference, pp. 181–187. ISEC 2017 (2017)
37. Satvat, K., et al.: EXTRACTOR: extracting attack behavior from threat reports. CoRR abs/2104.08618 (2021)
38. Sebastián, S., et al.: AVClass2: massive malware tag extraction from AV labels. In: Annual Computer Security Applications Conference, pp. 42–53. ACSAC 2020 (2020)

39. Syed, R.: Analyzing software vendors' patch release behavior in the age of social media. In: Proceedings of the International Conference on Information Systems - Transforming Society with Digital Innovation, ICIS (2017)
40. Takanobu, R., et al.: A hierarchical framework for relation extraction with reinforcement learning. Proc. AAAI Conf. Artif. Intell. **33**(01), 7072–7079 (2019)
41. The Hugging Face Team: Huggingface: Transformers (2020). https://huggingface.co/transformers/
42. Wåreus, E., et al.: Automated CPE labeling of CVE summaries with machine learning. In: Detection of Intrusions and Malware, and Vulnerability Assessment, pp. 3–22 (2020)
43. Yang, S., et al.: Unsupervised fake news detection on social media: a generative approach. Proc. AAAI Conf. Artif. Intell. **33**(01), 5644–5651 (2019)
44. Zhu, Z., et al.: FeatureSmith: automatically engineering features for malware detection by mining the security literature. In: Proceedings of the 2016 ACM SIGSAC Conference on Computer and Communications Security, pp. 767–778. CCS 2016 (2016)
45. Zhu, Z., et al.: ChainSmith: automatically learning the semantics of malicious campaigns by mining threat intelligence reports. In: 2018 IEEE European Symposium on Security and Privacy (EuroS&P), pp. 458–472 (2018)

Symmetric-Key Cryptography

Birthday-Bound Slide Attacks on TinyJAMBU's Keyed-Permutations for All Key Sizes

Ferdinand Sibleyras[✉], Yu Sasaki[✉], Yosuke Todo[✉],
Akinori Hosoyamada[✉], and Kan Yasuda[✉]

NTT Social Informatics Laboratories, Tokyo, Japan
{sibleyras.ferdinand.ez,yu.sasaki.sk,yosuke.todo.xt,
akinori.hosoyamada.bh,kan.yasuda.hy}@hco.ntt.co.jp

Abstract. We study the security of the underlying keyed-permutations of NIST LWC finalist TinyJAMBU. Our main findings are key-recovery attacks whose data and time complexities are close to the birthday bound 2^{64}. The attack idea works for all versions of TinyJAMBU permutations having different key sizes, irrespective of the number of rounds repeated in the permutations. Most notably, the attack complexity is only marginally increased even when the key size becomes larger. Concretely, for TinyJAMBU permutations of key sizes 128, 192, and 256 bits, the data/time complexities of our key-recovery attacks are about 2^{65}, 2^{66}, and $2^{69.5}$, respectively. Our attacks are on the underlying permutations and not on the TinyJAMBU AEAD scheme; the TinyJAMBU mode of operation limits the applicability of our attacks. However, our results imply that TinyJAMBU's underlying keyed-permutations cannot be expected to provide the same security levels as robust block ciphers of the corresponding block and key sizes. Furthermore, the provable security of TinyJAMBU AEAD scheme should be carefully revisited, where the underlying permutations have been assumed to be almost ideal.

Keywords: TinyJAMBU · NIST LWC · keyed-permutation · slide attack

1 Introduction

The Lightweight Cryptography standardization by NIST (NIST LWC) [9] is one of the most actively discussed topics recently in the symmetric-key cryptography community. In March 2021, out of 56 candidates NIST kept 10 finalists [10] whose evaluations would take approximately 12 months [11].

In this paper we target TinyJAMBU [16], one of the finalists of NIST LWC. TinyJAMBU was designed by Wu and Huang. Roughly speaking, TinyJAMBU (Fig. 2) can be seen as the duplex construction [2] with its public permutation replaced by a 128-bit keyed-permutations; or again as similar to SAEB [8].

C.-M. Cheng and M. Akiyama (Eds.): IWSEC 2022, LNCS 13504, pp. 107–127, 2022.
https://doi.org/10.1007/978-3-031-15255-9_6

TinyJAMBU has one of the smallest hardware footprints of all the finalists. One reason is its small 128 bits of internal state which is near optimal.
Moreover, the round function (Fig. 1) consists of a non-linear feedback shift
register (NLFSR) with only four XOR operations and a single NAND operation. To optimize throughput, TinyJAMBU varies the number of rounds of the
keyed-permutations throughout the mode. $P1$ denotes a permutation with fewer
rounds, and $P2$ the one with more rounds.

Table 1. Summary of attacks. KP, CP, and ACP represent known-plaintexts, chosen-
plaintexts, and adaptively-chosen plaintexts, respectively. †: This corresponds to the
Type-2 difference with a probability of 2^{-47} [15]. In [16], this analysis was deleted by
considering the difficulty of exploiting it through the mode. Because our interest is $P2$
as a standalone primitive without the mode, this analysis is of our interest.

Approach	Rounds	Key size	Setting	Data	Time	Memory	Reference
differential	512†		CP	2^{48}	-	-	[14,15]
differential	640	any	CP	2^{84}	-	-	[16]
linear	512		KP	2^{60}	-	-	[14,16]
			KP	2^{65}	2^{65}	2^{64}	Section 3.1
		128	KP	2^{64}	2^{65}	2^{64}	Section 3.2
slide	infinite		ACP	$2^{72.5}$	$2^{72.5}$	negl.	Section 3.2
		192	ACP	2^{65}	2^{66}	2^{65}	Section 4.4
			CP	2^{67}	2^{69}	2^{66}	Section A.1
		256	ACP	$2^{67.5}$	$2^{69.5}$	$2^{67.5}$	Section 5

Because of its minimalist design, the security of TinyJAMBU needs to be
carefully assessed. For instance, the security proof of TinyJAMBU assumes that
both $P1$ and $P2$ are ideal keyed-permutations, while deliberately making $P1$
weaker. As a matter of fact, the designers have already increased the number of
rounds of $P1$ from 384 to 640 following a forgery attack over a 338 rounds $P1$
by Saha et al. [14]. Unlike the old $P1$, $P2$ seems to resist those cryptanalyses
due to a larger number of rounds.

In this paper, we focus on slide attacks on TinyJAMBU keyed-permutation
which cannot be thwarted by increasing the number of rounds. As a matter
of fact, the designers do not make any claim on sliding property in the single-
key setting. Moreover, we are interested in sliding property that leads to actual
key-recovery attacks and their total complexity.

1.1   Our Contributions

In this paper, we study the security of the underlying keyed-permutation of
TinyJAMBU as a standalone primitive. Particularly, we investigate all the details
of the sliding property of the keyed-permutation to show that the sliding property

actually leads to efficient key-recovery attacks for all key sizes. Intuitively, by ignoring constant factors, the keyed-permutation can be attacked with about 2^{64} queries and computational cost. Most notably, the attack complexity is only marginally increased even when the key size becomes larger.

We begin with a slide attack on the keyed-permutation of TinyJAMBU-128 because of its simplicity. Slide attacks need to detect a slid pair by using the birthday paradox, which makes it inevitable to make 2^{64} queries. The simplest attack scenario requires almost no extra overhead from this minimum requirement, which results in the data, time, and memory complexities of 2^{65}, 2^{65}, and 2^{64}, respectively. We then discuss a small observation to halve the data complexity and apply the memoryless meet-in-the-middle attack to achieve the data and time complexities of $2^{72.5}$, while the required memory amount is negligible.

However, the simple attack on TinyJAMBU-128 cannot be trivially applied to a larger key size as the keyed-permutation for a k-bit key has a periodical structure in every k rounds weakening the key materials recovered by a slid pair. Nevertheless, the information loss for a large key can be compensated for by generating more slid pairs. Such a challenge has already been discussed in the pioneering work [4], and the technique of making a chain of queries was proposed. The same technique has been exploited by many following works [1,3,6]. In this paper, we present a new technique called "splitting longer chains" that generates more slid pairs than the previous method.

Then, we recover the key from multiple input and output pairs of P_k by applying linear algebra. In particular, we experimentally verified the correctness of our key-recovery algorithm by assuming an access to several slid pairs. As a result, we show that the keyed-permutation of TinyJAMBU-192 and TinyJAMBU-256 can be attacked with a marginally increased complexity than the case with TinyJAMBU-128. The complexities of our attacks are summarized in Table 1.

Lastly, we show several observations on the keyed-permutation: a combination of probability 1 differential characteristics and slide attacks to avoid adaptively-chosen-plaintext queries, a transformation of P_k to the iterative FX-construction [7], extension of our attacks so that the number of rounds that is not a multiple of the key-length can be attacked, and implication of our attacks to the authenticated-encryption with associated data (AEAD) schemes.

Note that results presented in this paper do not violate the security claim of TinyJAMBU, which is only for the entire scheme including the mode. Nevertheless, security of the keyed-permutation is of interest, because it is assumed to be ideal in the security proof. We believe that the security analysis in this paper will be valuable for the NIST to choose the winner(s) of NIST LWC.

2   Specifications

TinyJAMBU is a family of AEAD schemes that supports the key sizes of 128, 192, and 256 bits. Each version is called TinyJAMBU-128, TinyJAMBU-192, and TinyJAMBU-256, respectively. TinyJAMBU uses an n-round keyed-permutation P_n as a building block.

2.1 Keyed-Permutation P_n

The keyed-permutation P_n uses an internal state of 128 bits for all the key sizes, which is represented by $s_0, s_1, \ldots, s_{127}$. Let $k_0, k_1, \ldots, k_{klen-1}$ denote the $klen$-bit key. The internal state is updated by applying the following NLFSR n times by increasing i from 0 to $n-1$.

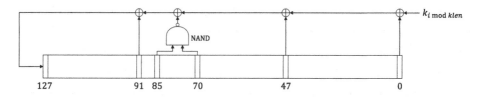

Fig. 1. Step-update function of TinyJAMBU for a $klen$-bit key.

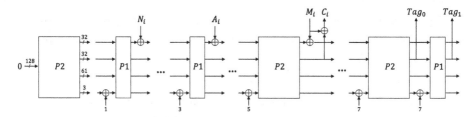

Fig. 2. The mode of TinyJAMBU. $P2$ is P_{1024}, P_{1152}, and P_{1280} for TinyJAMBU-128, TinyJAMBU-192, and TinyJAMBU-256. $P1$ is P_{640}, which was updated from previous P_{384} at the last-round design tweak in NIST LWC.

$$\text{feedback} \leftarrow s_0 \oplus s_{47} \oplus (\neg(s_{70} \wedge s_{85})) \oplus s_{91} \oplus k_{i \bmod klen}$$
$$\text{for } j \text{ from 0 to 126} : s_j \leftarrow s_{j+1}$$
$$s_{127} \leftarrow \text{feedback}$$

where '$\oplus$,' '$\wedge$,' and '$\neg$,' are XOR, AND, and NOT, respectively. The NLFSR is depicted in Fig. 1. Note that the tapping bit-positions were chosen so that 32 rounds of P_n can be computed in parallel on 32-bit CPUs.

2.2 AEAD Mode

The computation structure of TinyJAMBU is described in Fig. 2, which resembles the duplex mode with the keyed-permutation P_n. The details of the mode are omitted in this paper because our target is P_n. To process the nonce, the associated data, and the second half of the tag, the round number n is 640 for all key lengths, which is denoted by $P1$. During the initialization, the encryption, and the first half of the tag, the round number n is 1024, 1152, and 1280 for TinyJAMBU-128, TinyJAMBU-192, and TinyJAMBU-256, respectively, which is denoted by $P2$.

The main reason our attack strategy hardly applies to the AEAD mode is that an attacker can only observe 32 bits out of the 128-bit input and output of any permutation calls to $P1$ and $P2$.

2.3 Security Claim

64-bit security for authentication and 112-, 168-, and 224-bit security for encryption are claimed for TinyJAMBU-128, TinyJAMBU-192, and TinyJAMBU-256 respectively, against nonce-respecting adversaries who make at most 2^{50} bytes of queries.

Security of TinyJAMBU mode was proven assuming that $P1$ and $P2$ are ideal keyed-permutations. Nevertheless, the designers reported the existence of a differential characteristic with a probability of 2^{-471} and a linear characteristic with a bias of 2^{-30} for 512 rounds [15], which is sufficient to conclude that P_{384}, the original round number for $P1$, can be distinguished from an ideal object. Note that no analysis has been known for more than 512 rounds. In particular, it seems that differential and linear cryptanalysis cannot be applied to P_{1024}, P_{1152}, and P_{1280} used in $P2$.

2.4 Self-similarity of P_n

The keyed-permutation P_n does not use any round constant. Moreover, the bits from the key are computed by $k_{i \bmod klen}$. Hence, as mentioned by the designers [16], the state-update function of P_n has some sliding property, which is shown to be exploited with two related keys.[2]

Given that the internal state size is 128 bits, TinyJAMBU-128 shows the best fit because P_n is iterative in every 128 rounds and each state bit is updated exactly once with each key bit. In the following, we first describe the attack for TinyJAMBU-128 and later extend the attack to TinyJAMBU-192 and TinyJAMBU-256.

3   Slide Attacks on TinyJAMBU-128

This section presents a slide attack on TinyJAMBU-128. Because of its simplicity, it bears some similarity with other works, e.g. Bar-on et al. [1, Alg.1]. We first describe a key-recovery attack with 2^{65} known-plaintext queries, 2^{65} offline computations of P_{128}, and a memory to store 2^{64} queries. We then discuss an idea to halve the data complexity and further discuss a memoryless variant of

---

[1] This corresponds to the Type-2 difference [15]. In [16], the analysis about the Type-2 difference was deleted due to the difficultly of exploiting it through the mode. Our interest is $P2$ as a standalone primitive, so the Type-2 difference is of our interest.

[2] The designers did not give any details of this related-key attack, but when $K' = K \lll 1$, key bits for K' from round 1 to n equal the key bits for K from round 2 to $n+1$. Hence, a plaintext M processed by E_K and a plaintext $P_1^K(M)$ processed by $E_{K'}$ are actually the 1-round slid pair.

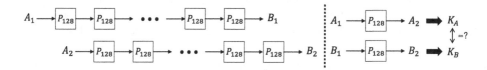

Fig. 3. Overview of slide attacks on the keyed-permutation of TinyJAMBU-128.

the attack. Note that the attack can work for 128t rounds for any positive integer $t > 1$ including $P1$ and $P2$ of TinyJAMBU-128, and the attack works in the single-key setting.

3.1   Overview of the Simple Slide Attack

The core of the slide attack (Fig. 3) is to find a slid pair; a pair of plaintext-ciphertext pairs (A_1, B_1) and (A_2, B_2), in which A_2 is the internal state after the first application of P_{128} for A_1, or $A_2 = P_{128}(A_1)$. This simultaneously ensures that $B_2 = P_{128}(B_1)$. A slid pair is generated by using the birthday paradox. The attacker makes 2^{64} queries of A_1 and of A_2 to obtain the corresponding B_1 and B_2. Then, among all the 2^{128} pairs, one pair will be a slid pair with good probability. The slid pair can be detected via a 113-bit filter and a collision-finding algorithm with a computational cost of 2^{64}.

Computing 113-Bit Filter. For a given pair of plaintext-ciphertext pairs (A_1, B_1) and (A_2, B_2), we want to know whether the induced key for $A_2 = P_{128}(A_1)$ and for $B_2 = P_{128}(B_1)$ collides. We do a collision-finding algorithm on values computed separately from (A_1, B_1) and (A_2, B_2), which is denoted by $G_1(A_1, B_1)$ and $G_2(A_2, B_2)$. We denote $G_x(A_x, B_x)$, $x \in \{1, 2\}$ with respect to the i-th bit by $G_x(A_x, B_x)[i]$.

Let $a_0, a_1, \ldots, a_{127}$ and $a_{128}, a_{129}, \ldots, a_{255}$ denote A_1 and A_2, respectively and $b_0, b_1, \ldots, b_{127}$ and $b_{128}, b_{129}, \ldots, b_{255}$ denote B_1 and B_2, respectively. If (A_1, A_2) is a slid pair then so is (B_1, B_2) and k_i is computed as follows:

$$k_i = a_{i+128} \oplus a_i \oplus a_{i+47} \oplus (\neg(a_{i+70} \wedge a_{i+85})) \oplus a_{i+91}$$
$$= b_{i+128} \oplus b_i \oplus b_{i+47} \oplus (\neg(b_{i+70} \wedge b_{i+85})) \oplus b_{i+91}.$$

Bit Positions 0 to 36. For $i = 0, 1, \ldots, 36$, we let $G_1(A_1, B_1)[i]$ and $G_2(A_2, B_2)[i]$ be the XOR sum of the terms belonging to (A_1, B_1) and (A_2, B_2) with respect to the i-th bit, respectively, i.e.,

$$G_1(A_1, B_1)[i] := a_i \oplus a_{i+47} \oplus (\neg(a_{i+70} \wedge a_{i+85})) \oplus a_{i+91} \oplus$$
$$b_i \oplus b_{i+47} \oplus (\neg(b_{i+70} \wedge b_{i+85})) \oplus b_{i+91},$$
$$G_2(A_2, B_2)[i] := a_{i+128} \oplus b_{i+128}.$$

$G_1(A_1, B_1)[i]$ and $G_2(A_2, B_2)[i]$ can be computed independently from the other pair, hence a collision on 37 bits of $k_0, k_1, \ldots, k_{36}$ can be observed.

Bit Positions 37 to 42. For $i = 37, 38, \ldots, 42$, notice that the term a_{i+91} belongs to A_2. The same applies to B_2. Hence, we have

$$G_1(A_1, B_1)[i] := a_i \oplus a_{i+47} \oplus (\neg(a_{i+70} \wedge a_{i+85})) \oplus b_i \oplus b_{i+47} \oplus (\neg(b_{i+70} \wedge b_{i+85})),$$
$$G_2(A_2, B_2)[i] := a_{i+91} \oplus a_{i+128} \oplus b_{i+91} \oplus b_{i+128}.$$

No Filter for Bit Positions 43 to 57. For $i = 43, 44, \ldots, 57$, one of the inputs to the AND operation, a_{i+85} (resp. b_{i+85}), belongs to A_2 (resp. B_2), while the other input bit, a_{i+70} (resp. b_{i+70}), belongs to A_1 (resp. B_1). Hence, the output of the AND operation cannot be computed independently.

Bit Positions 58 to 80 and 81 to 127. Following the same strategy, equations for $i = 58, 59, \ldots, 80$ are defined as

$$G_1(A_1, B_1)[i] := a_i \oplus a_{i+47} \oplus b_i \oplus b_{i+47},$$
$$G_2(A_2, B_2)[i] := (\neg(a_{i+70} \wedge a_{i+85})) \oplus a_{i+91} \oplus a_{i+128} \oplus (\neg(b_{i+70} \wedge b_{i+85})) \oplus b_{i+91} \oplus b_{i+128},$$

and equations for $i = 80, 81, \ldots, 127$ are defined as

$$G_1(A_1, B_1)[i] := a_i \oplus b_i,$$
$$G_2(A_2, B_2)[i] := a_{i+47} \oplus (\neg(a_{i+70} \wedge a_{i+85})) \oplus a_{i+91} \oplus a_{i+128} \oplus$$
$$b_{i+47} \oplus (\neg(b_{i+70} \wedge b_{i+85})) \oplus b_{i+91} \oplus b_{i+128}.$$

Summary. For each A_1 and its query-output B_1, the attacker can compute a 113-bit value to match with $G_1(A_1, B_1)[i]$ for $i = \in \{0, 1, \ldots, 127\} \backslash \{43, 44, \ldots, 57\}$. Similarly, for (A_2, B_2), the 113-bit value to match can be computed with $G_2(A_2, B_2)$.

Attack Procedure. The pseudo-algorithm to recover the key of TinyJAMBU-128 is described in Algorithm 1. For simplicity, here we assume that a table T of size 2^{64} is available.

Analysis. In the above attack procedure, the attacker makes 2^{64} queries of A_1 and A_2, thus the data complexity is 2^{65} known-plaintexts. The bottleneck of the time complexity is to compute $G_1(A_1, B_1)$ and $G_2(A_2, B_2)$, which is 2^{65} computations of P_{128}. The attack requires a memory of size 2^{64} for the table. (The table for Step 2 can be omitted by checking the collision in an online manner when a value of $G(A_2, B_2)$ is obtained.) In Step 3, 2^{128} pairs are examined and $2^{128-113} = 2^{15}$ pairs will pass this filter, and a valid pair will be detected by matching the remaining 15 bits.

Algorithm 1. A simple slide attack on TinyJAMBU-128 with 2^{64} memory.

1: Generate 2^{64} distinct values for A_1, obtain all the respective B_1 with 2^{64} queries, compute $G_1(A_1, B_1)$ for the 113 bits, and store $(A_1, B_1, G_1(A_1, B_1))$ in the table.
2: Generate 2^{64} distinct values for A_2, obtain all the respective B_2 with 2^{64} queries, compute $G_2(A_2, B_2)$ for the 113 bits, and store $(A_2, B_2, G_2(A_2, B_2))$ in the table.
3: Find collisions of $G_1(A_1, B_1)$ and $G_2(A_2, B_2)$ for all $2^{64} \times 2^{64} = 2^{128}$ pairs.
4: **for** all pairs with $G_1(A_1, B_1) = G_2(A_2, B_2)$ **do**
5:     Derive $k_{43}, \ldots, k_{57}$, with $A_2 = P_{128}(A_1)$ and also with $B_2 = P_{128}(B_1)$.
6:     **if** $k_{43}, \ldots, k_{57}$ from $A_2 = P_{128}(A_1)$ and from $B_2 = P_{128}(B_1)$ collide **then**
7:         **return** K.
8:     **end if**
9: **end for**

3.2 Reducing Data or Memory Complexity

Halving Data Complexity. Algorithm 1 assumes that queries in Step 1 correspond to the input to P_{128} and queries in Step 2 correspond to the output from P_{128}. However, we can reuse the data of Step 1 in Step 2 and look for a collision the same way. This would halve the data complexity from 2^{65} to 2^{64}.

A Memoryless Variant. As in [1], the 2^{64} memory requirement of Algorithm 1 can be removed with the standard memoryless collision-finding algorithm [13], which exploits a cycle-detection algorithm for the query chain. To do so, we start with a 113-bit value v_0, pads it to 128 bits to get A_0, and query to obtain B_0. Then, we compute either $G_1(A_0, B_0)$ or $G_2(A_0, B_0)$ depending on a bit of v_0 (LSB for instance). Set the result as v_1 and iterate this procedure to generate the chain of $v_0, v_1, v_2, \ldots$.

On the memory side, we only store some particular values for instance store the 100 values starting with the most 0 bits. When the chain length reaches about $2^{113/2}$, a newly computed v_i will eventually collide with one of the stored values. The exact colliding point can be found by starting from the stored points before the observed collision. If a collision is between $G_1(A_i, B_i)$ and $G_2(A_j, B_j)$, A_i and A_j is a slid pair candidate. If a collision is between $G_b(A_i, B_i)$ and $G_b(A_j, B_j)$ for the same $b \in \{1, 2\}$, the algorithm is repeated from scratch by changing v_0.

The procedure will be repeated twice on average to find a slid pair candidate which makes $2 \times 2^{113/2} = 2^{57.5}$ queries. And the candidate is a slid pair with probability 2^{-15}, thus we need 2^{15} candidates, which makes the total data complexity of $2^{15} \times 2^{57.5} = 2^{72.5}$ adaptively-chosen-plaintext queries. For each query, the attacker computes G_1 or G_2, thus the time complexity is $2^{72.5}$ computations of P_{128}. The memory amount is negligible when there are sufficiently few stored 113-bit values.

The memoryless meet-in-the-middle attack is an extreme case to optimize the memory complexity. A more general tradeoff for data, time, and memory complexities can be achieved by the parallel collision search [12].

4 Attacks Against a Larger Key

The same filter will not work for longer key versions TinyJAMBU-192 and TinyJAMBU-256 as the permutation repeats only after a number of rounds equal to the key length. However, we show that we can build a $113 - \kappa$-bit filter for $128 + \kappa$-bit key permutation and still do a key recovery from a slid pair.

4.1 Building a Filter

Concretely, for a given pair of plaintext-ciphertext pairs (A_1, B_1) and (A_2, B_2), we want to know whether the key for $A_2 = P_{128+\kappa}(A_1)$ and for $B_2 = P_{128+\kappa}(B_1)$ will collide. Hence, just like in Sect. 3.1, we want to compute colliding values separately from (A_1, B_1) and (A_2, B_2) to efficiently look for a collision.

Similarly, let us denote the bit states s_i for $i \in [0, 255 + \kappa]$ such that s_{127} to s_0 is the input, $s_{255+\kappa}$ to $s_{128+\kappa}$ is the output and $s_{127+\kappa}$ to s_{128} are κ bits of internal computations. By definition of the permutation we have:

$$k_i = s_{i+128} \oplus s_i \oplus s_{i+47} \oplus (\neg(s_{i+70} \wedge s_{i+85})) \oplus s_{i+91}.$$

We look for relations of key bits that only depend on input and output bits, that is on s_i for $i \in [0, 127] \cup [128 + \kappa, 255 + \kappa]$.

First, we ignore all key bits whose AND term $(\neg(s_{i+70} \wedge s_{i+85}))$ is not computable given either the input or output bits. There are 113 remaining key bits that are k_i for $i \in [0, 42] \cup [58 + \kappa, 127 + \kappa]$. Indeed, every AND term is unique, so there is no linear combination that can hope to cancel it.

	s_0	s_1	s_2	$\ldots$	s_{127}	s_{128}	$\ldots$	$s_{126+\kappa}$	$s_{127+\kappa}$	$s_{128+\kappa}$	$\ldots$	$s_{255+\kappa}$
k_0	1	0	0	$\ldots$	0	1	$\ldots$	0	0	0	$\ldots$	0
k_1	0	1	0	$\ldots$	0	0	$\ldots$	0	0	0	$\ldots$	0
k_2	0	0	1	$\ldots$	0	0	$\ldots$	0	0	0	$\ldots$	0
$\vdots$	$\vdots$	$\vdots$	$\vdots$	$\ddots$	$\vdots$	$\vdots$	$\ddots$	$\vdots$	$\vdots$	$\vdots$	$\ddots$	$\vdots$
$k_{126+\kappa}$	0	0	0	$\ldots$	0	0	$\ldots$	1	0	0	$\ldots$	0
$k_{127+\kappa}$	0	0	0	$\ldots$	0	0	$\ldots$	0	1	0	$\ldots$	1

Fig. 4. Construction of the $113 \times (256 + \kappa)$ binary matrix M.

Then, we build a binary matrix M with 113 rows, one row for each considered k_i, and $256 + \kappa$ columns, one column for each state bit s_i. Let $M(i, j) = 1$ if s_j linearly appears in the formula for the ith retained bit key and $M(i, j) = 0$ otherwise, as illustrated in Fig. 4. For instance, $M(0, j) = 1$ for $j \in \{128, 91, 47, 0\}$ and $M(0, j) = 0$ otherwise.

Then, we use row-wise Gaussian elimination on M to put zeroes on the columns 128 to $127 + \kappa$ that correspond to internal computation state bits.

s_0 s_1 s_2 $\cdots$ s_{127}	s_{128} $\cdots$ $s_{126+\kappa}$ $s_{127+\kappa}$	$s_{128+\kappa}$ $\cdots$ $s_{255+\kappa}$
$E^1_{\kappa \times 128}$	$I_{\kappa \times \kappa}$	$S^1_{\kappa \times 128}$
$E^2_{(113-\kappa) \times 128}$	$0_{(113-\kappa) \times (113-\kappa)}$	$S^2_{(113-\kappa) \times 128}$

Fig. 5. The $113 \times (256+\kappa)$ binary matrix M after Gaussian elimination. I is the identity matrix, 0 is the zero matrix and E^1, E^2, S^1, and S^2 are binary matrices resulting from the Gaussian elimination.

Assuming the 128 to $127 + \kappa$-column submatrix is a full rank $113 \times \kappa$ matrix, we will at least recover $113 - \kappa$ rows with only zeroes on those columns that naturally correspond to $113 - \kappa$ relevant relationships as illustrated in Fig. 5.

The linear part of each relationship is recovered by looking at the other columns of M and the non-linear part must be also added by looking at the corresponding key bits involved. By construction, those $113 - \kappa$ relationships are linearly independent and will involve both input and output state bits and only those state bits. Each such row thus implies a relation between key bits, input bits and output bits that can be summarized as $\mathcal{R}(k) = \mathcal{R}_i(A_1) \oplus \mathcal{R}_o(A_2) = \mathcal{R}_i(B_1) \oplus \mathcal{R}_o(B_2)$; implying $\mathcal{R}_i(A_1) \oplus \mathcal{R}_i(B_1) = \mathcal{R}_o(A_2) \oplus \mathcal{R}_o(B_2)$ that can be used to efficiently filter a slid pair among many plaintext-ciphertext.

4.2   Enhancing a Filter with Chains of Queries

With the previous method, to attack P_{240} ($\kappa = 112$), we only have a 1-bit filter which is insufficient. Hence we need a way to leverage on the filter.

Basic Method. We use a technique by Biryukov and Wagner [5] to increase the number of filtering bits by generating more slid pairs. To multiply the number of filtering bits, the attacker can generate a chain of queries. That is, after querying A_1 and receiving B_1, the attacker queries B_1 to obtain C_1, then queries C_1 to obtain D_1, and so on. A similar chain is generated from each A_2. If (A_1, A_2) is a slid pair, then so are (B_1, B_2), (C_1, C_2) and (D_1, D_2). Thus, we have the relationship $\mathcal{R}(k) = \mathcal{R}_i(A_1) \oplus \mathcal{R}_o(A_2) = \mathcal{R}_i(B_1) \oplus \mathcal{R}_o(B_2) = \mathcal{R}_i(C_1) \oplus \mathcal{R}_o(C_2) = \mathcal{R}_i(D_1) \oplus \mathcal{R}_o(D_2) = \cdots$. When the length of the chains is ℓ, the $113 - \kappa$-bit filter is applied to ℓ pairs, which achieves a $\ell \cdot (113 - \kappa)$-bit filter. For P_{240} ($\kappa = 112$), we set $\ell = 128$ and gets a $128 \cdot (113 - 112) = 128$-bit filter to identify the right slid pair.

Advanced Method: Splitting Longer Chains. We can further chain the queries to efficiently create multiple chains of the required length. Concretely, chains of length $\ell + \beta$ values can be cut into $\beta + 1$ chains of length ℓ (Fig. 6).

However, comparing those $\beta + 1$ chains for any reasonable β won't yield any slid pairs since an n-bit permutation won't loop until about $\mathcal{O}(2^n)$ iterations. Nevertheless, comparing two independent chains of length $\ell + \beta$, we can expect to find a solution among the implied $2\beta + 2$ chains with probability $2(2\beta + 1)/2^{128}$ (fixing the first set of chains, there are $2\beta + 1$ starting points for the next set of chains that will provide a slid output and the same amount for a slid input solution). Hence a solution is expected to be found after collecting about $2^{64}/\sqrt{4\beta + 2}$ sets of $\beta + 1$ chains, which makes for a $2^{64}(\ell + \beta)/\sqrt{4\beta + 2}$ data complexity optimized for $\beta = \ell - 1$. For $\ell = 128$, the data complexity becomes $\sqrt{255/2} \cdot 2^{64} \simeq 2^{67.5}$.

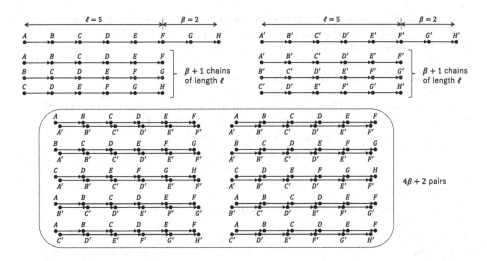

Fig. 6. Schematic representation of splitting longer chains for $\ell = 5$ and $\beta = 2$.

4.3   Key-Recovery from Input/Output Pairs

In this section, we explain how to efficiently extract the $128 + \kappa$-bit key from multiple input/output pairs of $P_{128+\kappa}$ in only about $\kappa \log(\kappa)$ operations where $0 \leq \kappa \leq 113$.

The key-recovery is described in Algorithm 2 which basically guesses the κ unseen bit states one by one. Let us explain the first iteration of the algorithm. We start by taking the matrix M after Gaussian elimination (Fig. 5) that was allegedly used to filter the pairs (A_1, A_2) and (B_1, B_2) both belonging to the set $\mathcal{P}$. We first guess k_0, the first key bit, which corresponds to the first row of our matrix M as it linearly depends on a_{128} and not on the rest of the unseen part. Hence, from k_0 we can deduce a_{128}, b_{128}, etc. for all known slid pairs. With the knowledge of the 128th state bit, a new AND term can be computed that is $a_{113} \wedge a_{128}$ corresponding to k_{43}. Thus, we add the linear term for k_{43} to the matrix M, which now contains 114 rows. Row-wise Gaussian elimination will restore the form of Fig. 5 but with 114 rows and, hence, a $(114 - \kappa)$-bit filter.

This additional bit of filter enables us to check whether the key guess was wrong. If the additional filter pass for all pairs, we proceed. Otherwise, we change our guess. Note that in the last 15 iterations, we can further deduce an additional AND term using a known output bit.

Algorithm 2. Efficient key-recovery after filtering on TinyJAMBU-$(128 + \kappa)$.

1: Let $\mathcal{P}$ be a list of multiple input/output pairs (S_1, S_2) whose internal (visible and invisible) bit states are denoted as s_i for i from 0 to $255 + \kappa$.
2: Let M be the filter producing matrix as in Fig. 5.
3: **for** i from 0 to $\kappa - 1$ **do**
4:     $g \leftarrow 0$
5:     Guess that the relation induced by the $(i + 1)$th row of M sums to g.
6:     $\forall (S_1, S_2) \in \mathcal{P}$: Deduce s_{128+i} from the guess.
7:     Add the relation of k_{43+i} in the matrix M.
8:     **if** $i \geq \kappa - 15$ **then**
9:         Add the relation of k_{58+i} in the matrix M.
10:     **end if**
11:     Perform row-wise Gaussian elimination with respect to column $128+i$ to $127+\kappa$.
12:     Consider the new computable relation (two relations if $i \geq \kappa - 15$).
13:     **if** $\forall (S_1, S_2) \in \mathcal{P}$: the relations are not equal **then**
14:         **if** $g = 0$ **then**
15:             $g \leftarrow 1$
16:             Go back to Step 5
17:         **else**
18:             No consistent key can be fond. **return** $\emptyset$.
19:         **end if**
20:     **end if**
21: **end for**
22: For some $(S_1, S_2) \in \mathcal{P}$ compute k such that :
23: $k_i = s_{i+128} \oplus s_i \oplus s_{i+47} \oplus (\neg(s_{i+70} \wedge s_{i+85})) \oplus s_{i+91}$
24: **return** k

The probability of success of this algorithm mainly depends on the probability of a wrong guess passing through the additional filter created which depends on the number of input/output pairs we have at hand. Notice that we can further compute additional input/output pairs by chaining the queries as in Sect. 4.2. Gathering around $\log(\kappa)$ input/output pairs will detect a wrong guess with about $1 - 1/\kappa$ probability. Hence, it will fully recover κ bits of key with good probability $((1 - 1/\kappa)^\kappa$ tends to $e^{-1} \simeq 36.8\%$ as κ grows) and deduce the full $128 + \kappa$ bits of key. Allowing back-tracking is probably efficient but hard to analyze. Notice that it is possible to know whether the additional filter passed because the guess is true or because it is independent of the guess. Indeed, the AND term we add depend both on a newly guessed key (computed state bit) and on a known state.

Table 2. Experimental reports about Algorithm 2. Success probability with different size of $\mathcal{P}$ on 1000 trials against a theoretical estimate.

$\|\mathcal{P}\|$	5	6	7	8	9	10	11	12	13	14
success prob. ($\kappa = 64$)	3.6	19.3	46.1	69.7	82.2	90.5	95.0	97.6	98.5	99.5
theoretical prob. ($\kappa = 64$)	4.0	20.8	46.1	68.0	82.5	90.9	95.3	97.6	98.8	99.4
success prob. ($\kappa = 112$)	0.4	4.1	19.9	44.7	69.6	83.8	90.5	95.1	97.7	99.1
theoretical prob. ($\kappa = 112$)	0.2	4.5	21.6	46.7	68.4	82.7	91.0	95.4	97.7	98.8

If the known state was 0, then the AND term does not depend on the guess but if the known state is 1 then the AND term depends linearly on the guess. Comparing both cases together will give us the correct guess; otherwise the filter always verifies independently of the guess.

Experimental Reports. We implemented Algorithm 2 and verified the required number of input/output pairs. We say Algorithm 2 succeeded when it returned the unique secret key. Table 2 summarizes the attack success probability with different sizes of $\mathcal{P}$ and $\kappa \in \{64, 112\}$. The theoretical estimation of the success probability is computed by $(1 - 2^{-(|\mathcal{P}|-1)})^{(\kappa-15)} \times (1 - 2^{-2 \times (|\mathcal{P}|-1)})^{15}$. It assumes there is a $1/2$ chance to detect a bad guess per filter per additional input/output pairs; we have one filter per step up to $\kappa - 15$ key bits, and two filters for the last 15 key bits. The theoretical estimation of $\log(\kappa)$ pairs required amounts to 6 and 7 for $\kappa = 64$ and $\kappa = 112$, respectively, and has indeed a good probability of success. The theoretical estimations well fit the success probability of our experiments.

4.4 Application on TinyJAMBU-192

The internal permutation of TinyJAMBU-192 is the case with $\kappa = 64$. With the technique in Sect. 4.1, we build a $113 - 64 = 49$-bit basic filter further enhanced by the technique of Sect. 4.2 with chain length $\ell = 2$. This builds a $2 \times 49 = 98$-bit filter and reduces 2^{128} candidate pairs to a sufficiently small size.

The pseudo-algorithm to recover the key of TinyJAMBU-192 is described in Algorithm 3. For simplicity, here we assume that a table T of size 2^{65} is available. In Step 1, we make 2^{65} queries, in which the first 2^{64} queries can be known-plaintexts queries, while the last 2^{64} queries must be adaptively-chosen-plaintext queries. In Step 2, we compute $\mathcal{R}_i$ for two pairs and $\mathcal{R}_o$ for two pairs, which is faster than $4 \times 2^{64} = 2^{66}$ computations of P_{192}. In Step 3, the match of 98 bits will be examined for 2^{128} pairs, hence 2^{30} pairs will remain after the filter. In Step 5, we further make $2 \times 2^{30} = 2^{31}$ adaptively-chosen-plaintext queries. Thanks to the additional 49-bit filter, only the right slid pair will remain after this step. In Step 7, we make additional queries to collect $\log \kappa = 6$ slid pairs, which is required by the key-recovery algorithm. The complexity of the key-recovery algorithm is $64 \times \log 64$, which is negligible. In summary, the bottleneck

Algorithm 3. An adaptively chosen-plaintext slide attack on TinyJAMBU-192.

1: Generate 2^{64} distinct values for A. Make 2^{64} queries of A to obtain B, and make 2^{64} queries of B to obtain C.
2: Compute $\mathcal{R}_i(A,B)$ and $\mathcal{R}_i(B,C)$ for the 98 bits, and compute $\mathcal{R}_o(A,B)$ and $\mathcal{R}_o(B,C)$ for the 98 bits. Store $(A,B,C,\mathcal{R}_i(A,B)\|\mathcal{R}_i(B,C),\mathcal{R}_o(A,B)\|\mathcal{R}_o(B,C))$ in the table.
3: Find collisions of $\mathcal{R}_i(A,B)\|\mathcal{R}_i(B,C)$ and $\mathcal{R}_o(A',B')\|\mathcal{R}_o(B',C')$ for all 2^{128} pairs.

4: **for** all pairs with $\mathcal{R}_i(A,B)\|\mathcal{R}_i(B,C) = \mathcal{R}_o(A',B')\|\mathcal{R}_o(B',C')$ **do**
5:     Make 2 queries of C and C' to obtain D and D'.
6:     **if** $\mathcal{R}_i(C,D) = \mathcal{R}_o(C',D')$ **then**
7:         Make additional queries to extend the chain length to be $\log \kappa = 6$.
8:         Run the key-recovery procedure in Sect 4.3.
9:         Return K.
10:     **end if**
11: **end for**

of the attack is Steps 1 and 2, which requires 2^{65} adaptively-chosen-plaintext queries, about 2^{66} computational cost, and a memory to store 2^{65} values.

5 Optimization for Attack on TinyJAMBU-256

When $\kappa = 128$, which is the parameter for TinyJAMBU-256, the technique of Sect. 4.1 can no longer construct a filter. Thus, we need additional tricks to attack TinyJAMBU-256. In this section, we optimize the attack on TinyJAMBU-256 by exploiting the structure of TinyJAMBU. First, we show a method to construct a 1-bit filter with only a 2-bit guess. In other words, the complexity is only increased by a factor 2^2. Next, we show an efficient method to recover the secret key given several plaintext-ciphertext pairs on P_{256}. The 15-bit key, i.e., $k_0, \ldots, k_{14}$, is recovered by exploiting the algebraic structure, and then, the other key bits are recovered by using Algorithm 2.

5.1 1-Bit Filter with a 2-Bit Guess

The trivial extension requires an additional 16-bit guess. However, we do not need to guess the whole 16-bit key, and only an additional 2-bit guess is enough to obtain a 1-bit filter. Concretely, guessing the 2 bits of key k_0 and k_{15} is enough. We derive the following equations from the step-update function.

$$s_{128} = s_0 \oplus s_{47} \oplus (\neg(s_{70} \wedge s_{85})) \oplus s_{91} \oplus k_0$$
$$s_{143} = s_{15} \oplus s_{62} \oplus (\neg(s_{85} \wedge s_{100})) \oplus s_{106} \oplus k_{15}$$

By guessing k_0 and k_{15}, we can compute s_{128} and s_{143}. Then, we obtain $k_{21} \oplus k_{58} \oplus k_{186} \oplus k_{233}$ from only known bits. These four key bits are computed as

$$k_{21} = s_{21} \oplus s_{68} \oplus (\neg(s_{91} \wedge s_{106})) \oplus s_{112} \oplus s_{149},$$
$$k_{58} = s_{58} \oplus s_{105} \oplus (\neg(s_{128} \wedge s_{143})) \oplus s_{149} \oplus s_{186},$$
$$k_{186} = s_{186} \oplus s_{233} \oplus (\neg(s_{256} \wedge s_{271})) \oplus s_{277} \oplus s_{314},$$
$$k_{233} = s_{233} \oplus s_{280} \oplus (\neg(s_{303} \wedge s_{318})) \oplus s_{324} \oplus s_{361},$$

and the sum is

$$k_{21} \oplus k_{58} \oplus k_{186} \oplus k_{233} = s_{21} \oplus s_{68} \oplus (\neg(s_{91} \wedge s_{106})) \oplus s_{112} \oplus s_{58} \oplus s_{105} \oplus (\neg(s_{128} \wedge s_{143})) \oplus$$
$$s_{314} \oplus (\neg(s_{256} \wedge s_{271})) \oplus s_{277} \oplus s_{361} \oplus s_{280} \oplus (\neg(s_{303} \wedge s_{318})) \oplus s_{324}.$$

Since s_{128} and s_{143} are known by guessing k_0 and k_{15}, we can get this 1-bit filter.

We want to use this 1-bit filter to detect slid pairs. Given a pair of plaintext-ciphertext pairs (A_1, B_1) and (A_2, B_2), we need to define the corresponding functions $G_1(A_1, B_1)$ and $G_2(A_2, B_2)$. Let $(a_0, a_1, \ldots, a_{127})$ and $(a_{256}, a_{257}, \ldots, a_{383})$ denote A_1 and A_2, respectively. Moreover, $(b_0, b_1, \ldots, b_{127})$ and $(b_{256}, b_{257}, \ldots, b_{383})$ denote B_1 and B_2, respectively. Then, two functions are defined as

$$G_1(A_1, B_1) := a_{21} \oplus a_{68} \oplus (\neg(a_{91} \wedge a_{106})) \oplus a_{112} \oplus a_{58} \oplus a_{105} \oplus (\neg(a_{128} \wedge a_{143})) \oplus$$
$$b_{21} \oplus b_{68} \oplus (\neg(b_{91} \wedge b_{106})) \oplus b_{112} \oplus b_{58} \oplus b_{105} \oplus (\neg(b_{128} \wedge b_{143}))$$
$$G_2(A_2, B_2) := a_{314} \oplus (\neg(a_{256} \wedge a_{271})) \oplus a_{277} \oplus a_{361} \oplus a_{280} \oplus (\neg(a_{303} \wedge a_{318})) \oplus a_{324} \oplus$$
$$b_{314} \oplus (\neg(b_{256} \wedge b_{271})) \oplus b_{277} \oplus b_{361} \oplus b_{280} \oplus (\neg(b_{303} \wedge b_{318})) \oplus b_{324}.$$

Note that $G_1(A_1, B_1)$ depends on the guess of k_0 and k_{15}, but $G_2(A_2, B_2)$ is independent of them.

5.2   Key-Recovery from Input/Output Pairs for P_{256}

Algorithm 2 accepts κ until 113. Therefore, Algorithm 2 cannot be applied to P_{256} directly. On the other hand, trivial extension is possible by guessing $15(= 128 - 113)$-bit key. Recall that Algorithm 2 is very efficient and the time complexity is $O(\kappa)$. Even if we additionally guess the 15-bit key, the impact on the time complexity is negligible compared with previous steps. Although the trivial extension is already efficient, we present a more efficient algorithm whose time complexity is still $O(\kappa)$.

In Algorithm 2, the corresponding row vector is not involved in the matrix if either of the NAND inputs is unknown. However, in practice, only one side of NAND inputs is known, so we can obtain an additional relationship. Considering the following NAND $\neg(s_t \wedge s_{t+15})$, the output of the NAND is always 1 independently of s_{t+15} when $s_t = 0$. On the other hand, when $s_t = 1$, the output of the NAND is $s_{t+15} \oplus 1$, i.e., the nonlinear output is linearized. By exploiting this property, we can recover the first 15-bit key efficiently.

The following is a concrete case to recover k_0. When $(s_{113}, s_{256}) = (0, 0)$, we can compute $k_6 \oplus k_{43} \oplus k_{171} \oplus k_{218}$ as

$$k_6 \oplus k_{43} \oplus k_{171} \oplus k_{218} = s_6 \oplus s_{53} \oplus (\neg(s_{76} \wedge s_{91})) \oplus s_{97} \oplus s_{43} \oplus s_{90} \oplus s_{262}$$
$$\oplus s_{299} \oplus s_{265} \oplus (\neg(s_{288} \wedge s_{303})) \oplus s_{309} \oplus s_{346}.$$

As the sum removes 3 uncomputable bits, i.e., s_{134}, s_{171}, and s_{218}. Moreover, when $(s_{113}, s_{256}) = (1, 0)$, we can compute $k_0 \oplus k_6 \oplus k_{43} \oplus k_{171} \oplus k_{218}$ as

$$k_0 \oplus k_6 \oplus k_{43} \oplus k_{171} \oplus k_{218} = s_0 \oplus s_{47} \oplus (\neg(s_{70} \wedge s_{85})) \oplus s_{91} \oplus s_6 \oplus s_{53}$$
$$\oplus (\neg(s_{76} \wedge s_{91})) \oplus s_{97} \oplus s_{43} \oplus s_{90} \oplus 1 \oplus (\neg(s_{241} \wedge s_{256}))$$
$$\oplus s_{262} \oplus s_{299} \oplus s_{265} \oplus (\neg(s_{288} \wedge s_{303})) \oplus s_{309} \oplus s_{346}.$$

As the sum removes 4 uncomputable bits, i.e., s_{128}, s_{134}, s_{171}, and s_{218}. Finally, the key bit k_0 is derived by summing these two equations. This procedure requires one input-output pairs satisfying each conditions, but the number of restricted bits is only 2. Therefore, we can recover k_0 by observing about 4 input-output pairs. This procedure can be used to recover k_x for $0 \leq x \leq 14$. Then, the restricted bits move to (s_{113+x}, s_{256+x}).

5.3   Complexity of TinyJAMBU-256

The attacker guesses 2-bit key k_0 and k_{15} and generates a 1-bit filter. Since a 1-bit filter is insufficient to detect a unique slid pair, the filter is enhanced with chains of queries. Thus, the attacker enhances the 1-bit filter to a 128-bit filter and detects only a right slid pair for each 2-bit guess. Deriving the key from a slid pair is very efficient by using Algorithm 2 with the technique shown in Sect. 5.2. Thus, the data complexity is $2^{67.5}$. The time complexity is $2^{69.5}$.

6   Conclusions

We have thoroughly analyzed the slide property of the keyed-permutation used as TinyJAMBU's underlying primitive. Our analysis shows that the slide property can be exploited to mount actual slide attacks with near-birthday-bound complexities for all proposed key sizes (128, 192, and 256 bits). The attacks exploit multiple (undesirable) properties of the primitive and work independently from the number of rounds repeated in the permutation.

The attacks do not directly contradict with the security goals to be achieved by TinyJAMBU [16] but invalidate the rationale that the underlying primitive is close to ideal. In particular, the attacks bring into question the (relatively high) 112/168/224-bit encryption/secret-key security goal for TinyJAMBU.

We emphasize that one should not treat TinyJAMBU's primitive as a standard block cipher like Advanced Encryption Standard (AES), as TinyJAMBU's keyed-permutation fails to provide the expected security level (the functionality of a keyed-permutation is the same as that of a block cipher.) The keyed-permutation is a dedicated primitive that should be used exclusively in Tiny-JAMBU's AEAD mode of operation.

A   Discussions and More Observations

A.1   Slide Attack with Deterministic Differential Characteristics

Overall Idea. The chain of queries in Sect. 4.2 efficiently increases the number of filtering bits, but requires adaptively chosen-plaintext. Here, we discuss another approach that was also discussed in [5] which avoids adaptively chosen-plaintext queries and show that it can be applied to recover a 192-bit key. The idea here is to combine differential characteristics with probability 1 with the slide attack. Suppose that there is an input and output difference of P_{192} denoted by α and β, which is satisfied with probability 1. For a slid pair (A_0, B_0) and (A_0', B_0') such that $A_0' = P_{192}(A_0)$ and $B_0' = P_{192}(B_0)$, we define that $A_1 = A_0 \oplus \alpha$ and $A_1' = A_0' \oplus \beta$. Then the pair (A_1, B_1) and (A_1', B_1') also satisfies $A_1' = P_{192}(A_1)$ and $B_1' = P_{192}(B_1)$ thanks to the probability 1 differential characteristic. Specifically, we obtain 2 slid pairs without using adaptively-chosen-plaintext queries. Moreover, the number of slid pairs can further increase to 2^n if n-many probability 1 differential characteristics are available, by assuming that it is possible to satisfy such n-many probability 1 characteristics simultaneously. This idea for the case with $n = 2$ is illustrated in Fig. 7.

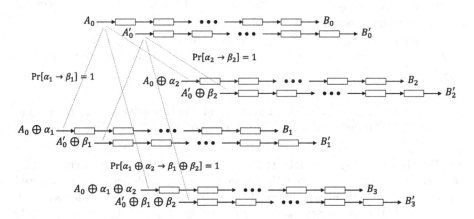

Fig. 7. Attacks on TinyJAMBU-192 with two deterministic differential characteristics.

Note that the previous attack on TinyJAMBU-192 in Sect. 4.4 required adaptively chosen-plaintext queries for not only query chains but also the bit-by-bit key-recovery explained in Sect. 4.3. Currently, we have not found an efficient key-recovery procedure that works in the chosen-plaintext setting. Hence, our approach to recover a 192-bit key is to first identify the valid slid pair and then guess the last 64 key bits. For this reason, we need to filter out all the wrong slid-pair candidates, and it is essential to have $n = 2$ distinct probability 1 characteristics to have a $49 \times 2^2 = 196$-bit filter.

Deterministic Differential Characteristic for P_{192}. In the keyed-permutation of TinyJAMBU, the only non-linear operation is the AND operation between s_{70} and s_{85}. Recall that in each step, the key bit only impacts s_{127}, thus during the first 43 rounds, the input to the AND operation is only dependent on the plaintext. Specifically, given the plaintext value, differential propagation for the first 43 rounds is deterministic. The same can be applied in the backward direction, i.e. given the ciphertext value, differential propagation for the last 70 rounds is deterministic. Moreover, we can set some plaintext and ciphertext bits to 0 to prevent the input difference to AND gates from propagating.

With these observations, we searched for such characteristics for P_{192} by using a refined MILP-based evaluation [14] by adding new constraints to ignore the active AND gates for the first 43 and last 70 rounds from the objective function. As a result, we found many probability 1 differential characteristics.[3] An example is explained in Table 3.

Table 3. An example of probability 1 differential characteristic for TinyJAMBU-192. Differential masks α, β are represented by hexadecimal numbers.

$\alpha : s_{127}, \ldots, s_1, s_0$	0000 0000 0004 0000 0000 0008 0000 0000
$\beta : s_{319}, \ldots, s_{193}, s_{192}$	0000 0008 1000 0000 0080 0000 0004 0000
conditions on plaintext (A_0)	$s_{97} = 0$
conditions on ciphertext (A'_0)	$s_{195} = 0, s_{225} = 0, s_{232} = 0, s_{262} = 0$

AND is active in rounds 12, 125, 140, 160, 177, and these output differences are 0.

We confirmed that the rotated variants of the characteristic in Table 3 are also satisfied with probability 1 for a left rotation by 1, 2, 3, 6, and 7 bits.

Application to TinyJAMBU-192. As mentioned above, using 2 characteristics is sufficient for a 192-bit key. Hence, we use one in Table 3 and its left-rotated version by 1 bit. When we choose 2^{64} distinct values of A_0, we fix $s_{97} = 0$ and $s_{98} = 0$. We also query $A_0 \oplus \alpha$, $A_0 \oplus (\alpha \lll 1)$, and $A_0 \oplus \alpha \oplus (\alpha \lll 1)$ along with A_0. Similarly, when we choose 2^{64} distinct values of A'_0, we fix 8 bits of $s_{195}, s_{225}, s_{232}, s_{262}, s_{196}, s_{226}, s_{233}, s_{263}$ to 0 to satisfy the conditions on the ciphertext, and we also query $A'_0 \oplus \beta$, $A'_0 \oplus (\beta \lll 1)$, and $A'_0 \oplus \beta \oplus (\beta \lll 1)$ along with A'_0. Those would derive a 196-bit filter. Hence, we only have a right slid pair after examining 2^{128} matching candidates. After detecting the slid pair, we exhaustively guess the last 64 key bits.

The complexity is $4 \times 2 \times 2^{64} = 2^{67}$ chosen-plaintext queries. The computational cost is less than $4 \times 2 \times 4 \times 2^{64} = 2^{69}$ computations of P_{192}, which is for computing 4 $\mathcal{R}_i$ or $\mathcal{R}_o$ functions for each query. The memory complexity is to store the queries for A_0 and associated quartets, which is 2^{66}. The memoryless attack is made possible by incurring slightly more computational cost.

---

[3] Run time was very short. It finished in a few seconds.

A.2   Attacks on Non-multiple Number of Rounds

In our attacks, we assumed that the total number of rounds was a multiple of the key-length, which is the case with $P2$ in all the members of TinyJAMBU. One may wonder that the attack can be prevented by setting the number of rounds to be a non-multiple the key-length. Here, we show that the restriction of the number of rounds to be a multiple of the key-length can easily be lifted for the attacks on P_{128} and P_{192} using the deterministic differential characteristics of Sect. A.1.

Let k be the key of length $klen$ and consider $klen \times m + s$ rounds of encryption for some strictly positive integers m and s. Then, a slid pair (A_0, B_0), (A'_0, B'_0) is such that $A'_0 = P^k_{klen}(A_0)$ and $B'_0 = P^{k \lll s}_{klen}(B_0)$. That is, B'_0 is the encryption of B_0 with $klen$ rounds but with a circular-shifted key. In that setting, one clearly cannot chain queries to enhance a filter because the key schedule does not cycle back to its initial state.

Attacking $klen = 128$ is mostly unchanged from Sect. 3. We simply derive equations on key bits independently for the unshifted and shifted cases that will give us a filter. The only difference is that the 15 unexploitable key bits (bit positions 43 to 57) are shifted in the second case, which can result in at most 30 unexploitable relationships. Nevertheless, we can always build a 98-bit filter and perform a key-recovery with the same complexity as before.

For $klen = 192$, the attack is very similar to Sect. A.1. Indeed, taking the notation of Fig. 7, we can still apply the same filter but only on the outputs $F(B_0, B_1) = F(B'_0, B'_1)$, $F(B_0, B_2) = F(B'_0, B'_2)$, $F(B_0, B_3) = F(B'_0, B'_3)$ and ignoring the relation induced by A_0 and A'_0. The actual shift s has no effect when only comparing relationship on outputs. More generally, in the shifted case, having n independent differential characteristics increase the filter $2^n - 1$ fold (instead of 2^n previously). For the 192-bit key case, a $49 \times 3 = 147$-bit filter is still more than enough to filter all the wrong pairs especially as A_0 and A'_0 can further help us in the guess stage for the remaining key bits.

A.3   Implication on the Security of the AEAD Schemes

Our results do not easily extend to attacks on TinyJAMBU AEAD schemes but bring their security into question. That is, they weaken the rationale to believe 112-bit (resp., 168-bit, or 224-bit) encryption/secret-key security goal being achieved by TinyJAMBU-128 (resp., TinyJAMBU-192, or TinyJAMBU-256); to believe so is essentially equivalent to regarding the security goal itself as an assumption. Neither the security of the primitive nor that of the mode implies security of the scheme; one is assuming that the combination of the two should achieve the security goal even though one is aware of the fact that the primitive is far from being ideal.

In other words, one is assuming that some features of the mode should "enhance" encryption/secret-key security to 112/168/224 bits even though the underlying primitive is vulnerable to birthday-bound (i.e., about 64 bits in any case) key-recovery attacks. The features may include, for example, the fact that "frame bits" [16][4] are inserted into states and that at most 32 bits of each state value are controllable by adversaries.

In fact, the underlying permutations are already known to be non-ideal. For instance, the designers show in the specifications that $P1$ in the AEAD mode (see Fig. 2) has a differential property of probability 2^{-83}. Nevertheless, we want to state that our attacks are the first to reveal that $P2$ of all the versions of TinyJAMBU is broken by a birthday-bound key-recovery attack, which make us less confident that the security proof of the mode by the designers can be regarded as a convincing reason for the security claim holding.

To be fair, we remark that our results do not significantly affect the privacy security (indistinguishability) shown by the designers or the authentication security goal stated by the designers [16]. This is due to the fact that both of these notions are up to the birthday bound of 64 bits and that our attacks require birthday-bound complexities.

References

1. Bar-On, A., Biham, E., Dunkelman, O., Keller, N.: Efficient slide attacks. J. Cryptol. **31**(3), 641–670 (2018)
2. Bertoni, G., Daemen, J., Peeters, M., Van Assche, G.: Duplexing the sponge: single-pass authenticated encryption and other applications. In: Miri, A., Vaudenay, S. (eds.) SAC 2011. LNCS, vol. 7118, pp. 320–337. Springer, Heidelberg (2012). https://doi.org/10.1007/978-3-642-28496-0_19
3. Biham, E., Dunkelman, O., Keller, N.: Improved slide attacks. In: Biryukov, A. (ed.) FSE 2007. LNCS, vol. 4593, pp. 153–166. Springer, Heidelberg (2007). https://doi.org/10.1007/978-3-540-74619-5_10
4. Biryukov, A., Wagner, D.: Slide attacks. In: Knudsen, L. (ed.) FSE 1999. LNCS, vol. 1636, pp. 245–259. Springer, Heidelberg (1999). https://doi.org/10.1007/3-540-48519-8_18
5. Biryukov, A., Wagner, D.: Advanced slide attacks. In: Preneel, B. (ed.) EUROCRYPT 2000. LNCS, vol. 1807, pp. 589–606. Springer, Heidelberg (2000). https://doi.org/10.1007/3-540-45539-6_41
6. Furuya, S.: Slide attacks with a known-plaintext cryptanalysis. In: Kim, K. (ed.) ICISC 2001. LNCS, vol. 2288, pp. 214–225. Springer, Heidelberg (2002). https://doi.org/10.1007/3-540-45861-1_17
7. Kilian, J., Rogaway, P.: How to protect DES against exhaustive key search (an analysis of DESX). J. Cryptol. **14**(1), 17–35 (2000). https://doi.org/10.1007/s001450010015
8. Naito, Y., Matsui, M., Sugawara, T., Suzuki, D.: SAEB: a lightweight blockcipher-based AEAD mode of operation. IACR Trans. Cryptogr. Hardw. Embed. Syst. **2018**(2), 192–217 (2018)
9. NIST: Submission Requirements and Evaluation Criteria for the Lightweight Cryptography Standardization Process (2018). https://csrc.nist.gov/Projects/lightweight-cryptography

---

[4] Indeed, the designers argue that the constants in the mode inserted between permutation calls should prevent slide attacks (refer to Fig. 2); it seems that the existence of constants should make it hard to extend our slide attacks to AEAD modes.

10. NIST: Lightweight Cryptography Standardization: Finalists Announced (2021). https://csrc.nist.gov/News/2021/lightweight-crypto-finalists-announced
11. NIST: Status Report on the Second Round of the NIST Lightweight Cryptography Standardization Process (2021). https://csrc.nist.gov/publications/detail/nistir/8369/final
12. van Oorschot, P.C., Wiener, M.J.: Parallel collision search with cryptanalytic applications. J. Cryptol. **12**(1), 1–28 (1999). https://doi.org/10.1007/PL00003816
13. Quisquater, J.-J., Delescaille, J.-P.: How easy is collision search. New results and applications to DES. In: Brassard, G. (ed.) CRYPTO 1989. LNCS, vol. 435, pp. 408–413. Springer, New York (1990). https://doi.org/10.1007/0-387-34805-0_38
14. Saha, D., Sasaki, Y., Shi, D., Sibleyras, F., Sun, S., Zhang, Y.: On the security margin of TinyJAMBU with refined differential and linear cryptanalysis. IACR Trans. Symmetric Cryptol. **2020**(3), 152–174 (2020)
15. Wu, H., Huang, T.: TinyJAMBU: A Family of Lightweight Authenticated Encryption Algorithms. Submitted to NIST, September 2019
16. Wu, H., Huang, T.: TinyJAMBU: A Family of Lightweight Authenticated Encryption Algorithms (Version 2). Submitted to NIST, May 2021

Quantum Key Recovery Attacks on 3-Round Feistel-2 Structure Without Quantum Encryption Oracles

Takanori Daiza and Kazuki Yoneyama$^{(\boxtimes)}$

Ibaraki University, Hitachi, Japan
`kazuki.yoneyama.sec@vc.ibaraki.ac.jp`

Abstract. The Feistel-2 (a.k.a, Feistel-KF) structure is a variant of the Feistel structure such that the i-th round function is given by $\mathsf{F}_i(k_i \oplus x)$, where F_i is a public random function and its input/output length is $n/2$ bits. Isobe and Shibutani showed a meet-in-the-middle attack in the classical setting with $(D, T) = (O(1), O(2^{n/2}))$ on the 3-round Feistel-2 structure where D and T are the numbers of online/offline queries, respectively. In their attack, since two round keys are recovered simultaneously, a naive application of Grover's algorithm for two keys needs $T = O(2^{n/2})$ in the quantum setting. In this paper, we introduce a new known plaintext attack and chosen plaintext attack on the 3-round Feistel-2 structure in the quantum setting using Grover's algorithm by recovering the round key one by one in $(D, T) = (O(1), O(2^{n/4}))$. Our attack does not need any quantum query to the encryption oracle (i.e., working in the Q1 model).

Keywords: Feistel-2 structure · Grover's algorithm · Q1 model

1 Introduction

1.1 Feistel Structure

Feistel structure is a popular design framework of block ciphers, and it is important both in theory and practice. The original r-round Feistel structure was introduced by Luby and Rackoff [1]. It takes a plaintext $P = (a_0, b_0)$ as an input, where $a_0, b_0 \in \{0,1\}^{n/2}$. Then, it computes $(a_{i+1}, b_{i+1}) = (b_i \oplus \mathsf{R}_i(a_i), a_i)$ (the left half of Fig. 1) for $i = 0, 1, \ldots, r-1$, where $\mathsf{R}_i : \{0,1\}^{n/2} \to \{0,1\}^{n/2}$ is a keyed round function. Finally it outputs a ciphertext $C = (a_r, b_r)$.

Luby and Rackoff [1] supposed that each round function R_i is an independent random function. Then, they showed that the 3-round construction is pseudo-random up to $2^{n/4}$ queries against chosen plaintext attacks (CPA) (i.e., a distinguisher can access to the permutation oracle), and the 4-round construction is pseudo-random up to $2^{n/4}$ queries against chosen ciphertext attacks (CCA) (i.e., a distinguisher can access to both the permutation oracle and the inverse permutation oracle).

T. Daiza—Presently, he is with Toppan Inc.

C.-M. Cheng and M. Akiyama (Eds.): IWSEC 2022, LNCS 13504, pp. 128–144, 2022.
https://doi.org/10.1007/978-3-031-15255-9_7

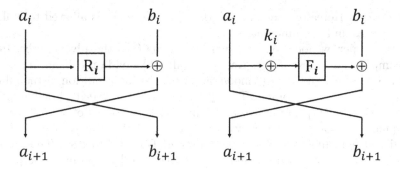

Fig. 1. Feistel/Feistel-2 structure

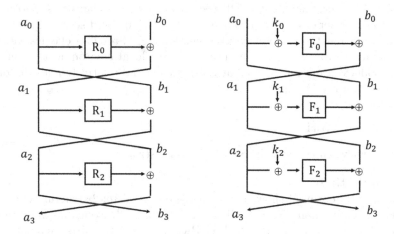

Fig. 2. 3-round Feistel/Feitel-2 structure

On the other hand, the Luby-Rackoff construction has a difficulty in implementations because it needs to design a key embedded random function R_i for each round key k_i. Feistel-2 (Feistel-KF) structure is an easy-to-implement variant of Feistel structure such that each round function $R_i(x)$ is replaced by $F_i(k_i \oplus x)$ (the right half of Fig. 1), where $F_i : \{0,1\}^{n/2} \to \{0,1\}^{n/2}$ is a public independent random function, and $k_i \in \{0,1\}^{n/2}$ is a round key. (Feistel-2 is also known as key-alternating Feistel cipher.)

1.2 Attack Scenarios for Quantum Setting

To compare attack performances, we consider oracle queries by separating into online and offline. An adversary needs online queries to obtain the result of processes using secret information such as the encryption/decryption process with the secret key. On the other hand, since public functions can be computed by anyone, the adversary can obtain results of processes of public functions by offline queries. Hereafter, we suppose that the adversary is allowed to make D online queries and T offline queries.

In this paper, we focus on the quantum setting (i.e., the adversary has quantum computational resources). Kaplan et al. [18] divide the quantum setting into the Q1 model and the Q2 model according to the condition of the allowed access to the encryption oracle. The Q2 model allows adversary's online queries to the (keyed) encryption oracle and offline queries to the other oracles both with quantum superposition. Kuwakado and Morii [17] and Kaplan et al. [18] showed distinguishing attacks on the 3-round Feistel structure. These distinguishing attacks are based on Simon's algorithm [16] by posing superposition states online queries to the encryption oracle. On the other hand, in the Q1 model, the adversary can only pose online queries to the encryption oracle in a classical manner whereas it is allowed to pose offline quantum superposition queries to the other oracles which have no information about secret keys. The Q1 model means that the adversary only make queries through a classical network but have access to quantum computers in their local environment. Therefore, the Q1 model is a more restricted attack scenario and relatively realistic for the adversary than the Q2 model.

1.3   Related Work

Here, we review known attacks on the Feistel-2 structure.

Classical Setting:

Lampe and Seurin [3] showed that the 3-round Feistel-2 structure is pseudorandom against non-adaptive CPA if $D + T \ll 2^{n/4}$. Isobe and Shibutani [4] showed a known plaintext attack (KPA) (i.e., a distinguisher cannot access to the permutation oracle nor the inverse permutation oracle) on the 3-round Feistel-2 structure along with the meet-in-the-middle approach. It works on $(D,T) = (O(1), O(2^{n/2}))$ and needs $M = O(2^{n/2})$ classical memory. Then, they extended their attack to 4 or more rounds [5]. Guo et al. [7] showed a Demirci-Selçuk meet-in-the-middle attack [6] on the 6-round Feistel-2 structure. Dinur et al., against more than 5 rounds, showed a dissection attack [8] and a more memory efficient attack [9]. Daiza and Kurosawa [10] showed KPA and CPA on the 3-round Feistel-2 structure working in $DT = O(2^{n/2})$ and $M = O(1)$.

Q1 Model:

Hosoyamada and Sasaki [13] showed a variant of the claw-finding algorithm and a CPA on the 6-round Feistel-2 structure by applying Grover's algorithm [11] to Guo et al.'s classical attack. Their attack works in $(D,T) = (O(2^{n/2}), O(2^{n/2}))$ and needs $Q = O(2^{n/2})$ qubits and $M = O(2^{n/2})$ memory.

Q2 Model:

Kuwakado and Morii [17] showed that the 3-round Feistel structure is not pseudo-random even if each R_i is a random permutation. Then, Kaplan et al.[18] showed that the 3-round Feistel structure is not pseudo-random even if each R_i is also a random function. Hosoyamada and Sasaki [13] showed quantum CPA (qCPA) on the r-round Feistel-2 structure ($r \geq 4$) in time $O(n^3 2^{(r-3)n/4})$, based on Leander and May's method [19] (which combines Grover's algorithm and Simon's algorithm). Cid et al. [20] showed qCPA in a polynomial time on the d-branch $(2d-1)$ round contracting Feistel-2 structure by solving $n/2 + 1$-bit Simon's problem.

1.4   Our Motivation

As in known quantum attacks, though an exponential speed up is achieved in the Q2 model, it is difficult in the Q1 model because the technique using Simon's algorithm by online queries cannot be used.

The classical key recovery attack on 3-round by Isobe and Shibutani [4] obtains two round keys simultaneously by the exhaustive search. Therefore, if we naively adapt their attack to the Q1 model using Grover's algorithm, it corresponds to the Grover search of the $n/2 \times 2 = n$-bit value in $T = O(2^{n/2})$. Since the twice encryption of the 3-round Feistel-2 structure can be regarded as 6 rounds, the Q1 key recovery attack by Hosoyamada and Sasaki [13] can be applied to the attack to the 3-round Feistel-2 structure. However, it needs $T = O(2^{n/2})$.

As far as we know, even against the 3-round, no Q1 key recovery attack on the Feistel-2 structure which is (approximately) more efficient than the classical one has been known. Therefore, as a milestone to explore the quantum security of the Feistel-2 structure, it is important to clarify if there is an more efficient attack on the (minimal) 3-round in the Q1 model than the classical model.

1.5   Our Contribution

In this paper, we introduce the first key recovery attacks on the 3-round Feistel-2 structure in the Q1 model, which are more efficient than the classical ones. Based on the classical attack by Daiza and Kurosawa [10], our attacks use Grover's algorithm and obtain the round key one by one. We first show a KPA in $(D, T) = (O(1), O(2^{n/4}))$. Next, we show a CPA (although it works in the same complexities approximately) which can decrease gates than the KPA. (see Table 1 for the comparison with previous works.)

Paper Organization. Section 2 shows some basics of the quantum computation, Grover's algorithm, and known related attacks. Section 3 shows our key recovery KPA and CPA on the 3-round Feistel-2 structure in the Q1 model. Section 4 shows the discussion on the non-triviality to improve our attacks using another quantum algorithms. Section 5 shows a conclusion and future works.

2   Preliminaries

For x, y such that $|x| = |y|$, we denote $x \oplus y$ bit-parallel XOR.

Table 1. Comparison among ours and known key recovery attacks on Feistel-2

	round	setting	type	D	T	Q	M
[4]	3	classical	KPA	$O(1)$	$O(2^{n/2})$	-	$O(2^{n/2})$
[10]	3	classical	KPA	$O(1)$	$O(2^{n/2})$	-	$O(1)$
[10]	3	classical	CPA	$O(2^{n/4})$	$O(2^{n/4})$	-	$O(1)$
[5]	4	classical	CPA	$O(1)$	$O(2^{n/2})$	-	$O(2^{n/2})$
[7]	6	classical	CPA	$O(2^{3n/4})$	$O(2^{3n/4})$	-	$O(2^{n/2})$
[13]	$r \geq 4$	Q2	qCPA	$O(2^{(r-3)n/4})$	$O(n^3 2^{(r-3)n/4})$	$O(n^2)$	$O(n)$
[20]	$2d-1$	Q2	qCPA	$O(Poly(n))$	$O(Poly(n))$	$O(Poly(n))$	$O(Poly(n))$
[13]	6	Q1	CPA	$O(2^{n/2})$	$O(2^{n/2})$	$O(2^{n/2})$	$O(2^{n/2})$
Ours (§3.1)	3	Q1	KPA	$O(1)$	$O(2^{n/4})$	$O(n)$	$O(1)$
Ours (§3.2)	3	Q1	CPA	$O(1)$	$O(2^{n/4})$	$O(n)$	$O(1)$

D is the number of plaintext/ciphertext pairs. T is the time complexity. Q is the qubit size. M is the classical memory size.

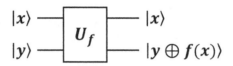

Fig. 3. Quantum circuit for oracle f

2.1 Quantum Gates

In this paper, we mainly use X, H and $CNOT$ gates. X gate is the bit-flip operator (i.e. the quantum version of the not-element) such that $X|b\rangle = |b \oplus 1\rangle$, where $b \in \{0,1\}$. H gate (the Hadamard transform) creates a superposition such that $H|b\rangle = \frac{1}{\sqrt{2}}(|0\rangle + (-1)^b|1\rangle)$, and n-bit parallel $H|0\rangle$ is also usually denoted as

$$H|0\rangle \otimes \cdots \otimes H|0\rangle = H^{\otimes n}|0^n\rangle = \frac{1}{\sqrt{2^n}} \sum_{x \in \{0,1\}^n} |x\rangle.$$

$CNOT$ gate leads to an entangled state such that $CNOT|x\rangle|y\rangle = |x\rangle|y \oplus x\rangle$, where $x, y \in \{0,1\}$.

2.2 Quantum Oracle

For a quantum oracle O_f computing the function $f : \{0,1\}^{l_1} \to \{0,1\}^{l_2}$, O_f is given as an unitary operator U_f below (see Fig. 3).

$$U_f|x\rangle|y\rangle = |x\rangle|y \oplus f(x)\rangle,$$

where $x \in \{0,1\}^{l_1}$ and $y \in \{0,1\}^{l_2}$.

2.3   Grover's Algorithm

Grover's algorithm [11], one of the most famous quantum algorithms, is used to search a target from a database containing N elements in time $O(N^{1/2})$.

The definition of the problem to be solved by Grover's algorithm for $N = 2^n$ is as follows.

Definition 1 (Grover's problem).   *Given function $g : \{0,1\}^n \rightarrow \{0,1\}$ such that $g(x_0) = 1$ for the particular input $x = x_0$ and $g(x) = 0$ for other $x \neq x_0$, find x_0.*

Grover's algorithm runs with an unitary operator U_g which represents the given g-oracle (like Sect. 2.2). The U_g operation is widely denoted as

$$U_g|x\rangle = (-1)^{g(x)}|x\rangle,$$

and this compact shape can be obtained by the following procedure:

1. Initialize a state $|0^n\rangle|1\rangle$.
2. Apply H gate and obtain

$$\left(\frac{1}{\sqrt{2^n}} \sum_{x\in\{0,1\}^n} |x\rangle \right) \otimes \frac{1}{\sqrt{2}}(|0\rangle - |1\rangle).$$

3. Apply U_g and obtain the following state. (Note that the last 1-bit is still the superposition between $|0\rangle$ and $|1\rangle$.)

$$\left(\frac{1}{\sqrt{2^n}} \sum_{x\in\{0,1\}^n} |x\rangle \right) \otimes \left(\frac{1}{\sqrt{2}}(|0 \oplus g(x)\rangle - |1 \oplus g(x)\rangle) \right).$$

Now, if $g(x) = 0$, the last 1-bit state is $\frac{1}{\sqrt{2}}(|0\rangle - |1\rangle) = \frac{(-1)^0}{\sqrt{2}}(|0\rangle - |1\rangle)$. Otherwise, $\frac{1}{\sqrt{2}}(|1\rangle - |0\rangle) = \frac{(-1)^1}{\sqrt{2}}(|0\rangle - |1\rangle)$. Thus, the total states can be denoted as

$$\frac{1}{\sqrt{2^n}} \sum_{x\in\{0,1\}^n} |x\rangle \otimes \frac{(-1)^{g(x)}}{\sqrt{2}}(|0\rangle - |1\rangle)$$

$$= \frac{1}{\sqrt{2^n}} \sum_{x\in\{0,1\}^n} (-1)^{g(x)}|x\rangle \otimes \frac{1}{\sqrt{2}}(|0\rangle - |1\rangle)$$

$$= \frac{1}{\sqrt{2^n}} \left(-|x_0\rangle + \sum_{x\neq x_0} |x\rangle \right) \otimes \frac{1}{\sqrt{2}}(|0\rangle - |1\rangle).$$

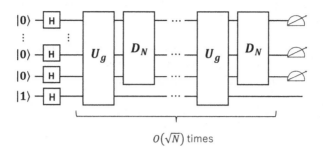

$O(\sqrt{N})$ times

Fig. 4. Grover search on a circuit

4. Then, increase the coefficient of the marked $|x_0\rangle$ state by applying the diffuser to the first n-bit. It is represented as the $N \times N$ matrix D_N such that

$$
D_N = \begin{bmatrix} \frac{2}{N} - 1 & \frac{2}{N} & \cdots & \frac{2}{N} \\ \frac{2}{N} & \frac{2}{N} - 1 & \cdots & \frac{2}{N} \\ \vdots & \vdots & \ddots & \vdots \\ \frac{2}{N} & \frac{2}{N} & \cdots & \frac{2}{N} - 1 \end{bmatrix}.
$$

5. Repeat Step 3 and 4 (Grover iterations).
6. Finally, measure the first n-bit.

It is known that the probability of measuring $x = x_0$ increases to nearly 1 when the number of repeating Grover iterations approaches $\left\lfloor \frac{\pi}{4}\sqrt{N} + \frac{1}{2} \right\rfloor$. In this case, the quantum complexity is $O(2^{n/2})$.

2.4 Hosoyamada and Sasaki's Claw-Finding Algorithm

Brassard et al. [12] showed a quantum algorithm finding the collision of a hash function (claw). Then, Hosoyamada and Sasaki [13] considered the following variant of the claw-finding problem.

Definition 2 (Hosoyamada and Sasaki's claw-finding problem). *Suppose that function $f : \{0,1\}^u \times \{0,1\}^v \to \{0,1\}^l$ and function $g : \{0,1\}^v \to \{0,1\}^l$ are given as black box, and there is the certain pair $(x, y) \in \{0,1\}^u \times \{0,1\}^v$ such that $f(x, y) = g(y)$. The g-oracle allows only classical queries. The f-oracle allows quantum queries. (i.e. the unitary operator of f is given on the quantum circuit). Then, find (x, y).*

They proposed an algorithm [13] solving the above problem with $Q = O((u + v)2^p)$ qubits for $p \leq v$ and $M = O(2^v)$ classical memory in time

$$
O(T^c_{g,all} + 2^{\frac{u}{2}+v-p} \cdot T^q_f),
$$

where $T^c_{g,all}$ is the time calculating $(y, g(y))$ with classical queries for each y and T^q_f is time to run the unitary operator of f once.

2.5   3-Round Feistel-2 Structure

Let $P = (a_0, b_0)$ ($\in \{0,1\}^{n/2} \times \{0,1\}^{n/2}$) be a plaintext. The 3-round Feistel-2 structure computes the ciphertext $C = (a_3, b_3)$ as follows.

$$(a_1, b_1) \leftarrow (b_0 \oplus \mathsf{F}_0(k_0 \oplus a_0), a_0)$$
$$(a_2, b_2) \leftarrow (b_1 \oplus \mathsf{F}_1(k_1 \oplus a_1), a_1)$$
$$(a_3, b_3) \leftarrow (b_2 \oplus \mathsf{F}_2(k_2 \oplus a_2), a_2)$$

Therefore, it holds that

$$
\begin{aligned}
b_3 &= a_2 \\
&= b_1 \oplus \mathsf{F}_1(k_1 \oplus a_1) \\
&= a_0 \oplus \mathsf{F}_1(k_1 \oplus \mathsf{F}_0(k_0 \oplus a_0) \oplus b_0)
\end{aligned}
\tag{1}
$$

$$
\begin{aligned}
a_3 &= b_2 \oplus \mathsf{F}_2(k_2 \oplus a_2) \\
&= a_1 \oplus \mathsf{F}_2(k_2 \oplus b_1 \oplus \mathsf{F}_1(k_1 \oplus a_1)) \\
&= b_0 \oplus \mathsf{F}_0(k_0 \oplus a_0) \oplus \\
&\quad \mathsf{F}_2(k_2 \oplus \mathsf{F}_1(k_1 \oplus \mathsf{F}_0(k_0 \oplus a_0) \oplus b_0) \oplus a_0).
\end{aligned}
\tag{2}
$$

Let the function $\mathsf{F}_0, \mathsf{F}_1$ and F_2 be public random functions. Since these functions contain no information for the secret key, the adversary can access $\mathsf{F}_0, \mathsf{F}_1$ and F_2-oracles in the offline classical or quantum computation.

2.6   Isobe and Shibutani's Classical MITM Attack on 3-Round Feistel-2 Structure

Isobe and Shibutani [4] showed a key recovery KPA by the meet-in-the-middle approach. Given two plaintext/ciphertext pairs (P_1, C_1) and (P_2, C_2), let $P_1 = (a_0, b_0)$ and $C_1 = (a_3, b_3)$. Their attack works as follows.

1. For each $j \in \{0,1\}^{n/2}$, query $j \oplus a_0$ to F_0-oracle and compute

$$a_{1,j} = \mathsf{F}_0(j \oplus a_0) \oplus b_0.$$

   Then, store $(j, a_{1,j})$ in table A_1.
2. For each $l \in \{0,1\}^{n/2}$, query $l \oplus b_3$ to F_2-oracle and compute

$$b_{2,l} = \mathsf{F}_2(l \oplus b_3) \oplus a_3.$$

   Then, store $(l, b_{2,l})$ in table A_2.
3. From A_1 and A_2, find (j, l) such that $a_{1,j} = b_{2,l}$. (see Fig. 5.)
4. From the candidates (j, l), select one of them as (k_0, k_2) by using (P_2, C_2).
5. For each $\kappa \in \{0,1\}^{n/2}$, query $\kappa \oplus a_{1,j}$ to F_1-oracle and verify if it holds that

$$\mathsf{F}_1(\kappa \oplus a_{1,j}) \oplus a_0 = b_3.$$

   Set κ satisfying the above equation as k_1 and output (k_0, k_1, k_2).

In this attack, $D = O(1)$ and the adversary makes $T = O(2^{n/2})$ offline queries to each F_i-oracle. Thus, the time complexity is $O(D + T) = O(2^{n/2})$ and the memory size is also $M = O(2^{n/2})$.

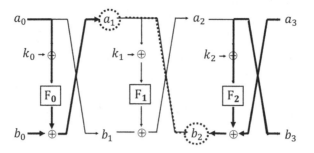

Fig. 5. MITM Attack on 3-round by Isobe and Shibutani [4]

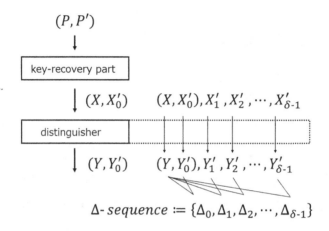

Fig. 6. Key-recovery part and distinguisher

2.7 Quantum DS-MITM Attack on 6-Round Feistel Constructions

Demirci-Selçuk MITM Attack. Demirci and Selçuk showed a meet-in-the-middle attack [6]. Given the encryption/decryption oracle, the adversary executes the distinguish part and the key-recovery part (see Fig. 6). The procedure is as follows.

1. Choose one-round for the key-recovery part and guess the subkey there.
2. Operate the Step from 3 to 5 in the classical setting.
3. Compute the input pair and output pair of the distinguisher $\Delta X = (X, X_0')$, $\Delta Y = (Y, Y_0')$.
4. Prepare $\delta - 1$ values by $X_i' := X_0' \oplus i$ for $i = 1, 2, \cdots, \delta - 1$. Then, obtain the output of the distinguisher Y_i' for the input X_i'.
5. For Y_i' ($i = 0, 1, \cdots, \delta - 1$), let Δ_i be the difference between Y and Y_i'. Then, store

$$\Delta\text{-}sequence := (\Delta_0, \Delta_1, \cdots, \Delta_{\delta-1})$$

in a list L.

6. In the other way, for various plaintext pairs (P, P'), make queries to prepare $(\Delta P, \Delta C)$ values where ΔP is the plaintext difference and ΔC is the ciphertext difference. If some of these are matched with Δ-sequence at the list L, the guessed subkey will be correct. Then, find a match at the list L.

Guo et al. [7] showed a key-recovery CPA with the DS-MITM approach on the 6-round Feistel-2 structure. Their attack works in $D = O(2^{3n/4}), T = O(2^{3n/4})$ and needs $M = O(2^{n/2})$ classical memory.

Quantum DS-MITM Attack on 6 Rounds in Q1 Model. Hosoyamada and Sasaki [13] showed a key-recovery CPA on the 6-round Feistel-2 structure in the Q1 model by applying Grover's algorithm to Guo et al.'s attack with the variant of the claw-finding algorithm in Sect. 2.4. Their attack works in $D = O(2^{n/2}), T = O(2^{n/2})$ and needs $Q = O(2^{n/2})$ qubits and $M = O(2^{n/2})$ classical memory.

3   Proposed Attacks

Isobe and Shibutani's key-recovery attack [4] on the 3-round Feistel-2 structure in Sect. 2.6 obtains two $n/4$-bit subkeys simultaneously by the exhaustive search. Therefore, if we extend their classical attack to the Q1 model using the Grover's algorithm directly, it needs a search for $2 * (n/2) = n$-bit in time $T = O(2^{n/2})$.

Hosoyamada and Sasaki's quantum key-recovery attack [13] in Sect. 2.7 works in $(D, T, Q, M) = (O(n2^{n/2}), O(n2^{n/2}), O(n2^{n/2}), O(n2^{n/2}))$. Since the two iterated 3-round encryption is regarded as 6 rounds, their attack can also be adapted on the 3-round Feistel-2 structure in the same complexities.

Though these known attacks need more than time $T = O(2^{n/2})$, we propose first quantum key-recovery attacks in time $T = O(2^{n/4})$ in the Q1 model. Our idea is simple but effective. We separate the Eq. (1) that

$$b_3 = F_1(k_1 \oplus F_0(k_0 \oplus a_0) \oplus b_0) \oplus a_0$$

into k_1 and $F_0(k_0 \oplus a_0)$. Then, we extract the input of F_0 by Grover's search to obtain the 1st-round key k_0. Our attack is a KPA and it is easily adapted to be a CPA. These attacks work in the Q1 model because no quantum query to the encryption oracle is necessary.

3.1   Our KPA

Let F_0, F_1, F_2 be public random functions. The adversary can query the F_i-oracle with a superposition in offline computations, and these are implemented as the unitary operator on a quantum circuit.

In the attack, the adversary is given plaintext/ciphertext pairs (P_1, C_1), (P_2, C_2) and (P_3, C_3). The outline is that the adversary obtains two values of

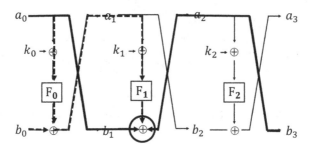

Fig. 7. Step 1 of our KPA

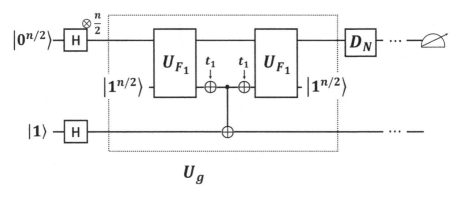

Fig. 8. Step 2 of our KPA

$k_1 \oplus F_0(k_0 \oplus a_0) \oplus b_0$ corresponding to the input of F_1 in Eq. (1), and removes k_1 by computing XOR of them. Let $P_i = (a_{i,0}, b_{i,0})$ and $C_i = (a_{i,3}, b_{i,3})$ $(i = 1, 2, 3)$. The procedure is as follows.

1. For (P_1, C_1) and (P_2, C_2), compute

$$a_{1,0} \oplus b_{1,3} = F_1(k_1 \oplus F_0(k_0 \oplus a_{1,0}) \oplus b_{1,0}),$$

$$a_{2,0} \oplus b_{2,3} = F_1(k_1 \oplus F_0(k_0 \oplus a_{2,0}) \oplus b_{2,0}).$$

(See Fig. 7). Let β_1, β_2 be

$$\beta_1 = k_1 \oplus F_0(k_0 \oplus a_{1,0}),$$

$$\beta_2 = k_1 \oplus F_0(k_0 \oplus a_{2,0}).$$

2. Let $t_1 := a_{1,0} \oplus b_{1,3}$. Obtain $\beta_1 \oplus b_{1,0}$ such that

$$F_1(\beta_1 \oplus b_{1,0}) = t_1$$

as follows: On the quantum circuit, we regard the following process as the function g in Definition 1. g takes $|x\rangle|b\rangle$ as the input, where $x \in \{0,1\}^{n/2}$ and $b \in \{0,1\}$. Pose offline query $|x\rangle|0^{n/2}\rangle$ to the F_1-oracle and obtain $|x\rangle|F_1(x)\rangle$. g outputs $|x\rangle|b\oplus1\rangle$ if $F_1(x) = t_1$, and outputs $|x\rangle|b\rangle$ if $F_1(x) \neq t_1$ such as Fig. 8. Hereafter, we call such a search process Grover's search. Then, calculate β_1.

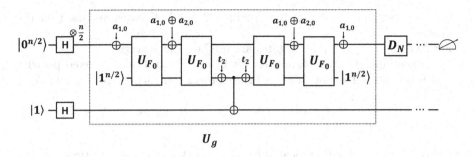

Fig. 9. Step 4 of our KPA

3. In the same way, obtain β_2 such that

$$F_1(\beta_2 \oplus b_{2,0}) = a_{2,0} \oplus b_{2,3}.$$

4. Computes $t_2 := \beta_1 \oplus \beta_2$. By Grover's search, obtain $k'_0 \in \{0,1\}^{n/2}$ such that

$$F_0(k'_0 \oplus a_{1,0}) \oplus F_0(k'_0 \oplus a_{2,0}) = t_2$$

such as Fig. 9.

5. Let $k'_1 := \beta_1 \oplus F_0(k'_0 \oplus a_{1,0})$. Then, for (P_1, C_1), let t_3, t_4 be

$$t_3 = F_1(k'_1 \oplus F_0(k'_0 \oplus a_{1,0}) \oplus b_{1,0}) \oplus a_{1,0},$$
$$t_4 = F_0(k'_0 \oplus a_{1,0}) \oplus b_{1,0}.$$

6. Obtain $k'_2 \in \{0,1\}^{n/2}$ such that

$$F_2(k'_2 \oplus t_3) \oplus t_4 = a_{1,3}$$

by Grover's search.

7. For the candidate (k'_0, k'_1, k'_2), check their validity whether Eqs. (1) and (2) hold with (P_3, C_3).

Analysis. In the attack, since three plaintext/ciphertext pairs are given, $D = O(1)$. The adversary operates Grover's search for a $n/2$-bit value in Step 2,3,4 and 6, i.e., each of them works in $O(2^{n/4})$. The adversary also make $O(1)$ classical queries to F_i-oracle in the offline computation. Therefore, the time complexity is $T = O(2^{n/4})$. Furthermore, the attack needs $Q = O(n)$ qubits for Grover's search. The required classical memory size is $M = O(1)$ because a few values are stored.

Because Step 4 (Fig. 9) is the dominant part for the circuit size (i.e., the number of quantum gates) of our KPA, we estimate the number of gates of Step 4 as follows.

1. For superposition state $H^{\otimes n/2}|0^{n/2}\rangle$ and state of auxiliary bits $|1^{n/2}\rangle$, $(n/2 + 1)$ H gates and $(n/2 + 1)$ X gates are used.

2. For XORing $a_{1,0}$ (and $a_{1,0} \oplus a_{2,0}$), $(2(n/2+1))$ X gates are used on the average.
3. For XORing t_2, $(n/2+1)$ X gates are used on the average.
4. For controlling the least significant bit by $n/2$ control bits, a mixed polarity multiple-control Toffoli (MPMCT) gate for $n/2$ control bits ($MPMCT(n/2+1)$) is used.[1]
5. For matrix D_N of Grover's algorithm, n H gates, n X gates and a $MPMCT(n/2)$ gate are used.

The above 2, 3, 4 and 5 are repeated by $\left\lfloor \frac{\pi}{4}\sqrt{2^{n/2}} + \frac{1}{2} \right\rfloor$ Grover iterations. Therefore, the total number of gates in Step 4 is

$$n + 2 + \{MPMCT(\frac{n}{2}+1) + MPMCT(\frac{n}{2}) + \frac{7n}{2} + 3\} \cdot \left\lfloor \frac{\pi}{4}\sqrt{2^{n/2}} + \frac{1}{2} \right\rfloor.$$

The attack is failed if a Grover's search in Step 2, 3, 4 or 6 is failed. Other steps work in probability 1. As explained in Sect. 2.3, the probability of the success of a Grover's search for a $n/2$-bit value is nearly 1 by $O(2^{n/4})$ time complexity. Therefore, our KPA succeeds with overwhelming probability.

3.2 Our CPA

Our KPA in Sect. 3.1 is easily extended to CPA, by replacing the given plaintext/ciphertext pairs to the process that the adversary chooses P_i and receives C_i from the encryption oracle. Besides, the adversary obtains $k_1 \oplus \mathsf{F}_0(k_0)$ from the first online query and let it be the next input of the encryption oracle to remove k_1. Thus, our attack is adaptive CPA. The procedure is as follows.

1. Query $(a_0, b_0) = (0^{n/2}, 0^{n/2})$ to the encryption oracle to receive (a_3, b_3), where $b_3 = \mathsf{F}_1(k_1 \oplus \mathsf{F}_0(k_0))$.
2. Obtain $\beta_1 \in \{0,1\}^{n/2}$ such that
$$\mathsf{F}_1(\beta_1) = b_3$$
   by Grover's search.
3. Query $(a_0, b_0) = (0\cdots01, \beta_1)$ to the encryption oracle to receive (a_3, b_3), where
$$b_3 \oplus a_0 = \mathsf{F}_1(k_1 \oplus \mathsf{F}_0(k_0 \oplus 0\cdots01) \oplus \beta_1).$$
   If it holds $\beta_1 = k_1 \oplus \mathsf{F}_0(k_0)$, then
$$b_3 \oplus a_0 = \mathsf{F}_1(\mathsf{F}_0(k_0 \oplus 0\cdots01) \oplus \mathsf{F}_0(k_0)).$$
4. Obtain $\beta_2 \in \{0,1\}^{n/2}$ such that
$$\mathsf{F}_1(\beta_2) = b_3 \oplus a_0$$
   by Grover's search.

---

[1] For example, how to efficiently dissect the MPMCT gate to atomic gates is shown in [21].

5. Obtain $k_0' \in \{0,1\}^{n/2}$ such that

$$F_0(k_0' \oplus 0 \cdots 01) \oplus F_0(k_0') = \beta_2$$

   by Grover's search.
6. Let $k_1' := \beta_1 \oplus F_0(k_0')$. Query $(a_0, b_0) = (F_1(k_1'), F_0(k_0' \oplus F_1(k_1')))$ to the encryption oracle to receive (a_3, b_3), where

$$a_3 = F_0(k_0 \oplus F_1(k_1')) \oplus F_0(k_0' \oplus F_1(k_1'))$$
$$\oplus\ F_2(k_2 \oplus F_1(k_1') \oplus F_1(k_1 \oplus F_0(k_0 \oplus F_1(k_1')) \oplus F_0(k_0' \oplus F_1(k_1')))).$$

   If it holds $(k_0', k_1') = (k_0, k_1)$, then

$$a_3 = F_2(k_2).$$

7. Obtain $k_2' \in \{0,1\}^{n/2}$ such that

$$F_2(k_2') = a_3$$

   by Grover's search.
8. Choose $(a_0, b_0) \in (\{0,1\}^{n/2})^2$ randomly and query to the encryption oracle to receive (a_3, b_3). For the candidate (k_0', k_1', k_2'), check their validity whether Eqs. (1) and (2) holds with this plaintext/ciphertext pair.

In Step 5, there is almost no process of bitwise XOR for the input of F_i-oracle on the quantum circuit. Thus, our CPA has the advantage of decreasing quantum gates against the KPA in Sect. 3.1, even though the (D, T, Q, M) complexities are asymptotically same.

Analysis. In the attack, the (D, T, Q, M) complexities are asymptotically same as our KPA in Sect. 3.1. In Step 5, there is almost no process of bitwise XOR for the input of F_i-oracle on the quantum circuit. Thus, our CPA has the advantage of decreasing quantum gates against the KPA. Specifically, in the dominant part (i.e., Step 5) for the circuit size, XORing $a_{1,0}$ (and $a_{1,0} \oplus a_{2,0}$) is not necessary. Therefore, the total number of gates in Step 5 is

$$n + 2 + \{MPMCT(\frac{n}{2} + 1) + MPMCT(\frac{n}{2}) + \frac{5n}{2} + 3\} \cdot \left\lfloor \frac{\pi}{4}\sqrt{2^{n/2}} + \frac{1}{2} \right\rfloor.$$

Also, our CPA succeeds with overwhelming probability as our KPA.

4 Non-triviality of Improving Our Attacks Using Another Quantum Algorithm

Here, we consider how to improve efficiency of our attacks against the Feistel-2 structure in the Q1 model by using another quantum algorithms than Grover's one.

In the Q2 model, it is known that Simon's algorithm [16] solves a problem defined below in a polynomial time.

Definition 3 (Simon's problem). *Given function* $f : \{0,1\}^n \to \{0,1\}^m$ *such that* $f(x) = f(x \oplus s)$ *for all* x *where* $s \in \{0,1\}^n \backslash \{0^n\}$, *find* s.

In distinguishing attacks on the Feistel-2 structure proposed by Kuwakado and Morii [17] and Kaplan et al. [18], the adversary obtains a period of the functions satisfying Simon's promise by querying in superposition the encryption oracle.

Moreover, in the Q2 model, variants of Simon's algorithm are introduced such as Leander and May's method [19] (which combines Grover's algorithm [11] and Simon's algorithm [16]) and Bonnetain et al.'s method [14] (which is called nested Simon's algorithm). Based on Leander and May's method, Hosoyamada and Sasaki showed qCPA on the r-round Feistel-2 structure ($r \geq 4$) [13]. Based on nested Simon's algorithm, Cid et al. showed qCPA on the 3-round Feistel-2 structure [20].

On the other hand, Bonnetain et al. [15] extended Leander and May's method to the Q1 model, and showed CPA on Even-Mansour cipher [2] with $D = O(2^{n/6})$, $T = O(2^{n/6})$ and $Q = Poly(n)$ as follows. The encryption function $E : \{0,1\}^{n/2} \to \{0,1\}^{n/2}$ is defined as $E(x) := P(k_1 \oplus x) \oplus k_2$ where $P : \{0,1\}^{n/2} \to \{0,1\}^{n/2}$ is a public random permutation, and $(k_1, k_2) \in \{0,1\}^{n/2} \times \{0,1\}^{n/2}$ is the secret key. Let a function $f : \{0,1\}^{n/2} \to \{0,1\}^{n/2}$ be

$$f(x) := E(x) \oplus P(x) = P(k_1 \oplus x) \oplus k_2 \oplus P(x),$$

then it holds that $f(x) = f(x \oplus k_1)$. In their attack, the adversary poses online classical queries to build an unitary operator simulating part of the encryption oracle. Then, the adversary runs the simulating operator and poses offline quantum queries to the P-oracle for constructing above f on the quantum circuit. It is important that the simulating operator is set before the offline query with quantum superposition of full of the domain. A promising direction is to apply their method to the 3-round Feistel-2 structure because no Q1 key recovery attack with $D = O(2^{n/6})$, $T = O(2^{n/6})$ and $Q = Poly(n)$.

Here, we consider a naive application of their method to the 3-round Feistel-2 structure. In the 3-round Feistel-2 structure, for example, a function f satisfying Simon's problem is given as follows. Let $(a_0, b_0) := (x, \mathsf{F}_0(x))$. Then, letting $f(x)$ be

$$f(x) := b_3 \oplus a_0 = \mathsf{F}_1(k_1 \oplus \mathsf{F}_0(k_0 \oplus x) \oplus \mathsf{F}_0(x)),$$

it holds that $f(x) = f(x \oplus k_1)$. In this case, the adversary runs the simulating operator after posing offline quantum queries. Since the number of online classical queries has to cover the range of F_0, D is more than $2^{n/2}$ and the total attack time is more than $2^{n/2}$. Hence, improving our attacks is not trivial and some additional technique is required.

5   Conclusion

We proposed new quantum key recovery attacks on the 3-round Feistel-2 structure by KPA and CPA in the Q1 model. For the first time, our attacks achieved a higher efficiency in the Q1 model than the known classical attacks.

As further research, in addition to the direction given in Sect. 4, it is interesting how to realize extending nested Simon's algorithm to the Q1 model.

References

1. Luby, M., Rackoff, C.: How to construct pseudorandom permutations from pseudorandom functions. SIAM J. Comput. **17**(2), 373–386 (1988)
2. Even, S., Mansour, Y.: A construction of a cipher from a single pseudorandom permutation. In: ASIACRYPT, pp 210–224 (1991)
3. Lampe, R., Seurin, Y.: Security analysis of key-alternating Feistel Ciphers. In: FSE, pp. 243–264 (2014)
4. Isobe, T., Shibutani, K.: All subkeys recovery attack on block ciphers: extending meet-in-the-middle approach. In: Knudsen, L.R., Wu, H. (eds.) SAC 2012. LNCS, vol. 7707, pp. 202–221. Springer, Heidelberg (2013). https://doi.org/10.1007/978-3-642-35999-6_14
5. Isobe, T., Shibutani, K.: Generic key recovery attack on Feistel scheme. In: ASIACRYPT, vol. 1, pp. 464–485 (2013)
6. Demirci, H., Aydin Selçuk, A.: A meet-in-the-middle attack on 8-round AES. In: FSE, pp.116–126 (2008)
7. Guo, J., Jean, J., Nikolic, I., Sasaki, Y.: Meet-in-the-middle attacks on generic Feistel constructions. In: ASIACRYPT, pp. 458–477 (2014)
8. Dinur, I., Dunkelman, O., Keller, N., Shamir, A.: New attacks on Feistel structures with improved memory complexities. In: CRYPTO, vol. 1, pp. 433–454 (2014)
9. Dinur, I., Dunkelman, O., Keller, N., Shamir, A.: Efficient dissection of Bicomposite problems with cryptanalytic applications. J. Cryptol. **32**(4), 1448–1490 (2018). https://doi.org/10.1007/s00145-018-9303-2
10. Daiza, T., Kurosawa, K.: Optimum attack on 3-round feistel-2 structure. In: IWSEC, pp. 175–192 (2021)
11. Grover, L.K.: A fast quantum mechanical algorithm for database search. In: STOC, pp. 212–219 (1996)
12. Brassard, G., Høyer, P., Tapp, A.: Quantum cryptanalysis of hash and claw-free functions. In: LATIN, pp. 163–169 (1998)
13. Hosoyamada, A., Sasaki, Yu.: Quantum demiric-Selçuk meet-in-the-middle attacks: applications to 6-round generic Feistel constructions. In: SCN, pp. 12–14 (2014)
14. Bonnetain, X., Naya-Plasencia, M., Schrottenloher, A.: On quantum slide attacks. In: SAC, pp. 492–519 (2019)
15. Bonnetain, X., Hosoyamada, A., Naya-Plasencia, M., Sasaki, YU., Schrottenloher, A.: Quantum attacks without superposition queries: the offline Simon's algorithm. In: ASIACRYPT, pp. 552–583 (2019)
16. Simon, D.R.: On the power of quantum computation. SIAM J. Comput. **26**(5), 1474–1483 (1997)
17. Kuwakado, H., Morii, M.: Quantum distinguisher between the 3-round Feistel cipher and the random permutation. In: ISIT, pp. 2682–2685 (2019)
18. Kaplan, M., Leurent, G., Leverrier, A., Naya-Plasencia, M.: Breaking symmetric cryptosystems using quantum period finding. In: CRYPTO, vol. 2, pp. 207–237 (2016)
19. Leander, G., May, A.: Grover meets Simon - Quantumly attacking the FX-construction. In: ASIACRYPT, vol. 2, pp. 161–178 (2017)

20. Cid, C., Hosoyamada, A., Liu, Y., Sim, S.M.: Quantum cryptanalysis on contracting Feistel structures and observation on related-key settings. In: INDOCRYPT, pp. 373–394 (2020)
21. Sasanian, Z., Miller, D.M.: Reversible and quantum circuit optimization: a functional approach. In: RC, pp. 112–124 (2012)

Post-quantum Cryptography

Improving Fault Attacks on Rainbow with Fixing Random Vinegar Values

Taku Kato[1]([✉]), Yutaro Kiyomura[2], and Tsuyoshi Takagi[1]

[1] Department of Mathematical Informatics, University of Tokyo, Tokyo, Japan
kato-taku243@g.ecc.u-tokyo.ac.jp
[2] NTT Social Informatics Laboratories, Tokyo, Japan

Abstract. Rainbow is an efficient variant of the unbalanced oil and vinegar scheme, which is a well-established digital signature scheme based on the difficulty of solving multivariate polynomials. It has been selected as one of the round 3 finalists in the National institute of standards and technology (NIST) post-quantum cryptography standardization project.

To investigate the practical security several fault attacks on Rainbow have been conducted. At PQCrypto 2011, Hashimoto et al. proposed a fault attack with fixing random vinegar values on Rainbow. Subsequently, Shim et al. showed that the complexity of the fault attack can be reduced by increasing the number of fixed random vinegar values. However, these attacks require exponential time, even though all the random vinegar values are fixed. In this paper, a polynomial time attack is proposed by further using the hidden information of the secret key, in the case that all random vinegar values are fixed. In addition, an improved attack is proposed in the case that some random vinegar values are fixed. Furthermore, the complexity of the proposed attack is demonstrated to be significantly smaller compared to that of Shim et al.'s attack. For instance, the proposed attack reduces the complexity by a factor of 2^{80} for the SL5 parameters of Rainbow.

Keywords: Post-quantum cryptography · Multivariate public key cryptography · Fault attack

1 Introduction

RSA cryptography [19] and elliptic curve cryptography [15,17] have been broken by the Shor's algorithm [21] when a large-scale quantum computer is realized. Therefore, in recent years, post-quantum cryptography (PQC) has been studied.

Multivariate public key cryptography (MPKC), a kind of PQC is based on the difficulty of multivariate quadratic (MQ) problems. The unbalanced oil and vinegar scheme (UOV) is a multivariate digital signature scheme proposed by Kipnis et al. [13]. UOV has essentially not been broken for over 20 years. Ding et al. [10] proposed Rainbow, which is a multilayered version of the UOV. Rainbow is one of the round 3 finalists in the National institute of standards and technology (NIST) post-quantum cryptography standardization project and has been garnering considerable attention recently.

C.-M. Cheng and M. Akiyama (Eds.): IWSEC 2022, LNCS 13504, pp. 147–165, 2022.
https://doi.org/10.1007/978-3-031-15255-9_8

Several cryptanalyses, such as Rank attacks [5], UOV attack [14], and Rainbow band separation (RBS) attack [11] have been conducted. Recently, Beullens proposed Simple attack and Combined attack on Rainbow. As a result, the SL3 and SL5 (192 and 256 bit security) parameters are rescaled to the SL1 and SL3 (128 and 192 bit security), respectively. In addition to these cryptanalyses, physical attacks also have been studied, in recent years. Side-channel attacks, which are a type of physical attack, include timing analysis and power analysis, as well as fault attacks. The focus of this paper is on the fault attacks against digital signature schemes. These attacks cause faults in the process of signature generation. Hashimoto et al. [12] proposed fault attacks with fixing random values against MPKC. Krämer et al. [16] applied Hashimoto et al.'s results to the UOV and Rainbow. Shim et al. [20] proposed a fault attack on Rainbow with fixing the random vinegar values used for the signature generation of Rainbow. The attacks proposed by Hashimoto et al., Krämer et al., and Shim et al. require exponential time with respect to the number of variables.

In this paper, two fault attacks on Rainbow have been proposed. As a model for the fault attacks, we consider the case that some random vinegar values that are used in the sign algorithm of Rainbow are fixed, which is the same as the model of Shim et al.'s attack. In this model, the two proposed attacks depend on the number of fixed vinegar values. The first one is an attack with fixing all random vinegar values. It is demonstrated that the attack takes only polynomial time. The second result is an attack with fixing some random vinegar values. It is shown that by using information from the fault, the complexity of MinRank attack [2,7], HighRank attack [8], UOV attack, RBS attack, Intersection attack, Rectangular MinRank attack, Simple attack, and Combined attack [6] is reduced. As the complexity of attacks depends on the number of fixed random vinegar values, in the proposed attack, the optimal attack is selected accordingly. The complexity of the proposed attack is approximately 2^{80} times smaller than that of Shim et al.'s attack for the SL5 parameters.

2   Preliminaries

In this section, the notations used in the rest of this paper are described. Subsequently, a review of the construction of Rainbow and the several known attacks on Rainbow is presented.

2.1   Notations

Let $\mathbb{N}$ be the set of natural numbers. Further, $\mathbb{F}_q$ denotes a finite field with q elements. Let $\mathbb{F}_q^n$ be the set of n-dimensional vectors over $\mathbb{F}_q$ for $n \in \mathbb{N}$. For $m, n \in \mathbb{N}$, the set of $(m \times n)$-matrices over $\mathbb{F}_q$ is denoted by $\mathbb{F}_q^{m \times n}$. For a matrix $A \in \mathbb{F}_q^{m \times n}$ and a positive integer $j \in \{1, \ldots, n\}$, $A_{(j)}$ denotes the j-th column of A. Let $A_{(i,j)}$ be the (i,j)-th entry of A for positive integers $i \in \{1, \ldots, m\}, j \in \{1, \ldots, n\}$. The transposed matrix of A is denoted by $A^\top$.

Algorithm 1. Signature generation for a message $\mu \in \{0,1\}^*$

1: $h \leftarrow \mathcal{H}(\mu)$
2: $y \leftarrow \mathcal{S}^{-1}(h)$
3: **for** $i \in V$ **do**
4:     $r_i \xleftarrow{\$} \mathbb{F}_q$
5:     $u_i \leftarrow r_i$
6: Compute $u_{v+1}, \ldots, u_n \in \mathbb{F}_q$ s.t. $\mathcal{F}(u_1, \ldots, u_v, u_{v+1}, \ldots, u_n) = y$
7: $\sigma \leftarrow \mathcal{T}^{-1}(u_1, \ldots, u_v, u_{v+1}, \ldots, u_n)$
8: **return** σ

For a finite set S, $x \xleftarrow{\$} S$ means that x is chosen uniformly randomly from S. For $n \in \mathbb{N}$, $\{0,1\}^n$ denotes the set of bitstrings of length n. Let $\{0,1\}^* := \bigcup_{n \geq 1} \{0,1\}^n$.

2.2 Rainbow

In this section, the concept of Rainbow [10], a multi-layer version of UOV [13], is explained. UOV is a digital signature scheme based on the MQ-based trapdoor function.

First, the notation used for Rainbow is defined. The parameters of Rainbow are (q, v, o_1, o_2). The number of variables is given by $n := v + o_1 + o_2$ and the number of equations is given by $m := o_1 + o_2$. The index sets are defined as follows. $V := \{1, \ldots, v\}$, $O_1 := \{v+1, \ldots, v+o_1\}$ and $O_2 := \{v + o_1 + 1, \ldots, n\}$. Let $W := \{x \in \mathbb{F}_q^m :^\forall i \in \{1, \ldots, o_1\}, x_i = 0\}$, $\mathcal{O}_1 := \{x \in \mathbb{F}_q^n :^\forall i \in \{1, \ldots, v\}, x_i = 0\}$ and $\mathcal{O}_2 := \{x \in \mathbb{F}_q^n :^\forall i \in \{1, \ldots, v+o_1\}, x_i = 0\}$. For $i \in V$, the variable u_i is called the vinegar variable.

Next, the public key and the secret key of Rainbow are explained. The invertible affine maps $\mathcal{S} \in \mathbb{F}_q^{m \times m}, \mathcal{T} \in \mathbb{F}_q^{n \times n}$ are selected randomly. A central map $\mathcal{F} = (\mathcal{F}^{(v+1)}, \ldots, \mathcal{F}^{(n)}) : \mathbb{F}_q^n \to \mathbb{F}_q^m$ is selected. o_1 polynomials $(\mathcal{F}^{(v+1)}, \ldots, \mathcal{F}^{(v+o_1)})$ are of the form

$$\mathcal{F}^{(k)}(u) = \sum_{i \in O_1, j \in V} \alpha_{ij}^{(k)} u_i u_j + \sum_{i,j \in V, i \leq j} \beta_{ij}^{(k)} u_i u_j + \sum_{i \in V \cup O_1} \gamma_i^{(k)} u_i + \eta^{(k)} \quad (1)$$

and o_2 polynomials $(\mathcal{F}^{(v+o_1+1)}, \ldots, \mathcal{F}^{(n)})$ are of the form

$$\mathcal{F}^{(k)}(u) = \sum_{i \in O_2, j \in V \cup O_1} \alpha_{ij}^{(k)} u_i u_j + \sum_{i,j \in V \cup O_1, i \leq j} \beta_{ij}^{(k)} u_i u_j + \sum_{i \in V \cup O_1 \cup O_2} \gamma_i^{(k)} u_i + \eta^{(k)}. \quad (2)$$

Further, the public key of Rainbow is $\mathcal{P} := \mathcal{S} \circ \mathcal{F} \circ \mathcal{T}$, and the secret key of Rainbow consists of $(\mathcal{S}, \mathcal{F}, \mathcal{T})$. S, T denote the representation matrices of $\mathcal{S}, \mathcal{T}$, and $F^{(k)}$ denotes the representation matrix of a quadratic map $\mathcal{F}^{(k)}$.

Note that there is no quadratic monomial of $u_i u_j$ $(i, j \in O_1 \bigcup O_2)$ in (1) and there is no quadratic monomial $u_i u_j$ $(i, j \in O_2)$ in (2). Using this structure,

$\mathcal{F}$ can be inverted as follows. First, the vinegar variables $u_1, \ldots, u_v$ are fixed with random values. Then, the polynomials in (1) are linear in the first oil variables $u_{v+1}, \ldots, u_{v+o_1}$. Hence, $u_{v+1}, \ldots, u_{v+o_1}$ can be computed by Gaussian elimination. Next, the polynomials in (2) are linear in the second oil variables $u_{v+o_1+1}, \ldots, u_n$. So, we can compute $u_{v+o_1+1}, \ldots, u_n$ by Gaussian elimination. Using this process, $\mathcal{F}$ can be inverted efficiently.

Furthermore, the signature algorithm and the verification algorithm of Rainbow are reviewed. Let $\mathcal{H} : \{0,1\}^* \rightarrow \mathbb{F}_q^m$ be a hash function. To sign a message $\mu \in \{0,1\}^*$, first $h = \mathcal{H}(\mu)$ is computed. Next, v random vinegar values $r_1, \ldots, r_v \in \mathbb{F}_q$ are selected and substituted for the vinegar variables $u_1, \ldots, u_v$. Then, using the previous process, $u_{v+1}, \ldots, u_n \in \mathbb{F}_q$ s.t. $\mathcal{F}(u_1, \ldots, u_v, u_{v+1}, \ldots, u_n) = h$ are computed. Subsequently, $\sigma = \mathcal{T}^{-1}(u_1, \ldots, u_v, u_{v+1}, \ldots, u_n) \in \mathbb{F}_q^n$ is computed. Algorithm 1 refers to the sign algorithm of Rainbow. A signature σ is accepted by the verifier if $\mathcal{P}(\sigma) = \mathcal{H}(\mu)$.

Here, the relation between Rainbow and the MQ problem is discussed. The MQ problem can be stated as finding $x \in \mathbb{F}_q^n$ such that $\mathcal{P}(x) = y$ given a system of quadratic polynomials $\mathcal{P} : \mathbb{F}_q^n \rightarrow \mathbb{F}_q^m$ and $y \in \mathbb{F}_q^m$. $MQ(q, n, m)$ denotes the complexity of solving a system consisting of m quadratic polynomials with n variables over $\mathbb{F}_q$. To forge a Rainbow signature, it is necessary to find σ such that the system of equations $\mathcal{P}(\sigma) = \mathcal{H}(\mu)$ is satisfied. This system can be regarded as an instance of the MQ problem.

Finally, the complexity of solving a system of quadratic polynomials is discussed. If $\mathcal{P}$ is a random system of quadratic polynomials, then $MQ(q, n, m)$ is estimated as follows.

$$\min_k O\left(q^k \cdot 3\binom{n-k}{2}\binom{d_{reg} + n - k}{d_{reg}}^2\right) \tag{3}$$

where d_{reg} is the degree of regularity of the system [4,9]. If the system is semiregular, the degree of regularity d_{reg} is the degree of the first non-positive term in the series $\frac{(1-z^2)^m}{(1-z)^{n-k}}$ [3]. In this paper, the special systems of quadratic polynomials have been treated. A case with two kinds of variables denoted by $x_1, \ldots, x_{n_1}$ and $y_1, \ldots, y_{n_2}$ is considered. It is assumed that there are m_1 quadratic polynomials in $x_1, \ldots, x_{n_1}$ and m_2 bilinear polynomials in $x_1, \ldots, x_{n_1}$ and $y_1, \ldots, y_{n_2}$. In this case, the complexity of solving the system is expressed as $MQ(q, n_1, n_2, m_1, m_2)$. Using the result of Smith-Tone et al. [18], $MQ(q, n_1, n_2, m_1, m_2)$ is estimated as follows.

$$\min_{k_1, k_2} O\left(q^{k_1+k_2} \cdot 3\binom{n_1 - k_1}{2}\left(\binom{a + n_1 - k_1}{a}\binom{b + n_2 - k_2}{b}\right)^2\right) \tag{4}$$

where $a, b \in \mathbb{N}$ is the bi-degree of the first non-positive term in the series $\frac{(1-z_1^2)^{m_1}(1-z_1 z_2)^{m_2}}{(1-z_1)^{n_1-k_1}(1-z_2)^{n_2-k_2}}$.

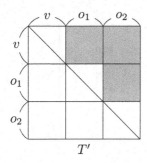
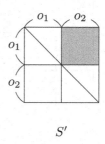

Fig. 1. Equivalent key for Rainbow

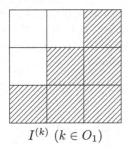
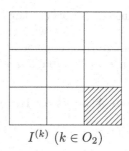

$I^{(k)}$ $(k \in O_1)$ $I^{(k)}$ $(k \in O_2)$

Fig. 2. Structure $I = \{I^{(k)}\}_{k \in O_1 \bigcup O_2}$

2.3 Equivalent Key and Good Key

In this section, the concept of equivalent keys and good keys is presented. These keys are used in the attacks on Rainbow. First, we define an equivalent key. We fix a structure $I = \{I^{(k)}\}_{k \in O_1 \bigcup O_2}$ where $I^{(k)} \subseteq \{u_i u_j : 1 \leq i, j \leq n\}$. We call $(\mathcal{S}', \mathcal{F}', \mathcal{T}')$ an equivalent key to $(\mathcal{S}, \mathcal{F}, \mathcal{T})$ if $\mathcal{S}' \circ \mathcal{F}' \circ \mathcal{T}' = \mathcal{S} \circ \mathcal{F} \circ \mathcal{T}$ and $\mathcal{F}'|_I = \mathcal{F}|_I$, that is $\mathcal{F}'$ and $\mathcal{F}$ share the same coefficients corresponding to the monomials in I. The equivalent keys play the same role in the sign algorithm as the secret key.

Figure 1 shows an example of an equivalent key for Rainbow with illustrations of the representation matrices of an equivalent key $\mathcal{T}', \mathcal{S}'$. The diagonal entries are 1; the white cells represent 0; and the gray cells represent arbitrary values. In this example, $I^{(k)}$ is the set of the quadratic monomials with zero coefficients in $\mathcal{F}^{(k)}$. Namely $I^{(k)} = \{u_i'' u_j'' : v + 1 \leq i, j \leq v + o_1\} \bigcup \{u_i'' u_j'' : 1 \leq i \leq n, v + o_1 + 1 \leq j \leq n\} \bigcup \{u_i'' u_j'' : v + o_1 + 1 \leq i \leq n - 1, 1 \leq j \leq v + o_1\}$ for $k \in O_1$ and $I^{(k)} = \{u_i'' u_j'' : v + o_1 + 1 \leq i, j \leq n\}$ for $k \in O_2$. In Fig. 2, the monomials in $I = \{I^{(k)}\}_{k \in O_1 \bigcup O_2}$ are represented by the shaded area.

Second, a good key is defined. We fix a structure $I = \{I^{(k)}\}_{k \in O_1 \bigcup O_2}$ where $I^{(k)} \subseteq \{u_i u_j : 1 \leq i, j \leq n\}$. In addition, we fix a partial structure $J = \{J^{(k)}\}_{k \in O_1 \bigcup O_2}$ where $J^{(k)} \subseteq I^{(k)}$. We call $(\mathcal{S}'', \mathcal{F}'', \mathcal{T}'')$ good key to $(\mathcal{S}, \mathcal{F}, \mathcal{T})$ if $\mathcal{S}'' \circ \mathcal{F}'' \circ \mathcal{T}'' = \mathcal{S} \circ \mathcal{F} \circ \mathcal{T}$ and $\mathcal{F}''|_J = \mathcal{F}|_J$.

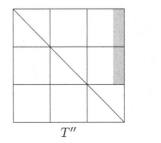
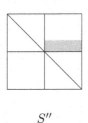

Fig. 3. Good key for Rainbow

Regarding the equivalent keys, the coefficients corresponding to all the monomials in I of $\mathcal{F}'$ coincide with those of $\mathcal{F}$. In contrast, regarding the good keys, $\mathcal{F}''$ and $\mathcal{F}$ share the same coefficients corresponding to certain monomials in I. Figure 3 shows an example of a good key for Rainbow.

2.4 Known Attacks on Rainbow

In this section, several known attacks on Rainbow are presented.

MinRank Attack. This attack finds a linear combination of m matrices of size n-by-n $P^{(1)}, \ldots, P^{(m)}$ which has rank at most $v + o_1$. Finding such a linear combination is called the MinRank problem. There are a few algorithms for solving the MinRank problem. In this paper, two algorithms are used for the MinRank problem. The algorithm proposed by Billet et al. [7] searches for the linear combination in $o_1 q^{v+1}(\frac{m^3}{3} - \frac{m^2}{6})$ time. Recently, Bardet et al. [2] proposed a new algorithm called the support minors modeling. This algorithm transforms the MinRank problem into an MQ problem. The dominant complexity is that of solving the MQ problem using XL algorithm [9]. The concrete complexity is described in section 2.3 of [5].

HighRank Attack. Coppersmith et al. [8] proposed HighRank attack. HighRank attack finds $T^{-1}\mathcal{O}_2$ The complexity of HighRank attack is $q^{o_2}n^3$.

UOV Attack. Kipnis et al. [14] proposed UOV attack on UOV. As Rainbow is a multilayered version of UOV, Rainbow can be regarded as UOV. Therefore, UOV attack can be applied to Rainbow. The complexity of UOV attack on Rainbow is $q^{n-2o_2-1}o_2^4$.

RBS Attack. Ding et al. [11] proposed Rainbow band separation (RBS) attack. The RBS attack constructs a system of quadratic polynomials in the good key of Fig. 3 and recovers an equivalent key from the solution of the equations.

In the system, there are $n - 1$ quadratic polynomials in $v + o_1$ variables of T' and m bilinear polynomials in $v + o_1$ variables of T' and o_2 variables of S'. Therefore, the complexity of RBS attack is $MQ(q, v + o_1, o_2, n - 1, m)$.

Intersection Attack. Beullens [5] proposed Intersection attack. Intersection attack is a generalization of RBS attack. An outline of this attack is presented below. First, two random linear combinations of $P_1, \ldots, P_m$ denoted by L_1, L_2 are randomly chosen. Then, the quadratic equations in $x \in L_1 T \mathcal{O}_2 \cap L_2 T \mathcal{O}_2$ and $y \in (S'^{-1})^\top W$ are constructed. From the conditions, $3o_2 - n$ and o_1 linear constraints can be posed on x and y respectively. These equations are solved using XL algorithm. For $n \geq 3o_2$, the probability that there exists $x \in \mathbb{F}_q^n$ such that $x \in L_1 T \mathcal{O}_2 \cap L_2 T \mathcal{O}_2$ is $\frac{1}{q^{n-3o_2+1}}$. Therefore, the aforementioned process is repeated q^{n-3o_2+1} times. The complexity of Intersection attack is $q^{n-3o_2+1} MQ(q, min\{2n - 3o_2, n - 1\}, o_2, 3m - 2, 2n)$.

Rectangular MinRank Attack. Beullens [5] proposed Rectangular MinRank attack. In this attack, the attacker uses a MinRank problem with $n - o_2 + 1$ matrices of size n-by-m with target rank o_2. This is a different type of MinRank problem from the above MinRank attack. Rectangular MinRank attack applies the algorithm proposed by Bardet et al. to the MinRank problem and constructs quadratic equations. Additional quadratic equations are also constructed from the condition $x \in T^{-1}\mathcal{O}_2$. The dominant part of the complexity is the complexity of solving these equations. The concrete complexity is described in section 7.1 of [5].

Simple Attack and Combined Attack. Beullens [6] proposed two new attacks called Simple attack and Combined attack. The attacks first compute a vector $x \in T^{-1}\mathcal{O}_2$ efficiently. From this vector, the second layer of Rainbow can be recovered. Then, the first layer can be regarded as a UOV map. Finally, the UOV map is attacked using known attacks on UOV. The difference between Simple attack and Combined attack is in the way in which $x \in T^{-1}\mathcal{O}_2$ is found. Simple attack constructs $m - 1$ quadratic equations in x, which have $v - 1$ variables and solves them using XL algorithm. Hence, the complexity of Simple attack is $MQ(q, v-1, m-1)$. Combined attack constructs the MinRank problem similar to Rectangular MinRank attack. The number of the matrices in the MinRank problem is v, the number of rows of the matrices is $n - 1$, the number of columns of the matrices is m, and the target rank is o_2. The concrete complexity is described in [6]. From the solution of the MinRank problem, $x \in T^{-1}\mathcal{O}_2$ can be computed. Simple attack is more efficient than Combined attack if $v - o_1$ is small. For example, the complexity of Simple attack is 2^{69} time for the SL1 parameters where $v - o_1 = 4$. However, for the SL3, SL5 parameters, Combined attack is more efficient. For example, the complexity of Combined attack is 2^{206} and 2^{157} time for the SL5 and SL3 parameters. This implies that the SL5 and SL3 parameters satisfy only 192 and 128 bit security, respectively.

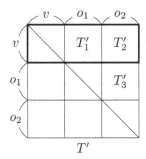 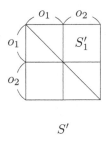

Fig. 4. Equivalent key T', S' $(d = v)$

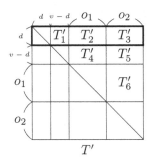 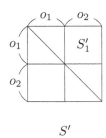

Fig. 5. Equivalent key T', S' $(d < v)$

2.5 Fault Attacks on Rainbow

In this section, fault attacks on Rainbow are explained. Hashimoto et al. [12] studied fault attacks with fixing random values. Krämer et al. [16] applied Hashimoto et al.'s result to UOV and Rainbow. Shim et al. [20] proposed a new fault attack on Rainbow which is explained as follows. In this attack, the adversary fixes d $(\leq v)$ random vinegar values of $r_1, \ldots, r_v$. From the signatures generated with the d fixed values, the attack recovers the partial information of an equivalent key. The information depends on the number of the fixed values d. Therefore, the case of $d = v$ is considered first and then the case of $d < v$ is considered.

The Case of $d = v$ [20]. In this case, the adversary uses an equivalent key, as shown in Fig. 4. From the faulty signatures, the adversary obtains the values of T'_1, T'_2 surrounded by the thick lines, as depicted in Fig. 4. The unknown variables in T', S' are T'_3, S'_1. Shim et al. proposed the method to recover T'_3, S'_1 using a good key. To recover T'_3, S'_1, the method constructs m quadratic equations as follows:

$$((T'^{-1})_{(n)})^\top P^{(k)} (T'^{-1})_{(n)} = 0 \ (k \in O_1 \bigcup O_2) \tag{5}$$

signature	v vinegar values in $\mathbb{F}_q$ used for signature generation								
$\sigma^{(1)}$	$r_1^{(1)}$	r_2^*	$r_3^{(1)}$	$\cdots$	r_j^*	$\cdots$	$r_{v-2}^{(1)}$	r_{v-1}^*	$r_v^{(1)}$
$\sigma^{(2)}$	$r_1^{(2)}$	r_2^*	$r_3^{(2)}$	$\cdots$	r_j^*	$\cdots$	$r_{v-2}^{(2)}$	r_{v-1}^*	$r_v^{(2)}$
$\vdots$	$\vdots$	$\vdots$	$\vdots$		$\vdots$		$\vdots$	$\vdots$	$\vdots$
$\sigma^{(N)}$	$r_1^{(N)}$	r_2^*	$r_3^{(N)}$	$\cdots$	r_j^*	$\cdots$	$r_{v-2}^{(N)}$	$r_{v-1}^{*\prime}$	$r_v^{(N)}$
		fixed			fixed			fixed	

Fig. 6. Illustration of the fault attack model

Since there are o_1 unknown variables in $(T'^{-1})_{(n)}$, Shim et al.'s attack requires $MQ(q, o_1, m)$ time, which is the exponential time.

The Case of $d < v$ [20]. In this case, the adversary uses an equivalent key, as shown in Fig. 5. From the faulty signatures, the adversary obtains the values of T_1', T_2', T_3' surrounded by the thick lines, as depicted Fig. 5. The unknown variables in T', S' are T_4', T_5', T_6', S_1'. Shim et al. proposed the method to recover T_4', T_5', T_6', S_1' using a good key. To recover T_5', T_6', S_1', the method constructs m quadratic equations and $n - 1$ bilinear equations as follows:

$$((T'^{-1})_{(n)})^\top P^{(k)}(T'^{-1})_{(n)} = 0 \ (k \in O_1 \bigcup O_2) \qquad (6)$$

$$(e_i)^\top (P^{(o_1)} - \sum_{l \in O_2} S'_{(o_1,l)} P^{(l)})(T'^{-1})_{(n)} = 0 \ (i \in \{1, \ldots, n-1\}) \qquad (7)$$

where e_i is a vector in $\mathbb{F}_q^n$ such that i-th coordinate is 1 and the other coordinates are 0. This system is essentially the same as that of RBS attack. Hence, Shim et al.'s attack can be considered as RBS attack. Since there are $v + o_1$ unknown variables in $(T'^{-1})_{(n)}$ and o_2 unknown variables in $(S'^{-1})_{(o_1)}$, Shim et al.'s attack requires $MQ(q, v + o_1, o_2, m, n - 1)$ time, which is the exponential time.

3   Proposed Fault Attacks with Fixing Random Vinegar Values

In this section, two fault attacks on Rainbow are proposed. In Sect. 3.1, the model of the proposed fault attacks with fixing the random vinegar values in the signature generation, which is the same model as Shim et al.'s fault attack [20] is discussed. Since our fault attacks depend on the number of fixed vinegar values, similar to Shim et al.'s fault attack, two cases are considered as follows. In Sect. 3.2 and 3.3, the case that all random vinegar values ($d = v$) are fixed and the case fixing only some random vinegar values ($d < v$) are fixed are discussed, respectively.

3.1 Fault Attack Model

In the following, the fault attack model on Rainbow by fixing the random vinegar values in the signature generation is described in detail to precisely explain the proposed fault attack. This is the same model as Shim et al.'s fault attack [20]. An illustration of the fault attack model is presented in Fig. 6. In this paper, we focus on the algebraic attack using faulty output, and we do not consider how to fix vinegar values physically.

At first, the signature σ on a message μ is generated by using the vinegar values $r_1, \ldots, r_v \in \mathbb{F}_q$ in the third line of Algorithm 1, which are randomly chosen in $\mathbb{F}_q$. We assume that the adversary accumulates N signatures $\sigma^{(1)}, \ldots, \sigma^{(N)} \in \mathbb{F}_q^n$, and the vinegar values for i-th signature $\sigma^{(i)}$ are denoted by $r_1^{(i)}, \ldots, r_v^{(i)}$ for $i \in \{1, \ldots, N\}$. Note that the messages for signatures $\sigma^{(1)}, \ldots, \sigma^{(N)} \in \mathbb{F}_q^n$ are not used in the attack model.

Subsequently, in the fault attack model, it is assumed that the d ($\leq v$) values of the random vinegar values are fixed during the signature generation, namely, the adversary fixes the d vinegar values in red squares, as depicted in Fig. 6. The fixed vinegar values in Fig. 6 are denoted by the values marked with an asterisk such as r_j^*. The other $v - d$ vinegar values of $r_1, \ldots, r_v \in \mathbb{F}_q$ are randomly chosen for each signature generation.

Note that by attacking certain registers of the output of the random number generator, the values at the registers could be fixed. This is considered as one of the cases in the fault attack model. Furthermore, the fault attack model also includes the case of the same values being used every time to generate a signature due to a defect of the implementer.

We remark that the algebraic way of the attack using the information about the indices of fixed vinegar values and the faulty signatures is analyzed in this paper. The physical way to fix vinegar values is out of the scope of this paper. The number of faulty signatures necessary to our fault attacks depend on the number of fixed vinegar values. This is further described in the following subsections.

3.2 Fixing All Random Vinegar Values $(d = v)$[1]

In this section, the case that all the random vinegar values are fixed by the adversary $(d = v)$ is considered and a polynomial time attack is proposed in this model.

We assume that the adversary fixes all the random vinegar values $r_1, \ldots, r_v$ to $r_1^*, \ldots, r_v^*$. Then, a description of the signature generation is given by Algorithm 2. Since the adversary fixes all the values in this case, Algorithm 2 does not generate random vinegar values. In the proposed fault attack, the adversary requires at least $N = n - v + 1 = m + 1$ signatures using Algorithm 2. Let $\sigma^{(1)}, \ldots, \sigma^{(m+1)} \in \mathbb{F}_q^n$ be the signatures the adversary obtains. We remark that if the adversary gets less than N faulty signatures, then the adversary cannot

---

[1] After this paper was submitted to IWSEC 2022, Aullbach et al. [1] have independently proposed the same attack in the case of $d = v$.

Algorithm 2. Signature generation for the message $\mu \in \{0,1\}^*$ in the case that all the vinegar values are fixed to $r_1^*, \ldots, r_v^*$

1: $h \leftarrow \mathcal{H}(\mu)$
2: $y \leftarrow \mathcal{S}^{-1}(h)$
3: **for** $i \in V$ **do**
4:     $u_i \leftarrow r_i^*$
5: Compute $u_{v+1}, \ldots, u_n \in \mathbb{F}_q$ s.t. $\mathcal{F}(u_1, \ldots, u_v, u_{v+1}, \ldots, u_n) = y$
6: $\sigma \leftarrow \mathcal{T}^{-1}(u_1, \ldots, u_v, u_{v+1}, \ldots, u_n)$
7: **return** σ

---

execute the proposed attack unless the adversary applies the exhaustive search. For each $i \in \{1, \ldots, m+1\}$, the same $r_1^*, \ldots, r_v^*$ are reused to generate the i-th signature $\sigma^{(i)}$.

First, the way to recover the partial information on an equivalent key is introduced. In this case, an equivalent key as depicted in Fig. 4 is used. Let T_v be the first v rows of T. Then, we have $T_v(\sigma^{(i)}) = (r_1^*, \ldots, r_v^*)^\top$ for all $i \in \{1, \ldots, m+1\}$. Let $\tilde{\sigma}^{(i)} := \sigma^{(i+1)} - \sigma^{(1)}$ for $i \in \{1, \ldots, m\}$. We have $T_v(\tilde{\sigma}^{(i)}) = 0$ for all $i \in \{1, \ldots, m\}$. Let $\Lambda := (\tilde{\sigma}^{(1)}, \ldots, \tilde{\sigma}^{(m)}) \in \mathbb{F}_q^{n \times m}$. Then, a basis of $\mathrm{Ker}\Lambda$ is computed. By computing the row reduced echelon form of $\mathrm{Ker}\Lambda$, T_1' and T_2' in Fig. 4 can be recovered.

Further, the approach for recovering an equivalent key T', S' from T_1', T_2' is demonstrated. Note that it suffices to compute T_3' and S_1'. Regarding T', $(T'^{-1})_{(j)}$ are revealed for $j \leq v+o_1$ and $(T'^{-1})_{(j)}$ include the unknown variables $(T_3')_{(j)}$ for $v + o_1 + 1 \leq j \leq n$.

Let $I = \{I^{(k)}\}_{k \in O_1 \bigcup O_2}$ be the set of the quadratic monomials with zero coefficients in $\mathcal{F}'$. Since $(S', \mathcal{F}', T')$ is an equivalent key, we have $I^{(k)} = \{u_i'' u_j'' : v+1 \leq i, j \leq v+o_1\} \bigcup \{u_i'' u_j'' : 1 \leq i \leq n, v+o_1+1 \leq j \leq n\} \bigcup \{u_i'' u_j'' : v+o_1+1 \leq i \leq n-1, 1 \leq j \leq v+o_1\}$ for $k \in O_1$ and $I^{(k)} = \{u_i'' u_j'' : v+o_1+1 \leq i, j \leq n\}$ for $k \in O_2$. Figure 2 shows $I = \{I^{(k)}\}_{k \in O_1 \bigcup O_2}$.

Next, equations in T'^{-1}, S'^{-1} are constructed. For $k \in O_1$, $\mathcal{F}'^{(k)} = (\mathcal{S}^{-1} \circ \mathcal{P})^{(k)} \circ T'^{-1}$ is considered. From the definition of $\mathcal{S}'$, the representation matrix of $(\mathcal{S}^{-1} \circ \mathcal{P})^{(k)}$ is $P^{(k)} - \sum_{l \in O_2} S_{(k,l)}' P^{(l)}$. Therefore, for $i, j \in \{1, \ldots, n\}$, we have

$$(F'^{(k)})_{(i,j)} = ((T'^{-1})_{(i)})^\top (P^{(k)} - \sum_{l \in O_2} S_{(k,l)}' P^{(l)})(T'^{-1})_{(j)}. \tag{8}$$

From this equation, equations in (T'^{-1}, S'^{-1}) are constructed and an equivalent key $(\mathcal{S}', T')$ is recovered.

First, $\mathcal{S}'$ is recovered. From Fig. 2, Eq. (8) for $v + 1 \leq i \leq j \leq v+o_1$ is as follows.

$$((T'^{-1})_{(i)})^\top (P^{(k)} - \sum_{l \in O_2} S_{(k,l)}' P^{(l)})(T'^{-1})_{(j)} = 0. \tag{9}$$

Since $(T'^{-1})_{(i)}, (T'^{-1})_{(j)}$ are revealed for $v+1 \leq i \leq j \leq v+o_1$, Eq. (9) is a linear equation in $S_{(k,l)}'$ ($l \in O_2$). From all the pairs (i,j), $\frac{o_1(o_1+1)}{2}$ linear equations

Algorithm 3. Signature generation for message $\mu \in \{0,1\}^*$ in the case that the first $d(< v)$ vinegar values are fixed to $r_1^*, \ldots, r_d^*$

1: $h \leftarrow \mathcal{H}(\mu)$
2: $y \leftarrow \mathcal{S}^{-1}(h)$
3: **for** $i = 1$ to d **do**
4:     $u_i \leftarrow r_i^*$
5: **for** $i = d+1$ to v **do**
6:     $\tilde{r}_i \xleftarrow{\$} \mathbb{F}_q$
7:     $u_i \leftarrow \tilde{r}_i$
8: Compute $u_{v+1}, \ldots, u_n \in \mathbb{F}_q$ s.t. $\mathcal{F}(u_1, \ldots, u_v, u_{v+1}, \ldots, u_n) = y$
9: $\sigma \leftarrow \mathcal{T}^{-1}(u_1, \ldots, u_v, u_{v+1}, \ldots, u_n)$
10: **return** σ

---

in o_2 variables are obtained. Since we have $\frac{o_1(o_1+1)}{2} \geq o_2$ for the parameters of Rainbow, the equations can be solved and $S'_{(k,l)}$ ($l \in O_2$) are recovered. Therefore, S' can be recovered by repeating this process for all $k \in O_1$.

Next, $\mathcal{T}'$ is recovered. We fix $j \in O_2$. From Fig. 2, Eq. (8) for $k \in O_1, 1 \leq i \leq v + o_1$ is

$$((T'^{-1})_{(i)})^\top (P^{(k)} - \sum_{l \in O_2} S'_{(k,l)} P^{(l)})(T'^{-1})_{(j)} = 0. \tag{10}$$

Since S' has already been recovered, the value of $\mathcal{S}'^{-1} \circ \mathcal{P}$ is known. Therefore, Eq. (9) is a linear equation in $(T'^{-1})_{(j)}$. Since $(T'^{-1})_{(j)}$ includes the unknown variables $(T_3')_{(j)}$, this linear equation has o_2 variables. From all the pairs (k, i), we have $o_1(v + o_1)$ linear equations in o_2 variables. Since we have $o_1(v + o_1) \geq o_2$ for the parameters of Rainbow, the equations can be solved and $(T_3')_{(j)}$ is recovered. Therefore, T_3' can be recovered by repeating this process for all $j \in O_2$. As a result, $\mathcal{T}'$ is recovered.

From $S', \mathcal{T}'$ and the public key $\mathcal{P}$, $\mathcal{F}'$ can be computed. Therefore, the equivalent key $(\mathcal{S}', \mathcal{F}', \mathcal{T}')$ can be recovered. Since only linear equations are solved in this process, the proposed attack is a polynomial time algorithm.

3.3   Fixing Some Random Vinegar Values ($d < v$)

In this section, the case that some random vinegar values are fixed by the adversary ($d < v$) is considered and an efficient attack is proposed in this model.

For the sake of simplicity, we assume that the first d vinegar values $r_1^{(i)}, \ldots, r_d^{(i)} \in \mathbb{F}_q$ ($i \in \{1, \ldots, N\}$) are fixed to $r_1^*, \ldots, r_d^* \in \mathbb{F}_q$, since the indices of the vinegar variables can be changed arbitrarily. Then, the description of the signature generation is outlined in Algorithm 3. In the proposed fault attack, the adversary requires at least $N = n - d + 1$ signatures using Algorithm 3. Let $\sigma^{(1)}, \ldots, \sigma^{(n-d+1)} \in \mathbb{F}_q^n$ be the signatures the adversary obtains. We remark that if the adversary gets less than N faulty signatures, then the adversary cannot execute the proposed attack unless the adversary applies the exhaustive search. For each $i \in \{1, \ldots, n - d + 1\}$, to generate the i-th signature $\sigma^{(i)}$, the same $r_1^*, \ldots, r_d^*$ are reused as the first d vinegar values, and the other $v - d$ vinegar values $r_{d+1}^{(i)}, \ldots, r_v^{(i)}$ are randomly chosen.

First, the approach to recover the partial information of an equivalent key is presented. In this case, an equivalent key depicted in Fig. 5 is used. Let T_d be the first d rows of T. Then, we have $T_d(\sigma^{(i)}) = (r_1^*, \ldots, r_d^*)^\top$ for all $i \in \{1, \ldots, n - d + 1\}$. Let $\tilde{\sigma}^{(i)} := \sigma^{(i+1)} - \sigma^{(1)}$ for $i \in \{1, \ldots, n - d\}$. We have $T_d(\tilde{\sigma}^{(i)}) = 0$ for all $i \in \{1, \ldots, n - d\}$. Let $\Lambda := (\tilde{\sigma}^{(1)}, \ldots, \tilde{\sigma}^{(n-d)}) \in \mathbb{F}_q^{n \times (n-d)}$. A basis of $\mathrm{Ker}\Lambda$ is computed. By computing the row reduced echelon form of $\mathrm{Ker}\Lambda$, T_1', T_2', T_3' in Fig. 5 can be recovered.

In the following, the way to recover an equivalent key T', S' from T_1', T_2', T_3' is demonstrated. Note that it suffices to compute T_4', T_5', T_6' and S_1'. First it is shown that by using T_1', T_2', T_3', a public key with smaller parameters can be constructed. Next, the complexity of the attacks described in Sect. 2.4 for new small public key is estimated. Finally, an attack in the case of $d < v$ is proposed.

Here, a public key with smaller parameters is constructed. In the proposed attack, an equivalent key S', T', as depicted in Fig. 5 is used. Let $\mathcal{F}' : \mathbb{F}_q^n \to \mathbb{F}_q^m$ be the corresponding central map. Let $\hat{F}'^{(k)}$ and $\hat{T}'$ be the lower right $((n - d) \times (n - d))$-matrix of $F'^{(k)}$ and T' respectively. Let $\hat{\mathcal{F}}'$ be the quadratic map $\mathbb{F}_q^{(n-d)} \to \mathbb{F}_q^m$ represented by $\{\hat{F}'^{(k)}\}_k$. Let $\hat{T}'$ be the map $\mathbb{F}_q^{(n-d)} \to \mathbb{F}_q^{(n-d)}$ represented by $\hat{T}'$.

Consider an element $\hat{x} \in \mathbb{F}_q^{(n-d)}$. For this $\hat{x}$, $x' \in \mathbb{F}_q^d$ is defined as $x' = -(T_1', T_2', T_3')\hat{x}$. Let $x \in \mathbb{F}_q^v$ be $(x'^\top, \hat{x}^\top)^\top$. Then, $T'x = (0, \ldots, 0, \hat{x}^\top)^\top$ is derived. Thus, we have $\mathcal{F}' \circ T'(x) = \hat{\mathcal{F}}' \circ \hat{T}'(\hat{x})$. Here, let $\hat{\mathcal{P}} : \mathbb{F}_q^{(n-d)} \to \mathbb{F}_q^m$ be $\hat{\mathcal{P}} := S' \circ \hat{\mathcal{F}}' \circ \hat{T}'$. Then, we have $\mathcal{P}(x) = \hat{\mathcal{P}}(\hat{x})$. Thus, $\hat{\mathcal{P}}$ can be computed using T_1', T_2', T_3' and a public key $\mathcal{P}$. $\hat{\mathcal{P}}$ can be regarded as the public key for parameters $(q, v - d, o_1, o_2)$. Therefore, $(S', \hat{T}')$ is the equivalent key to $\hat{\mathcal{P}}$. Figure 7 shows the equivalent key for $\mathcal{P}$ and the right lower section surrounded by the thick lines represents $\hat{T}'$. Since T_1', T_2', T_3' are revealed, the unknown variables are T_4', T_5', T_6' and S_1'. Thus, it suffices to recover $\hat{T}', S'$, which is an equivalent key to $\hat{\mathcal{P}}$.

Here, the proposed attack in this model $(d < v)$ is outlined. First, the known attacks are applied to $\hat{\mathcal{P}}$. Next, we recover an equivalent key to $\hat{\mathcal{P}}$ (denoted by $S', \hat{\mathcal{F}}', \hat{T}'$). Then, T' can be computed from T_1', T_2', T_3' and $\hat{T}'$. Finally, we recover the equivalent key $S', \mathcal{F}', T'$.

Now, the complexity of the attacks in Sect. 2.4 for smaller public key is estimated. For RBS attack, Shim et al.'s attack, as discussed in Sect. 2.5, is additionally considered.

MinRank Attack. Here, Billet et al.'s algorithm [7] and Bardet et al.'s algorithm [2] are considered. The complexity of Billet et al.'s algorithm is estimated as $o_1 q^{(v-d)+1} m^3$. Bardet et al.'s algorithm considers an instance of MinRank problem with m matrices of size $(n - d)$-by-$(n - d)$ with target rank $(v - d) + o_1$. Thus, as the number of fixed vinegar variables d increases, the size of matrices

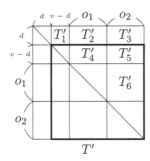 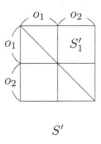

Fig. 7. Equivalent key T', S' $(d < v)$

and target rank decrease. Since the complexity of solving the MinRank problem depends on the number of matrices and the rank, the complexity of solving the MinRank problem is reduced.

HighRank Attack. The complexity is $q^{o_2}(n-d)^3$.

UOV Attack. The complexity is $q^{v-d+o_1-o_2-1}o_2^4$. This is the same result as Hashimoto et al. [12].

RBS Attack. In this case, RBS attack can be applied to $\hat{\mathcal{P}}$ and $(n-d)-1+m$ quadratic equations with $n-d$ variables can be derived. However, Shim et al. [20] have applied RBS attack to $\mathcal{P}$ directly and constructed the Eqs. (6), in which there are $n-1+m$ quadratic equations with $n-d$ variables. Although the number of variables are the same, the Eqs. (6) contains more equations than the case of applying RBS attack to $\hat{\mathcal{P}}$. Therefore, the Eqs. (6) can be solved more efficiently. As a result, the small public key $\hat{\mathcal{P}}$ is not used and RBS attack is applied to $\mathcal{P}$ directly. Further, the complexity of te proposed attack can be estimated as the complexity of solving the Eqs. (6), which is $MQ(q, (v-d)+o_1, o_2, m, (v-d)-1)$.

Intersection Attack. In this case, $2(n-d)$ bilinear equations in x and y, and $3m-2$ quadratic equations in x are obtained. As mentioned in Sect. 2.4, x has $min\{2(n-d)-3o_2, (n-d)-1\}$ unknown variables, and y has o_2 unknown variables. For $d \leq n - 3o_2$, the process is repeated q^{n-d-3o_2+1} times. However, for $d > n - 3o_2 + 1$, the equations are solved once. Therefore, the complexity is $q^{max\{0,(n-d)-3o_2+1\}}MQ(q, min\{2(n-d)-3o_2, (n-d)-1\}, o_2, 3m-2, 2(n-d))$.

Rectangular MinRank Attack. In this case, the MinRank problem where the number of matrices is $(n-d)-o_2+1$ and the number of rows is $(n-d)-1$ is constructed. As the number of fixed vinegar variables d increases, the number of the matrices and the size of the matrices decrease. Since the complexity of solving the MinRank problem depends on the number of matrices and the size, the complexity of solving the MinRank problem is reduced.

Simple Attack, Combined Attack. Simple attack solves $m - 1$ quadratic equations in $(v - d) - 1$ variables. Hence, the complexity of Simple attack is $MQ(q, (v - d) - 1, m - 1)$. Combined attack constructs the MinRank problem where the number of matrices is $v - d$ and the number of rows is $(n - d) - 1$. In addition, the size of UOV map in the first layer is reduced. Thus, the complexity decreases as d increases.

Using the previous results, an attack with fixing some random vinegar values $(d < v)$ is proposed. The attack with the smallest complexity amongst the aforementioned attacks depends on d. Therefore, the proposed attack chooses the optimal attack for each d and recovers an equivalent key with the attack. All the attacks except RBS attack are applied to the small public key $\hat{\mathcal{P}}$ to get an equivalent key for $\hat{\mathcal{P}}$. Subsequently, the equivalent key for $\mathcal{P}$ is recovered with the equivalent key for $\hat{\mathcal{P}}$. If RBS attack is optimal, then an equivalent key for $\mathcal{P}$ is directly recovered using RBS attack.

4   Complexity of the Proposed Attacks

In this section, the complexity of the proposed attacks with the fixing all random vinegar values $(d = v)$ and with the fixing some random vinegar values $(d < v)$ is evaluated.

4.1   Fixing All Random Vinegar Values ($d = v$)

In this section, the complexity of the proposed attack described in Sect. 3.2 is estimated. It is shown that the dominant part of the complexity of our attack is the complexity of solving the linear equations in equivalent key.

The Complexity of Recovering S'. For each $k \in O_1$, $\frac{o_1(o_1+1)}{2}$ Eqs. (9) in $S'_{(k,l)}$ ($l \in O_2$) are solved. Therefore, the total complexity of recovering S' is

$$o_1 \cdot \left(\frac{o_1(o_1 + 1)}{2} o_2^2 \right) = \mathrm{O}(n^5). \tag{11}$$

The Complexity of Recovering T'. For each $j \in O_2$, $o_1(v + o_1)$ Eqs. (10) in $(T'^{-1})_{(j)}$ are solved. Therefore, the total complexity of recovering T' is

$$o_2 \cdot \left(o_1(o_1 + 1) \cdot o_2^2 \right) = \mathrm{O}(n^5). \tag{12}$$

Table 1. Comparison of the complexity of Shim et al.'s attack [20] and the proposed attack (Section 3.2) with fixing all random vinegar values ($d = v$)

attack	complexity
Shim et al. [20]	$MQ(q, o_1, m)$ exponential time
Proposed attack (Section 3.2)	$O(n^5)$ **polynomial time**

The Complexity of Recovering $\mathcal{F}'$. For each $k \in O_1 \bigcup O_2$, let $P'^{(k)}$ be the representation matrix of $(\mathcal{S}'^{-1} \circ \mathcal{P})^{(k)}$. Note that the value of $P'^{(k)}$ is known since S' is known. Then, we have $F'^{(k)} = (T'^{-1})^{\top} P'^{(k)} T'^{-1}$. Therefore, $F'^{(k)}$ can be recovered by computing the products of matrices and its complexity is $O(n^3)$. Therefore, the total complexity of recovering $\mathcal{F}'$ is $O(n^4)$.

Therefore, the total complexity of recovering the equivalent key is $O(n^5)$, and it is a polynomial time algorithm with respect to the number of variables of Rainbow.

Table 1 shows the complexity of Shim et al.'s attack [20] and the proposed attack (Sect. 3.2) in the model of fixing all random vinegar values ($d = v$). Note that the outline of Shim et al.'s attack is described in Sect. 2.5 and it requires exponential time. Therefore, the proposed polynomial-time attack is more efficient than Shim et al.'s attack in terms of the complexity theory.

4.2 Fixing Some Random Vinegar Values ($d < v$)

In this section, the complexity of the proposed attack in the case of fixing some random vinegar values ($d < v$) is estimated. First, the complexity of the attacks mentioned in Sect. 3.3 is compared. The complexity for the SL5 parameters $(q, v, o_1, o_2) = (256, 96, 36, 64)$ is estimated. As previously mentioned, these parameters satisfy only 192 bit security. Figure 8 shows the complexity for each $d \in \{1, \ldots, 95\}$. The horizontal axis in Fig. 8 refers to the number of fixed vinegar values, and the vertical axis in Fig. 8 refers to the logarithm of the complexity. When estimating the complexity of MinRank attack, the smaller of the complexity of Billet et al.'s and Bardet et al.'s algorithms is selected. This graph shows that for $d \leq 8$, the complexity of Combined attack is the smallest; for $9 \leq d \leq 63$ and $d \geq 89$, the complexity of Simple attack is the smallest; and for $64 \leq d \leq 88$, the complexity of UOV attack is the smallest.

The proposed attack for the SL5 parameters $(q, v, o_1, o_2) = (256, 96, 36, 64)$ proceeds as follows. For $d \leq 8$, Combined attack is applied to $\hat{\mathcal{P}}$. For $9 \leq d \leq 63$ and $d \geq 89$, Simple attack is applied to $\hat{\mathcal{P}}$. For $64 \leq d \leq 88$, an equivalent key for $\hat{\mathcal{P}}$ is computed with UOV attack. Subsequently, an equivalent key for $\mathcal{P}$ is recovered.

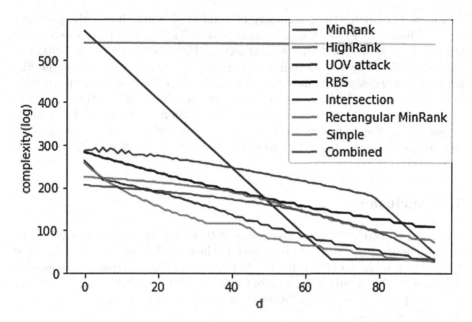

Fig. 8. Comparison of the complexity of eight attacks in Section 3.3 with fixing some random vinegar values $(d < v)$ for SL5 parameters of Rainbow $(v = 96)$

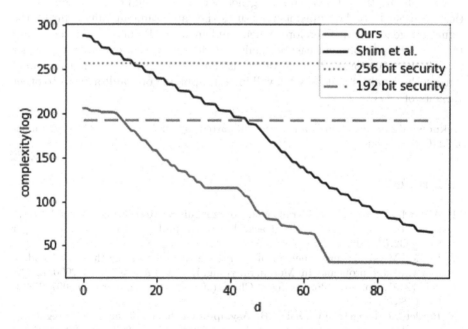

Fig. 9. Comparison of the complexity of Shim et al.'s attack [20] and the proposed attack (Section 3.3) with fixing some random vinegar values $(d < v)$ for SL5 parameters of Rainbow $(v = 96)$

Figure 9 compares the complexity of Shim et al.'s attack and the proposed attack. Similar to Fig. 8, the horizontal axis in Fig. 9 refers to the number of fixed vinegar values, and the vertical axis in Fig. 9 refers to the logarithm of the complexity. The gray dotted line represents the security level that the SL5 parameters are designed to have, and the gray broken line represents the security level considered for Beullens' attacks. It is confirmed in Fig. 9 that the complexity of the proposed attack is smaller than that of Shim et al.'s attack for all d. In particular, the complexity differs by approximately 2^{80} times for the SL5 parameters. In conclusion, the proposed attack is more efficient than Shim et al.'s attack.

5   Conclusion

In this paper, two fault attacks on Rainbow by fixing the random vinegar values in the signature generation are proposed. In the case of fixing all random vinegar values, the proposed attack is feasible in polynomial time in terms of the number of variables. When only some random vinegar values are fixed, the complexity of the proposed attack is significantly smaller than that of the previously most efficient Shim et al.'s attack.

From these results, it is concluded that Rainbow is less resistant to fault attacks than previously expected. The proposed fault attack model can be triggered by fixing the random number generator, which could cause in some practical cases such as the implementer reuses the same random values during the signature generation. Therefore, when implementing Rainbow, it is necessary to take sufficient countermeasures against fault attacks. For example, the signer records the values of the random values used in the past several signings to aboid reusing these values. Future work will include applying our fault attacks to other variants of UOV.

Acknowledgement. This work was supported by JST CREST Grant Number JPMJCR2113, Japan.

References

1. Aulbach, T., Kovats, T., Krämer, J., Marzougui, S.: Recovering rainbow's secret key with a first-order fault attack. IACR Cryptology ePrint Archive, Paper 2022/632 (2022)
2. Bardet, M., et al.: Improvements of algebraic attacks for solving the rank decoding and MinRank problems. In: Moriai, S., Wang, H. (eds.) ASIACRYPT 2020. LNCS, vol. 12491, pp. 507–536. Springer, Cham (2020). https://doi.org/10.1007/978-3-030-64837-4_17
3. Bardet, M., Faugère, J.C., Salvy, B.: Asymptotic behavior of the index of regularity of quadratic semi-regular polynomial systems. In: MEGA 2005–8th International Symposium on Effective Methods in Algebraic Geometry, pp. 1–17 (2005)
4. Bettale, L., Faugère, J.C., Perret, L.: Hybrid approach for solving multivariate systems over finite fields. J. Math. Cryptol. **3**, 177–197 (2009)

5. Beullens, W.: Improved cryptanalysis of UOV and rainbow. In: Canteaut, A., Standaert, F.-X. (eds.) EUROCRYPT 2021. LNCS, vol. 12696, pp. 348–373. Springer, Cham (2021). https://doi.org/10.1007/978-3-030-77870-5_13

6. Beullens, W.: Breaking rainbow takes a weekend on a laptop. IACR Cryptology ePrint Archive, Report 2022/214 (2022)

7. Billet, O., Gilbert, H.: Cryptanalysis of rainbow. In: De Prisco, R., Yung, M. (eds.) SCN 2006. LNCS, vol. 4116, pp. 336–347. Springer, Heidelberg (2006). https://doi.org/10.1007/11832072_23

8. Coppersmith, D., Stern, J., Vaudenay, S.: Attacks on the birational permutation signature schemes. In: Stinson, D.R. (ed.) CRYPTO 1993. LNCS, vol. 773, pp. 435–443. Springer, Heidelberg (1994). https://doi.org/10.1007/3-540-48329-2_37

9. Courtois, N., Klimov, A., Patarin, J., Shamir, A.: Efficient algorithms for solving overdefined systems of multivariate polynomial equations. In: Preneel, B. (ed.) EUROCRYPT 2000. LNCS, vol. 1807, pp. 392–407. Springer, Heidelberg (2000). https://doi.org/10.1007/3-540-45539-6_27

10. Ding, J., Schmidt, D.: Rainbow, a new multivariable polynomial signature scheme. In: Ioannidis, J., Keromytis, A., Yung, M. (eds.) ACNS 2005. LNCS, vol. 3531, pp. 164–175. Springer, Heidelberg (2005). https://doi.org/10.1007/11496137_12

11. Ding, J., Yang, B.-Y., Chen, C.-H.O., Chen, M.-S., Cheng, C.-M.: New differential-algebraic attacks and reparametrization of rainbow. In: Bellovin, S.M., Gennaro, R., Keromytis, A., Yung, M. (eds.) ACNS 2008. LNCS, vol. 5037, pp. 242–257. Springer, Heidelberg (2008). https://doi.org/10.1007/978-3-540-68914-0_15

12. Hashimoto, Y., Takagi, T., Sakurai, K.: General fault attacks on multivariate public key cryptosystems. In: Yang, B.-Y. (ed.) PQCrypto 2011. LNCS, vol. 7071, pp. 1–18. Springer, Heidelberg (2011). https://doi.org/10.1007/978-3-642-25405-5_1

13. Kipnis, A., Patarin, J., Goubin, L.: Unbalanced oil and vinegar signature schemes. In: Stern, J. (ed.) EUROCRYPT 1999. LNCS, vol. 1592, pp. 206–222. Springer, Heidelberg (1999). https://doi.org/10.1007/3-540-48910-X_15

14. Kipnis, A., Shamir, A.: Cryptanalysis of the oil and vinegar signature scheme. In: Krawczyk, H. (ed.) CRYPTO 1998. LNCS, vol. 1462, pp. 257–266. Springer, Heidelberg (1998). https://doi.org/10.1007/BFb0055733

15. Koblitz, N.: Elliptic curve cryptosystems. Math. Comput. **48**, 203–209 (1987)

16. Krämer, J., Loiero, M.: Fault attacks on UOV and rainbow. In: Polian, I., Stöttinger, M. (eds.) COSADE 2019. LNCS, vol. 11421, pp. 193–214. Springer, Cham (2019). https://doi.org/10.1007/978-3-030-16350-1_11

17. Miller, V.S.: Use of elliptic curves in cryptography. In: Williams, H.C. (ed.) CRYPTO 1985. LNCS, vol. 218, pp. 417–426. Springer, Heidelberg (1986). https://doi.org/10.1007/3-540-39799-X_31

18. Perlner, R., Smith-Tone, D.: Rainbow band separation is better than we thought. IACR Cryptology ePrint Archive, Report 2020/702 (2020)

19. Rivest, R.L., Shamir, A., Adleman, L.: A method for obtaining digital signatures and public-key cryptosystems. Commun. ACM **21**, 120–126 (1978)

20. Shim, K.A., Koo, N.: Algebraic fault analysis of UOV and rainbow with the leakage of random vinegar values. IEEE Trans. Inf. Forensics Secur. **15**, 2429–2439 (2020)

21. Shor, P.W.: Polynomial-time algorithms for prime factorization and discrete logarithms on a quantum computer. SIAM J. Comput. **26**, 1484–1509 (1997)

Quantum-Resistant 1-out-of-N Oblivious Signatures from Lattices

Jing-Shiuan You[1,2], Zi-Yuan Liu[1,2], Raylin Tso[1(✉)], Yi-Fan Tseng[1], and Masahiro Mambo[2]

[1] National Chengchi University, Taipei 11605, Taiwan
{zyliu,raylin,yftseng}@cs.nccu.edu.tw
[2] Kanazawa University, Kanazawa 920-1192, Japan
mambo@ec.t.kanazawa-u.ac.jp

Abstract. As business activities and information exchange increasingly move online, digital signatures, among other cryptographic techniques, have been developed to help authenticate the source and integrity of digital information when transferred. Various types of signature primitives, such as ring signatures and blind signatures, have been introduced to satisfy privacy protection needs spanning from ensuring anonymity of a signer to maintaining secrecy of the content to be signed from a signer. Among different signature schemes, the 1-out-of-N oblivious signature scheme, which was introduced by Chen (ESORICS' 94) and later formalized by Tso *et al.* (ISPEC' 08), provides a further basis of trust while preserving the signature requestor's privacy as blind signatures do. In this scheme, a recipient first selects a set of messages, one of which being the message he or she intends to obtain a signature for. After interacting with a signer, while the recipient will be able to obtain a signature on the predetermined message, the signer only knows that he or she signed one of the messages but remains oblivious to exactly which message was signed. However, all existing oblivious signature schemes are built upon the hardness of number-theoretic problems, which, as Shor demonstrated in 1994, cannot withstand attacks from quantum adversaries. To address this problem, this work proposes a novel quantum-resistant 1-out-of-N oblivious signature scheme based on SIS hard assumption. We also provide security proofs to demonstrate that the security requirements of ambiguity and strong unforgeability are satisfied under the random oracle model. To the best of our knowledge, the proposed scheme is the first 1-out-of-N oblivious signature that is secure against quantum adversaries.

Keywords: 1-out-of-N · Lattices · Oblivious signatures · Quantum-resistant

---

J.-S. You and Z.-Y. Liu—Equal contributions.

1 Introduction

The increasing sophistication of computing and the Internet has been transformative for many. For example, online search [18], social media [32,38], remote medical diagnosis [8,20], and even online voting (e-voting) [17,23,24] have replaced their conventional offline counterparts. Despite its many benefits, information technology has also created privacy and security challenges. In online transactions and digital contracts, a cryptographic technique called digital signatures is often adopted to guarantee the legality and authenticity of contracts [16]. In general, a digital signature scheme must meet the following basic characteristics: integrity, unforgeability, and public verifiability. On top of these criteria, signature schemes are designed to meet specific privacy protection needs in different use scenarios. For instance, if the identity of the signer must be hidden from the user, a group signature [10] or ring signature [31] can be implemented. A ring signature scheme has N signers forming a ring. When a signer in the ring receives a message to be signed, the signer can generate a ring signature with his or her secret key. A verifier can validate the signature with all public keys of the ring but will not be able to identify the signer. Group signatures are similar to ring signatures, with the main difference being the existence of a group manager, who is in charge of adding group members and has the ability to reveal the original signer's identity in the event of disputes. In addition, to further ensure the signer's anonymity, blind signatures [9] can be used when the recipient does not want to disclose to the signer the content of the message to be signed. The blind signature scheme allows a user to obtain a signature on a chosen message by interacting with the signer while keeping the actual content of the message concealed from the signer. At the end of the signature generation, the signer has never seen the message, and neither will he or she (or a verifier) be able to link the blinded message to its unblinded version based on information from the interactions between the signer and the user, thus granting user anonymity.

As far as user privacy is concerned, as in the above case of blind signatures, here we consider two more privacy protection needs on the user end. In cases where multiple signers are available, a user may hope to obtain a signature from a specific signer without disclosing which signer has been selected. That is, exactly which signer the user intends to request a signature from is sensitive information. This privacy need may occur, for example, in the case of getting access to sensitive databases, where a user hopes to access one of the multiple databases, each assigned to an administrator but intends to keep secret which database will be accessed. In other cases, a user may wish to get a signature for a specific item but does not want the signer to know which item he or she will be granting a signature on. This can apply in the example of a software permit purchase, where the buyer needs to obtain a certificate (a signature) from the software provider for legal use but prefers not to disclose to the seller which software item he or she is requesting a permit for.

To address these privacy protection requirements, Chen introduced the concept of oblivious signatures in 1994 [11]. Chen proposed two classes of oblivious signature schemes: one with N keys, and another with N messages. In the scheme with N keys, the signature is generated by a recipient $\mathcal{R}$ interacting with a group of possible signers $\mathcal{S}_1, \mathcal{S}_2, \cdots, \mathcal{S}_N$ (or a signer with N different keys). $\mathcal{R}$ sends a message to $\mathcal{S}$ which is then signed with one of the N keys. The signer's key is denoted as the accepted key. None of the possible $\mathcal{S}$ can know which key was used to sign the message. Furthermore, $\mathcal{R}$ can prove that he or she has obtained a signature with one of N keys without disclosing which key was used. In the scheme with N messages, $\mathcal{S}$ receives N messages from $\mathcal{R}$ where the recipient needs only one signature on one specific message among the N messages. During the signing process, $\mathcal{S}$ can read the content of all of the N messages but remains oblivious to which message he or she will be signing. Similar to the case with N keys, $\mathcal{R}$ can reveal that he or she has obtained a signature on one of these N messages without divulging which message was signed. This scheme can preserve recipient privacy in applications such as online shopping. For example, a recipient could choose N products but have only one of them signed by $\mathcal{S}$ without revealing the chosen product.

The merit of oblivious signatures stands out when we compare them with blind signatures. A key disadvantage of blind signatures is that the signer has absolutely no idea what message he or she is signing and thus risks providing a signature to information they may disapprove of. In contrast, the oblivious signature scheme allows the signer to view the content of all messages in the message set, providing a further basis of trust but still preserving the signature requestor's privacy as blind signatures do. Intuitively, one may think that the oblivious nature of an oblivious signature can be created using a blind signature scheme. That is, the recipient can request a blind signature on his or her preprocessed message (a so-called blinded message) accompanied with N messages to the signer, and claim that the content of the blinded message is the same as that of one of N messages. With this setup, the signer does have access to what information he or she is potentially signing. However, there is a security flaw. The signer is solely relying on a claim made by the recipient and has no way to verify whether the blinded message he or she signed indeed related to the N messages. Thus this setup is less reliable and potentially problematic.

Another option one may contemplate as an alternative that achieves the purposes of an oblivious signature scheme would be a general signature scheme that uses 1-out-of-N oblivious transfer [12, 29] to send back signatures generated by the signer. To elaborate, the recipient can request the signer to sign a set of messages and use a 1-out-of-N oblivious transfer to obtain a specific indexed signature without sharing the index number with the signer. Nevertheless, this alternative can be vulnerable to attacks by malicious signers. The malicious signer can generate N signatures on the same message belonging to the message set. If the signed message is not the one the recipient intends to obtain a signature for, naturally, the recipient would initiate the signature request process again to get the right signature. Thus by trying out one message at a time, until the signed message is the one preselected by the recipient, at which point the recipient will cease to initiate a new signature request process, the malicious signer will be able to identify which message is chosen by the recipient. In this case, the alternative setup fails to satisfy the oblivious property, which is the essential privacy premise an oblivious signature scheme offers.

1.1 Motivation and Contribution

To take into account the desired purposes and the security of the oblivious signature, Tso *et al.* [37] introduces a notion called "1-out-of-N oblivious signature scheme." Here, "1-out-of-N" indicates that the recipient either intends to obtain a signature for a specific message in his or her own preselected message set or intends to obtain a signature from a specific signer out of all possible signers. Tso *et al.* also formalized the security models of the scheme and proposed a more efficient 1-out-of-N oblivious signature scheme. Their scheme achieves a smaller signature size and its security is based on the discrete logarithm assumption, providing ground for further research and application. In addition, for special circumstances where both the message and the identity of the signer are sensitive, Tso [35,36] proposed a two-in-one system that combined two types of oblivious signature schemes into a single scheme. All existing oblivious signature schemes were introduced at an earlier time, and their securities are based on the hardness of number-theoretic problems. However, as early as 1994, Shor [33] introduced a quantum algorithm capable of solving the discrete logarithm problems in polynomial time, posing a major challenge to cryptographic schemes based on discrete logarithm problems, including the existing oblivious signature schemes. When quantum computers mature, oblivious signature schemes currently available will be broken. Several types of the quantum-resistant signature schemes based on lattices [15,27], isogeny [7,13], codes [5,34], and hash [6,21] assumptions have been introduced, but how to construct a quantum-resistant 1-out-of-N oblivious signature scheme remains an open problem.

Aiming to provide a solution, in this paper, we propose a novel 1-out-of-N oblivious signature scheme from lattices. The proposed scheme is inspired by Lyubashevsky's lattice-based signature [26], which has well-proven security and has been the basis for several extensions. We also present security proofs to demonstrate that the proposed scheme has strong unforgeability and ambiguity under random oracle. As its security proofs rely on the lattice-based hard assumption—short integer solution (SIS) [1], the proposed scheme is considered quantum-resistant. Furthermore, the theoretical comparison and efficiency analysis are provided to indicate the proposed scheme can be more secure when the execution time is reasonable.

1.2 Organization

This paper is organized as follows: Sect. 2 presents the notation used in this paper and background regarding the techniques used in the construction and security proofs. Section 3 defines the system model and security model of 1-out-of-N obvious signature scheme. Section 4 describes the proposed 1-out-of-N oblivious signature scheme using lattices. Section 5 presents the security proofs of the proposed scheme, including strong unforgeability and ambiguity. Section 6 provides a theoretical comparison and efficiency analysis of the proposed scheme. Section 7 summarizes the outcomes and provides directions for future work.

2 Preliminaries

2.1 Notation

For a positive integer N, a set $\{1, 2, \cdots, N\}$ is denoted by $[N]$. Let q be a prime; then, elements in $\mathbb{Z}_q$ denote integers in the range $[-\frac{q-1}{2}, \frac{q-1}{2}]$. When handling elements in $\mathbb{Z}_q$, all operations are performed modulo q. The notations $\mathcal{O}$ and ω are used to indicate the order (growth rate) of functions; for example, $f(n) = \mathcal{O}(g(n))$ if positive constants c and n_0 exist such that $0 \le f(n) \le cg(n)$ for all $n \ge n_0$, and $f(n) = \omega(g(n))$ if positive constants c and n_0 exist such that $0 \le cg(n) < f(n)$ for all $n \ge n_0$, where f, g are polynomial functions of n. For some n, $negl(n)$ is refereed as to the negligible function of n, and $1 - negl(n)$ means that a probability is overwhelming. Vectors and matrices are denoted by bold letters and bold capital letters, respectively. In addition, we presume all the vectors are column vectors, and $\|\mathbf{v}\|$ is defined as the ℓ_2 norm of the vector $\mathbf{v}$. The transpose of the vector $\mathbf{v}$ is denoted by $\mathbf{v}^\top$, and $[\mathbf{A}|\mathbf{B}] \in \mathbb{Z}^{m \times (n+k)}$ denotes the concatenation of matrices $\mathbf{A} \in \mathbb{Z}^{m \times n}$ and $\mathbf{B} \in \mathbb{Z}^{m \times k}$. For an element x and some distribution D, the notion $x \xleftarrow{\$} D$ indicates that x is randomly picked in accordance with D.

2.2 Lattices and the SIS Problem

Definition 1 (Lattices). *Let* $\mathbf{b}_1, \ldots, \mathbf{b}_n$ *be* n *linearly independent vectors in* $\mathbb{R}^n$. *An* n-*dimensional lattice* $\Lambda(\mathbf{B})$ *produced by a matrix* $\mathbf{B} = [\mathbf{b}_1, \cdots, \mathbf{b}_n]$ *is defined as:*

$$\Lambda(\mathbf{B}) := \left\{ \sum_{i=1}^{n} c_i \mathbf{b}_i \mid c_i \in \mathbb{Z} \right\}.$$

Here, the matrix $\mathbf{B}$ *is called the basis of lattice* $\Lambda(\mathbf{B})$.

In this paper, we only premeditate integer lattices, which means that for each entry of each vector $\mathbf{b}_i$ is in $\mathbb{Z}_q$.

Definition 2 (q-ary Lattices). *Given an integer* $q \ge 2$ *(q is often required to be a large prime), a positive integer* n, *and a matrix* $\mathbf{A} \in \mathbb{Z}_q^{n \times m}$, *we define three sets as follows:*

$$\Lambda_q(\mathbf{A}) := \{\mathbf{y} \in \mathbb{Z}^m \mid \mathbf{y} = \mathbf{A}^\top \mathbf{x} \bmod q, \text{ for some } \mathbf{x} \in \mathbb{Z}^n\};$$
$$\Lambda_q^\perp(\mathbf{A}) := \{\mathbf{y} \in \mathbb{Z}^m \mid \mathbf{A}\mathbf{y} = 0 \bmod q\};$$
$$\Lambda_q^\mathbf{u}(\mathbf{A}) := \{\mathbf{y} \in \mathbb{Z}^m \mid \mathbf{A}\mathbf{y} = \mathbf{u} \bmod q, \text{ for some } \mathbf{u} \in \mathbb{Z}_q^n\}.$$

We say that $\Lambda_q^\mathbf{u}(\mathbf{A})$ *is a coset of* $\Lambda_q^\perp(\mathbf{A})$. *If there is a vector* $\mathbf{t} \in \mathbb{Z}^m$ *such that* $\mathbf{A}\mathbf{t} = \mathbf{u}$, *then* $\Lambda_q^\mathbf{u}(\mathbf{A}) = \Lambda_q^\perp(\mathbf{A}) + \mathbf{t}$.

Definition 3 ($SIS_{q,n,m,\beta}$ Problem [26]**).** *Given a random matrix $\mathbf{A} \in \mathbb{Z}_q^{n \times m}$, the $SIS_{q,n,m,\beta}$ problem is to find out a non-trivial short vector $\mathbf{v} \in \mathbb{Z}^m$ such that $\mathbf{Av} = 0 \bmod q$ and $\|\mathbf{v}\| \leq \beta^1$.*

Definition 4 ($SIS_{q,n,m,d}$ Distribution [26]**).** *Choose a random matrix $\mathbf{A} \xleftarrow{\$} \mathbb{Z}_q^{n \times m}$ and a vector $\mathbf{s} \xleftarrow{\$} \{-d, \cdots, d\}^m$ and output $(\mathbf{A}, \mathbf{t})$, where $\mathbf{t} = \mathbf{As}$.*

Definition 5 ($SIS_{q,n,m,d}$ Search Problem [26]**).** *Given a pair $(\mathbf{A}, \mathbf{t})$ from the $SIS_{q,n,m,d}$ distribution, find a $\mathbf{s} \in \{-d, \cdots, d\}^m$ such that $\mathbf{As} = \mathbf{t}$.*

Definition 6 ($SIS_{q,n,m,d}$ Decision Problem [26]**).** *Given a pair $(\mathbf{A}, \mathbf{t})$ from the $SIS_{q,n,m,d}$ distribution, decide whether it came from the $SIS_{q,n,m,d}$ distribution or it was generated uniformly at random from $\mathbb{Z}_q^{n \times m} \times \mathbb{Z}_q^n$ with non-negligible advantage.*

Theorem 1 ([22,28]**).** *If d is polynomial in n, then there is a polynomial-time reduction from the $SIS_{q,n,m,d}$ search problem to the $SIS_{q,n,m,d}$ decision problem.*

Theorem 2 ([26]**).** *If $m = 2n$ and $4d\beta\sqrt{m} \leq q$, then there is a polynomial-time reduction from solving the $SIS_{q,n,m,d}$ decision problem to the $SIS_{q,n,m,\beta}$ problem.*

2.3   The Normal Distribution and Rejection Sampling

Definition 7 (Continuous Normal Distribution). *We define the function $\rho_{\mathbf{u},\sigma}^m(\mathbf{x}) = \left(\frac{1}{\sqrt{2\pi\sigma^2}}\right)^m e^{\frac{-\|\mathbf{x}-\mathbf{u}\|^2}{2\sigma^2}}$ as the continuous normal distribution over $\mathbb{R}^m$ centered at $\mathbf{u}$ with standard deviation σ. Here we note that we omit $\mathbf{u}$ (i.e., $\rho_\sigma^m(\mathbf{x})$) when $\mathbf{u} = 0$.*

Definition 8 (Discrete Normal Distribution). *We define the function $D_{\mathbf{u},\sigma}^m(\mathbf{x}) = \rho_{\mathbf{u},\sigma}^m(\mathbf{x})/\rho_\sigma^m(\mathbb{Z}^m)$ as the discrete normal distribution over $\mathbb{Z}^m$ centered at $\mathbf{u} \in \mathbb{Z}^m$ with standard deviation σ, where $\rho_{\mathbf{u},\sigma}^m(\mathbb{Z}^m) = \sum_{\mathbf{z} \in \mathbb{Z}^m} \rho_\sigma^m(\mathbf{z})$.*

Lemma 1 ([2,26]**).** *For any vector $\mathbf{v} \in \mathbb{R}^m$ and any $\sigma, r > 0$, $\Pr[|\langle \mathbf{x}, \mathbf{v} \rangle| > r \mid \mathbf{x} \xleftarrow{\$} D_\sigma^m] \leq 2e^{-\frac{r^2}{2\|\mathbf{v}\|^2\sigma^2}}$. We have properties as following:*

1. *For any $\eta > 0$, $\Pr[|x| > \eta\sigma \mid x \xleftarrow{\$} D_\sigma^1] \leq 2e^{\frac{-\eta^2}{2}}$;*
2. *For any $\mathbf{x} \in \mathbb{Z}^m$ and $\sigma \geq 3/\sqrt{2\pi}$, $D_\sigma^m(\mathbf{x}) \leq 2^{-m}$;*
3. *For any $\eta > 1$, $\Pr[\|\mathbf{x}\| > \eta\sigma\sqrt{m} \mid \mathbf{x} \xleftarrow{\$} D_\sigma^m] \leq \eta^m e^{\frac{m}{2}(1-\eta^2)}$.*

Rejection sampling, introduced by Lyubashevsky in [26], is used to prove the indistinguishability of two distributions of two different signatures from different secret keys. The main idea is to "reject" some elements of a distribution depending on the related secret. The following theorem expresses this idea.

---

[1] The solution $\mathbf{v}$ exists only when $\beta \geq \sqrt{m}q^{n/m}$.

172   J.-S. You et al.

Theorem 3 ([26]). *Let V be a subset of $\mathbb{Z}^m$ with that the norms of all items in V are less than T, and $\mathsf{H} : V \to \mathbb{R}$ be a probability distribution. Set $\sigma \in \mathbb{R}$ such that $\sigma = \omega(T\sqrt{\log m})$. Then there exists a constant $M = \mathcal{O}(1)$ such that the statistical distance between the distribution of the output of Algorithm 1 and the distribution of the output of Algorithm 2 is within $\frac{2^{-\omega(\log m)}}{M}$. In addition, with at least probability $\frac{1-2^{-\omega(\log m)}}{M}$, Algorithm 1 can output something. More precisely, for any positive α, if $\sigma = \alpha T$, namely $M = e^{12/\alpha+1/(2\alpha^2)}$, then the probability that Algorithm 1 outputs a result within a statistical distance $\frac{2^{-100}}{M}$ of output of Algorithm 2 is at least $\frac{1-2^{-100}}{M}$.*

Algorithm 1

1 : $\mathbf{v} \xleftarrow{\$} \mathsf{H}$

2 : $\mathbf{x} \xleftarrow{\$} D_{\mathbf{v},\sigma}^m$

3 : output $(\mathbf{x}, \mathbf{v})$ with probability $\min\left(\dfrac{D_\sigma^m(\mathbf{x})}{MD_{\mathbf{v},\sigma}^m(\mathbf{x})}, 1\right)$

Algorithm 2

1 : $\mathbf{v} \xleftarrow{\$} \mathsf{H}$

2 : $\mathbf{x} \xleftarrow{\$} D_\sigma^m$

3 : output $(\mathbf{x}, \mathbf{v})$ with probability $1/M$

2.4 Forking Lemma

The forking lemma was developed in [30], and formalized in [4]. It is utilized to prove the unforgeability of numerous signature schemes [3,15,19,26].

Definition 9 (Forking Lemma [4]). *Set an integer $t \geq 1$ and let H be a set with a size larger than 2. Let $\mathcal{A}$ be a randomized algorithm that takes a tuple of input $(x, h_1, \cdots, h_t)$ and returns a pair in which the first element is an integer in the range $\{0, \cdots, t\}$ while the other referred as a side output. Let $\mathcal{G}$ be a randomized algorithm termed input generator. Then, the accepting probability ζ of $\mathcal{A}$ is defined as the probability that $k \geq 1$ in the following experiment $\mathcal{E}_{FL}$. In addition, there is a randomized algorithm termed forking algorithm $\mathcal{F}_\mathcal{A}$ associated to $\mathcal{A}$. Then, let $\eta = \Pr[b = 1 \mid x \xleftarrow{\$} \mathcal{G}; (b, \mathsf{out}, \mathsf{out}') \leftarrow \mathcal{F}_\mathcal{A}(x)]$, we have $\eta \geq \zeta\left(\frac{\zeta}{t} - \frac{1}{|H|}\right)$. Alternatively, we have $\zeta \leq \frac{t}{|H|} + \sqrt{t \cdot \eta}$.*

Experiment $\mathcal{E}_{FL}$	Algorithm $\mathcal{F}_{\mathcal{A}}(x)$
1 : $x \xleftarrow{\$} \mathcal{G}$	1 : Picks coin ϕ for $\mathcal{A}$ at random
2 : $h_1, \cdots, h_t \xleftarrow{\$} H$	2 : $h_1, \cdots, h_t \xleftarrow{\$} H$
3 : $(k, \mathsf{out}) \xleftarrow{\$} \mathcal{A}(x, h_1, \cdots, h_t)$	3 : $(k, \mathsf{out}) \xleftarrow{\$} \mathcal{A}(x, h_1, \cdots, h_t; \phi)$
	4 : If $k = 0$, then returns $(0,0,0)$
	5 : $h'_k, \cdots, h'_t \xleftarrow{\$} H$
	6 : $(k', \mathsf{out}') \xleftarrow{\$} \mathcal{A}(x, h_1, \cdots, h_{k-1}, h'_k, \cdots, h'_t; \phi)$
	7 : If $k' = 0$, then returns $(0,0,0)$
	8 : If $(k = k'$ & $h_k \neq h'_k)$, then returns $(1, \mathsf{out}, \mathsf{out}')$
	9 : Else, returns $(0,0,0)$

3   1-out-of-N Oblivious Signature

In this section, we recall the definition and security models of the 1-out-of-N oblivious signature defined by Tso *et al.* [37].

3.1   Definition

A 1-out-of-N oblivious signature $\mathcal{OS}_1^N$ scheme has three participants: a signer $\mathcal{S}$, a recipient $\mathcal{R}$, and a verifier $\mathcal{V}$. Informally, $\mathcal{R}$ first selects a group of messages $\mathcal{M} = \{m_1, \cdots, m_N\}$, sets an index ℓ, and states that he or she wants to obtain a signature for message m_ℓ. For these messages, $\mathcal{S}$ generates corresponding "semi-signatures," and sends them to $\mathcal{R}$. Finally, $\mathcal{R}$ can convert these semi-signatures to a final result—a signature Σ for message m_ℓ. $\mathcal{S}$ cannot obtain any information regarding which signed message $\mathcal{R}$ obtains, and $\mathcal{R}$ can only obtain a signature for the chosen message m_ℓ. Moreover, any verifier $\mathcal{V}$ can use public information to verify the validity of the signature.

Formally, an $\mathcal{OS}_1^N$ comprises four algorithms $(\mathcal{G}, \mathsf{Sign}\text{-}\mathcal{S}, \mathsf{Sign}\text{-}\mathcal{R}, \mathcal{V})$, where $\mathcal{G}$ is a probabilistic polynomial-time algorithm, $\mathsf{Sign}\text{-}\mathcal{R}$ and $\mathsf{Sign}\text{-}\mathcal{S}$ are interactive Turing machines, and $\mathcal{V}$ is a deterministic polynomial-time algorithm. Each algorithm is defined as follows.

- $(pk, sk) \leftarrow \mathcal{G}(1^\lambda)$: Taking a security parameter λ as input, $\mathcal{G}$ outputs a key pair (pk, sk) for signer $\mathcal{S}$, where pk is the public key and sk is the secret key.
- $(\mathsf{completed}/\mathsf{notcompleted}, \Sigma/\bot) \leftarrow \langle \mathsf{Sign}\text{-}\mathcal{S}(pk, sk, \mathcal{M}), \mathsf{Sign}\text{-}\mathcal{R}(pk, m_\ell) \rangle$: This is an interactive signing protocol between $\mathcal{S}$ and $\mathcal{R}$ that uses the $\mathsf{Sign}\text{-}\mathcal{S}$ and $\mathsf{Sign}\text{-}\mathcal{R}$ algorithms, respectively. $\mathcal{S}$ takes the key pair (pk, sk), and the preselected N-message set $\mathcal{M} = \{m_1, \ldots, m_\ell, \cdots, m_N\}$ as inputs; $\mathcal{R}$ takes the public key pk, and one message $m_\ell \in \mathcal{M}$ as inputs. After a polynomial number of rounds of interactions through the protocol, $\mathcal{S}$ outputs $\mathsf{completed}$ or $\mathsf{notcompleted}$ and $\mathcal{R}$ outputs a valid signature Σ or an error $\bot$.

- $1/0 \leftarrow \mathcal{V}(pk, m_\ell, \Sigma)$: Taking the public key pk of signer $\mathcal{S}$, a message m_ℓ, and the signature Σ as inputs, $\mathcal{V}$ returns 1 if Σ is accepted, and 0 otherwise.

Completeness. After $\mathcal{S}$ and $\mathcal{R}$ have appropriately executed the signing protocol, we say that an $\mathcal{OS}_1^N$ scheme is complete if $\mathcal{S}$ outputs completed and $\mathcal{R}$ outputs a signature Σ with probability at least $1 - negl(\lambda)$ such that $\mathcal{V}(pk, m_\ell, \Sigma) = 1$ holds. The probability is obtained based on coin flips for $\mathcal{G}$, Sign-$\mathcal{S}$, and Sign-$\mathcal{R}$.

3.2   Securities Models

Here, we define the two required security properties and the corresponding security models for the $\mathcal{OS}_1^N$ scheme—strong unforgeability and ambiguity.

Strong Unforgeability. This security property ensures that a malicious recipient $\mathcal{R}^*$ cannot forge any new signature, even after obtaining several signatures generated through interacting with the signer $\mathcal{S}$. To model this security property, we define the following strong unforgeability game interacting between a challenger and an adversary (*i.e.*, $\mathcal{R}^*$). In this game, Sign-$\mathcal{R}^*$ is a probabilistic polynomial-time forging algorithm in the interactive signing protocol executed by $\mathcal{R}^*$, which aims to forge a new signature Σ^* on any message m^*.

Game - Strong Unforgeability
- **Initialization.** The challenger first runs $(pk, sk) \leftarrow \mathcal{G}(1^\lambda)$ and then sends pk to the adversary.
- **Query.** The adversary can adaptively choose a message set $\mathcal{M}_i = \{m_{i,1}, \cdots, m_{i,N}\}$ and a target message $m_{i,j} \in \mathcal{M}_i$. Then, Sign-$\mathcal{R}^*$ is executed during in the interactive signing protocol with the challenger. (The adversary can execute this step for an arbitrary polynomial-number of times and can decide when to stop). After the challenger outputs completed, the adversary can obtain a final valid signature Σ_i for the message $m_{i,j} \in \mathcal{M}_i$.
- **Forgery.** Finally, the adversary outputs a new signature Σ^* on any message m^*.

Definition 10 (Strong Unforgeability). *We say that an $\mathcal{OS}_1^N$ scheme satisfies strong unforgeability if, for any probabilistic polynomial-time adversary playing the strong unforgeability game, $\Pr[\mathcal{V}(pk, m^*, \Sigma^*) = 1] < negl(n)$ holds.*

Ambiguity. This security property ensures that a malicious signer $\mathcal{S}^*$ cannot distinguish which message that recipient $\mathcal{R}$ wanted to be signed. To model this security property, we define the following ambiguity game between a challenger and an adversary (*i.e.*, $\mathcal{S}^*$). In this game, Sign-$\mathcal{S}^*$ is a probabilistic polynomial-time distinguishing algorithm in the interactive signing protocol executed by $\mathcal{S}^*$, which aims to distinguish which message was signed.

Game - Ambiguity

- **Initialization.** The challenger first runs $(pk, sk) \leftarrow \mathcal{G}(1^{\lambda})$ and then sends (pk, sk) to the adversary.
- **Challenge.** The adversary $\mathcal{S}^*$ first randomly picks $\{m_0, m_1\}$. Then, the challenger and the adversary run the interactive signing protocol (completed/notcompleted, $\Sigma / \bot) \leftarrow \langle \mathsf{Sign}\text{-}\mathcal{S}^*(pk, sk, \mathcal{M} = \{m_0, m_1\}), \mathsf{Sign}\text{-}\mathcal{R}(pk, m_b)\rangle$, where b is kept secret from $\mathcal{S}^*$.
- **Guess.** After executing the interactive signing protocol, the adversary $\mathcal{S}^*$ outputs a bit $b^* \in \{0, 1\}$ according to the preceding steps. It means that $\mathcal{S}^*$ is not permitted to observe the eventual output of the signature Σ by $\mathcal{R}$.[2] If $b^* = b$, we say that adversary $\mathcal{S}^*$ wins the ambiguity game.

Definition 11 (Ambiguity). *We say that an $\mathcal{OS}_1^N$ scheme satisfies ambiguity, for any polynomial-time adversary playing the ambiguity game, $\Pr[b^* = b] - 1/2 \leq negl(n)$ holds.*

4 Proposed Oblivious Signature Scheme from Lattices

In this section, we propose our lattice-based 1-out-of-N oblivious signature scheme $\mathcal{OS}_1^N$ based on Lyubashevsky's lattice-based signature scheme [26].

Construction. On inputting a security parameter λ, the proposed 1-out-of-N oblivious scheme is parametrized by $n, m, q, k, d, \sigma, \rho$ which are described in the Sect. 2.2, by a matrix $\mathbf{B} \xleftarrow{\$} \mathbb{Z}_q^{n \times m}$, and by two collision-resistant hash functions $\mathsf{H} : \{0, 1\}^* \rightarrow \{\hat{\mathbf{e}}_i \mid \hat{\mathbf{e}}_i \in \{-1, 0, 1\}^k, \|\hat{\mathbf{e}}_i\|_1 \leq \rho\}$ as well as $\mathsf{H}_1 : \{0, 1\}^* \rightarrow \{-d, \cdots, d\}^m$. The public parameters are set as $\{n, m, q, k, d, \sigma, \rho, \mathsf{H}, \mathsf{H}_1, \mathbf{B}\}$.

Key Generation. With the aforementioned public parameters described, the algorithm uses the following steps to generate a key pair for the signer (pk, sk).

- Randomly chooses $\mathbf{S} \xleftarrow{\$} \{-d, \cdots, d\}^{m \times k}$ and $\mathbf{A} \xleftarrow{\$} \mathbb{Z}_q^{n \times m}$.
- Computes $\mathbf{P} \leftarrow \mathbf{AS} \in \mathbb{Z}_q^{n \times k}$.
- Outputs the signer's public key $pk := \{\mathbf{A}, \mathbf{P}\}$ and secret key $sk := \mathbf{S}$.

Interactive Signing Protocol. The recipient $\mathcal{R}$ and signer $\mathcal{S}$ interact with a signing protocol (Fig. 1) as follows to generate a valid signature:

---

[2] Since the signer has obtained all messages from the recipient, if he or she is allowed to obtain the signature, there is an inevitable attack. He or she will be able to verify which message the signature corresponds to and find out which message was pre-selected by the recipient.

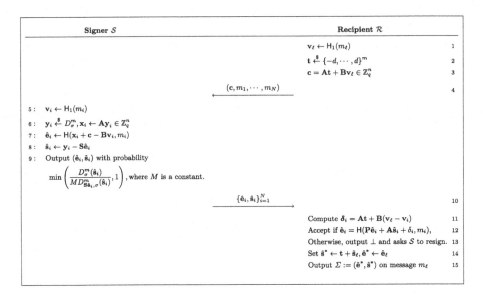

Fig. 1. The procedures of the proposed signing protocol.

- Assumes that $\mathcal{R}$ would like to obtain an oblivious signature Σ on message $m_\ell \in \mathcal{M} = \{m_1, \cdots, m_N\}$. $\mathcal{R}$ runs Sign-$\mathcal{R}(pk, m_\ell)$ as follows:
  - Computes $\mathbf{v}_\ell \leftarrow \mathsf{H}_1(m_\ell)$.
  - Randomly picks $\mathbf{t} \xleftarrow{\$} \{-d, \cdots, d\}^m$.
  - Computes $\mathbf{c} = \mathbf{At} + \mathbf{Bv}_\ell \in \mathbb{Z}_q^n$.
  - Sends tuple $(\mathbf{c}, m_1, \cdots, m_N)$ to $\mathcal{S}$.
- After receiving the request tuple, $\mathcal{S}$ then runs Sign-$\mathcal{S}(pk, sk, \mathcal{M})$ as follows for $i = 1, \cdots, N$:
  - Computes $\mathbf{v}_i \leftarrow \mathsf{H}_1(m_i)$.
  - Random picks $\mathbf{y}_i \xleftarrow{\$} D_\sigma^m$ and computes $\mathbf{x}_i \leftarrow \mathbf{Ay}_i \in \mathbb{Z}_q^n$.
  - Computes $\hat{\mathbf{e}}_i \leftarrow \mathsf{H}(\mathbf{x}_i + \mathbf{c} - \mathbf{Bv}_i, m_i)$.
  - Computes $\hat{\mathbf{s}}_i \leftarrow \mathbf{y}_i - \mathbf{S}\hat{\mathbf{e}}_i$.
  - Outputs pairs of $(\hat{\mathbf{e}}_i, \hat{\mathbf{s}}_i)$ with probability $\min\left(\frac{D_\sigma^m(\hat{\mathbf{s}}_i)}{MD_{\mathbf{S}\hat{\mathbf{e}}_i, \sigma}^m(\hat{\mathbf{s}}_i)}, 1\right)$, where M is a constant.

  Finally, $\mathcal{S}$ sends these semi-signatures $\{\hat{\mathbf{e}}_i, \hat{\mathbf{s}}_i\}_{i=1}^N$ back to $\mathcal{R}$.
- $\mathcal{R}$ then checks whether $\mathcal{S}$ generates these semi-signatures in a valid way as follows.
  - Computes $\delta_i = \mathbf{At} + \mathbf{B}(\mathbf{v}_\ell - \mathbf{v}_i)$, for $i = 1, \cdots, N$.
  - Accepts these semi-signatures if $\hat{\mathbf{e}}_i = \mathsf{H}(\mathbf{P}\hat{\mathbf{e}}_i + \mathbf{A}\hat{\mathbf{s}}_i + \delta_i, m_i)$, for $i = 1, \cdots, N$. Otherwise, outputs (notcompleted, $\bot$) and asks $\mathcal{S}$ to resign these messages again.
- If $\mathcal{R}$ accepts these semi-signatures, $\mathcal{R}$ then set $\hat{\mathbf{s}}^* \leftarrow \mathbf{t} + \hat{\mathbf{s}}_\ell$ as well as $\hat{\mathbf{e}}^* \leftarrow \hat{\mathbf{e}}_\ell$. Finally, $\mathcal{R}$ outputs a signature $\Sigma = (\hat{\mathbf{e}}^*, \hat{\mathbf{s}}^*)$ on m_ℓ.

Verification. To verify the validity of the signature, any verifier can checking whether $H(\mathbf{P}\hat{\mathbf{e}}^* + \mathbf{A}\hat{\mathbf{s}}^*, m_\ell) = \hat{\mathbf{e}}^*$. Then, it outputs 1 if the equation is satisfied, and outputs 0 otherwise.

Completeness. Given a valid signature $\Sigma = (\hat{\mathbf{e}}^*, \hat{\mathbf{s}}^*)$, the corresponding message m_ℓ and signer's public key pk. We have

$$
\begin{aligned}
H(\mathbf{P}\hat{\mathbf{e}}^* + \mathbf{A}\hat{\mathbf{s}}^*, m_\ell) &= H(\mathbf{A}\mathbf{S}\hat{\mathbf{e}}_\ell + \mathbf{A}(\mathbf{t} + \hat{\mathbf{s}}_\ell), m_\ell) \\
&= H(\mathbf{A}\mathbf{S}\hat{\mathbf{e}}_\ell + \mathbf{A}\mathbf{t} + \mathbf{A}(\mathbf{y}_\ell - \mathbf{S}\hat{\mathbf{e}}_\ell), m_\ell) = H(\mathbf{A}\mathbf{S}\hat{\mathbf{e}}_\ell + \mathbf{A}\mathbf{t} + \mathbf{A}\mathbf{y}_\ell - \mathbf{A}\mathbf{S}\hat{\mathbf{e}}_\ell, m_\ell) \\
&= H(\mathbf{A}\mathbf{t} + \mathbf{A}\mathbf{y}_\ell, m_\ell) = H(\mathbf{A}\mathbf{t} + \mathbf{x}_\ell, m_\ell) \\
&= H(\mathbf{x}_\ell + \mathbf{A}\mathbf{t} + \mathbf{B}\mathbf{v}_\ell - \mathbf{B}\mathbf{v}_\ell, m_\ell) = H(\mathbf{x}_\ell + \mathbf{c} - \mathbf{B}\mathbf{v}_\ell, m_\ell) \\
&= \hat{\mathbf{e}}_\ell = \hat{\mathbf{e}}^*.
\end{aligned}
$$

Therefore, Σ can pass the verification with overwhelming probability if function H is collision-resistant.

Parameters Restrictions. To make the proposed scheme work correctly and satisfy the security requirements, the following restrictions on the parameters should be held.

- To satisfy approximate 100 bits of security, $2^\rho \cdot \binom{k}{\rho} \geq 2^{100}$.
- To satisfy Lemma 3 in the security proof, $\sigma = \omega(d \cdot \rho \cdot \sqrt{m \log m})$.
- To satisfy Lemma 5 in the security proof, $m > 64 + n \cdot \log q / \log(2d + 1)$.

5   Security Proofs

In this section, we demonstrate that the proposed $\mathcal{OS}_1^N$ scheme satisfies strong unforgeability and ambiguity.

5.1   Unforgeability

Theorem 4. *The proposed scheme satisfies strong unforgeability if the $SIS_{q,n,m,\beta}$ problem is hard.*

Proof. According to the definition of strong unforgeability, we show that if there exists a polynomial-time forger $\mathcal{R}^*$, who queries the signing oracle at most s times and the random oracle H at most h times, winning the strong unforgeability game with probability ζ, then there exists a polynomial-time algorithm $\mathcal{A}$ that can use $\mathcal{R}^*$ as a black-box to solve the $SIS_{q,n,m,\beta}$ problem for $\beta = (2\eta\sigma + 2d\rho)\sqrt{m} = \tilde{O}(dn)$ with probability $\approx \frac{\zeta^2}{s(h+s)}$.

Our strategy is to begin by constructing two hybrids (described in Fig. 2), that is gradually modified from the proposed signing algorithm. More concretely, let $\mathcal{D}$ be a distinguisher querying the random oracle H and the signing oracle h

Proposed signing oracle	Hybrid 1	Hybrid 2
1: $\mathbf{v}_{i,j} \leftarrow H_1(m_{i,j})$	1: $\mathbf{v}_{i,j} \leftarrow H_1(m_{i,j})$	1: $\mathbf{v}_{i,j} \leftarrow H_1(m_{i,j})$
2: $\mathbf{y}_{i,j} \xleftarrow{\$} D_\sigma^m$	2: $\mathbf{y}_{i,j} \xleftarrow{\$} D_\sigma^m$	2: $\hat{\mathbf{e}}_{i,j} \xleftarrow{\$} \{\hat{\mathbf{e}}_{i,j} \in \{-1,0,1\}^k, \|\hat{\mathbf{e}}_{i,j}\|_1 \le \rho\}$
3: $\mathbf{x}_{i,j} \leftarrow A\mathbf{y}_{i,j} \in \mathbb{Z}_q^n$	3: $\hat{\mathbf{e}}_{i,j} \xleftarrow{\$} \{\hat{\mathbf{e}}_{i,j} \in \{-1,0,1\}^k, \|\hat{\mathbf{e}}_{i,j}\|_1 \le \rho\}$	3: $\hat{\mathbf{s}}_{i,j} \xleftarrow{\$} D_\sigma^m$
4: $\hat{\mathbf{e}}_{i,j} \leftarrow H(\mathbf{x}_{i,j} + \mathbf{c} - 2A\mathbf{v}_{i,j}, m_{i,j})$	4: $\hat{\mathbf{s}}_{i,j} \leftarrow \mathbf{y}_{i,j} - S\hat{\mathbf{e}}_{i,j}$	4: Outputs $\{\hat{\mathbf{e}}_{i,j}, \hat{\mathbf{s}}_{i,j}\}$ with probability $\frac{1}{M}$
5: $\hat{\mathbf{s}}_{i,j} \leftarrow \mathbf{y}_{i,j} - S\hat{\mathbf{e}}_{i,j}$	5: Outputs $\{\hat{\mathbf{e}}_{i,j}, \hat{\mathbf{s}}_{i,j}\}$ with	5: Programs $H(P\hat{\mathbf{e}}_{i,j} + A\hat{\mathbf{s}}_{i,j}, m_{i,j}) = \hat{\mathbf{e}}_{i,j}$
6: Outputs $\{\hat{\mathbf{e}}_{i,j}, \hat{\mathbf{s}}_{i,j}\}$ with	6: probability $\min\left(\frac{D_\sigma^m(\hat{\mathbf{s}}_{i,j})}{MD_{S\hat{\mathbf{e}}_{i,j},\sigma}^m(\hat{\mathbf{s}}_{i,j})}, 1\right)$	
probability $\min\left(\frac{D_\sigma^m(\hat{\mathbf{s}}_{i,j})}{MD_{S\hat{\mathbf{e}}_{i,j},\sigma}^m(\hat{\mathbf{s}}_{i,j})}, 1\right)$	7: Programs $H(P\hat{\mathbf{e}}_{i,j} + A\hat{\mathbf{s}}_{i,j}, m_{i,j}) = \hat{\mathbf{e}}_{i,j}$	

Fig. 2. The procedures of the proposed signing algorithm, Hybrid 1, and Hybrid 2.

and s times, respectively, the proof sequence is divided into three steps. First, in Lemma 2, we demonstrate that $\mathcal{D}$ can distinguish between the proposed signing algorithm and Hybrid 1 with an advantage of at most $\frac{s(h+s)}{q^n}$. Next, in Lemma 3, we further show that the statistical distance between the outputs of Hybrid 1 and Hybrid 2 is $s \cdot \frac{2^{-100}}{M}$. Finally, in Lemma 4, we prove that if there exists an polynomial-time forger $\mathcal{R}^*$ in the Hybrid 2 environment that can succeed in forging with probability ζ, then $\mathcal{A}$ can solve the $SIS_{q,n,m,\beta}$ problem with probability at least approximately $\frac{\zeta^2}{s(h+s)}$. Throughout the proofs of unforgeability, we adopt the following notations: $m_{i,j}$ denotes the jth message in the message set selected by $\mathcal{R}^*$ in the ith signing query, and $(\hat{\mathbf{e}}_{i,j}, \hat{\mathbf{s}}_{i,j})$ denoted the semi-signature on jth message in the message set selected by $\mathcal{R}^*$ in the ith query, where $i = 1, \cdots, s$ and $j = 1, \cdots, N$.

Lemma 2. *Suppose that the distinguisher $\mathcal{D}$ query h times random oracle H and s times signing oracle, it will get a valid matrix $\mathbf{A}$ with the probability at least $1 - e^{-\Omega(n)}$. And the advantage of $\mathcal{D}$ can distinguish between the proposed signing algorithm and Hybrid 1 is at most $\frac{s(h+s)}{q^n}$.*

Lemma 3. *The statistical distance between the outputs of Hybrid 1 and Hybrid 2 is $s \cdot \frac{2^{-\omega(\log m)}}{M}$, or more concretely, $s \cdot \frac{2^{-100}}{M}$.*

Lemma 4. *If there exists an adaptively chosen message polynomial-time adversary $\mathcal{R}^*$ who makes at most s queries to Hybrid 2 and h queries to the random oracle H and $\mathcal{R}^*$ wins unforgeability game with probability ζ, then there exists a $\mathcal{A}$ with the same polynomial-time algorithm as $\mathcal{R}^*$ that given $\mathbf{A} \xleftarrow{\$} \mathbb{Z}_q^{n \times m}$, can find out a non-zero $\mathbf{v} \in \mathbb{Z}^m$ such that $\|\mathbf{v}\| \le (2\eta\sigma + 2d\rho)\sqrt{m}$ and $\mathbf{A}\mathbf{v} = \mathbf{0}$ with probability at least*

$$\left(\frac{1}{2} - 2^{-100}\right)(\zeta - 2^{-100})\left(\frac{\zeta - 2^{-100}}{h + s} - 2^{-100}\right) \approx \frac{\zeta^2}{2(h + s)}.$$

$\square$

5.2   Ambiguity

Theorem 5. *The proposed scheme satisfies ambiguity if the $SIS_{q,n,m,d}$ decision problem is hard.*

Proof. Let $\mathcal{S}^*$ be a malicious signer who wants to distinguish which message that receiver wants to sign. The following we demonstrate that no matter which b is chosen from the challenger in the ambiguity game, for $\mathcal{S}^*$'s view, the transfer element $\mathbf{c} = \mathbf{At}_1 + \mathbf{Bv}_b$ is a randomness, where $\mathbf{v}_b \leftarrow \mathsf{H}_1(m_b)$.

Without loss of generality, suppose $b = 0$, then $\mathcal{S}^*$ obtains $\mathbf{At}_1 = \mathbf{c} - \mathbf{Bv}_0$; Otherwise, $\mathcal{S}^*$ obtains $\mathbf{At}_1 = \mathbf{c} - \mathbf{Bv}_1$. By Definition 6, since $\mathbf{t}_1 \xleftarrow{\$} \{-d, \cdots, d\}^m$, $(\mathbf{A}, \mathbf{c} - \mathbf{Bv}_0)$ and $(\mathbf{A}, \mathbf{c} - \mathbf{Bv}_1)$ are two instances of the decision SIS problem. Therefore, if the problem is hard, for $\mathcal{S}^*$'s view, $(\mathbf{A}, \mathbf{c} - \mathbf{Bv}_0)$ and $(\mathbf{A}, \mathbf{c} - \mathbf{Bv}_1)$ are generated uniformly at random from $\mathbb{Z}_q^{n \times m} \times \mathbb{Z}_q^n$. In other words, $\mathbf{c}$ reveals no information. The following we analyze the probability that $\mathcal{S}^*$ wins the game by directly guessing $\mathbf{t}$. Since $\mathbf{t}_1 \xleftarrow{\$} \{-d, \cdots, d\}^m$, the probability of guessing the $\mathbf{t}_1$ is equal to $(2d+1)^{-m}$. If we restrict the parameter $m > 64 + n \cdot \log q / \log(2d+1)$, we have

$$(2d + 1)^{-m} \leq (2d + 1)^{-64} \cdot (2d + 1)^{-n \log q / \log(2d+1)}$$
$$= (2d + 1)^{-64} \cdot q^{-n}$$
$$< 2^{-100} \cdot q^{-n}.$$

With the above analysis, the probability that $\mathcal{S}^*$ can distinguish which message is selected from the challenger is negligible.   □

6   Theoretical Comparison and Efficiency Analysis

In this section, we first theoretically compare the proposed scheme with other existing oblivious signatures in terms of the communication cost and computational cost. Then, we give a proof-of-concept implementation to demonstrate the running time of interactive signing and verification under different sizes of the message set.

As presented in Table 1, the communication cost of our oblivious signature scheme is lower than Chen's scheme [11], as our scheme only requires two steps of communication between the signer and the recipient, which is equivalent to that of Tso *et al.*'s scheme [37]. For the computational cost, shown in Table 2, since our proposed scheme relies on lattice-based cryptosystem, its operations are matrix multiplication operations; whereas Chen and Tso *et al.*'s scheme [37] require exponentiation operations.

For the efficiency analysis, the experiment was implemented in Python3 with SageMath[3] version 9.6 on macOS Monterey 12.3.1 with Intel(R) Core(TM) i5-9600K CPU clocked at 3.7 GHz and 32 GB of DDR4 system memory clocked

---

[3] https://www.sagemath.org/.

Table 1. Comparison of communication cost. N: the number of messages in the message set; N_r: the required steps to generate a signature; $\mathcal{S}$: signer; $\mathcal{R}$: recipient; $\mathcal{V}$: verifier; n, q: the parameters related to SIS assumption; p, q in Chen and Tso et $al.$'s works: two large primes such that $q|(p-1)$; k: the length of the output of the hash function.

Schemes	N_r	$\mathcal{R} \to \mathcal{S}$	$\mathcal{S} \to \mathcal{R}$	$\mathcal{R} \to \mathcal{V}$
Chen's [11]	3	$\lvert q \rvert$	$3N\lvert p\rvert + N\lvert q\rvert$	$7\lvert p\rvert + 2\lvert q\rvert$
Tso et $al.$'s [37]	2	$\lvert q \rvert$	$2N\lvert q\rvert$	$2\lvert q\rvert$
Ours	2	$n\lvert q\rvert$	$N(k+n)\lvert q\rvert$	$(k+n)\lvert q\rvert$

Table 2. Comparison of computational cost. N: the number of messages in the message set; E: the number of exponentiation operations; M: the number of matrix multiplication operations.

Schemes	$\mathcal{S}$	$\mathcal{R}$	$\mathcal{V}$
Chen's [11]	$3NE$	$(2N+10)E$	$8E$
Tso et $al.$'s [37]	$2NE$	$(2N+2)E$	$2E$
Ours	$3NM$	$(3N+2)M$	$2M$

at 2667 MHz. To achieve approximate 100-bit security, the parameter set ($i.e.$, $n = 512$; $q = 2^{25}$; $d = 1$; $k = 512$; $\eta = 1.1$; $m = 8139$; $\sigma = 15157$; $M = 2.72$) is chosen following [26]. The experiment result is illustrated by Fig. 3, which shows that the running time of generating signatures is proportional to the number of messages in the message set; whereas the running time of verification is not affected because only the target message needs to be verified.

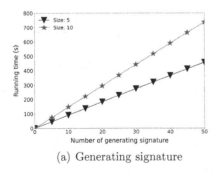

(a) Generating signature

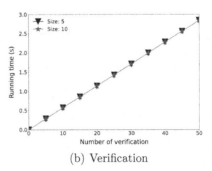

(b) Verification

Fig. 3. The running time of generating signature and verification under different number of messages in the message set.

7   Conclusion and Future Work

In this paper, we propose a 1-out-of-N oblivious signature scheme from lattices. The security requirements are satisfied under the SIS hard assumption by using the random oracle. To the best of our knowledge, this is the first quantum-resistant 1-out-of-N oblivious signature instantiation.

Below we describe two possible improvements and leave them for our future work. First, since the properties of the secret key it is more complex in terms of privacy and how it is generated, we speculate that there is no naive transformation from 1-out-of-N oblivious signature with N messages to 1-out-of-N oblivious signature with N keys. Therefore, how to construct a quantum-resistant 1-out-of-N oblivious signature with N keys is still an open problem. Second, our proposed scheme solely relies on Lyubashevsky's signature [26]. Many improved signature schemes in terms of efficiency and security have been proposed. For example, Ducas *et al.* [14] adopt bimodal Gaussian rejection sampling techniques to achieve shorter signature and public key sizes. Kiltz *et al.* [25] further introduced how to obtain a lattice-based signature that is secure under quantum ROM (QROM). How to construct a more efficient quantum-resistant 1-out-of-N oblivious signature scheme that satisfies stronger security is another interesting direction.

Acknowledgments. This research was supported by the Ministry of Science and Technology, Taiwan (ROC), under project numbers MOST 109-2221-E-004-011-MY3, MOST 110-2221-E-004-003-, MOST 110-2622-8-004-001-, and MOST 111-2218-E-004-001-MBK.

A   Proof of Lemma 2

Proof. For the view of $\mathcal{D}$, the only difference between the proposed signing algorithm and Hybrid 1 is the method of generating $\hat{\mathbf{e}}_{i,j}$. More specifically, $\hat{\mathbf{e}}_{i,j}$ are generated from the hash function H in our proposed signing algorithm; while in Hybrid 1, $\hat{\mathbf{e}}_{i,j}$ is chosen randomly from the set $\{-1, 0, 1\}^k$ and then programmed as the answer of $\mathsf{H}(\mathbf{P}\hat{\mathbf{e}}_{i,j} + \mathbf{A}\hat{\mathbf{s}}_{i,j}, m_{i,j}) = \mathsf{H}(\mathbf{A}\mathbf{y}_{i,j} + \mathbf{A}\mathbf{t}_i - \mathbf{B}\mathbf{v}_{i,j}, m_{i,j}) = \hat{\mathbf{e}}_{i,j}$ without checking whether $(\mathbf{A}\mathbf{y}_{i,j} + \mathbf{A}\mathbf{t}_i - \mathbf{B}\mathbf{v}_{i,j}, m_{i,j})$ were already set. Here $\mathbf{t}_i$ is a random vector picked by the forger $\mathcal{R}^*$ in the ith signing query. Therefore, the ability of $\mathcal{D}$ to distinguish between the original signing oracle and the Hybrid 1 depends on the probability of occurring collisions.

From the proposed signing algorithm, we have

$$\hat{\mathbf{e}}_{i,j} = \mathsf{H}(\mathbf{P}\hat{\mathbf{e}}_{i,j} + \mathbf{A}\hat{\mathbf{s}}_{i,j}, m_{i,j}) = \mathsf{H}(\mathbf{A}\mathbf{y}_{i,j} + \mathbf{A}\mathbf{t}_i - \mathbf{B}\mathbf{v}_{i,j}, m_{i,j}).$$

Since there are q^n elements in $\mathbb{Z}_q^n$, the probability of generating a $\mathbf{z}$ such that $\mathbf{z} = \mathbf{A}\mathbf{y}_{i,j} + \mathbf{A}\mathbf{t} - \mathbf{B}\mathbf{v}_{i,j}$ equals to one of the preceding values queried in Hybrid 1 is $\frac{1}{q^n}$. That is, for any $\mathbf{z} \in \mathbb{Z}_q^n$, we have

$$\Pr[\mathbf{z} = \mathbf{A}\mathbf{y}_{i,j} + \mathbf{A}\mathbf{t}_i - \mathbf{B}\mathbf{v}_{i,j} \mid \mathbf{z} \xleftarrow{\$} \mathbb{Z}_q^n] = \frac{1}{q^n}.$$

In addition, the probability of obtaining a collision each time is at most $\frac{(h+s)}{q^n}$ because at most $(h+s)$ values of $\hat{\mathbf{e}}_{i,j}$ have been set. Consequently, after querying s times of signing oracle, the probability of a collision appearing is at most $\frac{s(h+s)}{q^n}$. □

B   Proof of Lemma 3

Proof. This lemma is almost identical to Theorem 3, the output of Theorem 3 is $(\hat{\mathbf{s}}_{i,j}, \mathbf{v}_{i,j} = \mathbf{S}\hat{\mathbf{e}}_{i,j})$, whereas the outputs of both Hybrid 1 and Hybrid 2 are $(\hat{\mathbf{e}}_{i,j}, \hat{\mathbf{s}}_{i,j})$. For any $\mathbf{v}_{i,j}$, there always exists a $\hat{\mathbf{e}}_{i,j} \in \{-1, 0, 1\}^k$ such that $\mathbf{S}\hat{\mathbf{e}}_{i,j} = \mathbf{v}_{i,j}$, where $\|\hat{\mathbf{e}}_{i,j}\|_1 \leq \rho$. Therefore, the distribution is almost the same as that of $\hat{\mathbf{e}}_{i,j}$ in both hybrids from the distinguisher's perspective. □

C   Proof of Lemma 4

Proof. Let $D_{\mathsf{H}} = \{\hat{\mathbf{e}}_{i,\ell} \mid \hat{\mathbf{e}}_{i,\ell} \in \{-1, 0, 1\}^k, \|\hat{\mathbf{e}}_{i,\ell}\|_1 \leq \rho\}$ represent the range of the random oracle H, and let $t = h + s$ denote the scope on the number of times that the random oracle H is queried or programmed during $\mathcal{R}^*$'s attack. The oracle can be queried by $\mathcal{R}^*$ directly, or can be programmed by the signing algorithm when $\mathcal{A}$ inquires about the signature of a set of messages.

Given $\mathbf{A} \xleftarrow{\$} \mathbb{Z}_q^{n \times m}$, we pick $\mathbf{S} \xleftarrow{\$} \{-d, \cdots, d\}^{m \times k}$, $\mathbf{r}_1, \cdots, \mathbf{r}_t \xleftarrow{\$} D_{\mathsf{H}}$, a random coin ϕ for the forger $\mathcal{R}^*$; another random coin ψ for the signer $\mathcal{S}$; and finally compute the corresponding $pk = (\mathbf{A}, \mathbf{P} = \mathbf{AS})$. Now, we use $(\mathbf{A}, \mathbf{P}, \phi, \psi, \mathbf{r}_1, \cdots, \mathbf{r}_t)$ as the input for the algorithm $\mathcal{A}$. $\mathcal{A}$ initializes the forger $\mathcal{R}^*$ by providing the $pk = (\mathbf{A}, \mathbf{P})$ and the random coin ϕ. $\mathcal{A}$ executes the signing algorithm in Hybrid 2 and uses the random coin ψ for signer to generate a signature whenever $\mathcal{R}^*$ queries messages to be signed. The random oracle H is programmed during signing, and the reply from H is assigned to the first unused $\mathbf{r}_i$ in $(\mathbf{r}_1, \cdots, \mathbf{r}_t)$. $\mathcal{A}$ maintains a list recording all the results of queries to H; thus, a query may receive a previous $\mathbf{r}_i$ as a response if the same query was performed multiple times. Moreover, the forger $\mathcal{R}^*$ can query the random oracle H directly to obtain a reply of an unused $\mathbf{r}_i$ in $(\mathbf{r}_1, \cdots, \mathbf{r}_t)$, except for the query that had previously been performed. After $\mathcal{R}^*$ completes these queries and outputs a counterfeit signature with probability ζ, $\mathcal{A}$ simply outputs the output of $\mathcal{R}^*$.

After s times of queries, $\mathcal{R}^*$ outputs a signature corresponding a message $m_{i,\ell}$, that includes $(\hat{\mathbf{e}}_{i,\ell}, \hat{\mathbf{s}}_{i,\ell})$ such that $\|\hat{\mathbf{s}}_{i,\ell}\| \leq \eta \sigma \sqrt{m}$ and $\hat{\mathbf{e}}_{i,\ell} = ((\mathbf{P}\hat{\mathbf{e}}_{i,\ell} + \mathbf{A}\hat{\mathbf{s}}_{i,\ell}), m_{i,\ell})$ with probability ζ. If $(\mathbf{P}\hat{\mathbf{e}}_{i,\ell} + \mathbf{A}\hat{\mathbf{s}}_{i,\ell})$ was not generated by calling the random oracle H or was not programmed by the signing algorithm, then the probability $\mathcal{R}^*$ produces a $\hat{\mathbf{e}}_{i,\ell}$ such that $\hat{\mathbf{e}}_{i,\ell} \leftarrow \mathsf{H}((\mathbf{P}\hat{\mathbf{e}}_{i,\ell} + \mathbf{A}\hat{\mathbf{s}}_{i,\ell}), m_{i,\ell})$ is only has $1/|D_{\mathsf{H}}|$. Thus, $\hat{\mathbf{e}}_{i,\ell}$ is equal to an $\mathbf{r}_i$'s with probability of $1 - 1/|D_{\mathsf{H}}|$. Therefore, the probability that $\mathcal{R}^*$ succeeds in forging and that $(\mathbf{P}\hat{\mathbf{e}}_{i,\ell} + \mathbf{A}\hat{\mathbf{s}}_{i,\ell})$ is one of the $\mathbf{r}_i$'s is at least $\zeta - 1/|D_{\mathsf{H}}|$. Let such $\hat{\mathbf{e}}_{i,\ell} = \mathbf{r}_i$; then, $\mathbf{r}_i$ may have been obtained in two ways: either it was programmed during signing, or it was a reply from the random oracle queried by $\mathcal{R}^*$.

In the first case, suppose that $\mathcal{A}$ programmed the random oracle $\mathsf{H}((\mathbf{P}\hat{\mathbf{e}}_{i,\ell} + \mathbf{A}\hat{\mathbf{s}}'_{i,\ell}, m'_{i,\ell}) = \hat{\mathbf{e}}_{i,\ell}$ when it was signing a message $m'_{i,\ell}$ in the ith query. After the forger $\mathcal{R}^*$ outputs an effective forged "semi-signature" $(\hat{\mathbf{e}}_{i,\ell}, \hat{\mathbf{s}}_{i,\ell})$ for some (possibly different) messages $m_{i,\ell}$, we have $\mathsf{H}((\mathbf{P}\hat{\mathbf{e}}_{i,\ell} + \mathbf{A}\hat{\mathbf{s}}'_{i,\ell}), m'_{i,\ell}) = \mathsf{H}((\mathbf{P}\hat{\mathbf{e}}_{i,\ell} + \mathbf{A}\hat{\mathbf{s}}_{i,\ell}), m_{i,\ell})$. If $m_{i,\ell} \neq m'_{i,\ell}$ or $(\mathbf{P}\hat{\mathbf{e}}_{i,\ell} + \mathbf{A}\hat{\mathbf{s}}'_{i,\ell}) \neq (\mathbf{P}\hat{\mathbf{e}}_{i,\ell} + \mathbf{A}\hat{\mathbf{s}}_{i,\ell})$, then $\mathcal{R}^*$ has found a preimage of $\mathbf{r}_i$. However, this cannot occur because the hash fuction H is collision resistant. If $m_{i,\ell} = m'_{i,\ell}$ and $(\mathbf{P}\hat{\mathbf{e}}_{i,\ell} + \mathbf{A}\hat{\mathbf{s}}'_{i,\ell}) = (\mathbf{P}\hat{\mathbf{e}}_{i,\ell} + \mathbf{A}\hat{\mathbf{s}}_{i,\ell})$, we obtain $\mathbf{A}(\hat{\mathbf{s}}_{i,\ell} - \hat{\mathbf{s}}'_{i,\ell}) = \mathbf{0}$. We know that $\hat{\mathbf{s}}_{i,\ell} \neq \hat{\mathbf{s}}'_{i,\ell}$, otherwise $(\hat{\mathbf{e}}_{i,\ell}, \hat{\mathbf{s}}_{i,\ell})$ would be identical to the previous "semi-signature" $(\hat{\mathbf{e}}'_{i,\ell}, \hat{\mathbf{s}}'_{i,\ell})$. Because $\|\hat{\mathbf{s}}_{i,\ell}\|, \|\hat{\mathbf{s}}'_{i,\ell}\| \leq \eta\sigma\sqrt{m}$, we obtain $\|\hat{\mathbf{s}}_{i,\ell} - \hat{\mathbf{s}}'_{i,\ell}\| \leq 2\eta\sigma\sqrt{m}$.

For the second case, suppose $\mathbf{r}_k$ is a reply from random oracle queried by $\mathcal{R}^*$ for some kth query. We record the signature $(\mathbf{r}_k, \hat{\mathbf{s}}_{k,\ell})$ on the message $m_{k,\ell}$ and generate fresh items $\mathbf{r}'_k, \cdots, \mathbf{r}'_t \xleftarrow{\$} D_\mathsf{H}$. We next return the algorithm $\mathcal{A}$ with the refreshed inputs $(\mathbf{A}, \mathbf{P}, \phi, \psi, \mathbf{r}_1, \cdots, \mathbf{r}_{k-1}, \mathbf{r}'_k, \cdots, \mathbf{r}'_t)$. By Definition 9, the probability that $\mathbf{r}'_k \neq \mathbf{r}_k$ and that the answer of this random oracle $\mathbf{r}'_k$ was applied in $\mathcal{R}^*$'s counterfeit, is at least

$$\left(\zeta - \frac{1}{|D_\mathsf{H}|}\right)\left(\frac{\zeta - 1/|D_\mathsf{H}|}{h + s} - \frac{1}{|D_\mathsf{H}|}\right).$$

A signature $(\mathbf{r}'_k, \hat{\mathbf{s}}'_{k,\ell})$ for message $m_{k,\ell}$ with the aforementioned probability was output by $\mathcal{R}^*$ such that $(\mathbf{P}\hat{\mathbf{e}}'_{k,\ell} + \mathbf{A}\hat{\mathbf{s}}'_{k,\ell}) = (\mathbf{P}\hat{\mathbf{e}}_{k,\ell} + \mathbf{A}\hat{\mathbf{s}}_{k,\ell})$, where $\hat{\mathbf{e}}'_{k,\ell} = \mathbf{r}'_k$ and $\hat{\mathbf{e}}_{k,\ell} = \mathbf{r}_k$. Let $\mathbf{P} = \mathbf{A}\mathbf{S}$, we have $\mathbf{A}(\hat{\mathbf{s}}_{k,\ell} - \hat{\mathbf{s}}'_{k,\ell} + \mathbf{S}\hat{\mathbf{e}}_{k,\ell} - \mathbf{S}\hat{\mathbf{e}}'_{k,\ell}) = \mathbf{0}$. In addition, since $\|\mathbf{S}\hat{\mathbf{e}}_{k,\ell}\|, \|\mathbf{S}\hat{\mathbf{e}}'_{k,\ell}\| \leq d\rho\sqrt{m}$, we have $\|\hat{\mathbf{s}}_{k,\ell} - \hat{\mathbf{s}}'_{k,\ell} + \mathbf{S}\hat{\mathbf{e}}_{k,\ell} - \mathbf{S}\hat{\mathbf{e}}'_{k,\ell}\| \leq (2\eta\sigma + 2d\rho)\sqrt{m}$.

Now, we require to show that $(\hat{\mathbf{s}}_{k,\ell} - \hat{\mathbf{s}}'_{k,\ell} + \mathbf{S}\hat{\mathbf{e}}_{k,\ell} - \mathbf{S}\hat{\mathbf{e}}'_{k,\ell}) \neq \mathbf{0}$. Before proving this part, we must provide Lemma 5 first.

Lemma 5. *Given any $\mathbf{A} \in \mathbb{Z}_q^{n \times m}$, where $m > 64 + n \cdot \log q / \log(2d + 1)$, for any randomly chosen $\mathbf{S} \xleftarrow{\$} \{-d, \cdots, d\}^{m \times k}$, there exists another $\mathbf{S}' \in \{-d, \cdots, d\}^{m \times k}$ such that $\mathbf{A}\mathbf{S} = \mathbf{A}\mathbf{S}'$ with probability $1 - 2^{-100}$.*

Proof. Treat $\mathbf{A}$ as a linear transformation whose range is q^n. At most q^n elements $\mathbf{S} \in \{-d, \cdots, d\}^m$ do not collide with any other item in $\{-d, \cdots, d\}^m$. Notice that the set $\{-d, \cdots, d\}^m$ comprises $(2d + 1)$ elements. Randomly select an element that does not collide; then, the probability is at most

$$\frac{q^n}{(2d + 1)^m} \leq \frac{q^n}{(2d + 1)^{64 + n \log q / \log(2d+1)}} = \frac{1}{(2d + 1)^{64}} < 2^{-100}.$$

$\square$

Let the cth column be the column in which $\hat{\mathbf{e}}_{k,\ell,c} \neq \hat{\mathbf{e}}'_{k,\ell,c}$. By Lemma 5, we know that a different secret key $\mathbf{S}'$ exists with probability of at least $1 - 2^{-100}$ such that all the columns except for column c of $\mathbf{S}'$ are equal to the columns of $\mathbf{S}$, such that $\mathbf{A}\mathbf{S}' = \mathbf{A}\mathbf{S}$. Clearly, if $\hat{\mathbf{s}}_{k,\ell} - \hat{\mathbf{s}}'_{k,\ell} + \mathbf{S}(\hat{\mathbf{e}}_{k,\ell,c} - \hat{\mathbf{e}}'_{k,\ell,c}) = \mathbf{0}$, then $\hat{\mathbf{s}}_{k,\ell,c} - \hat{\mathbf{s}}'_{k,\ell,c} + \mathbf{S}'(\hat{\mathbf{e}}_{k,\ell,c} - \hat{\mathbf{e}}'_{k,\ell,c}) \neq \mathbf{0}$. That is, for every secret key $\mathbf{S}$ such that

$\hat{s}_{k,\ell,c} - \hat{s}'_{k,\ell,c} + \mathbf{S}(\hat{e}_{k,\ell,c} - \hat{e}'_{k,\ell,c}) = \mathbf{0}$, there is a distinct secret key $\mathbf{S}'$ that only differs from $\mathbf{S}$ in the ith column that results in $\hat{s}_{k,\ell,c} - \hat{s}'_{k,\ell,c} + \mathbf{S}'(\hat{e}_{k,\ell,c} - \hat{e}'_{k,\ell,c}) \neq \mathbf{0}$. Because $\mathcal{A}$ did not use these keys as input and did not put them to the signature oracle, $\mathcal{R}^*$ does not know if we are aware of a secret key such as $\mathbf{S}$ or $\mathbf{S}'$. Therefore, each secret key has an equal probability of being selected. $\qquad\square$

References

1. Ajtai, M.: Generating hard instances of lattice problems (extended abstract). In: STOC 1996, pp. 99–108. ACM (1996)
2. Banaszczyk, W.: New bounds in some transference theorems in the geometry of numbers. Mathematische Annalen **296**(1), 625–635 (1993)
3. Baum, C., Lin, H., Oechsner, S.: Towards practical lattice-based one-time linkable ring signatures. In: Naccache, D., Xu, S., Qing, S., Samarati, P., Blanc, G., Lu, R., Zhang, Z., Meddahi, A. (eds.) ICICS 2018. LNCS, vol. 11149, pp. 303–322. Springer, Cham (2018). https://doi.org/10.1007/978-3-030-01950-1_18
4. Bellare, M., Neven, G.: Multi-signatures in the plain public-key model and a general forking lemma. In: CCS 2006, pp. 390–399. ACM (2006)
5. Bellini, E., Caullery, F., Hasikos, A., Manzano, M., Mateu, V.: Code-based signature schemes from identification protocols in the rank metric. In: Camenisch, J., Papadimitratos, P. (eds.) CANS 2018. LNCS, vol. 11124, pp. 277–298. Springer, Cham (2018). https://doi.org/10.1007/978-3-030-00434-7_14
6. Bernstein, D.J., Hülsing, A., Kölbl, S., Niederhagen, R., Rijneveld, J., Schwabe, P.: The SPHINCS$^+$ signature framework. In: CCS 2019, pp. 2129–2146. ACM (2019)
7. Beullens, W., Kleinjung, T., Vercauteren, F.: CSI-FiSh: efficient isogeny based signatures through class group computations. In: Galbraith, S.D., Moriai, S. (eds.) ASIACRYPT 2019, Part I. LNCS, vol. 11921, pp. 227–247. Springer, Cham (2019). https://doi.org/10.1007/978-3-030-34578-5_9
8. Brickell, J., Porter, D.E., Shmatikov, V., Witchel, E.: Privacy-preserving remote diagnostics. In: CCS 2007, pp. 498–507. ACM (2007)
9. Chaum, D.: Blind signatures for untraceable payments. In: CRYPTO 1982, pp. 199–203. Plenum Press, New York (1982)
10. Chaum, D., van Heyst, E.: Group signatures. In: Davies, D.W. (ed.) EUROCRYPT 1991. LNCS, vol. 547, pp. 257–265. Springer, Heidelberg (1991). https://doi.org/10.1007/3-540-46416-6_22
11. Chen, L.: Oblivious signatures. In: Gollmann, D. (ed.) ESORICS 1994. LNCS, vol. 875, pp. 161–172. Springer, Heidelberg (1994). https://doi.org/10.1007/3-540-58618-0_62
12. Chu, C.-K., Tzeng, W.-G.: Efficient k-out-of-n oblivious transfer schemes with adaptive and non-adaptive queries. In: Vaudenay, S. (ed.) PKC 2005. LNCS, vol. 3386, pp. 172–183. Springer, Heidelberg (2005). https://doi.org/10.1007/978-3-540-30580-4_12
13. Decru, T., Panny, L., Vercauteren, F.: Faster SeaSign signatures through improved rejection sampling. In: Ding, J., Steinwandt, R. (eds.) PQCrypto 2019. LNCS, vol. 11505, pp. 271–285. Springer, Cham (2019). https://doi.org/10.1007/978-3-030-25510-7_15
14. Ducas, L., Durmus, A., Lepoint, T., Lyubashevsky, V.: Lattice signatures and bimodal Gaussians. In: Canetti, R., Garay, J.A. (eds.) CRYPTO 2013, Part I. LNCS, vol. 8042, pp. 40–56. Springer, Heidelberg (2013). https://doi.org/10.1007/978-3-642-40041-4_3

15. Ducas, L., et al.: Crystals-Dilithium: a lattice-based digital signature scheme. IACR Trans. Cryptogr. Hardw. Embed. Syst. **2018**(1), 238–268 (2018)

16. Fiat, A., Shamir, A.: How to prove yourself: practical solutions to identification and signature problems. In: Odlyzko, A.M. (ed.) CRYPTO 1986. LNCS, vol. 263, pp. 186–194. Springer, Heidelberg (1987). https://doi.org/10.1007/3-540-47721-7_12

17. Gibson, J.P., Krimmer, R., Teague, V., Pomares, J.: A review of E-voting: the past, present and future. Ann. Telecommun. **71**(7), 279–286 (2016). https://doi.org/10.1007/s12243-016-0525-8

18. Han, F., Qin, J., Hu, J.: Secure searches in the cloud: a survey. Future Gener. Comput. Syst. **62**, 66–75 (2016)

19. Hauck, E., Kiltz, E., Loss, J., Nguyen, N.K.: Lattice-based blind signatures, revisited. In: Micciancio, D., Ristenpart, T. (eds.) CRYPTO 2020, Part II. LNCS, vol. 12171, pp. 500–529. Springer, Cham (2020). https://doi.org/10.1007/978-3-030-56880-1_18

20. He, D., Zeadally, S., Kumar, N., Lee, J.H.: Anonymous authentication for wireless body area networks with provable security. IEEE Syst. J. **11**(4), 2590–2601 (2017)

21. Hülsing, A.: W-OTS+ – shorter signatures for hash-based signature schemes. In: Youssef, A., Nitaj, A., Hassanien, A.E. (eds.) AFRICACRYPT 2013. LNCS, vol. 7918, pp. 173–188. Springer, Heidelberg (2013). https://doi.org/10.1007/978-3-642-38553-7_10

22. Impagliazzo, R., Naor, M.: Efficient cryptographic schemes provably as secure as subset sum. J. Cryptol. **9**(4), 199–216 (1996). https://doi.org/10.1007/BF00189260

23. Kaim, G., Canard, S., Roux-Langlois, A., Traoré, J.: Post-quantum online voting scheme. In: Bernhard, M., et al. (eds.) FC 2021. LNCS, vol. 12676, pp. 290–305. Springer, Heidelberg (2021). https://doi.org/10.1007/978-3-662-63958-0_25

24. Khan, K.M., Arshad, J., Khan, M.M.: Empirical analysis of transaction malleability within blockchain-based E-voting. Comput. Secur. **100**, 102081 (2021)

25. Kiltz, E., Lyubashevsky, V., Schaffner, C.: A concrete treatment of Fiat-Shamir signatures in the quantum random-oracle model. In: Nielsen, J.B., Rijmen, V. (eds.) EUROCRYPT 2018, Part III. LNCS, vol. 10822, pp. 552–586. Springer, Cham (2018). https://doi.org/10.1007/978-3-319-78372-7_18

26. Lyubashevsky, V.: Lattice signatures without trapdoors. In: Pointcheval, D., Johansson, T. (eds.) EUROCRYPT 2012. LNCS, vol. 7237, pp. 738–755. Springer, Heidelberg (2012). https://doi.org/10.1007/978-3-642-29011-4_43

27. Lyubashevsky, V., Nguyen, N.K., Seiler, G.: SMILE: set membership from ideal lattices with applications to ring signatures and confidential transactions. In: Malkin, T., Peikert, C. (eds.) CRYPTO 2021, Part II. LNCS, vol. 12826, pp. 611–640. Springer, Cham (2021). https://doi.org/10.1007/978-3-030-84245-1_21

28. Micciancio, D., Mol, P.: Pseudorandom knapsacks and the sample complexity of LWE search-to-decision reductions. In: Rogaway, P. (ed.) CRYPTO 2011. LNCS, vol. 6841, pp. 465–484. Springer, Heidelberg (2011). https://doi.org/10.1007/978-3-642-22792-9_26

29. Naor, M., Pinkas, B.: Computationally secure oblivious transfer. J. Cryptol. **18**(1), 1–35 (2005). https://doi.org/10.1007/s00145-004-0102-6

30. Pointcheval, D., Stern, J.: Security arguments for digital signatures and blind signatures. J. Cryptol. **13**(3), 361–396 (2000). https://doi.org/10.1007/s001450010003

31. Rivest, R.L., Shamir, A., Tauman, Y.: How to leak a secret. In: Boyd, C. (ed.) ASIACRYPT 2001. LNCS, vol. 2248, pp. 552–565. Springer, Heidelberg (2001). https://doi.org/10.1007/3-540-45682-1_32

32. Schemer, C., Masur, P.K., Geiß, S., Müller, P., Schäfer, S.: The impact of Internet and social media use on well-being: a longitudinal analysis of adolescents across nine years. J. Comput. Mediat. Commun. **26**(1), 1–21 (2021)

33. Shor, P.W.: Algorithms for quantum computation: discrete logarithms and factoring. In: FOCS 1994, pp. 124–134. IEEE (1994)

34. Song, Y., Huang, X., Mu, Y., Wu, W., Wang, H.: A code-based signature scheme from the Lyubashevsky framework. Theor. Comput. Sci. **835**, 15–30 (2020)

35. Tso, R.: Two-in-one oblivious signatures secure in the random oracle model. In: Chen, J., Piuri, V., Su, C., Yung, M. (eds.) NSS 2016. LNCS, vol. 9955, pp. 143–155. Springer, Cham (2016). https://doi.org/10.1007/978-3-319-46298-1_10

36. Tso, R.: Two-in-one oblivious signatures. Future Gener. Comput. Syst. **101**, 467–475 (2019)

37. Tso, R., Okamoto, T., Okamoto, E.: 1-out-of-n oblivious signatures. In: Chen, L., Mu, Y., Susilo, W. (eds.) ISPEC 2008. LNCS, vol. 4991, pp. 45–55. Springer, Heidelberg (2008). https://doi.org/10.1007/978-3-540-79104-1_4

38. Zhang, Z., Gupta, B.B.: Social media security and trustworthiness: Overview and new direction. Future Gener. Comput. Syst. **86**, 914–925 (2018)

Advanced Cryptography

On Extension of Evaluation Algorithms in Keyed-Homomorphic Encryption

Hirotomo Shinoki[1] and Koji Nuida[2,3(✉)] (iD)

[1] Graduate School of Information Science and Technology, The University of Tokyo,
Tokyo, Japan
[2] Institute of Mathematics for Industry (IMI), Kyushu University, Fukuoka, Japan
nuida@imi.kyushu-u.ac.jp
[3] National Institute of Advanced Industrial Science and Technology (AIST),
Tokyo, Japan

Abstract. Homomorphic encryption (HE) is public key encryption that enables computation over ciphertexts without decrypting them, while it is known that HE cannot achieve IND-CCA2 security. To overcome this issue, the notion of keyed-homomorphic encryption (KH-PKE) was introduced, which has a separate homomorphic evaluation key and can achieve stronger security (Emura et al., PKC 2013).

The contributions of this paper are twofold. First, the syntax of KH-PKE assumes that homomorphic evaluation is performed for single operations, and its security notion called KH-CCA security was formulated based on this syntax. Consequently, if the homomorphic evaluation algorithm is enhanced in a way of gathering up sequential operations as a single evaluation, then it is not obvious whether or not KH-CCA security is preserved. In this paper, we show that KH-CCA security is in general not preserved under such modification, while KH-CCA security is preserved when the original scheme additionally satisfies circuit privacy.

Secondly, Catalano and Fiore (ACM CCS 2015) proposed a conversion method from linearly HE schemes into two-level HE schemes, the latter admitting addition and a single multiplication for ciphertexts. In this paper, we extend the conversion to the case of linearly KH-PKE schemes to obtain two-level KH-PKE schemes.

Keywords: Keyed-homomorphic encryption · KH-CCA security · Catalano–Fiore conversion

1 Introduction

Homomorphic encryption (HE) [32] is a kind of public key encryption that allows computation over encrypted data without knowing the secret key, and has several applications such as delegated computation on the clouds. Major classes of HE include additive HE [24,31] and multiplicative HE [16,33] that allow only a single kind of operations, and fully HE (FHE) [8–11,15,22,23] that allows arbitrary computation over encrypted data. Among them, there is a trade-off between

C.-M. Cheng and M. Akiyama (Eds.): IWSEC 2022, LNCS 13504, pp. 189–207, 2022.
https://doi.org/10.1007/978-3-031-15255-9_10

the efficiency (for additive/multiplicative HE) and the enhanced functionality (for FHE). As an intermediate class, there also exists leveled HE (or somewhat HE) where a limitation on the number of possible operations exists (typically for multiplication) while the efficiency is much better than FHE. In particular, there exist some constructions of two-level HE (2LHE) schemes [1,7,21,25] in which an arbitrary number of additions and a single multiplication are possible. Besides such direct constructions of 2LHE schemes, Catalano and Fiore [13] proposed a general conversion method from an additive HE scheme into a 2LHE scheme (with non-compact level-two ciphertexts). We refer to this method as "Catalano–Fiore conversion" in this paper.

For ordinary public key encryption (PKE) schemes, IND-CCA2 security is regarded as a standard security requirement due to e.g., Bleichenbacher's attack [5] and the implication of non-malleability from IND-CCA2 security [3]. However, in principle HE schemes cannot achieve IND-CCA2 security due to the ability of unrestricted computation over ciphertexts. To resolve the issue, Emura et al. [18,19] proposed the notion of *keyed-homomorphic PKE (KH-PKE)* in which the homomorphic evaluation on ciphertexts requires an evaluation key. They introduced a security definition for KH-PKE called KH-CCA security, which, roughly speaking, ensures IND-CCA2 security for adversaries not having the evaluation key and IND-CCA1 security for those having the evaluation key in advance. It is also known that KH-CCA security implies security against ciphertext validity attacks [17].

As concrete instantiations of KH-PKE, Emura et al. [18,19] proposed a multiplicative KH-PKE scheme based on the Decisional Diffie–Hellman (DDH) assumption and an additive KH-PKE scheme based on the Decisional Composite Residuosity (DCR) assumption. Multiplicative KH-PKE schemes are also proposed by Libert et al. [28] based on the Decisional Linear (DLIN) assumption and by Jutla and Roy [26] based on the Symmetric External Diffie–Hellman (SXDH) assumption. On the other hand, for fully homomorphic versions of KH-PKE called keyed-FHE, Lai et al. [27] proposed a construction using indistinguishability obfuscation (iO) [2] and recently Sato et al. [34,35] proposed a construction without iO. Moreover, recently Maeda and Nuida [29] proposed a two-level KH-PKE scheme based on the SXDH assumption. To the best of our knowledge, these are all of the known constructions of KH-PKE schemes in the literature, which are still few in comparison to ordinary (non-keyed) HE schemes. In particular, there exists only one known construction of leveled KH-PKE schemes.

On the other hand, we note that except for keyed-FHE, the homomorphic evaluation algorithm in KH-PKE was formulated in a way of corresponding to a single operation, say $C_1 + C_2$. When we perform two operations sequentially, say $(C_1 + C_2) + C_3$, some instantiation of KH-PKE (such as in [18,19]) performs a rerandomization at the end of the computation of $C' := C_1 + C_2$ and then another rerandomization at the end of the computation of $C' + C_3$. From the viewpoint of efficiency, we want to gather the two operations as a single operation and perform only one rerandomization at the end of the computation. Now, in order to formalize such a technique, the formulation of the homomorphic evaluation algorithm should be enlarged to also handle such sequential operations at once.

However, as an adversary in the KH-CCA game is supposed to have oracle access to the evaluation algorithm, and the modification of the evaluation algorithm as above also enhances the ability of the oracle, the adversary after the modification becomes, in theory, stronger than the original case. As a result, it is not obvious whether or not the KH-CCA security is preserved by this modification of the evaluation algorithm. (We note that, as a related work, Emura et al. [20] studied similar security issues when constructing "mis-operation resistant" searchable homomorphic encryption from keyed-homomorphic identity-based encryption. However, their work only concerned such an issue in some concrete schemes, and no argument was given in the same generality as the present paper.)

1.1 Our Contributions

Our contributions in this paper are twofold. First, we consider the modification of the evaluation algorithm to handle multiple operations at once as in the last paragraph; let $\mathcal{E}$ and $\mathsf{Comp}(\mathcal{E})$ denote the original and the modified KH-PKE schemes, respectively. We show that, in general, the KH-CCA security of $\mathcal{E}$ does not imply the KH-CCA security of $\mathsf{Comp}(\mathcal{E})$; under some reasonable assumptions, we construct a KH-CCA secure $\mathcal{E}$ for which $\mathsf{Comp}(\mathcal{E})$ is not KH-CCA secure (Theorem 1). We also show that, if $\mathcal{E}$ is moreover circuit private, then the KH-CCA security of $\mathcal{E}$ implies the KH-CCA security of $\mathsf{Comp}(\mathcal{E})$ (Theorem 2).

We explain a technical overview of our results above. As the counterexample, from any KH-CCA secure KH-PKE scheme $\mathcal{E}_0$ we construct a KH-CCA secure KH-PKE scheme $\mathcal{E}$ with the following property: $\mathcal{E}$ has a special ciphertext C_0 for which given the result $C + C_0$ of a homomorphic operation for C_0 and any ciphertext C, the original ciphertext C can be easily recovered. Now given a challenge ciphertext C^*, a KH-CCA adversary against $\mathsf{Comp}(\mathcal{E})$ asks the evaluation oracle to obtain at once the ciphertext $(C^* + C') + C_0$ where C' is another ciphertext. Due to the property above, now the adversary recovers the ciphertext $C^* + C'$ and knows its plaintext (and also knows the plaintext of C^* by using the plaintext of C') by querying $C^* + C'$ to the decryption oracle (which is not prohibited, as $C^* + C'$ itself was not returned by the evaluation oracle). Hence $\mathsf{Comp}(\mathcal{E})$ is not KH-CCA secure. On the other hand, the circuit privacy assumed in Theorem 2 guarantees that there exists no such special ciphertext C_0.

Secondly, we extend the Catalano–Fiore conversion for HE schemes to the case of KH-PKE schemes, to obtain a two-level KH-PKE scheme from a linearly KH-PKE scheme (Theorem 3). As a technical overview, we note that in the original Catalano–Fiore conversion, a level-2 ciphertext consists of a number of level-1 ciphertexts. Therefore, if we just apply it to a KH-PKE scheme, then a level-2 ciphertext of the resulting scheme is malleable even without the evaluation key, which violates the KH-CCA security. To resolve this issue, we modify level-2 ciphertexts by encrypting the whole of each level-2 ciphertext again (where the key for the latter encryption is included in the evaluation key). Assuming appropriate security properties for the latter encryption, an adversary cannot modify nor generate a level-2 ciphertext without using the evaluation key or the evaluation oracle. This property enables us to control the behaviors of ciphertexts well in our security proof.

1.2 Organization of the Paper

Section 2 summarizes basic definitions and properties used in this paper. Section 3 summarizes basic definitions for KH-PKE. In Sect. 4, we describe the first part of our results on the extended evaluation algorithm for multiple sequential operations. Section 5 summarizes the definitions for the original Catalano–Fiore conversion for non-keyed HE schemes. In Sect. 6, we describe the second part of our results on the extension of the Catalano–Fiore conversion to KH-PKE schemes.

2 Preliminaries

2.1 Basic Definitions and Properties

In this paper, "PPT" is an abbreviation of "probabilistic polynomial-time". We write $x \xleftarrow{\$} S$ to mean a uniformly random choice of an element x from a finite set S. We say that a function $f \colon \mathbb{N} \to \mathbb{R}$ is *negligible* (in security parameter λ) if for any integer $k > 0$, there exists an integer $\lambda_k > 0$ satisfying that for any $\lambda > \lambda_k$ we have $|f(\lambda)| < \lambda^{-k}$. For random variables X, Y on a finite set U, their statistical distance is defined by $\mathsf{SD}[X, Y] = \sum_{u \in U} |\Pr[u \leftarrow X] - \Pr[u \leftarrow Y]|$.

2.2 Homomorphic Encryption

We explain the syntax for *additively homomorphic encryption (HE)* consisting of the following four PPT algorithms.

- $\mathsf{Gen}(1^\lambda)$: Given the security parameter λ as input, it outputs a public key pk and a secret key sk.
- $\mathsf{Enc}(\mathsf{pk}, M)$: Given a public key pk and a plaintext M as input, it outputs a ciphertext C.
- $\mathsf{Dec}(\mathsf{sk}, C)$: Given a secret key sk and a ciphertext C as input, it outputs either a plaintext or a failure symbol $\bot$.
- $\mathsf{Add}(\mathsf{pk}, C_1, C_2)$: Given a public key pk and ciphertexts C_1, C_2 as input, it outputs either a ciphertext or $\bot$.

We require an additively HE scheme to satisfy the correctness as follows: for any $(\mathsf{pk}, \mathsf{sk}) \leftarrow \mathsf{Gen}(1^\lambda)$,

- for any plaintext M and any $C \leftarrow \mathsf{Enc}(\mathsf{pk}, M)$, we have $M \leftarrow \mathsf{Dec}(\mathsf{sk}, C)$;
- for any ciphertexts C_1, C_2, if $M_i \leftarrow \mathsf{Dec}(\mathsf{sk}, C_i)$ for $i = 1, 2$ and $C \leftarrow \mathsf{Add}(\mathsf{pk}, C_1, C_2)$, then we have $M_1 + M_2 \leftarrow \mathsf{Dec}(\mathsf{sk}, C)$.

By *linearly HE* we mean additive HE together with a PPT algorithm cMult(pk, m, C_0) that, given a public key pk, a plaintext m, and a ciphertext C_0 as input, outputs either a ciphertext or $\perp$. Now the correctness also requires that for any (pk, sk) $\leftarrow$ Gen(1^λ), any plaintext m, and any ciphertext C_0, if $M_0 \leftarrow$ Dec(sk, C_0) and $C \leftarrow$ cMult(pk, m, C_0), then we have $m \cdot M_0 \leftarrow$ Dec(sk, C).

By *two-level HE* we mean linearly HE together with the following three PPT algorithms (we write the original algorithms Add and cMult as Add_1 and cMult_1, respectively), where the ciphertexts are classified into level-1 and level-2, and the input and output ciphertexts for Add_1 and cMult_1 are of level-1:

- Mult(pk, C_1, C_2): Given a public key pk and level-1 ciphertexts C_1, C_2 as input, it outputs either a level-2 ciphertext or $\perp$. The correctness requires that for any (pk, sk) $\leftarrow$ Gen(1^λ) and any level-1 ciphertexts C_1, C_2, if $M_i \leftarrow$ Dec(sk, C_i) for $i = 1, 2$ and $C \leftarrow$ Mult(pk, C_1, C_2), then we have $M_1 \cdot M_2 \leftarrow$ Dec(sk, C).
- Add_2(pk, C_1, C_2): Given a public key pk and level-2 ciphertexts C_1, C_2 as input, it outputs either a level-2 ciphertext or $\perp$. The correctness condition is similar to the case of Add_1.
- cMult_2(pk, m, C_0): Given a public key, a plaintext m, and a level-2 ciphertext C_0 as input, it outputs either a level-2 ciphertext or $\perp$. The correctness condition is similar to the case of cMult_1.

2.3   Symmetric Key Encryption

We explain the syntax for symmetric key encryption (SKE) consisting of the following three PPT algorithms.

- Gen(1^λ): Given the security parameter λ as input, it outputs an encryption key K.
- Enc(K, M): Given an encryption key K and a plaintext M as input, it outputs a ciphertext C.
- Dec(K, C): Given an encryption key K and a ciphertext C as input, it outputs either a plaintext or a failure symbol $\perp$.

We require an SKE scheme to satisfy the correctness: for any K $\leftarrow$ Gen(1^λ), any plaintext M, and any $C \leftarrow$ Enc(K, M), we have $M \leftarrow$ Dec(K, C).

We explain two security definitions for SKE used in this paper.

Definition 1 (IND-CPA Security). *We say that an SKE scheme $\mathcal{SE} =$ (Gen, Enc, Dec) is (Left-or-Right) IND-CPA secure if for any PPT adversary $\mathcal{A}$, the advantage*

$$\left| \Pr \left[\text{K} \leftarrow \text{Gen}(1^\lambda); b \xleftarrow{\$} \{0,1\}; b' \leftarrow \mathcal{A}^{\mathcal{O}(b)} : b = b' \right] - \frac{1}{2} \right|$$

is negligible in λ, where $\mathcal{O}(b)$ denotes an oracle that, given two plaintexts m_0, m_1, returns an output of Enc(K, m_b).

Definition 2 (INT-CTXT Security). *We say that an SKE scheme* $\mathcal{SE} =$ (Gen, Enc, Dec) *is* INT-CTXT *secure if for any PPT adversary* $\mathcal{A}$, *the winning probability of* $\mathcal{A}$ *in the following game is negligible in* λ:

- *First, the challenger generates* $\mathsf{K} \leftarrow \mathsf{Gen}(1^\lambda)$ *and sets* List $= \emptyset$. *Then* $\mathcal{A}$ *performs the following two kinds of procedures, possibly adaptively and many times:*
  - $\mathcal{A}$ *sends a plaintext* m *to the challenger. The challenger sends an output* C *of* $\mathsf{Enc}(\mathsf{K}, m)$ *back to* $\mathcal{A}$ *and appends* C *to* List.
  - $\mathcal{A}$ *sends a ciphertext* C^* *to the challenger. When* $C^* \notin$ List *and* $\mathsf{Dec}(\mathsf{K}, C^*) \neq \perp$, $\mathcal{A}$ *wins the game. Otherwise, the challenger returns to* $\mathcal{A}$ *"valid" if* $\mathsf{Dec}(\mathsf{K}, C^*) \neq \perp$ *and "invalid" if* $\mathsf{Dec}(\mathsf{K}, C^*) = \perp$.

We note that an SKE scheme satisfying both IND-CPA and INT-CTXT security can be constructed from an IND-CPA secure SKE and an SUF-CMA secure message authentication code explained in the next subsection [4].

2.4 Message Authentication Codes

We explain the syntax for message authentication codes (MACs) consisting of the following three PPT algorithms.

- $\mathsf{Gen}(1^\lambda)$: Given the security parameter λ as input, it outputs a MAC key K.
- $\mathsf{Tag}(\mathsf{K}, M)$: Given a MAC key K and a plaintext M as input, it outputs a MAC tag τ.
- $\mathsf{Verify}(\mathsf{K}, M, \tau)$: Given a MAC key K, a plaintext M, and a MAC tag τ as input, it outputs 0 ("invalid") or 1 ("valid").

We require a MAC to satisfy the correctness: for any $\mathsf{K} \leftarrow \mathsf{Gen}(1^\lambda)$, any plaintext M, and any $\tau \leftarrow \mathsf{Tag}(\mathsf{K}, M)$, we have $1 \leftarrow \mathsf{Verify}(\mathsf{K}, M, \tau)$.

We explain the security definition for MAC used in this paper.

Definition 3 (SUF-CMA Security). *We say that a MAC* MAC $=$ (Gen, Tag, Verify) *is* SUF-CMA *secure if for any PPT adversary* $\mathcal{A}$, *the winning probability of* $\mathcal{A}$ *in the following game is negligible in* λ:

1. *The challenger generates* $\mathsf{K} \leftarrow \mathsf{Gen}(1^\lambda)$ *and sets* List $= \emptyset$.
2. $\mathcal{A}$ *sends a plaintext* m *to the challenger. The challenger generates* $\tau \leftarrow \mathsf{Tag}(\mathsf{K}, m)$, *sends* (m, τ) *back to* $\mathcal{A}$, *and appends* (m, τ) *to* List. *This procedure may be performed multiple times.*
3. $\mathcal{A}$ *sends a pair* (m^*, τ^*) *to the challenger.* $\mathcal{A}$ *wins the game if and only if* $(m^*, \tau^*) \notin$ List *and* $1 \leftarrow \mathsf{Verify}(\mathsf{K}, m^*, \tau^*)$.

3 Keyed-Homomorphic Public-Key Encryption

We explain the syntax and the security notion for keyed-homomorphic public key encryption (KH-PKE). The syntax for KH-PKE is given by modifying the syntax for (non-keyed) HE in the following manner:

- In addition to pk and sk, the key generation algorithm Gen also outputs an evaluation key ek.
- The homomorphic evaluation algorithms, such as Add and Mult, take ek instead of pk as a part of input.

The correctness condition for KH-PKE is basically the same as that for HE except for the differences mentioned above.

The standard security notion for KH-PKE is explained as follows.

Definition 4 (KH-CCA Security). *We say that a KH-PKE scheme is KH-CCA secure if for any PPT adversary $\mathcal{A}$, the advantage*

$$\left| \Pr\left[(\mathsf{pk}, \mathsf{sk}, \mathsf{ek}) \leftarrow \mathsf{Gen}(1^\lambda); (M_0^*, M_1^*, \mathsf{st}) \leftarrow \mathcal{A}^{\mathcal{O}}(\mathsf{find}, \mathsf{pk}); \right. \right.$$

$$\left. \left. b \xleftarrow{\$} \{0,1\}; C^* \leftarrow \mathsf{Enc}(\mathsf{pk}, M_b^*); b' \leftarrow \mathcal{A}^{\mathcal{O}}(\mathsf{guess}, \mathsf{st}, C^*) : b = b' \right] - \frac{1}{2} \right|$$

is negligible in λ. Here $\mathcal{O}$ denotes three oracles RevEK, Dec, and Eval defined as follows, and we set List $= \emptyset$ in the find phase and set List $= \{C^*\}$ at the beginning of the guess phase.

- *RevEK: It returns the evaluation key ek. This oracle can be used only once.*
- *Dec: For a ciphertext C as input, it returns $\perp$ if $C \in$ List, and otherwise it returns an output of Dec(sk, C). In the guess phase, this oracle cannot be used when RevEK has been used.*
- *Eval: For a type of possible operation F in the scheme (such as Add, cMult, and Mult) and a list of inputs $\boldsymbol{C}$ for F (e.g., $\boldsymbol{C} = (m, C_0)$ when $F =$ cMult) as input, it returns an output C of $F(\mathsf{ek}, \boldsymbol{C})$. Moreover, if at least one ciphertext in $\boldsymbol{C}$ is in List, then C is appended to List. This oracle cannot be used when RevEK has been used.*

We also extend the notion of circuit privacy for HE (following Catalano and Fiore [13]) to the case of linearly KH-PKE. The definition for the case of additively KH-PKE is similar and is omitted here.

Definition 5 (Circuit Privacy for KH-PKE). *We say that a linearly KH-PKE scheme is circuit private if there exist a PPT algorithm Sim and a negligible function ϵ satisfying the following condition: for any (pk, sk, ek) $\leftarrow$ Gen(1^λ),*

- *for any ciphertexts C_1, C_2, if $m_1 \leftarrow$ Dec(sk, C_1) and $m_2 \leftarrow$ Dec(sk, C_2), then we have SD[Add(ek, C_1, C_2), Sim(1^λ, ek, $m_1 + m_2$)] $\leq \epsilon(\lambda)$;*
- *for any plaintext m, and any ciphertext C_0, if $M_0 \leftarrow$ Dec(sk, C_0), then we have SD[cMult(ek, m, C_0), Sim(1^λ, ek, $m \cdot M_0$)] $\leq \epsilon(\lambda)$.*

4 On Extension of the Evaluation Algorithm

In this section, we introduce an extension of the evaluation algorithm in KH-PKE schemes to multiple sequential operations, and investigate the effect to the

196 H. Shinoki and K. Nuida

security. Here we focus only on the case of additively KH-PKE for the sake of simplicity, but similar results hold for a wider class of KH-PKE schemes as well; see the full version of this paper.

Our extension of the evaluation algorithm for KH-PKE is defined as follows.

Definition 6. *Let $\mathcal{E}$ be an additively KH-PKE scheme. Let $C(\mathsf{Add})$ denote the set of circuits for which the two-input addition is associated to each gate in the circuit. Now for each n-input circuit $f \in C(\mathsf{Add})$, we define the extended evaluation algorithm $\mathsf{Eval}(\mathsf{ek}, f, C_1, \ldots, C_n)$ by naturally composing the algorithm Add in $\mathcal{E}$. We write the resulting scheme with the extended evaluation algorithm as $\mathsf{Comp}(\mathcal{E})$.*

For example, if f is a circuit $(C_1 + C_2) + C_3$, then

$$\mathsf{Eval}(\mathsf{ek}, f, C_1, C_2, C_3) = \mathsf{Add}(\mathsf{ek}, \mathsf{Add}(\mathsf{ek}, C_1, C_2), C_3) .$$

We also naturally extend the KH-CCA security to such a scheme $\mathsf{Comp}(\mathcal{E})$ by modifying the evaluation oracle accordingly. A motivation of considering such an extension $\mathsf{Comp}(\mathcal{E})$ is that the extended evaluation algorithm can sometimes be implemented more efficiently without changing the output distribution. For example, when the algorithm Add in the original scheme $\mathcal{E}$ performs a rerandomization for each output, the computation of $\mathsf{Eval}(\mathsf{ek}, f, C_1, C_2, C_3)$ in the example above can be simplified by omitting the first rerandomization at the end of $\mathsf{Add}(\mathsf{ek}, C_1, C_2)$.

Now the extension from $\mathcal{E}$ to $\mathsf{Comp}(\mathcal{E})$ also changes the security definition in a direction of enhancing an oracle, hence strengthening the ability of adversaries. Therefore, it is not obvious whether or not KH-CCA security of $\mathcal{E}$ implies KH-CCA security of $\mathsf{Comp}(\mathcal{E})$. In fact, we have the following non-implication result.

Theorem 1. *Assume that there exist a KH-CCA secure additively KH-PKE scheme and an SUF-CMA secure MAC. Then there exists a KH-CCA secure additively KH-PKE scheme $\mathcal{E}$ for which $\mathsf{Comp}(\mathcal{E})$ is not KH-CCA secure.*

Proof (Sketch; see the full version for details). Take an additively KH-PKE scheme $\mathcal{E}_0$ and a MAC MAC as in the hypothesis of the statement. We construct an additively KH-PKE scheme $\mathcal{E}$ by modifying $\mathcal{E}_0$ as follows. The evaluation key for $\mathcal{E}$ is a pair of the evaluation key for $\mathcal{E}_0$ and the key for MAC. The ciphertext space of $\mathcal{E}$ consists of non-tagged ciphertexts (i.e., those in $\mathcal{E}_0$), tagged ciphertexts (by MAC), and a special symbol S for which $\mathsf{Dec}(\mathsf{sk}, S) := 0$ and $\mathsf{Add}(\mathsf{ek}, S, S) := S$. Enc outputs only non-tagged ciphertexts. Dec with tagged input ciphertext works in the same way as $\mathcal{E}_0$ if the tag is valid, and otherwise it rejects the input. For Add, it rejects the input if some input ciphertext has an invalid tag. In the other case, when the input involves S, Add removes the tag if the other ciphertext is tagged, and appends a fresh tag if the other ciphertext is non-tagged. When the input does not involve S, Add works in the same way as $\mathcal{E}_0$ (i.e., outputting a non-tagged ciphertext).

Now the correctness of $\mathcal{E}$ follows from the correctness of $\mathcal{E}_0$ and MAC. On the other hand, the KH-CCA security of $\mathsf{Comp}(\mathcal{E})$ does not hold; given a challenge ciphertext C^*, an adversary can generate $C_0 \leftarrow \mathsf{Enc}(\mathsf{pk}, m_0)$ with $m_0 \neq 0$, make an extended evaluation query to obtain $(C, \tau) \leftarrow \mathsf{Add}(\mathsf{ek}, \mathsf{Add}(\mathsf{ek}, C^*, C_0), S)$ at once, make a decryption query to obtain $\mathsf{Dec}(\mathsf{sk}, C)$ which is equal to $\mathsf{Dec}(\mathsf{sk}, C^*) + m_0$ by the construction of $\mathcal{E}$, and finally obtain $\mathsf{Dec}(\mathsf{sk}, C^*)$ by subtracting m_0.

Our remaining task is to show that $\mathcal{E}$ is KH-CCA secure. For any PPT adversary $\mathcal{A}_\mathcal{E}$ for the KH-CCA game of $\mathcal{E}$, consider a PPT adversary $\mathcal{B}_{\mathcal{E}_0}$ that plays the role of the challenger in the KH-CCA game of $\mathcal{E}$ with $\mathcal{A}_\mathcal{E}$ by generating a MAC key by itself and utilizing the own queries in the KH-CCA game of $\mathcal{E}_0$ (for example, on receiving a query $\mathsf{Add}(C_1, (C_2, \tau))$ from $\mathcal{A}_\mathcal{E}$, $\mathcal{B}_{\mathcal{E}_0}$ verifies the tag τ, makes a query $\mathsf{Add}(C_1, C_2)$ to its challenger, and forwards the challenger's response to $\mathcal{A}_\mathcal{E}$). Let List_0 denote the list List in the KH-CCA game of $\mathcal{E}_0$. Now if $\mathcal{B}_{\mathcal{E}_0}$ is able to simulate all the responses to $\mathcal{A}_\mathcal{E}$'s queries correctly, then $\mathcal{B}_{\mathcal{E}_0}$ has the same advantage as $\mathcal{A}_\mathcal{E}$, therefore the KH-CCA security of $\mathcal{E}_0$ implies that the advantage of $\mathcal{A}_\mathcal{E}$ is negligible. Hence, in order for $\mathcal{A}_\mathcal{E}$ to break the KH-CCA security of $\mathcal{E}$, $\mathcal{A}_\mathcal{E}$ has to make, with non-negligible probability, a query that cannot be responded by $\mathcal{B}_{\mathcal{E}_0}$. Such a query is necessarily of the form $\mathsf{Dec}(\widetilde{C})$ with $\widetilde{C} = C$ ($\neq S$) or (C, τ) with valid tag τ, satisfying that $\widetilde{C} \notin \mathsf{List}$ (i.e., $\mathcal{B}_{\mathcal{E}_0}$ cannot reject the query) and $\mathcal{B}_{\mathcal{E}_0}$ cannot determine the plaintext for C even by using its own decryption query.

We show that, for the purpose, $\mathcal{A}_\mathcal{E}$ has no advantage of using tagged ciphertexts $\widetilde{C} = (C, \tau)$. Namely, if $\widetilde{C} = (C, \tau)$ satisfies the conditions above, then $\mathcal{A}_\mathcal{E}$ should have received (C, τ) from $\mathcal{B}_{\mathcal{E}_0}$ at a previous step where $\mathcal{B}_{\mathcal{E}_0}$ generated the valid tag τ (in response to $\mathcal{A}_\mathcal{E}$'s query of the form $\mathsf{Add}(S, C)$ or $\mathsf{Add}(C, S)$), as otherwise $\mathcal{A}_\mathcal{E}$ with the new valid tag τ would break the SUF-CMA security of MAC. Now C was not in List at that previous step (otherwise $\widetilde{C}$ was appended to List at that time, a contradiction), while $\mathcal{B}_{\mathcal{E}_0}$ could not determine the plaintext of C at that time either (otherwise $\mathcal{B}_{\mathcal{E}_0}$ would have known the plaintext of $\widetilde{C}$ and could respond to the current query, a contradiction). Therefore, $\mathcal{A}_\mathcal{E}$ could have the same effect by instead making a query $\mathsf{Dec}(C)$ at that previous step.

Based on the previous paragraph, the tagged ciphertexts are essentially useless for $\mathcal{A}_\mathcal{E}$, therefore the situation is essentially equivalent to the scheme $\mathcal{E}$ without tagged ciphertexts, which is basically the same as $\mathcal{E}_0$. Hence the KH-CCA security of $\mathcal{E}_0$ implies that $\mathcal{A}_\mathcal{E}$ cannot have non-negligible advantage, concluding the proof (see the full version of this paper for a more rigorous argument).   □

On the other hand, we give the following affirmative result on preserving the KH-CCA security, with an additional assumption of circuit privacy.

Theorem 2. *If an additively KH-PKE scheme $\mathcal{E}$ is KH-CCA secure and circuit private, then $\mathsf{Comp}(\mathcal{E})$ is KH-CCA secure.*

Proof (Sketch; see the full version for details). For any PPT adversary $\mathcal{A}_\mathsf{Comp}$ for the KH-CCA game of $\mathsf{Comp}(\mathcal{E})$, consider a PPT adversary $\mathcal{B}_\mathcal{E}$ that plays the role of the challenger in the KH-CCA game of $\mathsf{Comp}(\mathcal{E})$ with $\mathcal{A}_\mathsf{Comp}$ by utilizing the own queries in the KH-CCA game of $\mathcal{E}$ (for example, on receiving a query $\mathsf{Eval}(f, C_1, C_2, C_3)$ from $\mathcal{A}_{\mathsf{Comp}}$ with f being the circuit $(x_1 + x_2) + x_3$, $\mathcal{B}_{\mathcal{E}}$ makes a query $\mathsf{Add}(C_1, C_2)$ to its challenger and obtains the response C', makes a query $\mathsf{Add}(C', C_3)$ to its challenger and obtains the response C'', and forwards C'' to $\mathcal{A}_{\mathsf{Comp}}$). Let $\mathsf{List}_{\mathsf{Comp}}$ denote the list List in the KH-CCA game of $\mathsf{Comp}(\mathcal{E})$. Now if $\mathcal{B}_{\mathcal{E}}$ is able to simulate all the responses to $\mathcal{A}_{\mathsf{Comp}}$'s queries correctly, then $\mathcal{B}_{\mathcal{E}}$ has the same advantage as $\mathcal{A}_{\mathsf{Comp}}$, therefore the KH-CCA security of $\mathcal{E}$ implies that the advantage of $\mathcal{A}_{\mathsf{Comp}}$ is negligible. Hence, in order for $\mathcal{A}_{\mathsf{Comp}}$ to break the KH-CCA security of $\mathsf{Comp}(\mathcal{E})$, $\mathcal{A}_{\mathsf{Comp}}$ has to make, with non-negligible probability, a query that cannot be responded by $\mathcal{B}_{\mathcal{E}}$. Such a query is necessarily of the form $\mathsf{Dec}(C)$ satisfying that $C \notin \mathsf{List}_{\mathsf{Comp}}$ (i.e., $\mathcal{B}_{\mathcal{E}}$ cannot reject the query) and $\mathcal{B}_{\mathcal{E}}$ cannot determine the plaintext for C even by using its own decryption query (in particular, $C \in \mathsf{List}$). We call such a query by $\mathcal{A}_{\mathsf{Comp}}$ an *unallowable query*.

Now we modify the behavior of the challenger in the KH-CCA game of $\mathcal{E}$ in a way that on receiving a query of the form $\mathsf{Add}(C_1, C_2)$, the challenger computes $\mathsf{Sim}(1^\lambda, \mathsf{ek}, \mathsf{Dec}(\mathsf{sk}, C_1) + \mathsf{Dec}(\mathsf{sk}, C_2))$ instead of $\mathsf{Add}(\mathsf{ek}, C_1, C_2)$ where the algorithm Sim is as in the definition of the circuit privacy of $\mathcal{E}$. By the condition of Sim, this modification only affects the behavior of the game in a negligible way (note that as $\mathcal{B}_{\mathcal{E}}$ is PPT, the challenger receives only polynomially many such queries). After this modification, the behavior of $\mathcal{A}_{\mathsf{Comp}}$ becomes independent of the outputs of the algorithm Sim executed to generate intermediate ciphertexts in each of $\mathcal{A}_{\mathsf{Comp}}$'s evaluation queries (for example, $\mathsf{Add}(C_1, C_2)$ in the case of a query $\mathsf{Eval}(f, C_1, C_2, C_3)$ with f being the circuit $(x_1 + x_2) + x_3$).

We assume for the contrary that an unallowable query $\mathsf{Dec}(C)$ is made with non-negligible probability, say p. Then we have $C \in \mathsf{List} \setminus \mathsf{List}_{\mathsf{Comp}}$ as mentioned above. Now we note that such a difference between List and $\mathsf{List}_{\mathsf{Comp}}$ arises only when generating intermediate ciphertexts at some evaluation query by $\mathcal{A}_{\mathsf{Comp}}$. Therefore, the algorithm $\mathsf{Sim}(1^\lambda, \mathsf{ek}, m)$ where $m := \mathsf{Dec}(\mathsf{sk}, C)$ was performed when generating some intermediate ciphertext at some previous query by $\mathcal{A}_{\mathsf{Comp}}$, and that execution of $\mathsf{Sim}(1^\lambda, \mathsf{ek}, m)$ yielded the ciphertext C. As the behavior of $\mathcal{A}_{\mathsf{Comp}}$ is independent of that execution of $\mathsf{Sim}(1^\lambda, \mathsf{ek}, m)$ as mentioned above, it follows that $p \leq p_C$ where $p_C := \Pr[C \leftarrow \mathsf{Sim}(1^\lambda, \mathsf{ek}, m)]$.

However, the property $C \in \mathsf{List}$ implies that C is generated by a sequence of algorithms Add starting from the challenge ciphertext C^*, therefore for each $i \in \{0, 1\}$, $\mathcal{B}_{\mathcal{E}}$ can compute the plaintext m_i satisfying that C would have the plaintext m_i if the challenge bit b in the KH-CCA game is $b = i$. We also note that $m_0 \neq m_1$, as otherwise $\mathcal{B}_{\mathcal{E}}$ could determine the plaintext of C regardless of b and hence could respond to the unallowable query $\mathsf{Dec}(C)$, a contradiction. Therefore, now $\mathcal{B}_{\mathcal{E}}$ can increase its winning probability by modifying the behavior in a way that whenever $\mathcal{B}_{\mathcal{E}}$ detects an unallowable query $\mathsf{Dec}(C)$ (which is in fact possible, as $\mathcal{B}_{\mathcal{E}}$ can know the current status of the list List while $\mathcal{B}_{\mathcal{E}}$ itself maintains the list $\mathsf{List}_{\mathsf{Comp}}$), $\mathcal{B}_{\mathcal{E}}$ makes a RevEK query to obtain the evaluation key ek, and for each $i \in \{0, 1\}$, $\mathcal{B}_{\mathcal{E}}$ computes $C_i \leftarrow \mathsf{Sim}(1^\lambda, \mathsf{ek}, m_i)$ and outputs the bit i if $C_i = C$. By this modification, the winning probability increases by $p \cdot \Pr[C_b \leftarrow \mathsf{Sim}(1^\lambda, \mathsf{ek}, m_b) : C_b = C] = p \cdot p_C \geq p^2$ (as $m_b = m$ by the definition of m_0 and m_1), which is non-negligible as well as p. This contradicts the KH-CCA security of $\mathcal{E}$. Hence an unallowable query is made with only negligible probability. Therefore, the advantage of $\mathcal{A}_{\mathsf{Comp}}$ is negligible by the KH-CCA security of $\mathcal{E}$, concluding the proof (see the full version of this paper for a more rigorous argument).   □

5   Catalano–Fiore Conversion

In this section, we explain the original Catalano–Fiore conversion [13] for linearly HE schemes. Below we sometimes write the algorithms Add and cMult as the form of binary operators $\boxplus$ and $\boxdot$, respectively. The Catalano–Fiore conversion is applied to HE schemes that are *public-space*, meaning that a uniformly random plaintext can be efficiently sampled. Note that many HE schemes are public-space, and most of the known non-public-space HE schemes such as [6,7,14,30] can be easily converted to public-space schemes.

The conversion yields a two-level HE scheme, whose level-1 ciphertexts are the same as the original scheme and whose level-2 ciphertexts are composed of a number of ciphertexts in the original scheme. The conversion is described as follows.

Definition 7 (Catalano–Fiore Conversion). *Let $\mathcal{E}$ be a linearly HE scheme that is public-space in the sense described above. Then we define a new two-level HE scheme* $\mathsf{CF}(\mathcal{E}) = (\mathsf{Gen}', \mathsf{Enc}', \mathsf{Dec}_1', \mathsf{Dec}_2', \mathsf{Add}_1, \mathsf{Add}_2, \mathsf{cMult}_1, \mathsf{cMult}_2, \mathsf{Mult})$ *as follows, where for $i \in \{1, 2\}$, Dec_i', Add_i, and cMult_i are decryption, addition, and scalar multiplication algorithms for level-i ciphertexts, respectively.*

- *Gen', Enc', and Dec_1': The same as Gen, Enc, and Dec.*
- *$\mathsf{Dec}_2'(\mathsf{sk}, C)$: First, it parses the level-2 ciphertext C as $C = (\alpha, \beta_{11}, \beta_{21}, \ldots, \beta_{1n}, \beta_{2n})$ for some n, where each component of C is a ciphertext in $\mathcal{E}$. It computes*

$$m = \mathsf{Dec}(\mathsf{sk}, \alpha) + \sum_{i=1}^{n} \mathsf{Dec}(\mathsf{sk}, \beta_{1i}) \cdot \mathsf{Dec}(\mathsf{sk}, \beta_{2i})$$

and outputs m.
- *Add_1 and cMult_1: The same as Add and cMult.*
- *$\mathsf{Mult}(\mathsf{pk}, C_1, C_2)$: Given level-1 ciphertexts C_1 and C_2, it chooses plaintexts m_1 and m_2 uniformly at random, sets $\alpha \leftarrow \mathsf{Enc}(\mathsf{pk}, m_1 \cdot m_2)$, and for each $i = 1, 2$, sets $C_i' \leftarrow \mathsf{Enc}(\mathsf{pk}, -m_i)$ and $\beta_i \leftarrow C_i \boxplus C_i'$. Then it computes*

$$\gamma \leftarrow \alpha \boxplus (m_2 \boxdot \beta_1) \boxplus (m_1 \boxdot \beta_2)$$

(where the $\boxplus$'s are calculated from left to right), and outputs $(\gamma, \beta_1, \beta_2)$.
- *$\mathsf{Add}_2(\mathsf{pk}, C_1, C_2)$: First, it parses the level-2 ciphertexts C_1 and C_2 as*

$$C_1 = (\alpha, \beta_{11}, \beta_{21}, \ldots, \beta_{1i}, \beta_{2i}, \ldots, \beta_{1n_1}, \beta_{2n_1}),$$
$$C_2 = (\gamma, \delta_{11}, \delta_{21}, \ldots, \delta_{1j}, \delta_{2j}, \ldots, \delta_{1n_2}, \delta_{2n_2}).$$

Then it sets $\epsilon \leftarrow \alpha \boxplus \gamma$ and puts

$$C = (\epsilon, \beta_{11}, \beta_{21}, \ldots, \beta_{1n_1}, \beta_{2n_1}, \delta_{11}, \delta_{21}, \ldots, \delta_{1n_2}, \delta_{2n_2}) \, .$$

Finally, it outputs $C' \leftarrow \mathsf{Rerand}(\mathsf{pk}, C)$ where Rerand is as defined later.

- *$\mathsf{cMult}_2(\mathsf{pk}, m, C)$: First, it parses the level-2 ciphertext C as $C = (\alpha, \beta_{11}, \beta_{21}, \ldots, \beta_{1n}, \beta_{2n})$. Then it sets $\alpha' \leftarrow m \boxdot \alpha$ and for each $k = 1, \ldots, n$, sets $\beta'_{1k} \leftarrow m \boxdot \beta_{1k}$, $\beta'_{2k} \leftarrow \beta_{2k}$, and puts $C' = (\alpha', \beta'_{11}, \beta'_{21}, \ldots, \beta'_{1n}, \beta'_{2n})$. Finally, it outputs $C'' \leftarrow \mathsf{Rerand}(\mathsf{pk}, C')$ where Rerand is as defined later.*

Now the algorithm Rerand used in the construction of evaluation algorithms above is given as follows.

- *$\mathsf{Rerand}(\mathsf{pk}, C)$: First, it parses the input C as $C = (\alpha, \beta_{11}, \beta_{21}, \ldots, \beta_{1n}, \beta_{2n})$. For each $i = 1, 2$ and $j = 1, \ldots, n$, it chooses a plaintext m_{ij} uniformly at random and sets $\gamma_{ij} \leftarrow \mathsf{Enc}(\mathsf{pk}, m_{ij})$. Moreover, it sets $\beta'_{ij} \leftarrow \beta_{ij} \boxplus \gamma_{ij}$ and $\delta_j \leftarrow \mathsf{Enc}(\mathsf{pk}, -m_{1j} \cdot m_{2j})$. Then it sets*

$$\epsilon_j \leftarrow \delta_j \boxplus ((-m_{2j}) \boxdot \beta_{1j}) \boxplus ((-m_{1j}) \boxdot \beta_{2j})$$

and $\alpha' \leftarrow \alpha \boxplus \epsilon_1 \boxplus \cdots \boxplus \epsilon_n$, and outputs $C' = (\alpha', \beta'_{11}, \beta'_{21}, \ldots, \beta'_{1n}, \beta'_{2n})$.

6   Catalano–Fiore Conversion for KH-PKE

In this section, we extend the Catalano–Fiore conversion to the case of KH-PKE. In Sect. 6.1, we show that the original Catalano–Fiore conversion applied to a linearly KH-PKE scheme does not preserve KH-CCA security. In Sect. 6.2, we describe our proposed extension of the Catalano–Fiore conversion to the case of KH-PKE that preserves KH-CCA security under some additional condition.

We note that Catalano and Fiore also proposed in [12] a generalization of the conversion to obtain a (slightly restricted) $2d$-level HE scheme (i.e., that allows additions and $2d - 1$ multiplications) from a d-level HE scheme. Although not discussed in this paper, our proposed conversion can be also extended to the case of d-level KH-PKE schemes; see the full version of this paper for details.

6.1   Motivation: The Original Catalano–Fiore Conversion Fails

First, we consider a two-level KH-PKE scheme $\mathsf{CF}(\mathcal{E})$ obtained by simply applying the original Catalano–Fiore conversion to a KH-PKE scheme $\mathcal{E}$. In this case, $\mathsf{CF}(\mathcal{E})$ is in general not KH-CCA secure even if $\mathcal{E}$ is KH-CCA secure. Indeed, the following properties of $\mathsf{CF}(\mathcal{E})$ are contradictory to KH-CCA security:

- An adversary without the evaluation key, given a level-1 ciphertext C, can still generate a level-2 ciphertext $(C, \mathsf{Enc}(\mathsf{pk}, 0), \mathsf{Enc}(\mathsf{pk}, 0))$ with the same plaintext as C.
- An adversary without the evaluation key, given a level-2 ciphertext $C = (\alpha, \beta_1, \beta_2)$, can still generate another level-2 ciphertext $(\alpha, \beta_2, \beta_1)$ with the same plaintext as C.

6.2   Catalano–Fiore Conversion for KH-PKE

The essence of the attacks mentioned in Sect. 6.1 is that an adversary can handle each component of a level-2 ciphertext separately. Our idea to prevent such attacks is that we will encrypt the whole of a level-2 ciphertext again by an appropriate SKE scheme. The resulting conversion method is described as follows.

Definition 8 (Our Conversion for KH-PKE). *Let $\mathcal{E}$ be a linearly KH-PKE scheme that is public-space, and let $\mathcal{SE} = (\mathsf{Gen}_{\mathcal{SE}}, \mathsf{Enc}_{\mathcal{SE}}, \mathsf{Dec}_{\mathcal{SE}})$ be an SKE scheme. We write the algorithms* Add *and* cMult *of $\mathcal{E}$ as the form of binary operators* $\boxplus$ *and* $\boxdot$, *respectively. Then we define a new two-level KH-PKE scheme* $\mathsf{CF'}(\mathcal{E}, \mathcal{SE}) = (\mathsf{Gen'}, \mathsf{Enc'}, \mathsf{Dec'_1}, \mathsf{Dec'_2}, \mathsf{Add}_1, \mathsf{Add}_2, \mathsf{cMult}_1, \mathsf{cMult}_2, \mathsf{Mult})$ *as follows, where for $i \in \{1, 2\}$, $\mathsf{Dec'_i}$, Add_i, and cMult_i are decryption, addition, and scalar multiplication algorithms for level-i ciphertexts, respectively.*

– $\mathsf{Gen'}(1^\lambda)$: *It generates* $(\mathsf{pk}, \mathsf{sk}, \mathsf{ek})$ *by* $\mathsf{Gen}(1^\lambda)$ *and* K *by* $\mathsf{Gen}_{\mathcal{SE}}(1^\lambda)$, *and outputs* $(\mathsf{pk}, \mathsf{sk'}, \mathsf{ek'})$ *where* $\mathsf{sk'} = (\mathsf{sk}, \mathsf{K})$ *and* $\mathsf{ek'} = (\mathsf{ek}, \mathsf{K})$.
– $\mathsf{Enc'}$ *and* $\mathsf{Dec'_1}$: *The same as* Enc *and* Dec.
– $\mathsf{Dec'_2}(\mathsf{sk'}, C)$: *First, it computes* $C' \leftarrow \mathsf{Dec}_{\mathcal{SE}}(\mathsf{K}, C)$ *(it rejects the input if $C' = \perp$), and parses C' as $C' = \alpha||\beta_{11}||\beta_{21}||\cdots||\beta_{1n}||\beta_{2n}$ where "$||$" denotes the concatenation of strings. It computes*

$$m = \mathsf{Dec}(\mathsf{sk}, \alpha) + \sum_{i=1}^n \mathsf{Dec}(\mathsf{sk}, \beta_{1i}) \cdot \mathsf{Dec}(\mathsf{sk}, \beta_{2i})$$

and outputs m.
– $\mathsf{Add}_1(\mathsf{ek'}, C_1, C_2)$ *and* $\mathsf{cMult}_1(\mathsf{ek'}, m, C)$: *The same as* $\mathsf{Add}(\mathsf{ek}, C_1, C_2)$ *and* $\mathsf{cMult}(\mathsf{ek}, m, C)$.
– $\mathsf{Mult}(\mathsf{ek'}, C_1, C_2)$: *It chooses plaintexts m_1 and m_2 uniformly at random, sets $\alpha \leftarrow \mathsf{Enc}(\mathsf{pk}, m_1 \cdot m_2)$, and for each $i = 1, 2$, sets $C'_i \leftarrow \mathsf{Enc}(\mathsf{pk}, -m_i)$ and $\beta_i \leftarrow C_i \boxplus C'_i$. Then it computes*

$$\gamma \leftarrow \alpha \boxplus (m_2 \boxdot \beta_1) \boxplus (m_1 \boxdot \beta_2)$$

(where the $\boxplus$'s are calculated from left to right), and outputs

$$C \leftarrow \mathsf{Enc}_{\mathcal{SE}}(\mathsf{K}, \gamma||\beta_1||\beta_2) \ .$$

– $\mathsf{Add}_2(\mathsf{ek'}, C_1, C_2)$: *First, it computes $C'_1 \leftarrow \mathsf{Dec}_{\mathcal{SE}}(\mathsf{K}, C_1)$ and $C'_2 \leftarrow \mathsf{Dec}_{\mathcal{SE}}(\mathsf{K}, C_2)$ (it rejects the input if $C'_1 = \perp$ or $C'_2 = \perp$), and parses them as*

$$C'_1 = \alpha||\beta_{11}||\beta_{21}||\cdots||\beta_{1n_1}||\beta_{2n_1} \ ,$$
$$C'_2 = \gamma||\delta_{11}||\delta_{21}||\cdots||\delta_{1n_2}||\delta_{2n_2} \ .$$

Then it sets $\epsilon \leftarrow \alpha \boxplus \gamma$ and puts

$$C' = \epsilon||\beta_{11}||\beta_{21}||\cdots||\beta_{1n_1}||\beta_{2n_1}||\delta_{11}||\delta_{21}||\cdots||\delta_{1n_2}||\delta_{2n_2} \ .$$

Finally, it computes $C'' \leftarrow \mathsf{Rerand}(\mathsf{ek}, C')$ and outputs $C \leftarrow \mathsf{Enc}_{\mathcal{SE}}(\mathsf{K}, C'')$, where Rerand is as defined later.

- $\mathsf{cMult}_2(\mathsf{ek}', m, C)$: *First, it computes* $C' \leftarrow \mathsf{Dec}_{\mathcal{SE}}(\mathsf{K}, C)$ *(it rejects the input if* $C' = \bot$*), and parses* C' *as* $C' = \alpha||\beta_{11}||\beta_{21}||\cdots||\beta_{1n}||\beta_{2n}$*. Then it sets* $\alpha' \leftarrow m \boxdot \alpha$ *and for each* $k = 1, \ldots, n$*, sets* $\beta'_{1k} \leftarrow m \boxdot \beta_{1k}$*,* $\beta'_{2k} = \beta_{2k}$*, and puts* $C'_0 = \alpha||\beta'_{11}||\beta'_{21}||\cdots||\beta'_{1n}||\beta'_{2n}$*. Finally, it computes* $C''_0 \leftarrow \mathsf{Rerand}(\mathsf{ek}, C'_0)$ *and outputs* $C_0 \leftarrow \mathsf{Enc}_{\mathcal{SE}}(\mathsf{K}, C''_0)$ *where* Rerand *is as defined later.*

Now the algorithm Rerand *used in the construction of evaluation algorithms is given as follows.*

- $\mathsf{Rerand}(\mathsf{ek}, S)$: *First, it parses the input as* $S = \alpha||\beta_{11}||\beta_{21}||\cdots||\beta_{1n}||\beta_{2n}$*. For each* $i = 1, 2$ *and* $j = 1, \ldots, n$*, it chooses a plaintext* m_{ij} *uniformly at random and sets* $\gamma_{ij} \leftarrow \mathsf{Enc}(\mathsf{pk}, m_{ij})$*. Moreover, it sets* $\beta'_{ij} \leftarrow \beta_{ij} \boxplus \gamma_{ij}$ *and* $\delta_j \leftarrow \mathsf{Enc}(\mathsf{pk}, -m_{1j} \cdot m_{2j})$*. Then it sets*

$$\epsilon_j \leftarrow \delta_j \boxplus ((-m_{2j}) \boxdot \beta_{1j}) \boxplus ((-m_{1j}) \boxdot \beta_{2j})$$

and $\alpha' \leftarrow \alpha \boxplus \epsilon_1 \boxplus \cdots \boxplus \epsilon_n$*, and outputs* $\alpha'||\beta'_{11}||\beta'_{21}||\cdots||\beta'_{1n}||\beta'_{2n}$*.*

The correctness of $\mathsf{CF}'(\mathcal{E}, \mathcal{SE})$ follows from the correctness of $\mathcal{E}$ and $\mathcal{SE}$ and can be verified straightforwardly. Now we have the following result on the security of $\mathsf{CF}'(\mathcal{E}, \mathcal{SE})$.

Theorem 3. *Let* $\mathcal{E}$ *be a linearly KH-PKE scheme that is KH-CCA secure and circuit private, and let* $\mathcal{SE}$ *be an SKE scheme that is IND-CPA secure and INT-CTXT secure. Then* $\mathsf{CF}'(\mathcal{E}, \mathcal{SE})$ *is KH-CCA secure.*

Proof (Sketch; see the full version for details). For any PPT adversary $\mathcal{A}_{\mathsf{CF}'}$ for the KH-CCA game of $\mathsf{CF}'(\mathcal{E}, \mathcal{SE})$, consider a PPT adversary $\mathcal{B}_{\mathcal{E}}$ that plays the role of the challenger in the KH-CCA game of $\mathsf{CF}'(\mathcal{E}, \mathcal{SE})$ with $\mathcal{A}_{\mathsf{CF}'}$ by generating the key K for $\mathcal{SE}$ by itself and utilizing the own queries in the KH-CCA game of $\mathcal{E}$ in a way similar to the proof of Theorems 1 and 2. Let $\mathsf{List}_{\mathsf{CF}'}$ denote the list List in the KH-CCA game of $\mathsf{CF}'(\mathcal{E}, \mathcal{SE})$. Now if $\mathcal{B}_{\mathcal{E}}$ is able to simulate all the responses to $\mathcal{A}_{\mathsf{CF}'}$'s queries correctly, then $\mathcal{B}_{\mathcal{E}}$ has the same advantage as $\mathcal{A}_{\mathsf{CF}'}$, therefore the KH-CCA security of $\mathcal{E}$ implies that the advantage of $\mathcal{A}_{\mathsf{CF}'}$ is negligible. Hence, in order for $\mathcal{A}_{\mathsf{CF}'}$ to break the KH-CCA security of $\mathsf{CF}'(\mathcal{E}, \mathcal{SE})$, $\mathcal{A}_{\mathsf{CF}'}$ has to make, with non-negligible probability, a query that cannot be responded by $\mathcal{B}_{\mathcal{E}}$. Such a query is necessarily a decryption query satisfying that the input ciphertext C is not in $\mathsf{List}_{\mathsf{CF}'}$ and C is

- a level-1 ciphertext, and $\mathcal{B}_{\mathcal{E}}$ cannot determine the plaintext for C even by using its own decryption query (in particular, $C \in \mathsf{List}$); or
- a level-2 ciphertext, $C' \leftarrow \mathsf{Dec}_{\mathcal{SE}}(\mathsf{K}, C)$ satisfies that $C' \neq \bot$ and C' is correctly parsed as $C' = \alpha||\beta_{11}||\beta_{21}||\cdots||\beta_{1n}||\beta_{2n}$, and $\mathcal{B}_{\mathcal{E}}$ cannot determine the plaintext for some component of C' even by using its own decryption query (in particular, that component is in List).

We call such a query by $\mathcal{A}_{\mathsf{CF}'}$ an *unallowable query*. We suppose that $\mathcal{A}_{\mathsf{CF}'}$ is chosen in a way that it makes an unallowable query as early as possible.

We modify the behavior of the challenger in the KH-CCA game of $\mathcal{E}$ in a way that on receiving an evaluation query from $\mathcal{B}_\mathcal{E}$, the challenger executes the algorithm Sim (with correct input plaintext) in the definition of the circuit privacy of $\mathcal{E}$ instead of the evaluation algorithm itself. By the condition of Sim, this modification only affects the behavior of the game in a negligible way (note that as $\mathcal{B}_\mathcal{E}$ is PPT, the challenger receives only polynomially many such queries).

Moreover, we modify the behavior of $\mathcal{B}_\mathcal{E}$ in a way that at every time of computing $\mathsf{Enc}_{\mathcal{SE}}(\mathsf{K}, c)$ for some c (in responding to $\mathcal{A}_{\mathsf{CF'}}$'s evaluation query with level-2 output ciphertext), $\mathcal{B}_\mathcal{E}$ chooses a string c' with $|c'| = |c|$ uniformly at random and computes $\mathsf{Enc}_{\mathcal{SE}}(\mathsf{K}, c')$ instead. By the IND-CPA security of $\mathcal{SE}$, this modification only affects the behavior of $\mathcal{A}_{\mathsf{CF'}}$ in a negligible way. After the modification, the behavior of $\mathcal{A}_{\mathsf{CF'}}$ becomes independent of the outputs of the algorithm Sim executed by the challenger during $\mathcal{B}_\mathcal{E}$'s response to $\mathcal{A}_{\mathsf{CF'}}$'s evaluation queries.

We show that the first unallowable query made by $\mathcal{A}_{\mathsf{CF'}}$ is with level-1 input ciphertext. Assume for the contrary that it is with level-2 input ciphertext, say C. Then C has been generated by $\mathcal{B}_\mathcal{E}$ in responding to $\mathcal{A}_{\mathsf{CF'}}$'s previous query, as otherwise the valid ciphertext C in $\mathcal{SE}$ that was not previously generated by $\mathsf{Enc}_{\mathcal{SE}}$ would break the INT-CTXT security of $\mathcal{SE}$. Now the input ciphertexts of that previous query were not in $\mathsf{List}_{\mathsf{CF'}}$, as otherwise C has been appended to $\mathsf{List}_{\mathsf{CF'}}$ at that query, contradicting the condition for unallowable query. On the other hand, for at least one input ciphertext, say C_0, of that previous query, $\mathcal{B}_\mathcal{E}$ could not determine the plaintext for C_0, as otherwise $\mathcal{B}_\mathcal{E}$ could determine the plaintext for the output ciphertext C as well, contradicting the condition for unallowable query. This implies that $\mathcal{A}_{\mathsf{CF'}}$ could make an unallowable query with input ciphertext C_0 at that previous step, contradicting the assumption that $\mathcal{A}_{\mathsf{CF'}}$ makes an unallowable query as early as possible. Hence the first unallowable query made by $\mathcal{A}_{\mathsf{CF'}}$ is with level-1 input ciphertext.

We assume for the contrary that an unallowable query $\mathsf{Dec}(C)$, where C is a level-1 ciphertext C as discussed above, is made with non-negligible probability, say p. Then we have $C \in \mathsf{List} \setminus \mathsf{List}_{\mathsf{CF'}}$ by the condition for unallowable query. Now we note that such a difference between List and $\mathsf{List}_{\mathsf{CF'}}$ arises only when $\mathcal{B}_\mathcal{E}$ makes some evaluation query in order to respond to $\mathcal{A}_{\mathsf{CF'}}$'s evaluation query with level-2 output ciphertext. Therefore, the algorithm $\mathsf{Sim}(1^\lambda, \mathsf{ek}, m)$ where $m := \mathsf{Dec}(\mathsf{sk}, C)$ was performed at some previous query by $\mathcal{A}_{\mathsf{CF'}}$, and that execution of $\mathsf{Sim}(1^\lambda, \mathsf{ek}, m)$ yielded the ciphertext C. As the behavior of $\mathcal{A}_{\mathsf{CF'}}$ is independent of that execution of $\mathsf{Sim}(1^\lambda, \mathsf{ek}, m)$ as mentioned above, it follows that $p \leq p_C$ where $p_C := \Pr[C \leftarrow \mathsf{Sim}(1^\lambda, \mathsf{ek}, m)]$.

However, the property $C \in \mathsf{List}$ implies that C is generated by a sequence of evaluation algorithms starting from the challenge ciphertext C^*, therefore for each $i \in \{0, 1\}$, $\mathcal{B}_\mathcal{E}$ can compute the plaintext m_i satisfying that C would have the plaintext m_i if the challenge bit b in the KH-CCA game is $b = i$. We also note that $m_0 \neq m_1$, as otherwise $\mathcal{B}_\mathcal{E}$ could determine the plaintext of C regardless of b and hence could respond to the unallowable query $\mathsf{Dec}(C)$, a contradiction. Therefore, now $\mathcal{B}_\mathcal{E}$ can increase its winning probability by modifying the behavior in a way that whenever $\mathcal{B}_\mathcal{E}$ detects an unallowable query $\mathsf{Dec}(C)$ (which is in fact possible, as $\mathcal{B}_\mathcal{E}$ can know the current status of the list List while $\mathcal{B}_\mathcal{E}$ itself maintains the list $\mathsf{List_{CF'}}$), $\mathcal{B}_\mathcal{E}$ makes a RevEK query to obtain the evaluation key ek, and for each $i \in \{0, 1\}$, $\mathcal{B}_\mathcal{E}$ computes $C_i \leftarrow \mathsf{Sim}(1^\lambda, \mathsf{ek}, m_i)$ and outputs the bit i if $C_i = C$. By this modification, the winning probability increases by $p \cdot \Pr[C_b \leftarrow \mathsf{Sim}(1^\lambda, \mathsf{ek}, m_b) : C_b = C] = p \cdot p_C \geq p^2$ (as $m_b = m$ by the definition of m_0 and m_1), which is non-negligible as well as p. This contradicts the KH-CCA security of $\mathcal{E}$. Hence an unallowable query is made with only negligible probability. Therefore, the advantage of $\mathcal{A}_{\mathsf{CF'}}$ is negligible by the KH-CCA security of $\mathcal{E}$, concluding the proof (see the full version of this paper for a more rigorous argument).   □

Remark 1. *Similarly to the case of the original Catalano–Fiore conversion, we can also show that* $\mathsf{CF'}(\mathcal{E}, \mathcal{SE})$ *is circuit private if* $\mathcal{E}$ *is circuit private. Here we note that* $\mathsf{CF'}(\mathcal{E}, \mathcal{SE})$ *have two classes of ciphertexts, level-1 and level-2 ciphertexts, that are easily distinguishable (even if they have the same plaintext), and different level-2 ciphertexts may have different sizes, which become easily distinguishable as well. Therefore, in order to discuss the circuit privacy for* $\mathsf{CF'}(\mathcal{E}, \mathcal{SE})$, *we must modify the definition of circuit privacy, in a way that the algorithm* Sim *also takes the level of the ciphertext and its size (for the level-2 case) as a part of input; that is, roughly speaking, ciphertexts of the same level and the same size are indistinguishable to each other. See the full version of this paper for a proof of the circuit privacy of* $\mathsf{CF'}(\mathcal{E}, \mathcal{SE})$.

7   Conclusion

In this paper, first we showed that when extending the number of inputs for the homomorphic evaluation algorithm in a KH-PKE scheme, the KH-CCA security is not necessarily preserved; while the KH-CCA security is preserved when the original scheme also satisfies circuit privacy. Secondly, we extended the Catalano–Fiore conversion to the case of KH-PKE schemes, which results in conversion from linearly KH-PKE schemes to two-level KH-PKE schemes. This conversion is applicable to KH-PKE schemes with various security assumptions such as the DDH and the DCR assumptions for linearly KH-PKE schemes.

A drawback of our proposed conversion method (which is common to the original Catalano–Fiore conversion) is that in the resulting scheme, the homomorphic evaluation for level-2 ciphertexts increases the size of the ciphertext. In the original paper [13] of Catalano and Fiore, they proposed a primitive called 2S-DCED (two-server delegation of computation on encrypted data), and based on it, they constructed a two-server protocol for resolving the issue of non-compact ciphertexts. It is a future research topic to investigate possible extensions of their technique to our case of KH-PKE schemes. On the other hand, the original Catalano–Fiore conversion is known to preserve some more properties in addition to the IND-CPA security and circuit privacy. Studying similar properties in the case of our proposed conversion method is also a future research topic.

Acknowledgements. This work was supported by JSPS KAKENHI Grant Number 19H01109, Japan, by JST CREST Grant Number JPMJCR2113, Japan, and by JST AIP Acceleration Research JPMJCR22U5, Japan.

References

1. Attrapadung, N., Hanaoka, G., Mitsunari, S., Sakai, Y., Shimizu, K., Teruya, T.: Efficient two-level homomorphic encryption in prime-order bilinear groups and a fast implementation in WebAssembly. In: ASIACCS 2018, pp. 685–697 (2018)
2. Barak, B., et al.: On the (Im)possibility of obfuscating programs. In: Kilian, J. (ed.) CRYPTO 2001. LNCS, vol. 2139, pp. 1–18. Springer, Heidelberg (2001). https://doi.org/10.1007/3-540-44647-8_1
3. Bellare, M., Desai, A., Pointcheval, D., Rogaway, P.: Relations among notions of security for public-key encryption schemes. In: Krawczyk, H. (ed.) CRYPTO 1998. LNCS, vol. 1462, pp. 26–45. Springer, Heidelberg (1998). https://doi.org/10.1007/BFb0055718
4. Bellare, M., Namprempre, C.: Authenticated encryption: relations among notions and analysis of the generic composition paradigm. In: Okamoto, T. (ed.) ASIACRYPT 2000. LNCS, vol. 1976, pp. 531–545. Springer, Heidelberg (2000). https://doi.org/10.1007/3-540-44448-3_41
5. Bleichenbacher, D.: Chosen ciphertext attacks against protocols based on the RSA encryption standard PKCS #1. In: Krawczyk, H. (ed.) CRYPTO 1998. LNCS, vol. 1462, pp. 1–12. Springer, Heidelberg (1998). https://doi.org/10.1007/BFb0055716
6. Boneh, D., Boyen, X., Shacham, H.: Short group signatures. In: Franklin, M. (ed.) CRYPTO 2004. LNCS, vol. 3152, pp. 41–55. Springer, Heidelberg (2004). https://doi.org/10.1007/978-3-540-28628-8_3
7. Boneh, D., Goh, E.-J., Nissim, K.: Evaluating 2-DNF formulas on ciphertexts. In: Kilian, J. (ed.) TCC 2005. LNCS, vol. 3378, pp. 325–341. Springer, Heidelberg (2005). https://doi.org/10.1007/978-3-540-30576-7_18
8. Brakerski, Z.: Fully homomorphic encryption without modulus switching from classical GapSVP. In: Safavi-Naini, R., Canetti, R. (eds.) CRYPTO 2012. LNCS, vol. 7417, pp. 868–886. Springer, Heidelberg (2012). https://doi.org/10.1007/978-3-642-32009-5_50
9. Brakerski, Z., Gentry, C., Vaikuntanathan, V.: (Leveled) fully homomorphic encryption without bootstrapping. In: ITCS 2012, pp. 309–325 (2012)
10. Brakerski, Z., Vaikuntanathan, V.: Fully homomorphic encryption from Ring-LWE and security for key dependent messages. In: Rogaway, P. (ed.) CRYPTO 2011. LNCS, vol. 6841, pp. 505–524. Springer, Heidelberg (2011). https://doi.org/10.1007/978-3-642-22792-9_29
11. Canetti, R., Raghuraman, S., Richelson, S., Vaikuntanathan, V.: Chosen-ciphertext secure fully homomorphic encryption. In: Fehr, S. (ed.) PKC 2017. LNCS, vol. 10175, pp. 213–240. Springer, Heidelberg (2017). https://doi.org/10.1007/978-3-662-54388-7_8
12. Catalano, D., Fiore, D.: Boosting linearly-homomorphic encryption to evaluate degree-2 functions on encrypted data. Cryptology ePrint Archive, 2014/813 (2014)
13. Catalano, D., Fiore, D.: Using linearly-homomorphic encryption to evaluate degree-2 functions on encrypted data. In: ACM CCS 2015, pp. 1518–1529 (2015)

14. Cramer, R., Gennaro, R., Schoenmakers, B.: A secure and optimally efficient multi-authority election scheme. In: Fumy, W. (ed.) EUROCRYPT 1997. LNCS, vol. 1233, pp. 103–118. Springer, Heidelberg (1997). https://doi.org/10.1007/3-540-69053-0_9

15. van Dijk, M., Gentry, C., Halevi, S., Vaikuntanathan, V.: Fully homomorphic encryption over the integers. In: Gilbert, H. (ed.) EUROCRYPT 2010. LNCS, vol. 6110, pp. 24–43. Springer, Heidelberg (2010). https://doi.org/10.1007/978-3-642-13190-5_2

16. El Gamal, T.: A public key cryptosystem and a signature scheme based on discrete logarithms. IEEE Trans. Inf. Theory **31**(4), 469–472 (1985)

17. Emura, K.: On the security of keyed-homomorphic PKE: preventing key recovery attacks and ciphertext validity attacks. IEICE Trans. Fundam. Electron. Commun. Comput. Sci. **E104.A**(1), 310–314 (2021)

18. Emura, K., Hanaoka, G., Nuida, K., Ohtake, G., Matsuda, T., Yamada, S.: Chosen ciphertext secure keyed homomorphic public key cryptosystems. Des. Codes Crypt. **86**(8), 1623–1683 (2018)

19. Emura, K., Hanaoka, G., Ohtake, G., Matsuda, T., Yamada, S.: Chosen ciphertext secure keyed-homomorphic public-key encryption. In: Kurosawa, K., Hanaoka, G. (eds.) PKC 2013. LNCS, vol. 7778, pp. 32–50. Springer, Heidelberg (2013). https://doi.org/10.1007/978-3-642-36362-7_3

20. Emura, K., Hayashi, T., Kunihiro, N., Sakuma, J.: Mis-operation resistant searchable homomorphic encryption. In: ASIACCS 2017, pp. 215–229 (2017)

21. Freeman, D.M.: Converting pairing-based cryptosystems from composite-order groups to prime-order groups. In: Gilbert, H. (ed.) EUROCRYPT 2010. LNCS, vol. 6110, pp. 44–61. Springer, Heidelberg (2010). https://doi.org/10.1007/978-3-642-13190-5_3

22. Gentry, C.: Fully homomorphic encryption using ideal lattices. In: STOC 2009, pp. 169–178 (2009)

23. Gentry, C., Sahai, A., Waters, B.: Homomorphic encryption from learning with errors: conceptually-simpler, asymptotically-faster, attribute-based. In: Canetti, R., Garay, J.A. (eds.) CRYPTO 2013. LNCS, vol. 8042, pp. 75–92. Springer, Heidelberg (2013). https://doi.org/10.1007/978-3-642-40041-4_5

24. Goldwasser, S., Micali, S.: Probabilistic encryption. J. Comput. Syst. Sci. **28**, 270–299 (1984)

25. Herold, G., Hesse, J., Hofheinz, D., Ràfols, C., Rupp, A.: Polynomial spaces: a new framework for composite-to-prime-order transformations. In: Garay, J.A., Gennaro, R. (eds.) CRYPTO 2014. LNCS, vol. 8616, pp. 261–279. Springer, Heidelberg (2014). https://doi.org/10.1007/978-3-662-44371-2_15

26. Jutla, C.S., Roy, A.: Dual-system simulation-soundness with applications to UC-PAKE and more. In: Iwata, T., Cheon, J.H. (eds.) ASIACRYPT 2015. LNCS, vol. 9452, pp. 630–655. Springer, Heidelberg (2015). https://doi.org/10.1007/978-3-662-48797-6_26

27. Lai, J., Deng, R.H., Ma, C., Sakurai, K., Weng, J.: CCA-secure keyed-fully homomorphic encryption. In: Cheng, C.-M., Chung, K.-M., Persiano, G., Yang, B.-Y. (eds.) PKC 2016. LNCS, vol. 9614, pp. 70–98. Springer, Heidelberg (2016). https://doi.org/10.1007/978-3-662-49384-7_4

28. Libert, B., Peters, T., Joye, M., Yung, M.: Non-malleability from malleability: simulation-sound Quasi-adaptive NIZK proofs and CCA2-secure encryption from homomorphic signatures. In: Nguyen, P.Q., Oswald, E. (eds.) EUROCRYPT 2014. LNCS, vol. 8441, pp. 514–532. Springer, Heidelberg (2014). https://doi.org/10.1007/978-3-642-55220-5_29

29. Maeda, Y., Nuida, K.: Chosen ciphertext secure keyed two-level homomorphic encryption. Cryptology ePrint Archive, 2021/722 (2021)
30. Okamoto, T., Uchiyama, S.: A new public-key cryptosystem as secure as factoring. In: Nyberg, K. (ed.) EUROCRYPT 1998. LNCS, vol. 1403, pp. 308–318. Springer, Heidelberg (1998). https://doi.org/10.1007/BFb0054135
31. Paillier, P.: Public-key cryptosystems based on composite degree residuosity classes. In: Stern, J. (ed.) EUROCRYPT 1999. LNCS, vol. 1592, pp. 223–238. Springer, Heidelberg (1999). https://doi.org/10.1007/3-540-48910-X_16
32. Rivest, R., Adleman, L., Dertouzos, M.: On data banks and privacy homomorphisms. Found. Secure Comput. 4(11), 169–180 (1978)
33. Rivest, R., Shamir, A., Adleman, L.: A method for obtaining digital signatures and public-key cryptosystems. Commun. ACM 21(2), 120–126 (1978)
34. Sato, S., Emura, K., Takayasu, A.: Keyed-fully homomorphic encryption without indistinguishability obfuscation. Cryptology ePrint Archive, 2022/017 (2022)
35. Sato, S., Emura, K., Takayasu, A.: Keyed-fully homomorphic encryption without indistinguishability obfuscation. In: ACNS 2022 (2022, to appear)

Computational Irrelevancy: Bridging the Gap Between Pseudo- and Real Randomness in MPC Protocols

Nariyasu Heseri[1] and Koji Nuida[2,3(✉)]

[1] Graduate School of Information Science and Technology, The University of Tokyo, Tokyo, Japan
[2] Institute of Mathematics for Industry (IMI), Kyushu University, Fukuoka, Japan
nuida@imi.kyushu-u.ac.jp
[3] National Institute of Advanced Industrial Science and Technology (AIST), Tokyo, Japan

Abstract. Due to the fact that classical computers cannot efficiently obtain random numbers, it is common practice to design cryptosystems in terms of real random numbers and then replace them with cryptographically secure pseudorandom ones for concrete implementations. However, as pointed out by the previous work (Nuida, PKC 2021), this technique may lead to compromise of security in secure multiparty computation (MPC) protocols, due to the property that a seed for a pseudorandom generator (PRG) is visible by an adversary in the context of MPC. Although this work suggested to use information-theoretically secure protocols (together with PRGs with high min-entropy) to alleviate the problem, yet it is preferable to base the security on computational assumptions rather than the stronger information-theoretic ones. By observing that the contrived constructions in the aforementioned work use MPC protocols and PRGs that are closely related to each other, we notice that it may help to alleviate the problem by using protocols and PRGs that are "unrelated" to each other. In this paper, we propose a notion called "computational irrelevancy" to formalise the term "unrelated" and under this condition provide a security guarantee under computational assumptions.

Keywords: Secure multiparty computation · pseudorandom generators · relativisation

1 Introduction

It is a widely known fact that classical computers are not able to generate random numbers. When necessary, random numbers are generated from noise of the environment, OS statistics, user inputs, etc. However, in most cryptographic schemes where very long random bit sequences are required, these random sources are not efficient enough to generate them. To this end, pseudorandom generators (PRGs) are used to expand a short real random bit sequence into a long one that looks random. In order to provide randomness for cryptographic purposes, it is recommended to use PRGs satisfying a standard cryptographic security condition, where the output distribution of the PRG is computationally indistinguishable from a uniformly random bit sequence.

Under the observation that if the use of PRGs compromises security of a cryptographic scheme then the scheme can be modified to a distinguisher against the PRGs, one may naïvely believe that when a cryptographically secure PRG is used in a secure cryptographic scheme, the resulting scheme is also secure. However, this naïve reduction only works in settings where the seeds for the PRGs are not explicitly known to the adversaries, since the distinguishers in the security notion for PRGs are formalised in a way of not viewing the seed for the PRG. In fact, as pointed out by a recent work [9], the security definition of secure multiparty computation (MPC) protocols (in the semi-honest model) forms a counterexample of the naïve reduction. Indeed, protocol-PRG pairs are explicitly constructed by [9] in a way that the protocol and the PRG are secure themselves but the protocol becomes insecure when the PRG is used. Since it has become so common a paradigm in cryptography to design cryptographic schemes in terms of real random numbers and use the output of PRGs for concrete implementations, it is urgent to find ways to avoid such problems.

To this end, it is proved also in [9] that using PRGs with very high min-entropy can help avoiding the problem provided that the original MPC protocol is information-theoretically secure. This requirement of information-theoretic security for the underlying MPC protocol is in fact a significant disadvantage of the previous result, since it is believed that achieving information-theoretic security for all parties is very hard and with severe limitations. For example, it is shown in [2] that, in terms of boolean functions, information-theoretic security for majority of the participating parties is achievable for only a limited subset of boolean functions. Therefore, instead of requiring information-theoretic security for the underlying protocols, it is more desirable to ensure security in terms of computational security assumptions.

By taking a close look at the constructions of the counterexamples in [9], it is easy to observe that these contrived constructions use MPC protocols and PRGs that are closely related to each other; the PRG for each counterexample was artificially designed in order to compromise the security of the specific MPC protocol when applied. One may develop an intuition that it helps to alleviate the problem to use PRGs "unrelated" to the MPC protocol. However, to realize the intuition as the form of a theorem, we have to formalise the meaning that a PRG and an MPC protocol are "unrelated".

1.1 Our Contributions

In this paper, we propose new sufficient conditions for an MPC protocol and a PRG to ensure that the use of the PRG to generate randomness for a party in the protocol does not compromise the security. The proposed sufficient conditions are more practical than the one in the previous work [9] in a way that our conditions require the protocol to have only computational security, while the condition in [9] requires the protocol to have information-theoretic security.

In order to develop such sufficient conditions, it might be helpful as mentioned above to formalise the meaning that a PRG and a protocol are "unrelated". To this end, in this paper we propose a notion called "computational irrelevancy" by utilising a paradigm called "relativisation", which is intensely studied in the literature of complexity theory. As an informal description, an MPC protocol or a PRG is considered computationally irrelevant from a PRG if the security of the former is preserved even if the corresponding distinguisher is given oracle access to the inverter of the latter. See Sect. 3 for the details. We note that as a related work, [3] discussed a notion called "computationally independent one-way functions" to avoid problems in interactive proof systems. Some relation between our notion of computational irrelevancy (extended from PRGs to one-way functions) and the computationally independent one-way functions is studied in Sect. 6.3.

Based on the notion of computational irrelevancy, we provide sufficient conditions for an MPC protocol and a PRG to preserve the security as mentioned above. Here we focus on the simplest (and non-trivial) case where there exists a single corrupted party $\mathcal{P}$ and the same party uses a PRG $\mathcal{R}$ in an MPC protocol π. Roughly speaking, our proposed sufficient condition for this case is as follows:

- π is computationally secure and is computationally irrelevant from $\mathcal{R}$.
- The simulator in the security definition for π simulates the view of $\mathcal{P}$ in a way that it uses a part of its random tape as the randomness part of the simulated view *as is*. (We note that this technical condition is common to the previous work [9].)
- Among the bit strings of the same length as outputs of $\mathcal{R}$, the ratio of the size of the range of $\mathcal{R}$ is asymptotically larger than an inverse polynomial.
- The output distribution of $\mathcal{R}$ is computationally indistinguishable from the uniform distribution over the range of $\mathcal{R}$ (instead of the bit strings of the same length as outputs of $\mathcal{R}$, as in the usual security definition for PRGs) even if the distinguisher is given access to the oracle that inverts $\mathcal{R}$.

The precise statement for the case of a single corrupted party (and possibly multiple PRGs) as well as the proof is given in Sect. 4. Moreover, in contrast to the previous work [9] where only the case of a single adversary is studied, we extend the result to a more general case where there exist many corrupted parties. The result is given in Sect. 5. We also discuss some relation between the sufficient conditions in our result here and the sufficient conditions in the result of [9]; see Sect. 6.1 for the details.

Regarding the computational irrelevancy condition in our proposed sufficient conditions, constructing protocols that are computationally secure even assuming access to the oracles inverting some PRGs apparently requires some computational problems that are hard even with access to some oracles. A class of problems called "the gap-problems", proposed by [10], can be considered a class of computational problems that are hard relative to an oracle solving the corresponding decision problem. This class of problems proved to be very useful and cryptographic schemes have been constructed and security of existing schemes has been proved under the computational hardness assumptions of these problems (e.g., [6,7,10]). In addition, the relativisation paradigm has been used to prove some negative results in the literature of cryptography (e.g., [5]). Hence here we argue that such relativised computational problems are interesting in their own right and security or computational hardness assumptions relative to a family of the inverters of some PRGs, which are essential for the concrete implementations of our proposed sufficient conditions, are hopefully further studied in future works.

2   Preliminaries

2.1   Basic Notations

In this paper, for a finite set S, we write $s \leftarrow_R S$ to denote that s is assigned a uniformly sampled value from the set S. Let "PPT" be an abbreviation of "probabilistic polynomial-time". We say that a function $f \colon \mathbb{N} \to \mathbb{R}_{\geq 0}$ is *negligible* if for any positive polynomial p, there exists a $\lambda_0 \in \mathbb{N}$ for which for any $\lambda > \lambda_0$ we have $f(\lambda) < 1/p(\lambda)$. We say that a function $f \colon \mathbb{N} \to \mathbb{R}_{\geq 0}$ is *noticeable* if there exists a positive polynomial p and a $\lambda_0 \in \mathbb{N}$ for which for any $\lambda > \lambda_0$ we have $f(\lambda) \geq 1/p(\lambda)$.

2.2   Pseudorandom Generators

We review the definition of pseudorandom generators (PRGs) and their security definition as well as introduce notations about PRGs for later use.

Definition 1. *A deterministic polynomial-time algorithm is called a* pseudorandom generator (PRG) *if on input* $(1^\lambda, s)$ *where* $\lambda \in \mathbb{N}$ *and* s *is a bit string of fixed length, it outputs a bit string* r *of fixed length* $|r| > |s|$. *Here* λ *is called the* security parameter, s *is called the* seed, *and* $l_{in}(\lambda) := |s|$ *and* $l_{out}(\lambda) := |r|$ *are called the* input length *and* output length, *respectively. When multiple PRGs are used, we use* $l_{in}(\lambda, i)$ *and* $l_{out}(\lambda, i)$ *to denote the input length and output length of the PRG indexed by* i.

Definition 2. *A PRG* $\mathcal{R}$ *is said to be* uniformly (*resp.* non-uniformly) secure *if for any PPT uniform (resp. non-uniform) distinguisher* $\mathcal{D}$, *the advantage*

$$\left| \Pr\left[\mathcal{D}(1^\lambda, \mathcal{R}(1^\lambda, s))\right] - \Pr\left[\mathcal{D}(1^\lambda, r)\right] \right|$$

is negligible where $s \leftarrow_R \{0,1\}^{l_{in}(\lambda)}$ *and* $r \leftarrow_R \{0,1\}^{l_{out}(\lambda)}$.

2.3   Secure Multiparty Computation

We review security definitions for multiparty computation (MPC) protocols. While the notion of secure multiparty computation was first conceived and formalised by Yao [11,12], the modern formalisation of security of MPC protocols that is used in more recent literature was proposed by [4]. In this paper, we shall deal with the semi-honest adversarial model in [4].

Definition 3. *Let π be an n-party protocol and $\vec{f} = (f_1, f_2, \ldots, f_n)$ be a probabilistic functionality to be computed by π. Let $I = \{i_1, i_2, \ldots, i_m\} \subset \{1, 2, \ldots, n\}$ ($i_1 < i_2 < \cdots < i_m$). We say π is* secure *against coalition of parties $\mathcal{P}_i$ with $i \in I$, or simply,* secure *against parties $\mathcal{P}_I := (\mathcal{P}_i)_{i \in I}$, if there exists a PPT simulator $\mathcal{S}$ for which for any PPT non-uniform distinguisher $\mathcal{D}$, the advantage*

$$\left| \Pr\left[\mathcal{D}\left(\mathcal{S}(1^\lambda, \vec{x}_I, \vec{f}_I(\vec{x})), \vec{f}(\vec{x})\right) = 1 \right] - \Pr\left[\mathcal{D}\left(\mathrm{VIEW}_I(\vec{x}; \vec{r}), \pi(1^\lambda, \vec{x}; \vec{r})\right) = 1 \right] \right|$$

is negligible where

- *x_i is an input of party $\mathcal{P}_i$, $\vec{x} = (x_1, x_2, \ldots, x_n)$, and $\vec{x}_I = (x_{i_1}, x_{i_2}, \ldots, x_{i_m})$;*
- *$\vec{f}(\vec{x}) = (f_1(\vec{x}), f_2(\vec{x}), \ldots, f_n(\vec{x}))$ and $\vec{f}_I(\vec{x}) = (\vec{f}_{i_1}(\vec{x}), \vec{f}_{i_2}(\vec{x}), \ldots, \vec{f}_{i_m}(\vec{x}))$;*
- *r_i is a random bit sequence used by $\mathcal{P}_i$ and $\vec{r} = (r_1, r_2, \ldots, r_n)$;*
- *$\mathrm{VIEW}_i(\vec{x}; \vec{r})$ denotes the view of $\mathcal{P}_i$ consisting of x_i, r_i, and a list of messages $\vec{m}_i(1^\lambda, \vec{x}; \vec{r})$ received by $\mathcal{P}_i$ during an execution of the protocol π with input $\vec{x}$ and randomness $\vec{r}$; and*
- *$\mathrm{VIEW}_I(\vec{x}; \vec{r}) = (\mathrm{VIEW}_{i_1}(\vec{x}; \vec{r}), \mathrm{VIEW}_{i_2}(\vec{x}; \vec{r}), \ldots, \mathrm{VIEW}_{i_m}(\vec{x}; \vec{r}))$.*

3   Formalising Computational Irrelevancy

In this section, we formalise what is meant by saying that a PRG $\mathcal{R}$ (or a family of PRGs) is *computationally irrelevant* to an MPC protocol π or to another PRG $\mathcal{R}'$. Roughly speaking, our proposed condition here is that the ability of inverting the PRG $\mathcal{R}$ does not affect the security of π or $\mathcal{R}'$. To explain it more clearly, we introduce relativised versions (with respect to some oracles) of the security of MPC protocols and of PRGs.

Definition 4. *In the setting of Definition 3, we additionally let $\mathcal{O}$ be a family of oracles. We say the protocol π is* secure *against parties $\mathcal{P}_I$ relative to $\mathcal{O}$ if the condition in Definition 3 holds even if the distinguisher $\mathcal{D}$ is given access to the oracles $\mathcal{O}$.*

Definition 5. *In the setting of Definition 2, we additionally let $\mathcal{O}$ be a family of oracles. We say the PRG $\mathcal{R}$ is* uniformly *(resp. non-uniformly)* secure relative *to $\mathcal{O}$ if the condition in Definition 2 holds even if the distinguisher $\mathcal{D}$ is given access to the oracles $\mathcal{O}$.*

Then our notion of computational irrelevancy is described by using these definitions and an oracle $\mathcal{I}_\mathcal{R}$ that inverts an output of a given PRG $\mathcal{R}$. More precisely, given a security parameter 1^λ and an input string $r \in \{0,1\}^{l_{out}(1^\lambda)}$, if there exists a seed $s \in \{0,1\}^{l_{in}(1^\lambda)}$ satisfying $\mathcal{R}(1^\lambda, s) = r$ then the oracle $\mathcal{I}_\mathcal{R}$ returns such an s chosen uniformly at random, and otherwise it returns $\perp$.

Based on the definition of $\mathcal{I}_\mathcal{R}$, we say a family of PRGs $(\mathcal{R}_j)_j$ is *computationally irrelevant* to a secure MPC protocol π (resp. a secure PRG $\mathcal{R}'$) if π (resp. $\mathcal{R}'$) is still secure relative to the oracle family $(\mathcal{I}_{\mathcal{R}_j})_j$.

4   Main Theorem: Case of a Single Adversary

In this section, we state and prove our main theorem for the case where there exists a single adversary $\mathcal{P}_i$ among the n parties. To state our theorem, we assume without loss of generality that every party $\mathcal{P}_j$ uses its own PRG $\mathcal{R}_j$ to generate the party's randomness in a protocol π. In fact, when some party does not use a PRG, we instead regard the party as using an identity function id as its PRG; this does not affect our assumption about the computational irrelevancy, since any PRG is computationally irrelevant to id (due to the information-theoretic security of id) and id is computationally irrelevant to any protocol and any PRG (due to the fact that inverting id is a trivial operation). Let $\pi \circ \vec{\mathcal{R}}$ denote the protocol where each party $\mathcal{P}_j$ first generates $r_j \leftarrow \mathcal{R}_j(1^\lambda, s_j)$ from a uniformly random seed s_j and then executes the protocol π using r_j as its randomness.

4.1   Additional Definitions

We prepare some additional definitions used in the statement of our theorem. The first definition here basically states that a random output of a PRG looks uniformly random over its range, instead of over all bit strings of the fixed length as in the original definition.

Definition 6. *Let $\mathcal{R}$ be a PRG. Let* range$(\mathcal{R}, \lambda)$ *denote the set of all outputs of $\mathcal{R}$ under security parameter λ:*

$$\mathrm{range}(\mathcal{R}, \lambda) := \left\{ \mathcal{R}(1^\lambda, s) \mid s \in \{0,1\}^{l_{in}(\lambda)} \right\}.$$

Let $\mathcal{O}$ be a family of oracles. We say $\mathcal{R}$ is uniformly *(resp. non-uniformly) indistinguishable in its range relative to $\mathcal{O}$ if for any PPT uniform (resp. non-uniform) distinguisher $\mathcal{D}$,*

$$\left| \Pr\left[\mathcal{D}^\mathcal{O}\left(1^\lambda, \mathcal{R}(1^\lambda, s)\right) = 1 \right] - \Pr\left[\mathcal{D}^\mathcal{O}\left(1^\lambda, r\right) = 1 \right] \right|$$

is negligible where $s \leftarrow_R \{0,1\}^{l_{in}(\lambda)}$, $r \leftarrow_R$ range$(\mathcal{R}, \lambda)$, and $\mathcal{D}^\mathcal{O}$ indicates that $\mathcal{D}$ is given access to the oracles $\mathcal{O}$.

The second definition here basically states that the simulator in the security of an MPC protocol outputs its own random bits as is to generate the corrupted party's random tape. Note that this definition is introduced by the previous work [9] and is proved to be necessary also in the setting of the previous work.

Definition 7 ([9]). *Let π be an n-party protocol that is secure against $\mathcal{P}_i$ with simulator $\mathcal{S}$. We say $\mathcal{S}$ is with raw randomness if there exists a PPT algorithm $\mathcal{T}$ for which for any $\lambda \in \mathbb{N}$ we have*

$$\mathcal{S}(1^\lambda, x_i, f_i(\vec{x}); r_i, \tau_i) = \langle r_i, \mathcal{T}(1^\lambda, x_i, f_i(\vec{x}), r_i; \tau_i) \rangle$$

where the notation $\langle r_i, y \rangle$ means that components of the tuple (r_i, y) are rearranged in a way that r_i corresponds to the simulated random tape part.

4.2 The Statement

We state our first main theorem as follows. See Sects. 3 and 4.1 for the terminology used in the statement. The proof is given in the next subsection.

Theorem 1. *Let π be an n-party protocol, and $\vec{\mathcal{R}} = (\mathcal{R}_j)_{j=1}^n$ be a family of non-uniformly secure PRGs. Let $i \in \{1, 2, \ldots, n\}$. Suppose that the following conditions hold:*

- *π is secure against party $\mathcal{P}_i$ relative to $\mathcal{I}_{\mathcal{R}_i}$ with raw randomness (in particular, $\mathcal{R}_i$ is computationally irrelevant to π).*
- *$|\mathrm{range}(\mathcal{R}_i, \lambda)| / 2^{l_{out}(\lambda, i)}$ is noticeable.*
- *$\mathcal{R}_i$ is non-uniformly indistinguishable in its range relative to $\mathcal{I}_{\mathcal{R}_i}$.*

Then $\pi \circ \vec{\mathcal{R}}$ is secure against party $\mathcal{P}_i$ with raw randomness.

Remark 1. We note that the last condition "$\mathcal{R}_i$ is non-uniformly indistinguishable in its range relative to $\mathcal{I}_{\mathcal{R}_i}$" in the statement is not a contradictory condition. If the term "in its range" were not put, then the use of the oracle $\mathcal{I}_{\mathcal{R}_i}$ could trivially distinguish an output of $\mathcal{R}_i$ from a uniformly random bit string r since the oracle can determine whether r is in the range of $\mathcal{R}_i$. However, the term "in its range" changes the setting in a way that r is always in the range of $\mathcal{R}_i$, therefore the trivial attack above is not applicable to the current setting.

Remark 2. If we require $\pi \circ \vec{\mathcal{R}}$ to be also secure relative to $\mathcal{I}_{\mathcal{R}_i}$, then we have to suppose moreover that $\mathcal{R}_i$ is also computationally irrelevant to other PRGs $\mathcal{R}_j$, $j \neq i$, i.e., $\mathcal{R}_j$ is also secure relative to $\mathcal{I}_{\mathcal{R}_i}$. The proof is basically the same as the proof given below.

4.3 Proof of Theorem 1

Here we give a proof of Theorem 1. Our proof consists of the following two parts:

1. If π is secure against party $\mathcal{P}_i$ relative to $\mathcal{I}_{\mathcal{R}_i}$ with raw randomness, then the protocol $\pi^{\langle i \rangle}$ obtained by replacing party $\mathcal{P}_i$'s randomness with an output of $\mathcal{R}_i$ is also secure against party $\mathcal{P}_i$ relative to $\mathcal{I}_{\mathcal{R}_i}$ with raw randomness.
2. If π is secure against party $\mathcal{P}_i$ with raw randomness, then for any $j \neq i$, the protocol $\pi^{\langle j \rangle}$ obtained by replacing party $\mathcal{P}_j$'s randomness with an output of $\mathcal{R}_j$ is also secure against party $\mathcal{P}_i$ with raw randomness.

If these two claims are proved, then the original statement follows by recursively applying the part 1 (to replace party $\mathcal{P}_i$'s randomness) and then the part 2 $n-1$ times (to replace the other parties' randomness one by one).

For the part 2, the seed of the PRG $\mathcal{R}_j$ is not explicitly known to the adversary $\mathcal{P}_i$, therefore we can perform a standard security reduction. We present this in the following lemma for completeness.

Lemma 1. *In the setting of Theorem 1, for any $j \neq i$, the protocol $\pi^{\langle j \rangle}$ defined as above is secure against party $\mathcal{P}_i$ with raw randomness.*

Proof. Let $\mathcal{S}$ be the simulator for party $\mathcal{P}_i$ in the security of π. We show that this simulator can also be used to prove the security of $\pi^{\langle j \rangle}$. For any PPT distinguisher $\mathcal{D}$ against $\mathcal{S}$ and any input $\vec{x}$, by the triangle inequality, the advantage of $\mathcal{D}$ for the case of protocol $\pi^{\langle j \rangle}$ is bounded from above by the sum of

$$\left| \Pr\left[\mathcal{D}(\mathcal{S}(1^\lambda, x_i, f_i(\vec{x})), \vec{f}(\vec{x})) = 1 \right] \right.$$
$$\left. - \Pr\left[\mathcal{D}(x_i, r_i, \vec{m}_i(1^\lambda, \vec{x}; \langle r_j \rangle_j), \pi(1^\lambda, \vec{x}; \langle r_j \rangle_j)) = 1 \right] \right|$$

and

$$\left| \Pr\left[\mathcal{D}(x_i, r_i, \vec{m}_i(1^\lambda, \vec{x}; \langle r_j \rangle_j), \pi(1^\lambda, \vec{x}; \langle r_j \rangle_j)) = 1 \right] \right.$$
$$\left. - \Pr\left[\mathcal{D}(x_i, r_i, \vec{m}_i(1^\lambda, \vec{x}; \langle \mathcal{R}_j(1^\lambda, s_j) \rangle_j), \pi(1^\lambda, \vec{x}; \langle \mathcal{R}_j(1^\lambda, s_j) \rangle_j)) = 1 \right] \right|,$$

where $r_i \leftarrow_R \{0,1\}^{l_{out}(\lambda,i)}$, $r_j \leftarrow_R \{0,1\}^{l_{out}(\lambda,j)}$, $s_j \leftarrow_R \{0,1\}^{l_{in}(\lambda,j)}$, and $\langle a \rangle_j$ in the randomness part of the inputs means that party $\mathcal{P}_j$ takes randomness a and others take uniformly distributed random bits (as specified in π). The former quantity is negligible by the security of π against $\mathcal{P}_i$, while the latter quantity is negligible by the non-uniform security of $\mathcal{R}_j$. □

Thus the problem is reduced to prove the part 1 above. To prove the part 1, let $\mathcal{S}$ be the simulator for party $\mathcal{P}_i$ in the security of π. Since $\mathcal{S}$ is with raw randomness, we can write $\mathcal{S}(1^\lambda, x_i, f_i(\vec{x}); r_i, \tau_i) = \langle r_i, \mathcal{T}(1^\lambda, x_i, f_i(\vec{x}), r_i; \tau_i) \rangle$. Consider a simulator $\tilde{\mathcal{S}}$ defined as

$$\tilde{\mathcal{S}}(1^\lambda, x_i, f_i(\vec{x}); s_i, \tau_i) := \langle s_i, \mathcal{T}(1^\lambda, x_i, f_i(\vec{x}), \mathcal{R}_i(1^\lambda, s_i); \tau_i) \rangle.$$

For any PPT distinguisher $\tilde{\mathcal{D}}$ (with oracle access to $\mathcal{I}_{\mathcal{R}_i}$) against $\tilde{\mathcal{S}}$, define distinguisher $\mathcal{D}$ (with oracle access to $\mathcal{I}_{\mathcal{R}_i}$) against $\mathcal{S}$ as in Algorithm 1, which is PPT as well as $\tilde{\mathcal{D}}$.

Algorithm 1. Distinguisher $\mathcal{D}$ against $\mathcal{S}$

1: **procedure** $\mathcal{D}^{\mathcal{I}_{\mathcal{R}_i}}(x_i^\dagger, r_i^\dagger, \vec{m}_i^\dagger, y_i^\dagger)$
2:     $s_i^\dagger \leftarrow \mathcal{I}_{\mathcal{R}_i}(r_i^\dagger)$
3:     **if** $s_i^\dagger \neq \perp$ **then**
4:         **return** $\tilde{\mathcal{D}}^{\mathcal{I}_{\mathcal{R}_i}}(x_i^\dagger, s_i^\dagger, \vec{m}_i^\dagger, y_i^\dagger)$
5:     **else**
6:         **return** 0
7:     **end if**
8: **end procedure**

Let $r_i \leftarrow_R \{0,1\}^{l_{out}(\lambda,i)}$, and let E be the event $\mathcal{I}_{\mathcal{R}_i}(r_i) \neq \perp$, i.e., r_i is in the range of $\mathcal{R}_i$. Since $\mathcal{D}$ outputs 0 when E does not occur, the advantage of $\mathcal{D}$ is equal to $\Pr[E] \cdot \mathsf{adv}'_{\mathcal{D}}$ where

$$\mathsf{adv}'_{\mathcal{D}} := \left| \Pr\left[\mathcal{D}^{\mathcal{I}_{\mathcal{R}_i}}(\mathcal{S}(1^\lambda, x_i, f_i(\vec{x}); r_i, \tau_i), \vec{f}(\vec{x})) = 1 \mid E\right] \right.$$
$$\left. - \Pr\left[\mathcal{D}^{\mathcal{I}_{\mathcal{R}_i}}(x_i, r_i, \vec{m}_i(1^\lambda, \vec{x}; \langle r_i \rangle_i), \pi(1^\lambda, \vec{x}; \langle r_i \rangle_i)) = 1 \mid E\right] \right|$$

(here $\langle a \rangle_i$ in the randomness part of the inputs means that party $\mathcal{P}_i$ takes randomness a and others take uniformly distributed random bits (as specified in π)). Since $\Pr[E]$ is noticeable by the second assumption in the theorem and $\Pr[E] \cdot \mathsf{adv}'_{\mathcal{D}}$ is negligible by the security of π, it follows that $\mathsf{adv}'_{\mathcal{D}}$ is negligible.

Note that the conditional distribution of r_i conditioned on the event E is the uniform distribution over range($\mathcal{R}_i, \lambda$). Then by the definitions of $\mathcal{D}$ and $\tilde{\mathcal{S}}$, we have

$$\mathsf{adv}'_{\mathcal{D}} = \left| \Pr\left[\tilde{\mathcal{D}}^{\mathcal{I}_{\mathcal{R}_i}}(\tilde{\mathcal{S}}(1^\lambda, x_i, f_i(\vec{x}); \mathcal{I}_{\mathcal{R}_i}(r_i^\dagger), \tau_i), \vec{f}(\vec{x})) = 1\right] \right.$$
$$\left. - \Pr\left[\tilde{\mathcal{D}}^{\mathcal{I}_{\mathcal{R}_i}}(x_i, \mathcal{I}_{\mathcal{R}_i}(r_i^\dagger), \vec{m}_i(1^\lambda, \vec{x}; \left\langle r_i^\dagger \right\rangle_i), \pi(1^\lambda, \vec{x}; \left\langle r_i^\dagger \right\rangle_i)) = 1\right] \right|$$

where $r_i^\dagger \leftarrow_R$ range($\mathcal{R}_i, \lambda$) (here the security parameter 1^λ in $\mathcal{I}_{\mathcal{R}}$ is omitted). Now since $\mathcal{R}_i$ is non-uniformly indistinguishable in its range relative to $\mathcal{I}_{\mathcal{R}_i}$ by the third assumption in the theorem, it follows that replacing the $r_i^\dagger$'s in the equality for $\mathsf{adv}'_{\mathcal{D}}$ above by $\mathcal{R}_i(s_i^\dagger)$ with $s_i^\dagger \leftarrow_R \{0,1\}^{l_{in}(\lambda,i)}$ (where the security parameter 1^λ in $\mathcal{R}_i$ is omitted) yields only negligible difference for the value of the right-hand side from the original. That is, the following

$$\mathsf{adv}''_{\mathcal{D}} := \left| \Pr\left[\tilde{\mathcal{D}}^{\mathcal{I}_{\mathcal{R}_i}}(\tilde{\mathcal{S}}(1^\lambda, x_i, f_i(\vec{x}); \mathcal{I}_{\mathcal{R}_i}(\mathcal{R}_i(s_i^\dagger)), \tau_i), \vec{f}(\vec{x})) = 1\right] \right.$$
$$\left. - \Pr\left[\tilde{\mathcal{D}}^{\mathcal{I}_{\mathcal{R}_i}}(x_i, \mathcal{I}_{\mathcal{R}_i}(\mathcal{R}_i(s_i^\dagger)), \vec{m}_i(1^\lambda, \vec{x}; \left\langle \mathcal{R}_i(s_i^\dagger) \right\rangle_i), \pi(1^\lambda, \vec{x}; \left\langle \mathcal{R}_i(s_i^\dagger) \right\rangle_i)) = 1\right] \right|$$

is negligible as well as $\mathsf{adv}'_{\mathcal{D}}$. Moreover, we use the following lemma.

Lemma 2. *In the setting, $\mathcal{I}_{\mathcal{R}_i}(\mathcal{R}_i(s_i^\dagger))$ is uniformly random over $\{0,1\}^{l_{in}(\lambda,i)}$.*

Proof. Let $\xi \in \{0,1\}^{l_{in}(\lambda,i)}$, $\zeta := \mathcal{R}_i(\xi)$, and let c be the number of $\xi' \in \{0,1\}^{l_{in}(\lambda,i)}$ with $\mathcal{R}_i(\xi') = \zeta$. Then

$$\Pr\left[\mathcal{I}_{\mathcal{R}_i}(\mathcal{R}_i(s_i^\dagger)) = \xi\right] = \Pr\left[\mathcal{R}_i(s_i^\dagger) = \zeta\right] \cdot \Pr\left[\mathcal{I}_{\mathcal{R}_i}(\zeta) = \xi\right]$$

$$= \frac{c}{2^{l_{in}(\lambda,i)}} \cdot \frac{1}{c} = \frac{1}{2^{l_{in}(\lambda,i)}} .$$

Hence the claim holds. □

By putting $s_i := \mathcal{I}_{\mathcal{R}_i}(\mathcal{R}_i(s_i^\dagger))$ which is uniformly random over $\{0,1\}^{l_{in}(\lambda,i)}$ as above, we have $\mathcal{R}_i(s_i^\dagger) = \mathcal{R}_i(s_i)$ and hence

$$\mathsf{adv}''_{\mathcal{D}} = \left| \Pr\left[\tilde{\mathcal{D}}^{\mathcal{I}_{\mathcal{R}_i}}(\tilde{\mathcal{S}}(1^\lambda, x_i, f_i(\vec{x}); s_i, \tau_i), \vec{f}(\vec{x})) = 1\right] \right.$$

$$\left. - \Pr\left[\tilde{\mathcal{D}}^{\mathcal{I}_{\mathcal{R}_i}}(x_i, s_i, \vec{m}_i(1^\lambda, \vec{x}; \langle\mathcal{R}_i(s_i)\rangle_i), \pi(1^\lambda, \vec{x}; \langle\mathcal{R}_i(s_i)\rangle_i)) = 1\right] \right| .$$

By the definition of the protocol $\pi^{\langle i \rangle}$, this is nothing but the advantage of the distinguisher $\tilde{\mathcal{D}}^{\mathcal{I}_{\mathcal{R}_i}}$ for the simulator $\tilde{\mathcal{S}}$ in the security of $\pi^{\langle i \rangle}$, which is negligible as above. Therefore $\pi^{\langle i \rangle}$ is secure against party $\mathcal{P}_i$ relative to $\mathcal{I}_{\mathcal{R}_i}$ with raw randomness. This completes the proof of Theorem 1.

5   Main Theorem: Case of Multiple Adversaries

In this section, we state and prove our main theorem for the case where there exist multiple colluding adversaries $\mathcal{P}_I$, $I \subset \{1,2,\ldots,n\}$ among the n parties. Similarly to Sect. 4, we assume without loss of generality that every party $\mathcal{P}_j$ uses its own PRG $\mathcal{R}_j$ to generate the party's randomness in a protocol π.

To state the theorem, we extend the definition of raw randomness (Definition 7) to the case of multiple adversaries.

Definition 8. *Let π be an n-party protocol that is secure against parties $\mathcal{P}_I$, $I = \{i_1, i_2, \ldots, i_m\} \subset \{1, 2, \ldots, n\}$, with simulator S. We say S is with raw randomness if there exists a PPT algorithm T for which for any $\lambda \in \mathbb{N}$ we have*

$$S(1^\lambda, \vec{x}_I, \vec{f}_I(\vec{x}); r_{i_1}, r_{i_2}, \ldots, r_{i_m}, \tau)$$

$$= \left\langle r_{i_1}, r_{i_2}, \ldots, r_{i_m}, T(1^\lambda, \vec{x}_I, \vec{f}_I(\vec{x}), r_{i_1}, r_{i_2}, \ldots, r_{i_m}; \tau) \right\rangle$$

where the notation $\langle r_{i_1}, r_{i_2}, \ldots, r_{i_m}, y \rangle$ means that components of the tuple $(r_{i_1}, r_{i_2}, \ldots, r_{i_m}, y)$ are rearranged in a way that each r_{i_k} corresponds to the simulated random tape part.

Now we state our second main theorem as follows.

Theorem 2. *Let π be an n-party protocol, and $\vec{\mathcal{R}} = (\mathcal{R}_j)_{j=1}^n$ be a family of non-uniformly secure PRGs. Let $I \subset \{1, 2, \ldots, n\}$. Suppose that the following conditions hold:*

- *π is secure against parties $\mathcal{P}_I$ relative to $(\mathcal{I}_{\mathcal{R}_j})_{j \in I}$ with raw randomness.*
- *For any $i \in I$, $|\mathrm{range}(\mathcal{R}_i, \lambda)| / 2^{l_{out}(\lambda, i)}$ is noticeable.*
- *For any $i \in I$, $\mathcal{R}_i$ is non-uniformly indistinguishable in its range relative to $(\mathcal{I}_{\mathcal{R}_j})_{j \in I}$.*

Then $\pi \circ \vec{\mathcal{R}}$ is secure against parties $\mathcal{P}_I$ with raw randomness.

Remark 3. Similarly to Remark 2, if we require $\pi \circ \vec{\mathcal{R}}$ to be also secure relative to $(\mathcal{I}_{\mathcal{R}_j})_{j \in I}$, then we have to suppose moreover that $(\mathcal{R}_j)_{j \in I}$ is also computationally irrelevant to other PRGs $\mathcal{R}_k$, $k \notin I$.

Proof (Theorem 2). We reduce the problem to the case of Theorem 1 by considering an $(n - |I| + 1)$-party protocol $\tilde{\pi}$ obtained from π in a way that now a single party $\tilde{\mathcal{P}}$, with input $\vec{x}_I$ and randomness $\vec{r}_I := (r_i)_{i \in I}$, simulates all the protocol executions by parties $\mathcal{P}_I$ in π. Now:

- Let $\tilde{\mathcal{R}}$ be the PRG obtained by concatenating the outputs of PRGs $\mathcal{R}_i$, $i \in I$. Then a hybrid argument implies that $\tilde{\mathcal{R}}$ is non-uniformly secure as well as the PRGs $\mathcal{R}_i$, $i \in I$.
- The ability of the oracle $\mathcal{I}_{\tilde{\mathcal{R}}}$ inverting $\tilde{\mathcal{R}}$ is polynomial-time equivalent to the family of oracles $(\mathcal{I}_{\mathcal{R}_i})_{i \in I}$. Hence $\tilde{\pi}$ is also secure against party $\tilde{\mathcal{P}}$ relative to $\mathcal{I}_{\tilde{\mathcal{R}}}$ with raw randomness. Indeed, given a simulator $\mathcal{S}$ for π, a simulator $\tilde{\mathcal{S}}$ for $\tilde{\pi}$ is obtained by just ignoring internal messages for parties $\mathcal{P}_I$ (that is, messages in π from some party inside I to some party inside I).
- The ratio $\left|\mathrm{range}(\tilde{\mathcal{R}}, \lambda)\right| / 2^{l_{out}(\lambda)}$ (where $l_{out}(\lambda)$ denotes the output length of $\tilde{\mathcal{R}}$) is the product of all $|\mathrm{range}(\mathcal{R}_i, \lambda)| / 2^{l_{out}(\lambda, i)}$, $i \in I$. Hence the ratio $\left|\mathrm{range}(\tilde{\mathcal{R}}, \lambda)\right| / 2^{l_{out}(\lambda)}$ is also noticeable.
- By the equivalence of $\mathcal{I}_{\tilde{\mathcal{R}}}$ and $(\mathcal{I}_{\mathcal{R}_i})_{i \in I}$, each $\mathcal{R}_i$ ($i \in I$) is non-uniformly indistinguishable in its range relative to $\mathcal{I}_{\tilde{\mathcal{R}}}$. Hence by a hybrid argument, $\tilde{\mathcal{R}}$ is also non-uniformly indistinguishable in its range relative to $\mathcal{I}_{\tilde{\mathcal{R}}}$.

Thus the protocol $\tilde{\pi}$ satisfies the assumptions in Theorem 1, therefore $\tilde{\pi} \circ \vec{\mathcal{R}}'$ (where $\vec{\mathcal{R}}'$ is the family of PRG $\tilde{\mathcal{R}}$ and the other PRGs $\mathcal{R}_k$, $k \notin I$) is secure against party $\tilde{\mathcal{P}}$ with raw randomness. Moreover, we note that the internal messages for parties $\mathcal{P}_I$ in π can be recovered from the other messages and the randomness for parties $\mathcal{P}_I$. Due to this property, a simulator (with raw randomness) to prove the security of $\pi \circ \vec{\mathcal{R}}$ against parties $\mathcal{P}_I$ can be constructed from the simulator in the security of $\tilde{\pi} \circ \vec{\mathcal{R}}'$ against party $\tilde{\mathcal{P}}$. This completes the proof of Theorem 2.   □

6   Related Works

6.1   Relation to Information-Theoretic Assumptions

We discuss the relation between our proposed sufficient conditions to preserve the security and the information-theoretic ones used in the previous work [9]. Since [9] only considered the case of a single adversary, we compare its result with Theorem 1 (rather than Theorem 2). We note that [9] only considered two-party protocols, but its result is easily extendible to n-party protocols (with a single adversary), therefore below we deal with the n-party version of the result in [9]. The statement in [9] is as follows.

Theorem 3 ([9]). *Let π be an n-party protocol. Let $i \in \{1, 2, \ldots, n\}$, and let $\mathcal{R}$ be a PRG used by party $\mathcal{P}_i$. Let $\pi \circ_i \mathcal{R}$ denote the protocol obtained from π by replacing party $\mathcal{P}_i$'s randomness with a random output of $\mathcal{R}$. Suppose that the following conditions hold:*

- π *is information-theoretically secure against party $\mathcal{P}_i$ with raw randomness, i.e., the real and the simulated views have negligible statistical distance.*
- $l_{out}(\lambda) - H_\infty(\mathcal{R}(1^\lambda, \cdot)) \in O(\log \lambda)$, *where $H_\infty(\mathcal{R}(1^\lambda, \cdot))$ is the min-entropy of $\mathcal{R}$ defined as*

$$H_\infty(\mathcal{R}(1^\lambda, \cdot)) := -\max_{r \in \{0,1\}^{l_{out}(\lambda)}} \log_2 \Pr\left[\mathcal{R}(1^\lambda, s) = r\right]$$

where $s \leftarrow_R \{0, 1\}^{l_{in}(\lambda)}$.

Then $\pi \circ_i \mathcal{R}$ is information-theoretically secure against party $\mathcal{P}_i$ with raw randomness.

Theorem 3 assumes information-theoretically secure protocols with raw randomness. This is a stronger assumption than the first assumption of Theorem 1 since it is a well-known fact that statistical closeness implies computational indistinguishability and its proof relativises to any family of oracles.

Next we show that the min-entropy condition on the PRG in Theorem 3 is stronger than our second assumption of Theorem 1.

Proposition 1. *Let $\mathcal{R}$ be a PRG. If $l_{out}(\lambda) - H_\infty(\mathcal{R}(1^\lambda, \cdot)) \in O(\log \lambda)$, then $|\mathrm{range}(\mathcal{R}, \lambda)| / 2^{l_{out}(\lambda)}$ is noticeable.*

Proof. By definition, we may focus on the range of $\mathcal{R}$ when considering min-entropy:

$$H_\infty(\mathcal{R}(1^\lambda, \cdot)) = -\max_{r \in \mathrm{range}(\mathcal{R}, \lambda)} \log_2 \Pr\left[\mathcal{R}(1^\lambda, s) = r\right].$$

For a finite set, the uniform distribution yields the highest min-entropy among all distributions over this set, thus

$$H_\infty(\mathcal{R}(1^\lambda, \cdot)) \leq -\max_{r \in \mathrm{range}(\mathcal{R}, \lambda)} \log_2 \Pr\left[U_{\mathrm{range}(\mathcal{R}, \lambda)} = r\right]$$

$$= \log_2 |\mathrm{range}(\mathcal{R}, \lambda)|$$

where U_S denotes the uniform distribution over a finite set S. The assumption in the proposition can be rewritten as $2^{l_{out}(\lambda)}/2^{H_\infty(\mathcal{R}(1^\lambda,\cdot))} \leq p(\lambda)$ for some positive polynomial p and any sufficiently large λ's. Thus

$$\frac{2^{l_{out}(\lambda)}}{|\mathrm{range}(\mathcal{R},\lambda)|} = \frac{2^{l_{out}(\lambda)}}{2^{\log_2|\mathrm{range}(\mathcal{R},\lambda)|}} \leq \frac{2^{l_{out}(\lambda)}}{2^{H_\infty(\mathcal{R}(1^\lambda,\cdot))}} \leq p(\lambda) .$$

Taking the inverse on both sides yields the desired result.   □

6.2   On Random Oracle Vs. Hash Function Ensembles

Here we note that the technique used above seems unlikely to resolve the problem that occurs when a random oracle is replaced with a hash function ensemble [1]. For a cryptosystem that is secure under the random oracle model, if we want to prove (based on this fact) the security when the random oracle is replaced with a hash function ensemble with similar techniques, we have to rely on some computational indistinguishability between them. However, no well-known security requirements (one-wayness, collision resistance, etc.) on hash functions seem to provide such indistinguishability in any sense. A seemingly promising indistinguishability requirement might be that

$$\left| \Pr_{\mathscr{O}_k, s \leftarrow_R \{0,1\}^k} \left[\mathcal{D}^{\mathscr{O}_k}(1^k, s) \right] - \Pr_{s \leftarrow_R \{0,1\}^k} \left[\mathcal{D}^{f_s}(1^k, s) \right] \right|$$

be negligible, where $\mathscr{O}_k$ denotes (the distribution of) random oracles outputting strings of length $l_{out}(k)$ and f_s denotes the element with index s of a hash function ensemble. Note that we have to pass the seed s to the distinguisher since all parties (including adversaries) are supposed to know the seed in an implementation of random oracles by hash functions. However, a distinguisher can easily distinguish the two by computing $f_s(x)$ itself with arbitrary x and compare with the result of the oracle query.

Since both adversaries and appropriate users (or honest parties) have access to the same random oracle or hash functions, one may think that the notion of indistinguishability, which assumes that the random bits are private to each party, is anyway not suitable to be used in the random oracle vs. hash function setting. A less naïve notion called "indifferentiability", proposed by [8], is a generalisation of indistinguishability to deal with public and private interfaces. However, even this notion cannot be applied to the random oracle vs. hash function setting – no hash function ensemble is indifferentiable from a random oracle.

Thus we can see there seems to exist a huge gap between the random oracle model and reality (in the sense that even trivial algorithms can distinguish them). Indeed, [1] presents stronger negative results on the random oracle vs. hash functions than does [9] on real randomness vs. pseudorandomness.

6.3 Relation to Computational Independency of One-Way Functions

It has been noticed by previous works that use of closely related cryptographic primitives may cause problems. [3] discussed a notion called "computationally independent one-way functions" to avoid the problems in interactive proof systems. Here we briefly discuss the relationship between our proposed computational irrelevancy of pairs of PRGs (Sect. 3) and computational independency of pairs of one-way functions proposed by [3].

A straightforward adaptation of the computational irrelevancy for one-way functions can be formalised as follows.

Definition 9. *Let f be a one-way function, and let $\mathcal{O}$ be a family of oracles. We say f is one-way relative to $\mathcal{O}$ if for any PPT inverter $\mathcal{I}$ for f, the success probability*

$$\Pr\left[\mathcal{I}^{\mathcal{O}}\left(1^{\lambda}, f(x)\right) \in f^{-1}(f(x))\right]$$

is negligible where $x \leftarrow_R \{0,1\}^{\lambda}$.

Definition 10. *Let f_1 and f_2 be one-way functions. We say f_1 and f_2 are computationally irrelevant if for each $i \in \{1,2\}$, f_i is one-way relative to $\mathcal{I}_{f_{3-i}}$, where the oracle $\mathcal{I}_f$ is the inverter of f specified in the same way as in Sect. 3.*

For comparison, we restate the definition of pairs of computationally independent one-way functions.

Definition 11 ([3]). *Let f_1 and f_2 be one-way functions. We say f_1 and f_2 are computationally independent if the following conditions hold:*

- *(CI-a) $g(x) := (f_1(x), f_2(x))$ is also one-way.*
- *(CI-b) For $i \in \{1,2\}$ and for any PPT algorithm $\mathcal{A}$, the probability*

$$\Pr\left[\mathcal{A}\left(1^{\lambda}, f_i(x)\right) = f_{3-i}(x)\right]$$

is negligible where $x \leftarrow_R \{0,1\}^{\lambda}$.

Our computational irrelevancy extended to one-way functions does not capture the condition (CI-a) since we originally considered PRGs only and different PRGs are supposed to use different seeds anyway. On the other hand, the computational irrelevancy is a stronger property than the condition (CI-b).

Proposition 2. *For pairs of one-way functions f_1, f_2, the computational irrelevancy implies (CI-b), i.e. if they are computationally irrelevant, then for $i \in \{1,2\}$ and for any PPT algorithm $\mathcal{A}$, the probability*

$$\Pr\left[\mathcal{A}\left(1^{\lambda}, f_i(x)\right) = f_{3-i}(x)\right]$$

is negligible where $x \leftarrow_R \{0,1\}^{\lambda}$.

Proof. Assume for some $i \in \{1,2\}$, there exists a PPT algorithm $\mathcal{A}$ that given $f_i(x)$ computes $f_{3-i}(x)$ with non-negligible probability. Then given access to the oracle $\mathcal{I}_{f_{3-i}}$, an inverter of f_i can be obtained by calling $\mathcal{A}$ on $f_i(x)$ and calling $\mathcal{I}_{f_{3-i}}$ on the output of $\mathcal{A}$. The success probability is the same as that of $\mathcal{A}$, which is non-negligible as above, therefore f_i is not one-way relative to $\mathcal{I}_{f_{3-i}}$. □

7 Conclusion

In this paper, we formalised the notion of computational irrelevancy between PRGs and MPC protocols using the relativisation paradigm. Also, based on this notion, for both the case of a single adversary and the case of multiple adversaries in the semi-honest model, we provided sufficient conditions under which security of an MPC protocol is preserved even if PRGs are used for generating the parties' randomness. Our sufficient conditions are more practical than that proposed in the previous work [9] in a way that our conditions require an MPC protocol to have only computational security, while the condition in [9] requires the protocol to have information-theoretic security.

It remains open to construct protocols and PRGs that satisfy these computational irrelevancy conditions. We note here that constructing such examples theoretically is very easy. For example, in terms of protocols that are irrelevant from PRGs, information-theoretically secure ones always satisfy these conditions; for the ones that are not necessarily information-theoretically secure, replacing the underlying computational hardness assumptions with the ones relativised to the inverters of PRGs directly results in the protocols with the desired properties. However, whether these relativised assumptions can be considered "reasonable" requires further study in the literature. Since, as noted before, the relativisation paradigm has been of great interest in both complexity theory and cryptography and proved to be useful in previous works, we optimistically hope that subsequent works will stress this open problem.

Acknowledgements. This work was supported by JST CREST Grant Number JPMJCR2113, Japan, by JSPS KAKENHI Grant Number 22K11906, Japan, and by JST AIP Acceleration Research JPMJCR22U5, Japan.

References

1. Canetti, R., Goldreich, O., Halevi, S.: The random oracle methodology, revisited. J. ACM **51**(4), 557–594 (2004)
2. Chor, B., Kushilevitz, E.: A zero-one law for Boolean privacy. In: Proceedings of the Twenty-First Annual ACM Symposium on Theory of Computing, STOC 1989, New York, NY, USA, pp. 62–72. Association for Computing Machinery (1989)
3. Dutta, S., Sakurai, K.: Theory and application of computationally-independent one-way functions: interactive proof of ability—revisited. In: Giri, D., Ho, A.T.S., Ponnusamy, S., Lo, N.-W. (eds.) Proceedings of the Fifth International Conference on Mathematics and Computing. AISC, vol. 1170, pp. 97–109. Springer, Singapore (2021). https://doi.org/10.1007/978-981-15-5411-7_7

4. Goldreich, O.: Foundations of Cryptography, vol. 2. Cambridge University Press, Cambridge (2004)
5. Impagliazzo, R., Rudich, S.: Limits on the provable consequences of one-way permutations. In: Proceedings of the Twenty-First Annual ACM Symposium on Theory of Computing, STOC 1989, New York, NY, USA, pp. 44–61. Association for Computing Machinery (1989)
6. Kiltz, E.: Chosen-ciphertext security from tag-based encryption. In: Halevi, S., Rabin, T. (eds.) TCC 2006. LNCS, vol. 3876, pp. 581–600. Springer, Heidelberg (2006). https://doi.org/10.1007/11681878_30
7. Lynn, B.: On the Implementation of Pairing-based Cryptosystems. Ph.D. thesis, Stanford University (2007)
8. Maurer, U., Renner, R., Holenstein, C.: Indifferentiability, impossibility results on reductions, and applications to the random oracle methodology. In: Naor, M. (ed.) TCC 2004. LNCS, vol. 2951, pp. 21–39. Springer, Heidelberg (2004). https://doi.org/10.1007/978-3-540-24638-1_2
9. Nuida, K.: Cryptographic pseudorandom generators can make cryptosystems problematic. In: Garay, J.A. (ed.) PKC 2021. LNCS, vol. 12711, pp. 441–468. Springer, Cham (2021). https://doi.org/10.1007/978-3-030-75248-4_16
10. Okamoto, T., Pointcheval, D.: The gap-problems: a new class of problems for the security of cryptographic schemes. In: Kim, K. (ed.) PKC 2001. LNCS, vol. 1992, pp. 104–118. Springer, Heidelberg (2001). https://doi.org/10.1007/3-540-44586-2_8
11. Yao, A.C.: Protocols for secure computations. In: 23rd Annual Symposium on Foundations of Computer Science (SFCS 1982), pp. 160–164 (1982)
12. Yao, A.C.-C.: How to generate and exchange secrets. In: 27th Annual Symposium on Foundations of Computer Science (SFCS 1986), pp. 162–167 (1986)

Card-Based Secure Sorting Protocol

Rikuo Haga[1(✉)] , Kodai Toyoda[2(✉)] , Yuto Shinoda[2] ,
Daiki Miyahara[3,5(✉)] , Kazumasa Shinagawa[4] , Yuichi Hayashi[1,5(✉)] ,
and Takaaki Mizuki[2,5(✉)]

[1] Nara Institute of Science and Technology, Ikoma, Japan
haga.rikuo.hm5@is.naist.jp
[2] Tohoku University, Sendai, Japan
mizuki+lncs@tohoku.ac.jp
[3] The University of Electro-Communications, Chofu, Japan
[4] Ibaraki University, Hitachi, Japan
[5] National Institute of Advanced Industrial Science and Technology, Koto, Japan

Abstract. The research area of card-based cryptography, which relies on a deck of physical cards to perform cryptographic functionalities, has been growing in recent years, ranging from basic secure computations, such as secure AND and XOR evaluations, to more complex tasks, such as Yao's Millionaires' problem and zero-knowledge proof. In this paper, we propose a card-based "secure sorting" protocol; although sorting is probably the most fundamental problem in computer science, secure sorting has not been addressed in the field of card-based cryptography yet. Given a sequence of face-down cards representing a collection of keys with values (to be sorted), our proposed protocol sorts them without leaking any information. As imagined, secure sorting provides many applications; for instance, we show how to apply our protocol to implementing an auction. Since many algorithms for computational problems (say, graph algorithms) use sorting as subroutines, we expect that our secure sorting protocol will be useful when constructing card-based secure computations regarding computational problems.

1 Introduction

A *secure computation* allows players (holding individual private inputs) to obtain the output value of a predetermined function while keeping information about the individual inputs secret. Since Yao [42] proposed a secure computation solving the Millionaires' problem in 1982, various secure computation protocols have been proposed (refer to [3,6] for survey). While such cryptographic protocols are typically designed to be run on computers, there is another research direction where protocols should be run on daily physical tools (instead of computers). Because such physical cryptographic protocols are executed by human hands, they have the advantage that players do not need to trust a computer as a black box and that the correctness and security can be easily understood (cf. [11,14]).

1.1   Card-Based Cryptography

Among physical cryptographic protocols, many *card-based protocols* using a deck of physical cards, such as ♣ ♣ ··· ♡ ♡ ···, have been constructed since Den Boer [5] proposed the first card-based protocol, called the "five-card trick." Actually, the research area of *card-based cryptography* has been growing in recent years [22, 23], ranging from basic secure computations, such as secure AND and XOR evaluations (e.g., [1, 4, 16, 20, 24, 25, 27, 30, 41]), to more complex tasks, such as Yao's Millionaires' problem [21, 26, 29], secure ranking [40], and zero-knowledge proof (e.g., [2, 8, 35–37]).

1.2   Secure Sorting with Cards

In this study, we consider the fact that *secure sorting* (e.g., [7, 10]) has not been addressed in card-based cryptography yet although sorting is probably the most fundamental problem in computer science. Thus, we propose a *card-based secure sorting protocol* for the first time. Given a sequence of cards representing a collection of keys with values (to be sorted), our proposed protocol sorts them without leaking any information. We describe the problem and goal more concretely, as follows.

Given a sequence of n pairs

$$(1, x_1), (2, x_2), (3, x_3), \ldots, (n, x_n), \tag{1}$$

we want to sort them by taking the second elements $x_1, x_2, \ldots, x_n$ as keys: that is, we want to obtain a sorted sequence

$$(\sigma^{-1}(1), x_{\sigma^{-1}(1)}), (\sigma^{-1}(2), x_{\sigma^{-1}(2)}), (\sigma^{-1}(3), x_{\sigma^{-1}(3)}), \ldots, (\sigma^{-1}(n), x_{\sigma^{-1}(n)}) \tag{2}$$

such that a permutation $\sigma \in S_n$ satisfies the following:

$$x_{\sigma^{-1}(i)} \geq x_{\sigma^{-1}(i+1)} \text{ for every } i \in \{1, \ldots, n-1\}, \tag{3}$$

where S_n is the symmetric group of degree n.

In addition, we want to hide the individual values $x_1, x_2, \ldots, x_n$ themselves as well as the sorted sequence. As typically done in card-based cryptography, we use a pair of face-down cards ? ? to commit a one-bit value according to the following encoding:

$$\boxed{♣}\boxed{♡} = 0, \quad \boxed{♡}\boxed{♣} = 1. \tag{4}$$

Thus, assuming that $x_1, x_2, \ldots, x_n$ are m-bit values for some positive integer m, i.e., $x_1, x_2, \ldots, x_n \in \{0, 1\}^m$, each x_i is assumed to be committed to $2m$ face-down cards:

$$\boxed{?}\boxed{?} \leftarrow x_i[1]$$
$$\boxed{?}\boxed{?} \leftarrow x_i[2]$$
$$\vdots \qquad \vdots$$
$$\boxed{?}\boxed{?} \leftarrow x_i[m],$$

where $x[j]$, $1 \leq j \leq m$, means the j-th bit of an m-bit value $x \in \{0,1\}^m$ (throughout the paper). We call this a *commitment* to $x_i \in \{0,1\}^m$, denoted by

$$
\boxed{?}\,\boxed{?}
$$
$$
\boxed{?}\,\boxed{?}
$$
$$
\vdots
$$
$$
\underbrace{\boxed{?}\,\boxed{?}}_{x_i}.
$$

Since the first elements in the sequence (1) above serve indices, we prepare numbered cards $\boxed{1}\,\boxed{2}\cdots\boxed{n}$ (whose backs are also $\boxed{?}$) and place them along with n commitments to $x_1, x_2, \ldots, x_n \in \{0,1\}^m$, as follows:

$$
\boxed{1}\quad\boxed{2}\quad\cdots\quad\boxed{n}
$$
$$
\boxed{?}\boxed{?}\,\boxed{?}\boxed{?}\cdots\boxed{?}\boxed{?}
$$
$$
\boxed{?}\boxed{?}\,\boxed{?}\boxed{?}\cdots\boxed{?}\boxed{?}
$$
$$
\vdots\qquad\vdots\qquad\vdots
$$
$$
\underbrace{\boxed{?}\boxed{?}}_{x_1}\underbrace{\boxed{?}\boxed{?}}_{x_2}\cdots\underbrace{\boxed{?}\boxed{?}}_{x_n}.
$$
(5)

This should be the input to a secure sorting protocol.

Given an input arrangement (5), after turning over the n numbered cards (on the first row), a secure sorting protocol should output the following arrangement without leaking any information about the input:

$$
\underset{\sigma^{-1}(1)}{\boxed{?}}\quad\underset{\sigma^{-1}(2)}{\boxed{?}}\quad\cdots\quad\underset{\sigma^{-1}(n)}{\boxed{?}}
$$
$$
\boxed{?}\boxed{?}\,\boxed{?}\boxed{?}\cdots\boxed{?}\boxed{?}
$$
$$
\vdots\qquad\vdots\qquad\vdots
$$
$$
\underbrace{\boxed{?}\boxed{?}}_{x_{\sigma^{-1}(1)}}\underbrace{\boxed{?}\boxed{?}}_{x_{\sigma^{-1}(2)}}\cdots\underbrace{\boxed{?}\boxed{?}}_{x_{\sigma^{-1}(n)}},
$$
(6)

such that the permutation $\sigma \in S_n$ satisfies the condition (3) above. Here,

$$
\underset{i}{\boxed{?}}
$$

(appearing on the first row in the arrangement (6)) for i, $1 \leq i \leq n$, represents a face-down numbered card whose face is $\boxed{i}$. Thus, the arrangement (6) serves a hidden form of the sorted sequence (2).

1.3   Contribution

In this paper, we present a concrete construction of a card-based secure sorting protocol. In other words, we construct a protocol that performs secure sorting using a physical deck of cards. Specifically, given an input arrangement as shown in (5) together with some additional cards, our protocol transforms it into an output arrangement as shown in (6) via a series of actions such as shuffling and revealing cards.

Actually, our protocol performs a *stable sort*, meaning that the resulting permutation σ satisfies the following property in addition to the condition (3):

for every $i \in \{1, \ldots, n-1\}$, if $x_{\sigma^{-1}(i)} = x_{\sigma^{-1}(i+1)}$, $\sigma^{-1}(i) < \sigma^{-1}(i+1)$.

That is, our protocol preserves the original order if two input commitments have the same value. For example, if the input sequence is $(1, 10), (2, 11), (3, 11), (4, 10)$, the output will be $(2, 11), (3, 11), (1, 10), (4, 10)$ because the order of $(1, 10)$ and $(4, 10)$ as well as the order of $(2, 11)$ and $(3, 11)$ should be kept.

Beyond just the purpose of sorting, our protocol has many applications. For example, consider an auction (sealed bid), and we would like to ensure that the information on the prices other than the successful bidder's one is not leaked to anyone. This can be achieved by our proposed secure sorting protocol (as will be seen in Sect. 4.1). In addition, a wide range of functions can be implemented by our protocol, from basic secure computations such as the multi-input AND computation and majority decision, to the Millionaires' problem and secret lottery protocol [39]. That is, our protocol serves a generic protocol in a sense.

1.4   Related Work

As mentioned above, in the field of card-based cryptography, basic operations such as logical computation [1,5,9,13,17–19,25] and applied computation protocols covering a wide range of applications have been proposed. The applied computation protocols include: a millionaire protocol [21,26,29] that reveals who is richer between two players while keeping their money information secret, a ranking protocol [40] that outputs only the ranking information while keeping the money information of multiple players secret, and a card-based covert lottery protocol [39], which determines the first and second moves of a game based on two players' secret preferences. In addition, there are applications to zero-knowledge proofs, which prove the existence of a solution to a puzzle problem without divulging any information about the solution [31–34,37].

2   Preliminaries

In this section, we explain a deck of cards and shuffling operations which will be used in our proposed protocol.

2.1 Deck of Cards

As already seen, we use black cards ♣ ♣ ⋯ , red cards ♡ ♡ ⋯ , and numbered cards 1 2 ⋯ n . In addition, our protocol uses white cards ☐ ☐ ⋯ and marker cards ⋆ ⋆ ⋯ . We assume that the sizes of all these cards are the same, and their backs, denoted by ? , are identical. That is, they are indistinguishable except for designs on their fronts.

2.2 Pile-Scramble Shuffle

A *pile-scramble* shuffle [12] is a shuffling action that completely randomizes the order of multiple piles consisting of the same number of cards. For a positive integer d, applying a pile-scramble shuffle to a sequence of d piles $(\mathsf{pile}_1, \mathsf{pile}_2, \dots, \mathsf{pile}_d)$ results in $(\mathsf{pile}_{\pi^{-1}(1)}, \mathsf{pile}_{\pi^{-1}(2)}, \dots, \mathsf{pile}_{\pi^{-1}(d)})$, where $\pi \in S_d$ is a uniformly distributed random permutation:

Note that no one can know which permutation was applied.

Implementation methods for a pile-scramble shuffle have been discussed in the literature, e.g., [12,40]. A typical implementation is to use envelopes; each pile of cards is fixed by using envelopes, and then players jointly shuffle them by hands (until the players are all satisfied).

2.3 Pile-Shifting Shuffle

Another shuffling action is a *pile-shifting* shuffle, which cyclically and randomly shifts the order of piles consisting of the same number of cards [28,38]. For a positive integer d, by applying a pile-shifting shuffle to d piles $(\mathsf{pile}_1, \mathsf{pile}_2, \dots, \mathsf{pile}_d)$, we obtain $(\mathsf{pile}_{1+(r\%d)}, \mathsf{pile}_{1+(1+r\%d)}, \dots, \mathsf{pile}_{1+(d+r\%d)})$, where $r \in \{0, 1, \dots, d-1\}$ is a random number, and $\%$ denotes the remainder.

Similar to the pile-scramble shuffle explained in Sect. 2.2, a pile-shifting shuffle can be implemented by using envelopes.

2.4 Koch–Walzer Sort Protocol

In 2022, Koch and Walzer [15] proposed the "coupled sorting sub-protocol" that sorts multiple piles of cards according to the order of given numbered cards.

We note that the distribution of the numbers written on the numbered cards is known in their protocol; in contrast, our protocol sorts multiple commitments to multi-bit values whose distribution is unknown; below is the more specific explanation.

Let us apply their idea to the input arrangement (5); turn over all the numbered cards, apply a pile-scramble shuffle to the arrangement, reveal all the commitments, and sort the whole piles according to the order of the revealed values:

Then, we obtain sorted indices

$$\underset{\sigma^{-1}(1)}{\boxed{?}} \quad \underset{\sigma^{-1}(2)}{\boxed{?}} \quad \cdots \quad \underset{\sigma^{-1}(n)}{\boxed{?}} \; ,$$

but the distribution of the key values $x_1, x_2, \ldots, x_n$ are leaked. It is non-trivial to sort the arrangement (5) without leaking any information; we will construct a protocol to overcome this difficulty.

3   Our Proposed Secure Sorting Protocol

In this section, we construct a card-based secure sorting protocol. In Sect. 3.1, we illustrate an overall flow of our protocol. In Sect. 3.2, by showing a working example, we present the idea of how to securely sort commitments. In Sect. 3.3, we give the complete description of our protocol. In Sect. 3.4, we prove the security of our protocol.

3.1   Overall Flow

Take the sequence

$$(1, 1011), (2, 0110), (3, 1101)$$

Table 1. Overall flow of our protocol

	(a)			(b)			(c)		
	1	2	3	1	3	2	1	2	3
1st-bit →	♡♣	♣♡	♡♣	♡♣	♡♣	♣♡	♡♣	♣♡	♡♣
2nd-bit →	♡♣	♡♣	♣♡	♡♣	♣♡	♡♣	♡♣	♡♣	♣♡
3rd-bit →	♣♡	♡♣	♡♣	♣♡	♡♣	♡♣	♣♡	♡♣	♡♣
4th-bit →	♡♣	♣♡	♡♣	♡♣	♡♣	♣♡	♡♣	♣♡	♡♣

	(d)			(e)		
	2	3	1	3	1	2
	♣♡	♡♣	♡♣	♡♣	♡♣	♣♡
	♡♣	♣♡	♡♣	♣♡	♡♣	♡♣
	♡♣	♡♣	♣♡	♡♣	♣♡	♡♣
	♣♡	♡♣	♡♣	♡♣	♡♣	♣♡

as a working example (to be sorted). As mentioned in Sect. 1.2, we use commitments (consisting of face-down cards) to represent such an input: That is, we now have

$$
\begin{array}{ccc}
\boxed{1} & \boxed{2} & \boxed{3} \\
\boxed{?}\boxed{?} & \boxed{?}\boxed{?} & \boxed{?}\boxed{?} \\
\boxed{?}\boxed{?} & \boxed{?}\boxed{?} & \boxed{?}\boxed{?} \\
\boxed{?}\boxed{?} & \boxed{?}\boxed{?} & \boxed{?}\boxed{?} \\
\boxed{?}\boxed{?} & \boxed{?}\boxed{?} & \boxed{?}\boxed{?} \\
\underbrace{\quad}_{1011} & \underbrace{\quad}_{0110} & \underbrace{\quad}_{1101}
\end{array}
\tag{7}
$$

as an input arrangement, whose front sides satisfy (a) in Table 1.

In our protocol, we sort the commitments (together with the numbered cards on the first row) bit by bit in a stable manner. Thus, we first apply a stable sort based on the first bit, i.e., the least significant bit; then, the resulting sequence is

$$(1, 1011), (3, 1101), (2, 0110),$$

which corresponds to (b) in Table 1. Next, we apply a stable sort based on the second bit, resulting in

$$(1, 1011), (2, 0110), (3, 1101),$$

which corresponds to (c) in Table 1. In the same manner, we have

$$(2, 0110), (3, 1101), (1, 1011)$$

corresponding to (d) and then

$$(3, 1101), (1, 1011), (2, 0110)$$

corresponding to (e).

In this way, we sort the input arrangement. In the next subsection, we show how to transform the arrangement without leaking any information about the input.

3.2 How to Securely Sort

Assume that we want to perform a stable sort based on the first bits, given the arrangement (7) above. We here use additional white cards $\boxed{}\boxed{}\boxed{}$ and numbered cards $\boxed{1}\boxed{1}\boxed{2}\boxed{2}\boxed{3}\boxed{3}$.

First, place the three white cards as follows, and turn over the cards on the first row:

Next, after turning over the additional numbered cards $\boxed{1}\boxed{1}\boxed{2}\boxed{2}\boxed{3}\boxed{3}$, we apply a pile-scramble shuffle as follows:

where (r_1, r_2, r_3) is a random rearrangement of $(1, 2, 3)$ generated by the pile-scramble shuffle. Then, place these six cards above the arrangement, as follows:

We say that a column is *white* if its second cards is $\boxed{}$; thus, in this case, the second, forth, and sixth columns are white.

Remember that we want to perform a stable sort based on the first bits; however, we cannot open the cards corresponding to the first bits (i.e., the cards on the third row), of course. Therefore, we apply a pile-scramble shuffle to each commitment (together with the four cards above it):

$$
\begin{bmatrix} ? \\ ? \\ ? \\ ? \\ ? \\ ? \end{bmatrix}
\begin{bmatrix} ? \\ ? \\ ? \\ ? \\ ? \\ ? \end{bmatrix}
\begin{bmatrix} ? \\ ? \\ ? \\ ? \\ ? \\ ? \end{bmatrix}
\begin{bmatrix} ? \\ ? \\ ? \\ ? \\ ? \\ ? \end{bmatrix}
\begin{bmatrix} ? \\ ? \\ ? \\ ? \\ ? \\ ? \end{bmatrix}
\begin{bmatrix} ? \\ ? \\ ? \\ ? \\ ? \\ ? \end{bmatrix}.
$$

As known from the encoding rule (4), now, revealing the cards on the third row does not leak any information (because each bit value was negated with a probability of exactly $1/2$); therefore, reveal those cards:

$$
\begin{matrix}
? & ? & ? & ? & ? & ? \\
? & ? & ? & ? & ? & ? \\
\heartsuit & \clubsuit & \heartsuit & \clubsuit & \clubsuit & \heartsuit \\
? & ? & ? & ? & ? & ? \\
? & ? & ? & ? & ? & ? \\
? & ? & ? & ? & ? & ?
\end{matrix}.
$$

Then, we perform a stable sort according to the revealed values (based on $\heartsuit > \clubsuit$) while keeping the order of cards inside each column unchanged:

$$
\begin{matrix}
? & ? & ? & ? & ? & ? \\
? & ? & ? & ? & ? & ? \\
\heartsuit & \heartsuit & \heartsuit & \clubsuit & \clubsuit & \clubsuit \\
? & ? & ? & ? & ? & ? \\
? & ? & ? & ? & ? & ? \\
? & ? & ? & ? & ? & ?
\end{matrix}.
$$

Next, using the existing technique [40] (as the details will be explained in Step 5. of our protocol presented in Sect. 3.3), we take out all the white columns:

$$\begin{array}{ccc} \boxed{?}\boxed{?}\boxed{?} & \boxed{?}\boxed{?}\boxed{?} \\ \boxed{?}\boxed{?}\boxed{?} & \Box\Box\Box \\ \boxed{?}\boxed{?}\boxed{?} & \boxed{?}\boxed{?}\boxed{?} \\ \boxed{?}\boxed{?}\boxed{?} & \boxed{?}\boxed{?}\boxed{?} \\ \boxed{?}\boxed{?}\boxed{?} & \boxed{?}\boxed{?}\boxed{?} \\ \boxed{?}\boxed{?}\boxed{?} & \boxed{?}\boxed{?}\boxed{?} . \end{array}$$

Finally, reveal all the cards on the first row, and move each white column so that the commitment is restored. Note that the cards in the first row are shuffled so that no information is leaked when they are turned over:

$$\begin{array}{c} \boxed{3}\boxed{3}\boxed{1}\boxed{1}\boxed{2}\boxed{2} \\ \boxed{?}\Box\boxed{?}\Box\boxed{?}\Box \\ \boxed{?}\boxed{?}\boxed{?}\boxed{?}\boxed{?}\boxed{?} \\ \boxed{?}\boxed{?}\boxed{?}\boxed{?}\boxed{?}\boxed{?} \\ \boxed{?}\boxed{?}\boxed{?}\boxed{?}\boxed{?}\boxed{?} \\ \boxed{?}\boxed{?}\boxed{?}\boxed{?}\boxed{?}\boxed{?} . \end{array}$$

3.3 Description of Our Protocol

In this subsection, we give the complete description of our secure sorting protocol.

Given an arrangement as shown in Eq. (5) along with additional n white cards $\Box\Box\cdots\Box$ and $2n$ numbered cards $\boxed{1}\boxed{1}\boxed{2}\boxed{2}\cdots\boxed{n}\boxed{n}$, our protocol proceeds as follows.

1. To the input arrangement, add the n white cards as below, and turn over all the cards on the first row:

$$\begin{array}{c}
\boxed{1}\Box\,\boxed{2}\Box\cdots\boxed{n}\Box \\
\boxed{?}\boxed{?}\,\boxed{?}\boxed{?}\cdots\boxed{?}\Box \\
\boxed{?}\boxed{?}\,\boxed{?}\boxed{?}\cdots\boxed{?}\Box \\
\vdots\quad\vdots\qquad\vdots \\
\underbrace{\boxed{?}\boxed{?}}_{x_1}\,\underbrace{\boxed{?}\boxed{?}}_{x_2}\cdots\underbrace{\boxed{?}\Box}_{x_n}
\end{array}
\rightarrow
\begin{array}{c}
\boxed{?}\boxed{?}\,\boxed{?}\boxed{?}\cdots\boxed{?}\boxed{?} \\
\boxed{?}\boxed{?}\,\boxed{?}\boxed{?}\cdots\boxed{?}\boxed{?} \\
\boxed{?}\boxed{?}\,\boxed{?}\boxed{?}\cdots\boxed{?}\boxed{?} \\
\vdots\quad\vdots\qquad\vdots \\
\boxed{?}\boxed{?}\,\boxed{?}\boxed{?}\cdots\boxed{?}\boxed{?} .
\end{array} \qquad (8)$$

Set $j := 1$.

2. Turn over the additional $2n$ numbered cards $\boxed{1}\,\boxed{1}\,\boxed{2}\,\boxed{2}\,\cdots\,\boxed{n}\,\boxed{n}$, and apply a pile-scramble shuffle as follows:

$$\boxed{?}\boxed{?}\boxed{?}\boxed{?}\cdots\boxed{?}\boxed{?} \;\rightarrow\; \left[\boxed{?}\boxed{?}\,\middle|\,\boxed{?}\boxed{?}\,\middle|\cdots\middle|\,\boxed{?}\boxed{?}\right] \;\rightarrow$$
$$\underset{r_1\;\;r_1\;\;r_2\;\;r_2\qquad\quad r_n\;\;r_n}{\boxed{?}\boxed{?}\boxed{?}\boxed{?}\cdots\boxed{?}\boxed{?}},$$

where $(r_1, r_2, \ldots, r_n)$ is a random rearrangement of $(1, 2, \ldots, n)$ generated by the pile-scramble shuffle. Then, place these $2n$ cards above the arrangement (8), as follows:

$$\underset{r_1\;\;r_1\;\;r_2\;\;r_2\qquad r_n\;\;r_n}{\boxed{?}\boxed{?}\boxed{?}\boxed{?}\cdots\boxed{?}\boxed{?}}$$

3. Apply a pile-scramble shuffle to the $(2i-1)$-th and $2i$-th columns for every i, $1 \le i \le n$:

4. Reveal the cards corresponding to the j-th bits and perform a stable sort as follows:

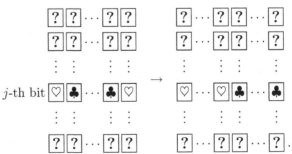

5. Take out all the white columns, as follows:

   (a) Turn all the face-up cards face down, and place to the left a new column consisting of marker cards, as follows:

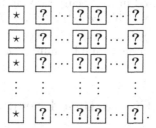

   (b) Turn all the face-up cards face-down, and apply a pile-shifting shuffle to the whole columns. Then, turn over the card on the second row of the first column; if it is a white card ▢, then the column is white and hence, remove it. If the total number of removed white columns reaches n, proceed to the next step. Otherwise, return to the beginning of this step.

6. Reveal all the cards on the first row; then, ignore the marker column. Restore each commitment by placing the white columns at the appropriate positions:

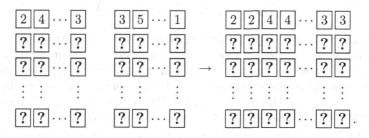

7. Remove the cards in the first row.
8. Set $j := j + 1$. If $j < m$, return to Step 2.

3.4   Security

Information about inputs and outputs is generally leaked when revealing cards in card-based protocols; thus, we focus on Steps 4, 5, and 6 of our protocol. In Step 4, we reveal the n bit-values on the j-th bit. Since each bit-value is randomized by the shuffle in Step 3, no information about the values is leaked. In Step 5(b), because a pile-shifting shuffle is applied before the second card is revealed, the revealed card does not leak information. Similarly, in Step 6, no information leaks. In conclusion, the proposed protocol is information-theoretically secure.

3.5   Optimization

Because Steps 5(b) has a repetition, our protocol is a Las-Vegas protocol. We note that our protocol can be converted to a finite-runtime protocol by applying the existing technique used in the secure ranking protocols [40].

Remember that in Step 5(b), we extract the n white columns from the $2n+1$ ones. The above-mentioned technique enables us to achieve the same task in finite runtime using two pile-scramble shuffles, n pile-shifting shuffles, and n^2 additional cards.

4   Applications of Card-Based Secure Sorting

In this section, we show how to apply our secure sorting protocol proposed in Sect. 3 to achieving an auction and secure computation of threshold functions. Recall that the proposed protocol outputs an arrangement shown in Eq. (6).

4.1   Auction

Let auction be the functionality of auction. Since auction only needs to output the maximum bid price and its bidder, it can be written as follows using a permutation σ corresponding to a stable sort:

$$\text{auction}(x_1, \ldots, x_n) = (x_{\sigma^{-1}(1)}, \sigma^{-1}(1)).$$

That is, auction can be realized by revealing the first commitment and its numbered card after executing our secure sorting protocol; the former indicates the price and the latter indicates the winner. In the case where there is a player who bids the same price as the winning bid price, the player can confirm by turning the second price and the numbered card. Therefore, ties can also be detected. Alternatively, using the existing XOR and OR protocols (e.g., [25]), the players can determine whether the second commitment has the same value as the first one without revealing its value.

4.2   Secure Threshold Function Evaluation

We define a threshold function thr_n^t that outputs 1 if and only if the sum of n bits $x_1, \ldots, x_n \in \{0, 1\}$ is greater than or equal to $t \in \{1, \ldots, n\}$:

$$\text{thr}_n^t(x_1, \ldots, x_n) := \begin{cases} 1 & \text{if } \sum_{i=1}^{n} x_i \geq t, \\ 0 & \text{otherwise.} \end{cases}$$

Using the permutation σ corresponding to a stable sort, we have the following:

$$\text{thr}_n^t(x_1, \ldots, x_n) = x_{\sigma^{-1}(t)}.$$

Therefore, thr_n^t can be realized by turning over the t-th commitment after executing the proposed protocol with $m = 1$.

5   Conclusion

In this paper, we proposed a card-based secure sorting protocol. The protocol itself is useful as well as it can provide various applications. The protocol is based on the representation of each player's value as a binary string, and sorts the values bit by bit from the least significant bit. As examples of the application of our protocol, we showed how to implement an auction and secure computations of threshold functions. This protocol can also be applied to a computation similar to a ranking computation [40] and to a covert lottery protocol [39] (although we omit the details).

Acknowledgements. We thank the anonymous referees, whose comments have helped us improve the presentation of the paper. We would like to thank Hideaki Sone for his cooperation in preparing a Japanese draft version at an earlier stage of this work. This work was supported in part by JSPS KAKENHI Grant Numbers JP21K11881 and JP19H01104.

References

1. Abe, Y., Hayashi, Y., Mizuki, T., Sone, H.: Five-card AND computations in committed format using only uniform cyclic shuffles. New Gener. Comput. **39**, 97–114 (2021). https://doi.org/10.1007/s00354-020-00110-2
2. Bultel, X., Dreier, J., Dumas, J.G., Lafourcade, P.: Physical zero-knowledge proofs for Akari, Takuzu, Kakuro and KenKen. In: Demaine, E.D., Grandoni, F. (eds.) Fun with Algorithms. LIPIcs, vol. 49, pp. 8:1–8:20. Schloss Dagstuhl, Dagstuhl, Germany (2016). https://doi.org/10.4230/LIPIcs.FUN.2016.8
3. Cramer, R., Damgård, I.B., et al.: Secure Multiparty Computation and Secret Sharing. Cambridge University Press, Cambridge (2015). https://ir.cwi.nl/pub/23529
4. Crépeau, C., Kilian, J.: Discreet solitary games. In: Stinson, D.R. (ed.) CRYPTO 1993. LNCS, vol. 773, pp. 319–330. Springer, Heidelberg (1994). https://doi.org/10.1007/3-540-48329-2_27
5. Den Boer, B.: More efficient match-making and satisfiability the five card trick. In: Quisquater, J.-J., Vandewalle, J. (eds.) EUROCRYPT 1989. LNCS, vol. 434, pp. 208–217. Springer, Heidelberg (1990). https://doi.org/10.1007/3-540-46885-4_23
6. Evans, D., Kolesnikov, V., Rosulek, M.: A pragmatic introduction to secure multiparty computation. Found. Trends Privacy Secur. **2**(2–3), 70–246 (2018). https://doi.org/10.1561/3300000019
7. Goodrich, M.T.: Randomized shellsort: a simple data-oblivious sorting algorithm. J. ACM **58**(6), 1–26 (2011). https://doi.org/10.1145/2049697.2049701
8. Gradwohl, R., Naor, M., Pinkas, B., Rothblum, G.N.: Cryptographic and physical zero-knowledge proof systems for solutions of Sudoku puzzles. Theory Comput. Syst. **44**(2), 245–268 (2009). https://doi.org/10.1007/s00224-008-9119-9
9. Haga, R., Hayashi, Y., Miyahara, D., Mizuki, T.: Card-minimal protocols for three-input functions with standard playing cards. In: Progress in Cryptology–AFRICACRYPT 2022. LNCS, Springer, Cham (2022, to appear)

10. Hamada, K., Kikuchi, R., Ikarashi, D., Chida, K., Takahashi, K.: Practically efficient multi-party sorting protocols from comparison sort algorithms. In: Kwon, T., Lee, M.-K., Kwon, D. (eds.) ICISC 2012. LNCS, vol. 7839, pp. 202–216. Springer, Heidelberg (2013). https://doi.org/10.1007/978-3-642-37682-5_15
11. Hanaoka, G.: Towards user-friendly cryptography. In: Phan, R.C.-W., Yung, M. (eds.) Mycrypt 2016. LNCS, vol. 10311, pp. 481–484. Springer, Cham (2017). https://doi.org/10.1007/978-3-319-61273-7_24
12. Ishikawa, R., Chida, E., Mizuki, T.: Efficient card-based protocols for generating a hidden random permutation without fixed points. In: Calude, C.S., Dinneen, M.J. (eds.) UCNC 2015. LNCS, vol. 9252, pp. 215–226. Springer, Cham (2015). https://doi.org/10.1007/978-3-319-21819-9_16
13. Isuzugawa, R., Toyoda, K., Sasaki, Yu., Miyahara, D., Mizuki, T.: A card-minimal three-input AND protocol using two shuffles. In: Chen, C.-Y., Hon, W.-K., Hung, L.-J., Lee, C.-W. (eds.) COCOON 2021. LNCS, vol. 13025, pp. 668–679. Springer, Cham (2021). https://doi.org/10.1007/978-3-030-89543-3_55
14. Koch, A.: The landscape of security from physical assumptions. In: 2021 IEEE Information Theory Workshop (ITW), Los Alamitos, CA, USA, pp. 1–6. IEEE (2021). https://doi.org/10.1109/ITW48936.2021.9611501
15. Koch, A., Walzer, S.: Private function evaluation with cards. New Gener. Comput. 40, 115–147 (2022). https://doi.org/10.1007/s00354-021-00149-9
16. Koch, A., Walzer, S.: Private function evaluation with cards. New Gener. Comput. 40, 115–147 (2022). https://doi.org/10.1007/s00354-021-00149-9
17. Koyama, H., Miyahara, D., Mizuki, T., Sone, H.: A secure three-input AND protocol with a standard deck of minimal cards. In: Santhanam, R., Musatov, D. (eds.) CSR 2021. LNCS, vol. 12730, pp. 242–256. Springer, Cham (2021). https://doi.org/10.1007/978-3-030-79416-3_14
18. Koyama, H., Toyoda, K., Miyahara, D., Mizuki, T.: New card-based copy protocols using only random cuts. In: ASIA Public-Key Cryptography Workshop, APKC 2021, pp. 13–22. ACM, New York (2021). https://doi.org/10.1145/3457338.3458297
19. Kuzuma, T., Toyoda, K., Miyahara, D., Mizuki, T.: Card-based single-shuffle protocols for secure multiple-input AND and XOR computations. In: ASIA Public-Key Cryptography, pp. 51–58. ACM, New York (2022). https://doi.org/10.1145/3494105.3526236
20. Manabe, Y., Ono, H.: Card-based cryptographic protocols with malicious players using private operations. New Gener. Comput. 40, 67–93 (2022). https://doi.org/10.1007/s00354-021-00148-w
21. Miyahara, D., Hayashi, Y., Mizuki, T., Sone, H.: Practical card-based implementations of Yao's millionaire protocol. Theor. Comput. Sci. 803, 207–221 (2020). https://doi.org/10.1016/j.tcs.2019.11.005
22. Mizuki, T.: Preface: special issue on card-based cryptography. New Gener. Comput. 39, 1–2 (2021). https://doi.org/10.1007/s00354-021-00127-1
23. Mizuki, T.: Preface: special issue on card-based cryptography 2. New Gener. Comput. 40, 47–48 (2022). https://doi.org/10.1007/s00354-022-00170-6
24. Mizuki, T., Kumamoto, M., Sone, H.: The five-card trick can be done with four cards. In: Wang, X., Sako, K. (eds.) ASIACRYPT 2012. LNCS, vol. 7658, pp. 598–606. Springer, Heidelberg (2012). https://doi.org/10.1007/978-3-642-34961-4_36
25. Mizuki, T., Sone, H.: Six-card secure AND and four-card secure XOR. In: Deng, X., Hopcroft, J.E., Xue, J. (eds.) FAW 2009. LNCS, vol. 5598, pp. 358–369. Springer, Heidelberg (2009). https://doi.org/10.1007/978-3-642-02270-8_36

26. Nakai, T., Misawa, Y., Tokushige, Y., Iwamoto, M., Ohta, K.: How to solve millionaires' problem with two kinds of cards. New Gener. Comput. **39**, 73–96 (2021). https://doi.org/10.1007/s00354-020-00118-8
27. Niemi, V., Renvall, A.: Secure multiparty computations without computers. Theor. Comput. Sci. **191**(1–2), 173–183 (1998). https://doi.org/10.1016/S0304-3975(97)00107-2
28. Nishimura, A., Hayashi, Y., Mizuki, T., Sone, H.: Pile-shifting scramble for card-based protocols. IEICE Trans. Fundam. Electron. Commun. Comput. Sci. **101**(9), 1494–1502 (2018). https://doi.org/10.1587/transfun.E101.A.1494
29. Ono, H., Manabe, Y.: Efficient card-based cryptographic protocols for the millionaires' problem using private input operations. In: Asia Joint Conference on Information Security (AsiaJCIS), pp. 23–28 (2018). https://doi.org/10.1109/AsiaJCIS.2018.00013
30. Ono, H., Manabe, Y.: Card-based cryptographic logical computations using private operations. New Gener. Comput. **39**, 19–40 (2021). https://doi.org/10.1109/AsiaJCIS.2018.00013
31. Robert, L., Miyahara, D., Lafourcade, P., Mizuki, T.: Physical zero-knowledge proof for suguru puzzle. In: Devismes, S., Mittal, N. (eds.) SSS 2020. LNCS, vol. 12514, pp. 235–247. Springer, Cham (2020). https://doi.org/10.1007/978-3-030-64348-5_19
32. Robert, L., Miyahara, D., Lafourcade, P., Mizuki, T.: Interactive physical ZKP for connectivity: applications to Nurikabe and Hitori. In: De Mol, L., Weiermann, A., Manea, F., Fernández-Duque, D. (eds.) CiE 2021. LNCS, vol. 12813, pp. 373–384. Springer, Cham (2021). https://doi.org/10.1007/978-3-030-80049-9_37
33. Robert, L., Miyahara, D., Lafourcade, P., Libralesso, L., Mizuki, T.: Physical zero-knowledge proof and NP-completeness proof of Suguru puzzle. Inf. Comput. **285**, 104858 (2021). https://doi.org/10.1016/j.ic.2021.104858. https://www.sciencedirect.com/science/article/pii/S0890540121001905
34. Robert, L., Miyahara, D., Lafourcade, P., Mizuki, T.: Card-based ZKP for connectivity: applications to Nurikabe, Hitori, and Heyawake. New Gener. Comput. **40**, 1–23 (2022). https://doi.org/10.1007/s00354-022-00155-5
35. Ruangwises, S.: Two standard decks of playing cards are sufficient for a ZKP for Sudoku. New Gener. Comput. **40**, 49–65 (2022). https://doi.org/10.1016/j.tcs.2021.09.034
36. Ruangwises, S., Itoh, T.: Physical zero-knowledge proof for Ripple Effect. Theor. Comput. Sci. **895**, 115–123 (2021). https://doi.org/10.1016/j.tcs.2020.05.036
37. Sasaki, T., Miyahara, D., Mizuki, T., Sone, H.: Efficient card-based zero-knowledge proof for Sudoku. Theor. Comput. Sci. **839**, 135–142 (2020). https://doi.org/10.1016/j.tcs.2020.05.036
38. Shinagawa, K., et al.: Card-based protocols using regular polygon cards. IEICE Trans. Fundam. **E100.A**(9), 1900–1909 (2017). https://doi.org/10.1587/transfun.E100.A.1900
39. Shinoda, Y., Miyahara, D., Shinagawa, K., Mizuki, T., Sone, H.: Card-based covert lottery. In: Maimut, D., Oprina, A.-G., Sauveron, D. (eds.) SecITC 2020. LNCS, vol. 12596, pp. 257–270. Springer, Cham (2021). https://doi.org/10.1007/978-3-030-69255-1_17
40. Takashima, K., et al.: Card-based protocols for secure ranking computations. Theor. Comput. Sci. **845**, 122–135 (2020). https://doi.org/10.1016/j.tcs.2020.09.008

41. Toyoda, K., Miyahara, D., Mizuki, T., Sone, H.: Six-card finite-runtime XOR protocol with only random cut. In: ACM Workshop on ASIA Public-Key Cryptography, APKC 2020, pp. 2–8. ACM, New York (2020). https://doi.org/10.1145/3384940.3388961
42. Yao, A.C.: Protocols for secure computations. In: Foundations of Computer Science, Washington, DC, USA, pp. 160–164. IEEE Computer Society (1982). https://doi.org/10.1109/SFCS.1982.88

Author Index

Printed in the United States
by Baker & Taylor Publisher Services